7/22/97

To Dave and Judi.

We've enjoyed your
visit - Come back to
us soon -

Sincerely
Bob Wildmore

D0805661

Call Forth The Mighty Men

Samuel Davis
Hanged at Pulaski, Tennessee, November 27, 1863.

NOTE: This picture of Sam Davis has never before appeared in a publication.

Photo courtesy of Mike Minor, Sevierville, Tennessee.

Call Forth

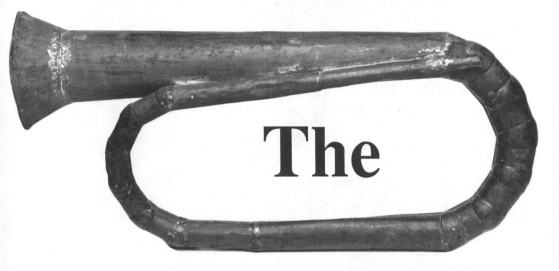

The

Mighty Men

by

Bob Womack

Colonial Press

Also by Bob Womack
The Echo of Hoof Beats; History of the Tennessee Walking Horse

Publisher's Special Acknowledgment

Special appreciation to the following for their kindness in furnishing photographs for use in this book:

Mrs. Sam Bone, Lebanon, Tenn.
J. V. Drake
Wanda and Ethel Elmore, Eagleville, Tenn.
William Fanning, Lynchburg, Tenn.
Ms. Shirley Farris Jones, Murfreesboro, Tenn.
Mike Miner, Sevierville, Tenn.
Herb Peck, Nashville, Tenn.
Hon. Harry Phillips, Cincinnati, Oh.
Frank Rankin, Louisville, Ky.
Jim Puckett, Murfreesboro, Tenn.
Mrs. Margaret Sullivan, Fayetteville, Tenn.

Special gratitude to Pat & Walter Atkinson of Bayou Graphics, Covington, Louisiana for editing, typography, and design.

Copyright © 1987 by Bob Womack

All rights reserved.

Colonial Press, 1237 Stevens Road, SE, Bessemer, AL 35023.
(205) 428-8327

Printed in United States of America.

Library of Congress Catalog Number: 86-72014
ISBN 0-938991-02-7

This book is dedicated to the staff and students of Middle Tennessee State University who have, during the past thirty years, assisted in gathering the materials upon which it is based.

Acknowledgments

It would be impossible to acknowledge all the people who have contributed to the completion of this work. Below is a partial list of those who have given so graciously of their time and energy. To those inadvertently omitted, my deepest appreciation.

For their valuable assistance, thanks to Jill Garrett, Columbia, Tennessee; Ms. Mary Ella Burke, Nashville; Dr. James Lee McDonough, Nashville; Lowell Reidenbaugh, St. Louis, Missouri; Marshall Krolick, Chicago; Gordon Whitney, Madison, Indianna; Lee A. Wallace, Jr., Falls Church Virginia; Joy Bailey Dunn, Tullahoma, Tennessee; and from Middle Tennessee State University, Dr. William Windham, Dr. James Huhta, Dr. Robert Bullen, Dr. Ralph White, Dr. Robert Eaker, Dr. Joe Nunley, Dr. King Jamison, Dr. Richard Lindsley, Dr. Robert Jones, Dr. John Harris, Neal Pistole, and Mr. Jack Ross.

Contents

Illustrations

Publisher's Preface

Call Forth The Mighty Men is a touching and historically accurate account of the actions and experiences of the magnificent men and women who soldiered the causes espoused by the politicians of the 1860's. The needless and senseless nature of a civil war, fought for intangible ideals of questionable value, is brought to light by Dr. Womack's compilation of over thirty years of exhaustive research.

Never before has a work of this magnitude been written —from the point of view of both sides—in such an unbiased and unemotional presentation. Through the use of a wealth of unpublished materials, such as personal diaries, he skillfully portrays the changes which occurred in the people of Tennessee as they battled to survive the war of their arrogant politicians.

What begins as a valiant and glorified march to war by men of high ideals in flashy dress uniforms, deteriorates into a desperate, and oftentimes futile, effort to survive, as half-naked soldiers from opposing sides—soldiers who comingle and share the necessities of life between battles—charge each other to the death for reasons they do not understand. The helpless frustrations of women like Virginia French and Betty Bobo are revived and lend understanding to the reasons why citizens who watched old veterans from both sides march in reunion parades as late as the Twentieth Century, could "still see the fire in the old boys eyes."

Walter B. Atkinson
Editor in Chief, Colonial Press

Proclaim ye this among the gentiles; prepare war, wake up the mighty men, let all the men of war draw near; beat your plough-shares into swords, and your pruning hooks into spears: let the weak say, I am strong.

3rd Chapter of Joel

But war is only the final flower of an evil tree.

Bertrand Russell

Chapter I

There was a call to arms

By late spring in 1861 only the formalities were needed to place Tennessee in a state of war. The difficult and uncertain part had already been accomplished by the politicians. Like expert harpists they had strummed the emotions of the people until, in most areas of the state, there was an almost complete unison in the wish for, and expectation of, war. Tears streamed from the eyes of citizens who stood in town squares and heard the politicians extol the virtues of the South and recite the heroic deeds of its people. The air became charged with emotion as local leaders recalled the sacrifices of those who had established the social order now being threatened by outsiders.

Ever-so-skillfully, the citizens were led from the realm of sentimentality into the realm of hate. Tears turned to wrath as the politician pictured the "Lincolnites" invading Tennessee homes, murdering Tennessee men, stealing and burning property, and insulting Tennessee women. The keen eye of the politician saw in these tears, and in this wrath, a power he believed strong enough to give birth to and sustain a new nation. Only one spark was needed to set this power in motion — a spark supplied by Abraham Lincoln when he asked for two thousand volunteers from Tennessee to help subdue the rebellion that had begun in South Carolina.

Lincoln's call for troops met a wave of indignant protest from the majority of people in Tennessee. Previously, on February 9th, Tennesseans had expressed a desire at the polls to remain in the Union, but they were not prepared to pay the price now being asked for that privilege. Men who had spent hours on end attempting to convince their neighbors that secession was not the proper answer to the nation's problem now openly urged withdrawal from the Union. The choice had become one between national and sectional pride and, in a nation not yet mature enough to see that one was inseparable from the other, people tended to fix their allegiances where an immediate advantage seemed obvious. For most influential Tennesseans this meant sectionalism and the South.

Governor Isham G. Harris, a native of Franklin County, set the tone in response to Lincoln's call for troops. On April 17, he answered Lincoln's request by replying, "Tennessee will not furnish a single man for coercion, but fifty thousand if necessary for the defense of our rights or those of our Southern brothers."[1] The "rights" of which Harris spoke concerned the independence of action which he believed resided with the separate states, regardless of the national government's attitude. Harris immediately convened the legislature and declared a declaration of independence from the United States.

Most of the people in Middle and West Tennessee applauded the governor's action, but as the level land of these regions gradually ascended toward the mountains of East Tennessee, so did the sentiments of the people change from rabid Southern Nationalism to ardent Unionism. In all three regions there were those who sided against the majority, adding to the intensity of feeling already existing. The result was that the people of Tennessee found themselves swept along in a tide of emotionalism in which there was little room for reason and deliberation. Unionists and secessionists agreed to meet and debate the issues in Knoxville, but the attempt ended when guns were drawn and made ready for use. Bloodshed was avoided only through the delicate persuasion of influential leaders.[2]

In Middle and West Tennessee there was little point in debate. The people of Franklin County, already dissatisfied with the results of the February 9th election, had met and expressed a wish to secede from Tennessee and join Alabama which had withdrawn from the Union in January. A Middle Tennessee newspaper reported on April 25th, "From all parts of the State we hear the most cheering intelligence in regard to the organizing of military companies for the defense of an oppressed people. Before one week from today there will be a force of fifty thousand brave Tennesseans organized to resist to the bitter end, the Goths and Vandals of the treacherous North."3 Newspapers throughout the area quoted Jefferson Davis in a speech at Stevenson, Alabama, as saying, "Your border States will gladly come into the Southern Confederacy within sixty days . . . England and France will recognize us, and a glorious future is before us."4

By April of 1861, most of the people in Tennessee accepted as inevitable the fact that the nation's problems would be settled through the medium of war. The possibility of war caused little gloom, especially among the secessionists whose thinking was so dominated by thoughts of "going to" war that the possibility of war "coming to" them was scarcely considered. They had heard the politician speak. This would be a short affair somewhere in Virginia in which one Southerner would whip five Yankees and all Southern soldiers would return home genuine heroes.

"In truth the public pulse was surging and the public brain reeling," recalled one observer of the times. "The young men of the village were fired and recruiting was easy, although as they marched by home with the light of patriotism and a great determination on their faces old eyes were watching wistfully from the doorways." In Middle and West Tennessee bands played martial airs amid the shouts and demonstrations of people whose emotions soared with each successive tune. The fertile ground of reason had been eroded by the torrential floods of verbalisms that poured from the lips of men who held their audiences spellbound with visions of glory and prosperity. Years later it was written, "As Gibbon truthfully observed, experience has proved that the mechanical operation of sounds, by quickening the circulation of the blood and spirits, will act on the human machine more forcibly than the eloquence of reason and honor."[5]

In some Middle Tennessee counties the prospect of war sent the people into a festive state of mind. Said one participant, "Early in the Spring of 1861, after the fall of Fort Sumter, and the call of President Lincoln for troops from Tennessee, war was the only thing discussed in Lincoln County. Old gray haired men, devoted wives, sisters and mothers talked of war until the whole atmosphere was full of it."[6] Children screamed in the night as they dreamed of Yankee blood pouring down the stairway, and they trembled in their beds as they remembered the tales told by their parents. Old saws, hoes, or anything else appropriate were put to the grindstone to make large, ugly, ill-shaped knives to be used by men and boys to meet the insolent foe.

One Confederate soldier later wrote that speeches were long and loud, and "what was wanting in quality was made up in quantity. On some occasions we remember well to have heard men try to make war speeches who never before or since lifted their voices in strains of eloquent patriotism to stir the souls of their countrymen."[7]

After listening to the passionate speeches of Tennessee's politicians and reading the venom-spiked editorials of the state's leading newspapers, secessionists viewed with pity what they envisioned as the inevitable fate of their adversary. The climate of confidence became adamant. One newspaper writer said, "If there is a man in Tennessee today, who hesitates as to his duty, between Lincoln and the South, he ought to leave the South forthwith. There can be no room here now for any man every throb of whose heart is not a beat for Southern Independence."[8] By early spring "Sectionalism had crystalized until the fatal 'Mason and Dixon's line' was too often looked upon as a sort of reverential division line by both sections, and the result was jealousy, embittered feeling and distrust of each other."[9] The atmosphere in most Middle and West Tennessee counties was electric with southern patriotism and the people who disagreed kept their mouths shut or confided only to those they knew could be trusted.

The image of the Northerner prevalent among Tennessee secessionists was a rather pale-faced individual who had no thoughts of his own, but like a filthy vulture waited around to do Abe Lincoln's dirty work. The supposed character of the Yankee soldier was represented in a drugstore tale in which a company of Northern troops were walking down the road when someone yelled, "Stop thief," whereupon every member of the company darted toward the nearest hiding place. More often than not, the Northern soldier was pictured as a hired murderer whose overpowering urge was to satisfy an unquenchable thirst for blood from the veins of Tennessee's "noble sons and defenseless women."

Amidst this climate of irrational imagination young men from the farms of Middle and West Tennessee left their plows in the field to join local companies. Young plowmen found it difficult to find contentment behind a mule when at the county seat flags were waving, bands were playing, and beautiful girls were showering affection on those who entered their names on company rolls. As one veteran wrote, "In the month of April, 1861, came the first call for volunteers in the Confederate service, the drum tapped, and the shrill notes of the fife and bugle rang out the call to arms. Immediately four companies were organized in Lincoln County, four in Franklin, one in Grundy, and one in Coffee. These ten companies met at Winchester, Tennessee, on April 27, 1861, and the 1st Tennessee Regiment was organized."[10]

From all points of the state, and from all walks of life, men began making their way toward camps of instruction. A recruit from Warren County wrote in his diary, "All was life, fun, and gayety; very few, if any, imagining for one moment the requirements of the stupendous undertaking they are now engaging in. Notwithstanding we have enlisted for the defense of Tennessee for twelve months, yet it is believed by very few that our services will be wanted in the field half that period. The idea is prevalent that the Seceded States will be an independent Government and her soldiers returned home before the expiration of six months."[11]

There was ample opportunity for everyone in the community to become involved in the process of preparing for war. Entire families loaded into wagons or carriages and made their way to town squares where battle flags were being presented to local companies. Beautiful young ladies of high breeding stood on elaborately decorated platforms and challenged the men-folk to march out and subdue the insolent foe. Sometimes disagreements arose as to just which young lady was to receive the honor of presenting these colorful emblems and on rare occasions such disagreements threatened the serenity of the rituals. Usually such misunderstandings were settled peaceably and the soldiers marched away to concentrate all their wrath toward the enemy rather than dividing it among themselves.

Young ladies often became more ardent in their warlike tendencies than the prospective soldiers they were attempting to inspire. During a ceremony in which a flag was being presented to a company of the 8th Tennessee Regiment, a feminine sponsor exhorted, "The once quiet and happy homes of our 'Sunny South' are invaded by myrmidons of the Black Republican usurper of the South. They insolently demand our homes. They would desecrate our altars and overthrow our institutions. Your defiant, yet noble, answer to this menace is clearly expressed in the indignant flash of those cloudless eyes. The heritage is ours: God gave it to our fathers . . . And now, when they would enforce their impious designs you are buckling on your armor to resist the unholy crusade."[12]

After one such speech, the captain of the Lynchburg Rangers lifted the flag above his head and shouted, "Then if we fall let this banner bathed in the tears and consecrated in the prayers of the ladies of Lynchburg and vicinity be our winding sheet."[13] If, in later years, the enthusiasm for the cause symbolized by such flags wavered, the allegiance to the flag itself would not.

Many new recruits had little to say about their enlistment. They had attended political rallies out of curiosity, but suddenly awoke to find their honor threatened unless they volunteered in a local company. Political rallies took on the appearance of religious revivals in which the character of the Yankee devil was colorfully described, after which "men of courage and patriotism" were invited to come forth and join the noble group whose mission it would be to protect southern property and the honor of southern womanhood. The pressure generated on such occasions left little opportunity for a potential soldier to examine his true feelings; before he realized what was happening, he was caught in an emotional web in which other people vaunted their patriotism by urging him into the Army.

J.G. Carrigan, a Confederate soldier from Fayetteville, Tennessee, wrote, "On many occasions, when a call was made for volunteers, young ladies would walk out and fall in line, and this was the signal for all men present to fall in. With this element of wild fire sweeping over the country, is it at all strange or beyond proper explanation, that old men, the middle-aged men, and the young men of the country rushed into the ranks of the Confederate army, not knowing or dreaming what awaited them."[14]

Nelse Rainey, of Columbia, Tennessee, was one of those whose enthusiasm ran ahead of his reason. He later recalled, "In our community the boys were enlisting for the war; they were eager for war. They were full of patriotism. How few of them understood or appreciated why or what it was all about. I know that neither Joe [a brother] nor I did, yet we enrolled our names on the roster of one of the three companies raised in Columbia — Joe 17 the December before; I just 16. Pa having more sense than we, ordered our names erased from the roll." [15]

Marcus Toney

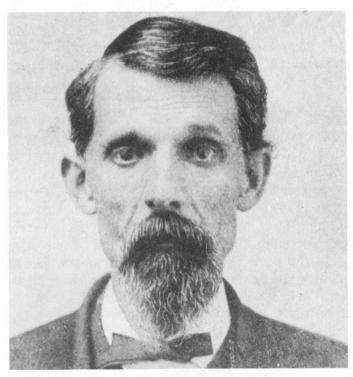

Thomas Head

John Johnson, a member of the 6th Tennessee Regiment from West Tennessee, said he enlisted because, "there was now a call to arms . . . Speeches were made . . . at the close of the speaking a call was made for volunteers. I had no taste for war, but I remember feeling the conviction that somebody ought to go and if so it was as much my duty as anyone else's . . . and I walked up and signed my name among the first." [16]   James Cooper, a member of the 20th Tennessee Regiment, wrote, "Were I asked to explain the reason for going into the army, I do not know that I could do it. I had not much idea of patriotism. I was a mere boy and carried away by boyish enthusiasm. I was ambitious and felt that I should be disgraced if I remained at home while other boys no older than myself were out fighting for the South . . . I was tormented by feverish anxiety before I joined my regiment for fear the fighting would be over before I got into it."[17]

Gaily clad young ladies gathered at points of embarkation to cheer their heroes on. Picnics were arranged where potential recruits were feted with an abundance of food for both mind and body. Town bands played *The Girl I Left Behind Me,* while politicians passed the muster rolls. Marcus Toney of Nashville was "too young to be leaving a girl behind me; so I marched out with light step and joyous heart, not dreaming of the shock of battle, the roar of cannon, the hissing of bullets, and the groans of the wounded and dying."[18]   Toney marched out of Nashville in a company of one hundred and three men, thirty two of whom were to come home four years later.

During the months before the actual face of war made its appearance in Tennessee, bravery was everywhere to be heard. To be brave was to have a good imagination and an attentive audience. The long-knife vogue grew until almost every man appeared in public wearing one or more at his side. Nelse Rainey witnessed men "wearing knives made of horseshoe files, knives as long as their arms." As Rainey remembered such individuals they were "brave with their mouths," and "strutted around full of braggadocio . . . their cry 'Just let em come; I can whip a dozen of the cowardly Yankees!'" Many years later Rainey observed, "We noticed that none of these longknife braves volunteered. No, they, when the Yankees did come, joined the Yankees and were meaner, behind the Union blue, than any real Yankee that invaded our country."[19]

While the politicians and volunteers celebrated their newly-gained prominence and the general public drifted with the tide of excitement which engulfed their communities, Amanda McDowell, a quiet schoolmarm in White County, seriously reflected, "Little thought have I had that I would ever live to see civil war in this, our goodly land, but it is so! The Southerners are so hot they can stand it no longer, and have already begun to make the break. There will be many a divided family in this once happy Union. There will be father against son and brother against brother. O God! that such things should be in a Christian land . . . There are thousands who will rush into the fury with blind enthusiasm, never stopping to question whether it be right or wrong, who, if they only understood it properly, would stay at home with their families and let those who started it fight it out."[20]

To Amanda McDowell a terrible thing was taking place, a thing she explained by saying, "the ignorant mass are so easily excited that an enthusiast who can make mountains out of molehills and raise a bussie about nothing can so stir them up and excite that they will run headlong into almost anything proposed to them."[21] Miss McDowell was among those in Tennessee to whom the threat of war meant more than the shrill notes of the fife and the muffled echo of the drum. Behind the cheering crowds and the brass bands, such people could hear the more realistic sounds of war — sounds that their neighbors were to hear some months later when the glamour of anticipation had been replaced by the goriness of reality.

Newly formed companies met to elect officers, and sometimes this process was disruptive in nature. Since soldiers from each community represented in a company or regiment wished to see their friends elected to the officers' ranks, competition could become fierce. When Amanda McDowell's brother Fayette joined the 25th Tennessee Regiment at Cookeville, such a situation developed. A neighbor of the McDowells who was on the scene told Amanda that "they made a great split of it and came very near breaking up. A great many of them wanted Fayette to be captain, but he would not have it.... They elected Shaw [Christopher] for capt., and John Young lieutenant, and some of them would not go out under John Young . . . if it had not been for Fayette, there would not have been a dozen men left together; he being a friend to all contrived to keep about forty together." It was explained that "The company was composed partly of those from the vicinity of Cookeville and partly of those from the lower end of the county. They agreed to join and each was to have two of the commissioned officers. The upper end, having the majority, elected three of them and the lower end would not stand for it."[22]

In describing the dress of his regiment, a member of the 8th Tennessee Regiment observed that "it ranged from the butternut jeans up to the finest article of French cloth, the butternut, however, largely predominating. Our large bloody-looking knives were the only things possessing any similarity, and a failure to have one of these pieces of war cutlery dangling at your side was almost a certain sign of weakness in the knees."[23]

Discipline was almost non-existent in many companies. Many officers were more anxious to be popular than efficient and even those who attempted to conduct themselves in a military manner oftentimes learned that such behavior was not appreciated by the men in the ranks. At least a few conscientious officers were rewarded for their efforts by receiving the "blanket toss," a ritual during which bossy officers were placed on a blanket held by four stalwart troopers, who gleefully tossed them in the air until the officers promised to forget about drills and such things. Many of the first officers were little more than local politicians. Thomas Head of

McMinnville, Tennessee, noted "The first officers were good men, though they were selected more through their standing and influence in private life than through efficiency."[24] Experience in battle would later expose the shocking lack of qualifications of such men, and they were voted out of office. In at least a few instances, this particular group of men, after losing their positions, lost their zeal for war and remained home during the war.

By May of 1861, Confederate volunteers were in camps of instruction which had been established throughout the state. The day of departure from hometowns would remain a memory for most. The scenes accompanying these departures became so confusing that military authorities sought to keep their exact time a secret — an undertaking almost as ambitious as the war itself.

The 6th Tennessee Regiment left Jackson on a Sunday afternoon in May. Although the departure had been planned in the utmost secrecy, Sunday morning found the town crowded to capacity with old men, wives, mothers, children, sweethearts, and neighbors. Robert Gates, a member of the regiment, wrote, "An entire people had assembled ... The line of march from the camp to the M. and O. depot, the distance of a mile and a half, was packed with people, the streets full, the houses covered, the very trees breaking with their human fruits. Now and then a cheer would break forth as the regiment with difficulty made its way through the throngs; but sobs and sounds of weeping, women screaming and fainting with mingled excitement and grief, gave to that first march a wild and mournful character." [25]

John Johnson later remembered how his company had met in West Tennessee, and that "Some weeks were spent in drilling and dress parades and undergoing the plaudits and admirations of our friends and sweethearts." Such pleasant experiences ended "about the first of May, when we received orders to go into camp at Jackson." Johnson learned on the day of departure from Jackson what other soldiers were to learn later: that regardless of the size of the crowd in attendance, leaving home is essentially a private matter. He wrote, "The church services being over, we were marched out and drawn up in line in front of the gate of the Church yard and facing the Church where Miss Emma Cobb presented the Company with a beautiful silk flag . . . This over we proceeded to tell our friends and loved-ones good-bye. And now came to me a great surprise — our Mothers and sisters, who up to this time had stood quietly by, now began to weep in the most mournful manner.

"I got along easily enough with the girls of the village — all of whom I believe kissed me good-bye. But when it came to dear Mama who was always quiet and patient in manner, she threw her arms around my brother and myself and gave vent to such heartfelt grief that I could not forget it if I had yet a hundred years to live."[26]

But not all was sadness. As the members of the 6th Tennessee Regiment stood by the train in Jackson, awaiting the moment of departure, their attention was attracted to a clamoring sound that was most unusual. Robert Gates explained, "The men were resting on their arms, the officers standing in little groups near their respective companies, and all were more or less silent and thoughtful, awaiting orders to board the train. At this juncture, at a considerable distance, an object was seen approaching through the camp. At first it was difficult to make out, so curious it looked and so encumbered it seemed. However, it soon became apparent that a soldier was approaching, equipped for war; and it turned out to be Lieut. John McDonald, of Company H. He was a small man, but he carried a large and full haversack, a large knapsack with a double-barreled shotgun strapped across it, in his right hand a Minie-rifle, belted around him a sword, a large knife (then common), two pistols, and a hatchet. He was a sight to behold, and, as he neared the regiment, was greeted with shouts of laughter." The young lieutenant explained that he had the "rations to sustain his strength and the weapons to execute his will on the enemy. His idea was to use the Minie at long range, then his shotgun, then his pistols; then, as the hostile lines came closer, to throw his tomahawk, and then, with sword in one hand and the big knife in the other, to wade in and dispatch the ten traditional Yankees."27

Once the new Confederates arrived in camps of instruction — they didn't call them training camps — they faced a serious shortage of weapons. Many soldiers had no guns at all, but such men were almost as well off as many who did. Some of the guns issued had been used in the War of 1812, and had not been fired since that time. To compensate for the lack of guns, sticks were utilized in drill, and sometimes, on guard duty. Those men who had brought guns from home were plagued by an almost total lack of ammunition, but such handicaps failed to dim the enthusiasm of volunteers who believed the natural superiority of the Southern fighting man would offset any obstacle.

The camps offered a new setting for young men accustomed to the freedom of open spaces. Usually such camps were laid out in an orderly fashion with tents facing out on streets named for famous Southern leaders. Located near an ample supply of water, many camp-sites were blessed with near-by groves of trees that offered relief from the steadily rising temperatures which accompanied the developing season. The most detestable part of the camp was the drill-field which, more often than not, was referred to in terms that would not have been flattering to any Southerner and so remained nameless, except for the improvised designators used by soldiers not appreciative of its unique contribution to the war effort.

The Army represented a new way of life for Confederate recruits and its demands placed them in frustrating situations. A soldier by the name of J. R. Thompson wrote in his diary about going to the drill field where the captain of his company sought to put his men through some basic movements. According to Thompson, "as we marched down near the woods wher their was a bunch of fine looking ladies   one of them threw the Capt a nice boca [bouquet] & it pleased him so well that he did not know how to behave himself."28

Young men away from home for the first time found it difficult to withstand the temptations that seemed to beckon on every hand.   The feeling of manhood which accompanied freedom from home restrictions, when combined with the boredom of camplife, often prompted the troops to drink too much whiskey.   The problem became so serious that General Felix Zollicoffer, a native of Columbia and former editor of the *Nashville Banner*, issued an order that no man, except himself, could pass the guard lines without a proper pass.   Matters progressed smoothly until a young soldier named Stevens was placed on guard duty.   As a comrade of Stevens remembered the situation, "The soldier-boy began his beat.   In a short while, sure enough, along came Gen. Zollicoffer, and as he approached the soldier's beat he was halted.   The General remarked that he was Gen. Zollicoffer, and had a right to pass. The soldier replied: 'You can't play that game on me;   if I should let you pass, in half an hour there would be forty Zollicoffers here to pass.' "29

In many regiments there were men skilled in the art of making whiskey and it was not unusual for at least one wagon to be equipped for the production of this most valued commodity.   Many were the Tennessee belles whose modesty was shocked by three-week veterans who had recently visited the special wagon.

While the men of war in Confederate Tennessee prepared to go forth and conquer new foes, the politicians began taking steps to make the whole thing legal.   Governor Isham G. Harris had already established an alliance with the Southern Confederacy and had authorized the mobilization of thousands of troops, but the citizens of the state had not yet given their official approval. In an effort to give Tennessee's war preparations official sanction, the legislature designated June 8, 1861, as the day for a referendum on secession. As that crucial date approached a new flurry of oratory echoed from town squares and cross-roads as politicians sought to explain the issue.

According to secessionists, the referendum would decide "whether Tennessee will single-handed attempt to resist the thieving Yankees, the low-down Dutch, and the 'Hessian scum' who are gathering in the north for the avowed purpose of devastating this fair land and murdering its brave men, its fair women, and its innocent children or join with other States of the South in one common mighty effort to resist the tide that is sweeping down upon us." [30] It was suggested to voters that this be an "open election" and they were told, "Don't roll up your ballot—don't make a rat tail of it, but leave it open."[31] Clarksville voters were told, "Let every man vote for 'Separation' or not vote at all."[32] Middle Tennessee newspapers strongly inferred that any man seen folding his ballot would be suspected of casting a Yankee vote.

Soldiers in camp were allowed to take part in the referendum. The night before the voting it was announced that all drill would be suspended; the entire day would be devoted to secession. The next day entire companies were called into formation and marched to the polling places. The absurdity of some scenes greatly amused the young soldiers. One recruit remembered, "It came Jack Turner's time to vote (he was only fourteen years old), when one of the officers of the election, an elderly man who perhaps thought there ought to be a limit somewhere between the age of Twenty-one and the cradle, asked Jack, 'How old are you young man?' Jack promptly replied 'Twenty-one years old sir.' We all laughed heartily and the balloting continued."[33]   Another soldier observed, "our regiment was allowed to vote, and strange to say, some of the boys voted against secession; but overwhelmingly the regiment voted for it."[34]

This was no ordinary election. The stakes were high and emotions even higher. In locations where Southern sentiments prevailed, officers of the election kept a watchful eye on the balloting. Ominous groups of local citizens looked threateningly dangerous to those whose political leanings were toward the Union. Many people who came to the polls to vote against secession suddenly decided not to vote at all and anxiously made their way from the scene.

The day following the election, Amanda Mc Dowell wrote in her diary, "Yesterday was the great election day in Tennessee. I guess it is voted 'out of the Union' by this time. But it would not have been had the people been allowed to vote their sentiments . . . Nearly all the Union men stayed home, not wishing to get into a brawl and deeming it a hopeless cause. And what did go did not vote . . . for fear of their lives."

The thinking of the people was clearly reflected in the vote on secession. In Middle and West Tennessee the people chose the Confederacy, but in East Tennessee the vote just as clearly indicated a desire to remain in the Union.

The announcement that Tennessee had withdrawn from the Union gave added impetus to the Confederate sympathizers in the state. But in East Tennessee the reaction was bitter. East Tennesseans met in convention and challenged the legality of the election — and the way it was conducted. They accused the newspapers of the state of encouraging death for people who voted against secession; they argued that thousands of unqualified voters had participated in the election; and they questioned the honesty of the people who counted the votes. It was obvious from the moment that the election results were made known that secession, instead of unifying Tennessee under one flag, had divided its people into irreconcilable adversaries.

Amanda McDowell, noting in her diary that the Secessionists were organizing companies at Sparta, Tennessee, wrote:

Why Christian men who live here in peace and plenty with nothing to interrupt their happiness should prefer to leave their peaceful homes and all that which binds them to their families and rush into a fight in which they cannot possibly gain anything and in which they may lose their lives is more than I can see. . . .

A month later on June 15, 1861, she wrote, "Oh, what a fair country and what a glorious government have politicians ruined."[35]

Recruiting for the Confederate Army took a sharp turn upward following the vote on secession and the swarms of volunteers descending on camps of instruction overtaxed the facilities for receiving them. A Cannon County soldier wrote, "Tennesseans were then offering their services faster than the state was prepared to arm and equip them. It was after hard begging that Governor Isham G. Harris gave his consent to have our company mustered into service; and as he could not receive more than twenty-six men, including officers, eight of our company had to return home."[36] A day would come when such a situation would seem like an unrealistic dream.

Training was accelerated during the months of June and July of 1861. The process was not simple. As one recruit noted, "Nearly every man, in the ranks at least, knew nothing but hard labor, and discipline was a difficult matter to learn. They knew exactly how to manage a plow, wield an axe, push a plane, or direct a hammer, and were splendid shots with the rifle; but to level themselves down to obedience, tactics, and rigid military discipline, was almost impossible; and this important fact was often overlooked by some swell-headed officers in command."[37] Many of the men considered drill a very unpleasant way to pass the time; they had joined the Army to fight Yankees, and until the Yankees showed their faces, the Rebs believed the Army should take it easy.

Officers faced problems other than discipline. A member of the 20th Tennessee wrote, "We at first stood guard duty with sticks for guns, later we procured a few antiquated muskets . . . and when we proudly walked our beats with real guns on our shoulders, we felt that we were indeed 'heroes,' but fancy the disgust of one of our young heroes when he drew rammer and dropped it into the barrel to hear it ring — instead of a ring it was a dull thud, the barrel being nearly full of home-made soap."[38]

A soldier from Lincoln County wrote, "The weather was growing warm, and often some of the boys would drill barefoot and without coats. And what a motley looking line of old men, middle-aged men and young men was here presented! Men from plow handles, out of work-shops, men who had never before seen a regiment of soldiers in line, and who knew as little about war as infants; flattering themselves that each was an invincible Hercules, and could slay his allotted five Yankees within the next ensuing sixty days and return home to his family, with the country saved, were then in full enjoyment of a blissful ignorance."[39] What was lacking in equipment was made up in spirit, and if the barefoot, dirty, and unshaven soldiers in Confederate camps lacked armament, they possessed the invaluable ingredients of determination and confidence which kept their attitude positive toward the conflict ahead.

2.

By mid-summer of 1861, Tennessee's Confederate troops had dispersed to other states. Several regiments were already in Virginia. When the Confederate Army encountered the enemy at the First Battle of Bull Run on July 18, 1861, the results were all that the South could have hoped for. The Union troops were routed and the spectators who had come out from Washington to view the affair raced their soldiers to escape the charging Rebs. The entire experience tended toward proving that the Southern Army was every bit as good as it thought it was.

When the news of Bull Run reached the troops in Tennessee, joy and jubilation reigned supreme. As Private J.R. Thompson made his way from the drill field, "a shout commenced at the Depo & in the tents that shook the air the nuse came to our second Lieut that the Northern and southern Army had met & the Southern army killed six hundred Lincolnites & our loss fifty & he gave the command to all howlow & we did . . . . We went ten or fifteen steps & they bursted off like a gang of wild horses & ran to wher the crowde was gathered & their was a sencible looking Genlemon upon a table with a dispatch that the Enemy came to Virginia & six hundred Lincornites was kill & fifty Southern men."[40] If Private Thompson's figures were greatly exaggerated, what they symbolized was not. The South had won a great victory.

The news from Virginia signaled that the war was underway, and Tennessee's Confederate soldiers moved from camps toward the scenes of action. More regiments went to Virginia, but the great bulk of men were sent to the Confederate defense line across southern Kentucky.

As Maney's 1st Tennessee Regiment moved toward Virginia it passed through Nashville. A young lady who identified herself only as "Mary" watched the men march down main street and the next day wrote,

> *Early in the morning the streets of Nashville were filled to overflowing with people. You could only pass through the streets with the utmost difficulty . . . It was past 2, all was excitement when the shouts of a thousand voices arose, "They are coming!" In the distance I hear the beating of drums and the playing of fifes. The drums*

*and fifes all at once cease to play . . . But now a brass
band of more than twenty pieces burst forth with my
favorite tune, "The Mocking Bird." The head of the
column of the regiment appears . . . Every head in the
vast crowd is uncovered. Of course we had to use our
hats to wave them a welcome they so well deserved . . .
What fine, manly fellows they were. Their guns, as
bright as silver, shone in the July sun with unsurpassed
splendor. Their upturned, sunburned faces, their eyes
beaming with unspeakable enthusiasm and joy, seem to
say, "It is sweet to endure and even sweet to die for a
country that gave us such homes, such people and such
womanhood." . . . My country is in danger and I can
only shed bitter tears for those poor boys. I know what
is before them, and my soul tells me many will never see
their homes and dear ones again. God be with them.
They are gone, yet their shouts of triumph with which
they answered our greeting are still ringing in my ears.
My heart is sore, a fearful presentiment has taken the
place of that hopeful spirit that animated me on
yesterday. I am crushed. I can only pray and weep.* [41]

The soldiers were glad to escape the monotony of camp life,
and buoyed by the prospect of meeting the enemy, they stepped
lively to the music of regimental bands. As they made their way
across the country, the men began to see new territory and to
experience some of the more attractive aspects of army life. The
opportunities for entertainment in Nashville, Knoxville, and
Chattanooga often proved too tempting to country boys, and the
results were less favorable than the generals would have
desired.

After the Warren County "Guards" of the 16th Tennessee
passed through Nashville, Jim Womack noted, "While there
many of the men and officers became beastly drunken, some of
whom had to be left in the city and many others were
remarkably troublesome."[42]   Later, when the same regiment

reached Knoxville, it was observed that few of the officers remained sober enough to stand their turn on duty. The 20th Tennessee also had problems. While making its way through Knoxville, the boys had too much free time and trouble came in bottled portions. One observer wrote, "a great many of the regiment indulged too freely in East Tennessee's apple brandy and became very boisterous. Our Colonel ordered the sober portion of the regiment to put the drunken portion in a mule pen near the depot; this was done with some difficulty and when the work was completed a large per cent of the regiment was in the pen."[43]

Troop trains were usually crowded far beyond their normal capacity. As the 1st Tennessee made its way to Virginia the men stood in box cars "as thick as pins in a pincushion. When a fellow got tired of standing, he could climb to the top of the car, lie flat like a lizard, and hold on to the running board. About every fifteen miles we had to water and wood, and in order to rest themselves many of the boys would crawl down and spread out on the ground."[44]

Such train trips in the middle of the summer often brought on serious health problems. But there was seldom a condition for which there was not a reasonable, and sometimes pleasant, remedy. As J.R. Thompson's company passed through Nashville "the cars was powerfully crowded   some had to stand up   we had like to sufficated for want of water   when we reached Nashville We formed in double file & marched through town over to Edgefield before we got any water & one man drank so much watter that his sistem collasped & he came near diing   they gave him peppermint (having no better remedy) & Lieut Bain went to the Doctor & the advise was give him enough whiskey to make him drunk."[45] To some men it seemed that only the reliable soldiers ever became ill. One man said, "the hardened old cupes or the swearing old fellows, who would walk a mile to steal a sheep, or to rob a henroost, seemed to be utterly beyond the ravages of all diseases."[46]

As Confederate Regiments continued their journey toward the enemy, many soldiers got their first look at other sections of the country. When trains stopped to refuel, the men unloaded from the overcrowded cars and lined up in formation to march through the throngs of people gathered along the streets. Men not accustomed to such attention thrilled under the glance of those who cheered them wildly as they proceeded in something less than a faultless military fashion. J.R. Thompson wrote his mother, "All along the road the Ladies were standing in the doors & gallerys waving handkerchiefs & flowers as we passed by & even the little boys were waving their hats & cheering as we passed."[47] A strong rumor persisted in Virginia that after a Tennessee Regiment passed through a town, not a drop of brandy could be found.

After several weeks of constant shifting and moving about, Tennessee Confederates began settling down. Most of the regiments were on the Kentucky defense line, which extended from Columbus on the left, to Cumberland Gap on the right. A few regiments were in Virginia and still others continued to train back home. Early fall found the Tennesseans in close proximity to the enemy, and each day brought with it the possibility of a fight. Loud cheers split the air each time the Yankees were reported near. The men waited impatiently to get the "big show" started.

There were aspects of the army that strained the understanding of the hill soldiers. They watched in awe and wonderment as comrades-to-be arrived in camps from the plantation areas of the state. It seemed to the hill soldier that such men were more appropriately equipped for a pleasure excursion than fighting a war. In some instances the boys from wealthy families were accompanied by their own individual wagons loaded with all the luxuries they had enjoyed at home. They wore fancy suits of clothing for every occasion, stores of fine food were available to satisfy the appetites of gentlemen accustomed to every delicacy, and there were sometimes as many as two slave body-servants to wait hand and foot on their demanding young masters. Much of the finery had disappeared as the troops moved to the front, but enough remained, especially the slaves, to make the hill soldier wonder aloud if such men could hold their own—even against Yankees.

Back at home, the people of Confederate Tennessee were in high spirits, especially those who did not have sons in the army. The politicians continued to enjoy their success. The flame of Southern Nationalism was burning brightly and the politician was its keeper. Already the heat from that flame had fired the imagination of men who envisioned a new nation all their own, while the light from that flame had attracted thousands of young men who, although they stood to gain nothing from a Southern victory, were deemed more than capable of achieving it. Anxiously, but confidently, the people waited.

3.

By September of 1861, a campaign was taking shape in Virginia. The Union Army had moved into the northwestern portion of the state, and from the rugged peaks of Cheat Mountain, peered threateningly at the country to the south.* General Robert E. Lee, then relatively unknown to Tennesseans, was assigned a force and ordered to dislodge the enemy from its stronghold. Five regiments of Tennessee soldiers were in Lee's command: Maney's 1st, the 7th, the 8th, the 14th, and 16th — all from Middle Tennessee.

Even before the Cheat Mountain campaign began, Tennessee soldiers had learned that politicians and recruiters had not told the whole story of army life. The troops had left home in summer and the possibility of changing seasons had not been properly considered. When the first chilling winds of fall appeared, the officers applied to Richmond for winter-gear, but none was forthcoming. Captain Jim Womack of the 16th Tennessee wrote, "In consequence of either the neglect or inability of the C.S. [Confederate States] government to supply our brigade with clothing, Capts. of companies are ordered to ascertain the wants of their respective commands, and report a

* After June 20, 1863, this portion of Virginia would comprise a part of what is now West Virginia.

34

list of same, to be sent by a detailed officer to our homes in Tennessee to solicit supplies from them."[48] It was while waiting for these anticipated supplies that the men set out on their first campaign.

The Tennesseans were brought together for the first time on September 10th, and the march toward the enemy began. Thomas Head wrote that "The men were cheerful and buoyant, and eager for the conflict, when they could test their prowess on the enemy's stronghold at Cheat Mountain."[49] The advance toward the enemy was not easy. There were no roads to follow and the progress was slow, and often-times painful. It was Lee's plan to surprise the Yankees and capture them before help could arrive. To accomplish this objective he must keep his army well concealed until the enemy's position was reached.

Men unused to marches under battle conditions wasted their food — or ate it all the first day. Cut off from all supplies, the men marched further and further into the mountains until by the end of the second day very little food remained. What bread there was crumbled into doughy balls in the rain-soaked packs the men carried on their backs. So constant was the rain that, during a slight let-up, one soldier looked up and wondered aloud "if something had gone wrong with the clouds." The men became so muddy that bright red flannel shirts worn by some Tennesseans were no longer distinguishable, and officers ordered strips of white cloth placed in the soldiers' hats so they would not be confused with the enemy.

Neither the countryside nor the people impressed Lee's soldiers. Of the country, one soldier wrote, "if steamships were selling at a shilling a piece, I would not give a gangway plank for the whole of it."[50] The people were described as resembling "Egyptian mummies just excavated from their graves after being dead seventeen hundred years or more."[51]

Details of men were sent ahead to carve out steps up the mountains. Even with the added assistance of such steps, the soldiers stumbled and slid as they made their way ever closer to the enemy. Following two days of such rugged progress the

Confederate troops were in position to carry out their surprise attack. But just when everything was in readiness something went wrong. The column assigned to deliver the first assault, which was to be the signal for a general advance, was fooled into believing the enemy was much stronger than it actually was. As a result, the attack was never launched. The element of surprise was lost and the Confederates were ordered to withdraw.

The unexpected withdrawal caught most of the Tennessee troops in a highly vulnerable position. Knowing of their situation, Lee mounted his horse and rode to warn them of the impending danger. J.G. Carrigan wrote, "Gen. Lee, learning of our critical situation, had ridden all night to get to us and lead us out of the jaws of death . . . is it any wonder that they hailed him as a deliverer? . . . he lifted his hat, and with a smile on his face, and bowing to the men on the left and on the right, he rode off and by many of us was never seen again."[52]

The Cheat Mountain expedition was a failure for the Confederate cause. The green and inexperienced troops had seen only a few Union soldiers, of which an insignificant number had been killed or wounded. But this would not be the aspect of the expedition they would remember. Cut off from supplies and untrained in the practical aspects of mountain warfare, they found out quickly that war, even stripped of its more gruesome characteristics, was a brutal, uncompromising, and ruthless mistress.

The withdrawal from Cheat Mountain was marked by severe suffering for all the men in Lee's small army. The main fare was saltless beef obtained by killing stray cattle found in the mountains. A steady diet of this unseasoned meat took its toll in the sick who hampered the trip toward safety. Clothing became so wet and torn that it literally fell from the backs of the men. Resinor Etter of the 16th Tennessee wrote in his diary, "I marched all day barefooted, and my feet bleeding in about twenty places."[53] Without tents, blankets, or warm clothing, the men stumbled along mountainsides looking in vain for the supply train that would never appear. Tempers became short, many soldiers became unruly, and on some occasions officers threatened to kill soldiers who disobeyed orders.

On the second day of the withdrawal, Resinor Etter wrote, "we waded water rump deep   it was so cold my legs was as red as roses when I got through . . . I stold some corn and eat it   it was the sweetest food that I ever eat." That night Etter wrote, "night has come again   I have lade myself on a humble bed that I have constructed to day   it three poles   one each side of me a small one in the middle so as to swag a little   some leaves on them."[54]

By the time the Confederates had made their way out of the mountains they were in no shape for further campaigning and, somewhat deflated by their disappointing experience, settled down for the remainder of the year.

At home, women met to knit socks, church groups gathered clothing, days were set aside for prayer, and already a few people were wondering about the wisdom of the war they had so eagerly supported during the spring months. Fathers and sons were divided on the issues, and in some cases, were in opposing armies. One of Amanda McDowell's brothers had joined the Confederate Army, another the Union Army. Friends who had sat side by side in church now, sometimes, watched each other suspiciously. In some instances neighbors who were divided on the political issues remained friends, but such cases were all too few.

In Virginia, David Phillips, a former school teacher from Watertown, wrote in his diary, "this morning begins the last six months of our services. Day gloomy and rainy. During the past six months we have endured innumerable ills such as soldiers alone are heir to.   May the next six be the consummation of peace is doubtless the wish of all."[55] It was well that Phillips, Resinor Etter, J. R. Thompson, and those with them could not see what the future held. To have done so would have seen the six months they anticipated lengthen into three and a half years, and the peace they longed for to come at the price of almost total annihilation. They would have seen the day when brigades could not combine to make regiments, and the calling of company rolls would only produce tragic memories of such places as Shiloh, Stone's River, Chickamauga, and Franklin. They would have seen neighbors become informers on each other and have seen men who had encouraged secession become trusted advisors to the enemy. They would have seen prominent Southern families, who had promised to take care of the Confederate soldier's children while he was away, selling their products and allegiance to the Union Army while the soldier's children went hungry.

The possibility of such things found no place in the thoughts of Confederate Tennesseans in 1861. The circumstances that would bring them about had not yet taken shape in Middle Tennessee. But in the mountains to the east, the demon of border war was already rearing its head and spitting out its venomous spray of fear and hate. This demon had only to wait to reap its victims, for Tennesseans, dislodged from the virtues which had formerly disciplined their lives, would perform its desolate work with a high degree of efficiency.

4.

When Tennessee felt the first sting of war it did not come from the North. It did not come in the form of Northern Armies burning and killing as the politician had predicted. It was not a war of great armies commanded by generals who planned brilliant strategy, or a war highlighted by sensational charges made by rank upon rank of screaming soldiers. Instead, it was a war which pitted neighbor against neighbor, which saw men hanged before the eyes of their own families, and found men led off to prison for no other reason than professing loyalty to a cause they believed right. In East Tennessee the demon of border war was about its work.

The situation in East Tennessee did not develop overnight, but was many months in the making. In 1860, four candidates had been selected to run for the presidency of the United States. The Whig Party selected John Bell of Tennessee. Abraham Lincoln was selected by the Republican Party, John C. Breckinridge by the southern wing of the Democratic Party, and Stephen A. Douglas by the northern wing of the Democratic Party. Only three electoral tickets were placed on the ballot in Tennessee. Mr. Lincoln's name did not appear.

In later years Southerners in particular would argue that slavery played only a minor role in the act of secession. An examination of speeches and issues of the time belie this assertion. Slavery was, for all practical purposes, the *only* issue for secessionists. Knowing that Lincoln represented the political party most opposed to slavery it was, according to Judge Oliver Temple of Knoxville, "openly proclaimed that the election of Mr. Lincoln would be a sufficient cause and should be the signal for withdrawing from the Union," of all the cotton states. [56]

Lincoln was elected to the presidency and was inaugurated on March 4, 1861. One of his first official acts was the calling for 75,000 volunteers to quell the rebellion which had started in South Carolina. As a result of this action, Tennessee officially withdrew from the Union on June 8th.

East Tennesseans had little objection to the institution of slavery. In fact, many of the most ardent supporters of the Union owned slaves. What they did object to was the dissolution of the Union. Leaders of the area continually referred to the role played by East Tennesseans at the Battle of King's Mountain at which the mountaineers won one of the battles that insured the nation's independence. They were not inclined to throw the fruits of that victory to a Southern Confederacy.

Nine days after the people of Tennessee voted themselves out of the Union a special convention was called in Greenville where a resolution was adopted asking that East Tennessee be allowed to form an independent state. Political leaders of the area argued that the vote on secession had not been legal and was therefore not binding. Such a plea went unheeded in Nashville where Governor Harris looked with contempt on East Tennessee Unionists. If the pro-Southern governor believed in secession it did not necessarily follow that he extended that privilege to counties. East Tennesseans must fight; their problem became one of deciding with whom they would fight.

To the mountain people of East Tennessee a government dominated by the plantation aristocracy of the South held little appeal. The thing they wanted most was for the Union to remain intact, the thing they desired next was to be left alone, the thing they wanted least was to become part of a Southern Confederacy.

The matter was not to be decided so simply. Although a minority in East Tennessee, the secessionists were vocal enough to force the issue and it soon became apparent that the men of that region must choose sides. Encouraged and bolstered by the victory at Manassas and the constant flow of Confederates on their way to Virginia, Confederate leaders became oppressive in their treatment of the unorganized Unionists and tensions continued to mount.

Throughout the summer and fall of 1861, Unionist leaders in East Tennessee left their homes and sought protection in Kentucky. Among these was Andrew Johnson. Soon, small bands of men from all points of the area headed north toward the safety of the Union Army. Such groups gradually increased in size until they became regular caravans seeking to escape Confederate authorities who steadily increased their pressures in behalf of the Confederate cause.

Summing up the state of affairs during the fall of 1861, one writer observed, "bitter feelings between those of opposing sentiments had been aroused, and crimination and recrimination was freely indulged. The Union men were accused of disloyalty to the South and called 'Lincolnites', 'Abolitionists', and 'Thugs'. They in turn accused those in opposition to the government, calling them 'rebels', 'traitors', and other epithets."[57]

Loyalty to the Union began to carry with it untold risks in East Tennessee following the arrival of Confederate troops. One Unionist reported, "Every unguarded word and act was duly reported by Southern sympathizers to headquarters, and this becoming known the most bitter feelings engendered, and threats were freely made. Thus the strongest friendships were broken and the closest ties of kindred were severed. Fathers, and sons, and brothers became estranged, and joining different armies, were arrayed in deadly hostility to each other. Confidence was lost and men knew not whom to trust. Suspicion and distrust ruled the hour."[58]

Through all the seething resentment of Confederate occupation there was one ray of hope for the Unionists in East Tennessee: they firmly believed that the authorities in Washington would send troops to their aid. Already such an army under the command of General George Thomas, a Virginian, was taking shape in Kentucky, and it was accepted as a matter of course that his army would come through the Cumberland Gap and drive the secessionists away. By October of 1861, enough East Tennesseans had escaped to form two infantry regiments, and hundreds of other mountaineers had swelled the ranks of regiments of other states. The fondest hope of these men was to be sent to their home areas to liberate their families.

Believing as they did that the Federal Army would soon come to their rescue, it became the objective of the Unionists to do all within their power to insure its success. In September a lone minister of the Gospel started to Washington with a plan he believed would be helpful. The Reverend William B. Carter called on President Lincoln and presented his plan. It called for

41

burning all the railroad bridges between Bristol, Tennessee, on the Virginia border to Bridgeport, Alabama. Carter was confident that such an operation would deny the Confederates the communication necessary to defend East Tennessee and would, in turn, insure the success of an invading army.

Lincoln liked the plan and gave it his unqualified support. Carter was promised the cooperation of the Federal Army and returned home to work out the details of the plan, convinced that he was about to strike the first blow for the liberation of his people.

Carter's plan called for the selection of one or two of the most trusted men in each locality where a bridge was to be burned. These men, in turn, would notify as many of the most discreet citizens in the neighborhoods involved as were needed in the operation. A leader was to be designated from the group and all orders were to come from him.

The plan went well at first. Trusted men were selected and informed of their roles in the daring undertaking and by the first of November matters were well enough in hand to set a date for the burnings. November 8th was the date set.

Unknown to Carter on the day before the bridges were to be burned General George Thomas sent a short note to Andrew Johnson in Kentucky in which it was stated, "I have done all in my power to get troops and transportation and means to advance into East Tennessee . . . Up to this time we have been unsuccessful . . . If the Tennesseans are not content and must go, then the risk of disaster will remain with them."[59]

Unaware of this development, the bridgeburners prepared to carry through their carefully laid plans. Nine bridges were included in the operation — the two most important being those over the Tennessee River at Loudon, Tennessee, and at Bridgeport, Alabama. Both were massive structures and their destruction would certainly paralyze Confederate transportation for weeks — an important factor in light of the supposed invasion of a Federal force from the north.

The bridge at Bridgeport was to be burned by two local

men chosen by A.M. Cate, one of the original planners. So secret was the operation that it was thirty-five years after the event before their closest friends knew who had taken part. The two men chosen for the daring deed approached the bridge, but finding it too closely guarded turned and made no attempt to fulfill their mission.

Not far away, A.M. Cate's brother burned two bridges across the Hiwassee River with the help of still another brother and some nearby residents. It was never known for sure if an attempt was made on the bridge at Loudon— in any event the structure remained undamaged. The two bridges which spanned the Tennessee River remained intact. At least eight bridges had been either destroyed or severly damaged, and the reaction which followed clearly indicates the concern of the Confederates.

The particular incident which caused the most excitement was the burning of the bridge across the Holston River at Bluff City. Daniel Stover, Andrew Johnson's son-in-law, led the raid which caused consternation among the Confederates.

On the day set for the burnings Stover called together those trusted with the original plans. Working at a feverish pitch they set out to inform their associates who had been selected to take part. Throughout the afternoon and evening, inconspicuous messengers dodged Confederate scouts to deliver the word that all participants would meet at Rueben Miller's barn. At the appointed time, thirty men came for additional directions. Every man knew the danger involved. They knew the enemy would leave no stone unturned to hunt them down, yet none declined to take part.

The raiding party made its way to the bridge. Members masked their faces and crept into position. Two Confederate guards were seen at the end of the bridge, but these were surprised and overcome with little difficulty. The operation accomplished its objective and soon the flames were leaping skyward. There had been only one slip, but it would prove to be a fatal one.

In the process of disarming the guards, the mask had slipped from the face of G.O. Collins, one of the raiders. He had been recognized by a guard named Jenkins who was also a resident of the community. Several members of the raiding party insisted that Jenkins be killed on the spot since a report by him to the Confederate authorities would mean certain death to many of the party. Other members of the Unionist group counseled moderation, and upon Jenkins' solemn pledge to reveal nothing he had seen, he was released. As soon as he was free, Jenkins hurried to Confederate headquarters and reported everything, including the names of those he had recognized.

As Oliver Temple remembered it, "Soon the news spread that the men engaged in this enterprise had been identified under oath, and that they were to be arrested and hung as bridgeburners."[60]

The next night and the following day, intense excitement developed throughout East Tennessee. Union men with knives, pistols, shotguns, and squirrel rifles rushed to meet the anticipated advance of the Federal Army. In their minds such men envisioned themselves falling into the ranks of the Union Army and joining in the fight to rid their communities of the detested Rebels. By noon of November 10th, over a thousand men had gathered near Elizabethton and before dark the group had grown by another five hundred.

Word spread quickly that Union men were being arrested for the bridge-burnings and the news set into motion farmers and business-men who gathered throughout the region. A feeling close akin to savagery overcame the mountaineers, who now resolved to fight the Southerners with or without the aid of the Federal Army. Every instrument that could serve as a weapon was collected and placed in the hands of Loyalists. One observer noted that "A reign of terror prevailed, and it really seemed as if the devil had been turned loose and was having everything his own way."[61]

The citizen army paused long enough to organize into a military body with Daniel Stover as colonel. Tired and excited from the day's activities, the men stopped for a night's rest. They found little. During this time, they were attacked by a company of Confederates who were, after a brisk fight, driven away. Unused to the fire of hostile forces some of the Unionists deserted their newly formed regiment and sought safety in the mountains while others stood their ground like veterans and bravely returned the fire of the Confederates with the weapons at hand.

By the following morning the Confederates were duly warned and organized. Although their commanders imagined themselves about to be attacked by thousands of armed mountaineers aided by well-trained Federal troops, they marched toward the scene of action. Messages of the most desperate kind were sent to Richmond, Virginia, as the Confederates planned strategy to cope with the awful thing they believed about to happen. Their fear was unfounded. The brisk fight that had taken place had convinced Unionist leaders that to put untrained mountain men against Confederate troops would be nothing short of tragic, and before noon Colonel Stover instructed his men to break up and go home or seek places of safety. Many of Stover's men left immediately for Kentucky, others hid in the mountains, and a few went home. Thus the "little rebellion against the big rebellion" ended.

From the day of the bridge-burnings, East Tennessee was to know only intervals of uneasy peace. It would be a time when neighbor would be hunted by neighbor, and only rarely did the light of human kindness cut its way through the ugliness of border war.

Four days after the bridges were burned, Governor Isham G. Harris wrote Jefferson Davis, "The burning of the railroad bridges in East Tennessee shows a deep-seated spirit of rebellion in that section. Union men are organizing. The rebellion must be crushed out instantly, the leaders arrested and summarily punished. I shall send immediately about ten thousand men to that section. If you can possibly send from Western Virginia a number of Tennessee regiments to East

Tennessee we can at once repair the bridges and crush the rebellion."[62]

In Richmond, the Confederate Secretary of War, Judah P. Benjamin, had some suggestions of his own. In reply to a dispatch from the Confederate Commander at Knoxville, Benjamin suggested, "all such men as can be identified as having engaged in bridge-burning are to be tried summarily by drum-head courtmartial, and if found guilty, executed on the spot by hanging. It would be well to leave their bodies hanging in the vicinity of the burned bridges."[63]

Confederate military units swept throughout the communities involved in the burnings and arrested every suspect they could find. It was not unusual for a neighbor of the accused to be riding in the group that arrested the suspects. Fear and anxiety gripped the thinking of men who had formerly lived peaceful, quiet, and orderly lives. One East Tennessean wrote, "Houses were searched and ransacked, and curses and abusive language used, even to women and aged and respected citizens . . . Such is the spirit aroused by civil war."[64]

It took only a short time for Confederate authorities to round up those suspected of burning the bridges. On November 30, 1861, a Confederate colonel sent a dispatch to Richmond stating, "Two insurgents have today been tried for bridge burning, found guilty and hanged."[65] The speed with which Confederate justice was rendered is evidenced by the fact that the trial and execution occurred the same day.

The two men referred to above were Jacob Hensie and Henry Fry who had burned the bridge over Lick Creek. The men were "swung from the projecting limb of a tree which stood north of the railroad and the depot in Greenville. This was in full sight of the railroad and the trains as they passed. The bodies . . . were left swinging from the tree for about twenty-four hours before they were taken down."[66]

At Knoxville, Jacob Harmon and his son Thomas were jailed on charges of bridge-burning, and after a short trial, both were sentenced to hang. Even the intervention of Confederate friends failed to delay the execution. On December 17th the men were led to a specially constructed gallows in North Knoxville, and while the father was forced to watch, the son was executed. In a few minutes the father was hanged with the same rope. This temporary gallows would be a prime target of East Tennessee troops when they entered Knoxville almost two years later.

Many other executions followed. In addition to those hanged, countless others were jailed in selected prisons throughout the South. Only rarely did the passions of men cool sufficiently for reason to reassert itself. Through the personal intervention of Jefferson Davis the life of Harrison Self was spared only minutes before he was to ascend the steps of the gallows. Such instances were few and far between. The demon of border war was loose on the land, feeding on the fears and emotions of people on both sides of the political fence.

Thus the year in which the war began came to an end. The terrible trail of blood which had begun in East Tennessee would eventually extend across the state and throughout the South. Locations unknown to the overwhelming majority of people waited patiently for their moment in history. Their day would come. It would come as a practical consequence of the actions of men who had abandoned the route of reason and were instead following the dictates of selfishness and emotion. It would come.

Robert Gates

William J. McMurray

Major Jesse Taylor

Chapter II

It was here we began to understand the seriousness of war

The opening days of 1862 found the overwhelming majority of Tennessee's Confederate troops clustered along a Southern defense line extending from Columbus, Kentucky, to Cumberland Gap. Three of the Tennessee regiments that had taken part in the Cheat Mountain campaign in Virginia were preparing to leave that theater of war to return home — Maney's 1st, the 8th, and 16th regiments. During the fall months, Tennessee had had two regiments in Virginia that called themselves the "1st." One was the regiment raised by Peter Turney at Winchester early in the spring, the other being a regiment raised by George Maney in Davidson County later in the year. To separate the two for administrative purposes, one was called "Maney's 1st", the other "Turney's 1st". When Maney's 1st left Virginia, its place was taken by Turney's 1st which left the numerical alignment intact.

As of yet, few Tennesseans had seen anything resembling a full-scale action. Tennessee men had been at Manassas but were afforded little opportunity to display their military talents. The troops in Virginia were tired of marching and those in Kentucky were tired of waiting, but both groups believed that when the enemy was finally engaged, it would be a swift, sure victory for the Southern Army.

Lt. Burton Warfield, a member of the 6th Tennessee Cavalry, wrote from Kentucky in January, "We went to Brownsville last Sunday on a scout and had the pleasure of seeing a few Yankies and hearing the balls from their Minnie Muskits whistle over our heads and among our feet . . . I shot six times at them. They have longer shooting guns than we have. We were close enough for them to have killed some of us and we them, but they were too cowardly to show themselves long at a time."[1] Such incidents served only to add to the complacency of boys who waited in boredom and disgust for the time they could get close enough to make the fire from their antiquated muskets hit the target.

A remarkable transition had taken place in Tennessee soldiers: they seemed to believe that they would actually enjoy killing Union men. Even the most refined individuals, men who had been exposed to the best cultural influences the region had to offer, spoke and wrote as if they relished the experience of taking aim and killing a man of whom they knew little except the color of his uniform. Few seemed to doubt that God was on their side and that the bullets projected from their guns would carry with them the blessing of the Almighty.

Back home, the people of Confederate Tennessee went about their business as if nothing of consequence was happening. The defense line across Kentucky would surely protect Tennessee soil from the invader and only a few more months would be needed to impress the Federals of their incompetency in subduing the South. Rebel sympathizers could find little cause for worry. There were some citizens who liked the economic aspects of the situation and were in no particular hurry for the good times to end. Secessionists continued to maintain an unbounded confidence in the brains of their generals and the valor of their troops. They waited patiently for the day when the Union Army would blunder into the range of Southern fighting men.

General Albert Sidney Johnston of "the old army" was in command in Kentucky and nothing could have been more reassuring to the secessionists. Johnston, a native of Kentucky, had been the commander of the Department of the Pacific during the months preceding the bombardment of Fort Sumter, but had resigned in May of 1861, to become a major general in the Confederate Army. The West Point graduate was considered by many to be the most brilliant military mind in the country and his presence in Kentucky was interpreted by Southerners as another good omen of things to come.

Johnston himself was more realistic than the people who looked to him for leadership. It took him only a short time to discover the deplorable condition of the army whose destiny he was to guide and without delay he appealed to Richmond for arms and ammunition which were so conspicuously lacking. He dispatched a messenger to Jefferson Davis with instructions to obtain all the help possible, but the messenger returned empty-handed. Davis asked, "My God! Why did General Johnston send you to me for arms and reinforcements when he must know that I have neither."[2]   Giving a forewarning of his efforts to assist the armies in the west, Davis added, "He has plenty of men in Tennessee, and they must have arms of some kind — shotguns, rifles, even pikes could be used . . ." [3]   Obviously the President of the Confederacy had overlooked some of the practical implications of the idealistic dream he had promoted the previous year.

Johnston did the best he could under the circumstances and divided his army into three main parts. His left was at Columbus, Kentucky, under General Leonidas Polk. Polk was a West Point graduate who had given up a military career to follow a life in the ministry and had risen to the rank of Bishop in the Episcopal Church of Louisiana. There would come a day when some of his superiors in the army would question how beneficial it had been for the South that the Bishop ever decided to take up arms again — but at least his credentials were impressive.

The center of Johnston's line was at Bowling Green, Kentucky, under the command of General W. J. Hardee.

Hardee was a native of Georgia; he had served in the Mexican war and as commandant of cadets at West Point. He was also the author of a standard text known as *Rifle and Light Infantry Tactics*. Unfortunately, the distinguished general had not included in his book a chapter on how an army of 25,000, the size of his own, could defeat one of twice that number — a situation he now faced. If such odds bothered Hardee, he found little sympathy among civilians in Confederate Tennessee who still believed their soldiers would win despite the odds.

The Confederate right was at Cumberland Gap on the Kentucky-East Tennessee border. Here Felix Zollicoffer, a native of Columbia, Tennessee, was in command. Zollicoffer had previously served as editor of the *Nashville Republican Banner* and subsequently represented his district for three terms in the U. S. House of Representatives. He was known as an impulsive, brilliant, and courageous man who had once fought a duel on the streets of Nashville with an opposing editor.[4] In spite of these impressive credentials, few people, even including himself, would have lauded Zollicoffer's qualifications to lead men in battle.

The first action on the Kentucky defense line came on the left at Columbus. Actually the action occurred at Belmont, Missouri, just across the Mississippi River. There, on November 7, 1861, General Ulysses S. Grant moved on the Confederate forces commanded by Polk. The fighting lasted from 10:30 in the morning until sunset and decided nothing. Both sides could find evidence of victory but substantively the situation remained unchanged.

The first significant contact with the enemy came at the other end of the line at a place called Mill Springs, Kentucky. During November, Zollicoffer left the Cumberland Gap guarded by a small force of his command and headed west. After traveling for approximately a hundred miles, he turned north into Kentucky. The Blue Grass State still insisted that it was neutral but Leonidas Polk disregarded that plea when he moved his men to Columbus, and now Zollicoffer did the same thing at

Mill Springs. Zollicoffer did at least write Kentucky Governor Beriah Magoffin, and told him that since his state was recruiting and training men for the Union Army, its claim of neutrality could no longer be honored.

Mill Springs was an insignificant village on the south bank of the Cumberland River. At this place the river formed a horseshoe curve into which Zollicoffer moved his men by crossing them to the north side. Immediately the horseshoe was fortified by constructing entrenchments in its open end and here the Confederates settled down in what they called Camp Beech Grove.

Felix Zollicoffer had many reasons to be a worried man. He had expected reinforcements which had not arrived; his men were tired, hungry, ill-clothed, and poorly equipped. When he had asked for help none came — not even advice. But there were other reasons why the former editor might be worried.

Zollicoffer's wife Louisa had died four years before Tennessee seceded form the Union. Although Louisa had given birth to thirteen children, only six had survived. Among the dead were the couple's five sons. Of the six surviving children the oldest was Virginia, who was, at the time of Mill Springs, twenty-four years of age. Just before taking his army to Kentucky, Zollicoffer wrote Virginia:

Jenny take care of your younger sisters — they are motherless and their father is now powerless to look after them. My only feeling of gloom is that I left my children homeless and under circumstances in which I cannot watch over their inexperience. I have a strong faith, though, that there is a just and merciful Omnipotence and I know you will do the utmost of your ability as a mother of the younger ones. In this great conflict which will tax our people to the utmost I will endeavor to do my duty. The responsibility is great. I

*feel my want of experience and knowledge of war for so
large a command — now about 10,000 men . . .* [5]

At Camp Beech Grove Zollicoffer had only 4,000 of the
men he had spoken of, and in the eyes of some observers the
"want of experience and knowledge of war" was beginning to
assert itself.[6]   In crossing his men to the north bank of the
river, he had placed his army between a river swollen by a series
of prolonged rains and an enemy force much larger than his
own. To compound Zolicoffer's problems, Jefferson Davis had
assigned General George Crittenden to East Tennessee to
assume overall command.

Crittenden really wasn't the man for the job. He had been
a Lieutenant Colonel in the old army but had resigned his
commission to cast his lot with the Confederacy. His brother,
Thomas, was a general in the Union Army, and although writers
found this situation romantic, it tended to raise eyebrows among
fighting men. There was also the rumor that George was a
drunkard and at least some of the evidence for the rumor had
been supplied by the general himself. In view of these
considerations, the appointment of the Kentucky native met with
little enthusiasm from the men he was sent to rescue.

Crittenden did not go to Camp Beech Grove immediately
but stopped in Knoxville from where he sent Zollicoffer orders
to cross his army to the south side of the river. Zollicoffer liked
the position he had selected and, believing it too late to change,
stayed where he was.

The cold weather and short supplies which had
accompanied the late fall months had brought displeasure and
discontent to Zollicoffer's ranks. The patriotism of some men
completely vanished with the appearance of winter and
desertions were not uncommon.

If desertions were not uncommon, neither were they a
source of pleasure for men who were caught. Such culprits
were punished by putting their heads through a hole cut in the
top of a barrel in such a way that the weight of the barrel rested

on their shoulders. Following this phase of the ceremony the regiment of the deserter was "formed on dress parade and the deserters were marched in front of the line in this condition, with the regimental band playing 'The Bob-tail Horse' behind them, they were escorted to our outer lines and let go." [7] In spite of this ritual, desertions continued to thin the ranks.

Crittenden eventually arrived at Zollicoffer's camp and to his consternation found the Confederates still in their camp north of the river. It was too late to move. At long last, a half-equipped, so-called "brigade", came from Knoxville under the command of General William Carroll to join Zollicoffer's men. As Crittenden mulled the situation, word was received that the Yankees under General George Thomas were moving toward them.

Crittenden learned that the Union force was divided by a river. He proposed to move out and attack before it could consolidate. If the Yankees got all their men together they would outnumber the Confederates by at least one-third — a situation that could not be allowed to develop. On the night of January 18th, the men at Camp Beech Grove abandoned their carefully constructed earthworks and moved toward their first major encounter with the enemy.

It was after midnight when the Rebs left their camp. The weather was miserable. Spencer Talley, a member of the 28th Tennessee, remembered the night as "very cold, and it had been raining, sleeting or snowing all night and many were the fence rails we had to burn on the roadside to keep form freezing." [8] The pelting rain quickly penetrated the scant clothing of the Southerners and they shivered uncontrollably as they sloshed their way along the narrow roads. The progress of the troops was slowed to a snail's pace and regiments attempting to stay closed up were soon spread along a line three miles long. To make matters worse, daylight came before the enemy's position was reached.

Crittenden's force was divided into two brigades with Zollicoffer's in the lead and Carroll's acting as a reserve.

Shortly after daylight, Zollicoffer's men spotted the enemy and deployed for an attack. In short order, the Union pickets were driven in and the fight began.

On each side of a country road, the Southerners pushed forward. Zollicoffer's brigade spread itself as thinly as possible but they found Yankees in superior numbers everywhere. In the mud and fog it appeared as if every tree shielded three or more of the enemy. At the very outset of the fighting the Rebs gained an advantage, but they were unable to maintain it. When the Southerners attempted to deliver a telling blow to the enemy they found that fully one-third of their weapons would not fire, and when they looked to their artillery for help they saw only two guns which had somehow made it over the muddy roads too late to be of service.

Inclement weather and faulty weapons were not alone responsible for the ultimate withdrawal of the Rebel force. Early in the fighting General Zollicoffer, dressed in a white raincoat, rode through his own lines and began giving orders to the Yankees. At first the Yankees were none the wiser, but when one of Zollicoffer's men attempted to correct his general's mistake, Zollicoffer was recognized and killed instantly.

Meanwhile, the battle continued to go badly for the Rebs. Their enemy was better equipped, better disciplined, and had better leadership. Describing the lack of preparation of his unit, W. J. Worsham of the 19th Tennessee, recalled, "Our brigade was never drilled or put in line of battle by any one until the morning of the memorable battle of Fishing Creek [one of the many names by which the battle is known]."

Perhaps of equal significance was the fact that the Confederates had almost no confidence in George Crittenden, and after Zollicoffer was killed, there was no-one to whom they could turn. The men constantly repeated the tales of the General's family history and of his love for whiskey. Many considered him both unpatriotic and dangerous, and in Zollicoffer's absence, his presence assumed more importance. Soon, men all along the line were yelling: "Crittenden is drunk a good portion of the time," "He has a brother in the Federal Army," "He is in sympathy with the North," "He will surrender us all to the Federals if he has a good opportunity."[9] The men in the 15th Mississippi worked themselves up to such a state that it was rumored that some planned to kill the general should the opportunity present itself.[10] Although much of such talk was probably little more than finding excuses for their own situations, it contributed to the Confederate line breaking. In a very short time the Rebs were running in wild confusion toward the rear.

The battle had been short in duration, but it served to initiate men to the demands of war. Although the Confederate forces had been routed from the field, many regiments had fought well. Front line regiments held, with those in the rear coming up, and together they had stood firm against the Yankee pressure being applied. Individual soldiers and officers had displayed astounding courage in the face of discouraging odds.

The impressions carried away from the battle by most Confederates were confined to their personal experiences. Spencer Talley remembered:

> *Our regiment was on the extreme left while the fighting was all on the right and when we were repulsed, our wing was about to be cut off and captured. We were formed through a dense thicket of undergrowth and grape vines, when our Col. gave orders to retreat in haste or we would be cut off. There was a rush to get out of this thicket and in leaving my foot caught in a vine. I fell in the pathway leading out of the thicket. I made many efforts to rise up but before I could rise some boy would step on me and I am sure that not less than twenty men ran over me before I could get to my feet ... I found that I had been kicked along and that my hat and gun were twenty feet behind me. I knew it would not do to lose my hat and gun, and when I had gone back for them, I found I was way behind and the 'Minnie balls'*

flying thick and fast about me. After leaving the thicket we had to cross an open field, the ground was soft and wet and covered with grass which made the mud stick fast to our feet. Before I reached the woodland on the opposite side of the field my feet felt as if there was twenty pounds to each foot and I was broken down and still behind my comrades and felt sure I would be captured. I had gone but a short distance in the woodland before a piece of fleeing artillery came passing by me with ten horses hitched to it. A man to each pair of horses was driving under whip and lash, as the cannon was passing I jumped astride of it and locked my arms around it and my gun to keep from falling off. I rode this cannon for half a mile right through a woods where there was no road . . . This was our first scrap with the Yanks and I am sure we had a few days of as much suffering and want as we experienced during the civil strife.[11]

Perhaps the memory that would linger longest in the minds of men in the 20th Tennessee was their attempt to flank the 4th Kentucky Regiment. Just when it appeared that the Tennesseans might accomplish their objective, they were met by a savage counter-stroke, which included two regiments of East Tennesseans fighting with the Yankees. It was the first opportunity the East Tennesseans had been afforded to demonstrate their contempt for their mid-state cousins and they entertained no idea of passing it by. The Tennessee Yankees emphatically hurled back the Tennessee Rebs, who soon found themselves engulfed by a flanking movement similar to the one they had attempted to execute.

One memory shared by all Confederates who occupied a position on the line was that of watching their fire fall short of its intended target. A. S. Marks of the 17th Tennessee wrote that the fire from the Confederate guns "was immediately observed to have no effect. The worthlessness of the guns

58

and the condition of the ammunition made the firing a farce . . . and for the first and last time during the war the Seventeenth Regiment retired before an enemy in disorder."12   Marks belonged to a regiment whose men had refused the summer before to accept the old flintlock muskets offered it, but reconsidered when assured that new guns would be forthcoming. The new guns never came.

W. J. Worsham watched his men take their guns and break them against the stumps that dotted the battlefield. But other memories were more sobering. He wrote:

> As we went into the battle . . . the writer picked up a Yankee overcoat and put it on for the rain was cold and falling fast. When nearly in the woods, we came upon one of our boys so badly wounded, who even with our help, could go no farther, we spread our Yankee overcoat on the wet ground and our wounded comrade lay down upon it to die. The wounded were taken from the field as fast as could be done, some left at the field hospital, others taken on the camp and from there to Monticello. The last one we helped on this sad morning was Charlie Clemenson, of Company E, 19th Tennessee, who fell mortally wounded about half way up the ridge after we had been driven from the woods. Pink Henderson, Clabe Perry and the writer carried Charlie from the field in a blanket. We had just reached the yard of the log cabin on the hill side where our hospital was located. Our men were now hurrying by as rapidly as they could, the road and woods were full, all in haste to be gone. Wood's Alabama regiment was trying to make a show of resistance but was as powerless as straw in the wind . . .
>
> Poor Charlie was dying when we laid him down. We can never forget the sad anxious expression of his face, as we left him on the last sad trial of the battle of life, dying alone, deserted by all whom he thought were

his friends, left on the cold ground with naught but the cold rain to wash the sweat of death from his brow. [13]

During the afternoon of their defeat Crittenden put his men behind the earthworks at Beech Grove. Meanwhile, he planned a way to cross to the south side of the river. By late afternoon the pursuit of the Federal troops had slackened and perhaps there was a good reason. One Northern writer explained:

> *The road which the retreating force followed was strewn with evidences that the retreat had degenerated into a panic. A piece of artillery was found abandoned in a mud hole, hundreds of muskets were strewn along the road and in the fields, and, most convincing proof of all, the flying foe had thrown away their haversacks filled with rations of corn pone and bacon. Those were the days when stories of 'regel atrocities' in the way of poisoning wells and food were current, and the pursuers, who had gone into the fight breakfastless, were doubtful about tasting the contents of the first haversacks they observed . . . Their great number, however, soon became a guarantee of good faith, and hungry soldiers seized on them with avidity.* [14]

By sunset Crittenden was ready to begin the evacuation of his demoralized army. A few days before, a small steamer named *Noble Ellis* had arrived at Camp Beech Grove with supplies from Nashville, and luckily it was still around. While the cavalrymen whooped and yelled to make their horses swim the river, the infantrymen crowded along the banks trying to get aboard the overtaxed little steamer. Each time the ship pulled away there was a rush to occupy the place from which it would take on its next cargo of exhausted soldiers. One man reckoned that if Yankees had fired a gun somewhere behind them the entire Rebel army would have jumped headlong into the swollen river. But such was not the case, and by daylight most of the men had crossed. With an almost apologetic attitude, the men paused long enough to set fire to the *Noble Ellis* which had saved them from disaster.

Very little of the Confederate equipment was saved. For the most part, even the attempt to save horses was futile. One man observed that "Very few horses ever crossed, many of them, perhaps, were drowned, but the greater part of them remained and were captured. Here were artillerymen without artillery, teamsters without teams and cavalrymen afoot. What a racket and confusion reigned here, and right in the face of the enemy."[15]

The conduct of some Tennessee troops on the march from Mill Springs left much to be desired. High ranking officers accused men of stealing horses and fleeing to Nashville, Knoxville, and other places of safety. The people at home were aware of "the intense excitement as well as gloom pervading Southern arms that the Battle of Fishing Creek created . . . and the 2:40 gate made by some of our panicked soldiers home"[16]

Perhaps if the home-front critics had been with the retreating soldiers they might have seen things differently.

W. J. McMurray said, "This march in the dead of winter, was one of the most severe that I experienced during the four years of war. We lived almost the entire ten days on parched corn."[17] Adding to the miseries of hunger and cold was a deep resentment which burned fiercely within the defeated men. As one of them said, "The men felt that without fault on their own part they had been subjected to a needless humiliation."[18] Their equipment had proved astoundingly inferior; no arrangements had been made to deliver supplies; and they seriously doubted the competency of the commanding general.

The retreating Confederates traveled in small groups as they made their way south and tried desperately to take their wounded home. Straw was placed in wagons and the wounded were arranged as comfortably as possible. In many instances the teams were so weak from hunger that they could hardly move the improvised ambulances in the bottomless mire created by the incessant rains. When such situations developed, able-bodied men rolled the wheels until firmer ground was reached. Each turn of the wheel was accompanied by the shouts of teamsters as they urged their horses forward. Such shouts blended inharmoniously with the groans of the wounded as the grim caravans crept slowly southward. At times, the suffering of the wounded became so unbearable that they begged the teamsters to stop the wagons and allow them to die in peace.

This aspect of war was, as of yet, unknown to the people of Confederate Tennessee. They were aware mostly of their own humiliation in the fact that their soldiers had retreated before the enemy. This was not the picture painted by the politicians the year before and the people at home were not prepared to accept the development in good grace.

Where were the soldiers who could whip ten Yankees? This particular bit of fancy had long since vanished from the minds of the muddy creatures making their way toward places where bands had played and politicians had shouted unbridled optimism only a few months before. For many of these water-logged volunteers the only appeal war had ever had was that of adventure, and this aspect had not proven nearly so exciting in reality as it had in camp-fire conversations and drug store dialogue.

In the North, citizens celebrated the victory at Fishing Creek. Some of this celebrating took a weird form. A Cincinnati reporter told his readers of seeing General Zollicoffer's body and that the General "lay by the side of the road along which we all passed, and all had a fair view of what was once Zollicoffer. I saw his lifeless body as it lay in a fence-corner by the side of the road, but Zollicoffer himself is now in hell. Hell is a fitting abode for all such arch-traitors."[19]

Actually Zollicoffer's body was treated with great respect. His remains, along with those of young Baylie Peyton, whose father was then serving in the U.S. Congress, were carefully wrapped and sent to Nashville. There an entire population turned out to pay its respects. The body was placed in the State

Capitol where thousands filed by to pay tribute to their first Confederate hero. Tales abounded of how the general actually died in a hail of bullets while leading his men in a gallant charge. And in the weeks that followed, controversies arose as to how many bullets pierced his body. In any event, the people of Nashville buried their hero amid all the sorrows of a grief-stricken city.

No sooner had the tear-stained eyes of the politicians been lifted from the bier of the martyred Zollicoffer, than they began to search for a scapegoat for Fishing Creek. The search was short and fruitful. Who was a known drunkard? Who had a brother in the Yankee Army? As if by previous design, all eyes fixed on the man who had watched his undisciplined and poorly equipped army disintegrate before his eyes, George Crittenden.

The mail to Richmond was crowded with letters from Tennesseans demanding that Crittenden be relieved from command. Governor Isham G. Harris stated as his opinion that Crittenden could never rally troops from Tennessee. Soon, Confederate authorities ordered Crittenden relieved from command. He never regained his former prominence.

Meanwhile, the soldiers from Mill Springs began arriving home. Some were deserters, but most were not. Public opinion had a hard time distinguishing one from the other. For the soldiers, the visit home was short and sometimes unpleasant. A few days at home and the remnant of the Mill Springs army began making its way toward Murfreesboro in Middle Tennessee.

2.

Tennesseans and the rest of the South had only a short time to mourn the loss at Fishing Creek. Even before the soldiers from that battle began arriving home, a Federal naval and land force was moving south toward Forts Henry and

Donelson in upper Middle Tennessee. Burton Warfield caught the temperament of the time when he wrote his mother, "It seems that the enemy is determined to get to Tennessee. But if every soldier we have will do his duty they can never get there to do us harm . . . They may run over us and dispoil us of our homes but from every hill top and from every secluded spot the mussiles of death will be sent into their ranks from a foe they can never overcome." [20]

When young Warfield said that the Yankees were determined to get inside Tennessee, he could have well been reading the mind of Ulysses S. Grant, commander of the land forces moving south along the course of the Tennesse River. To the leaders of the Union Army, the Tennessee River offered a natural entrance into the heartland of the South. As Federal General Lew Wallace explained:

> *The trend of the river; its navigability for large steamers; its offer of a highway to the rear of the Confederate hosts in Kentucky and the State of Tennessee; its silent suggestion of a secure passage into the heart of the billigerent land . . . must have been discerned by every military student who, in the summer of 1861, gave himself to the most cursory examination of the map.* [21]

Southerners were quite aware that the Tennessee and her companion stream the Cumberland represented potentially dangerous avenues over which armies and supplies could be transported. In upper Middle Tennessee the streams flowed roughly parallel, about fifteen miles apart, as they made their way north to empty into the Ohio. Realizing the situation, the Confederates began work during the fall of 1861 on Fort Henry on the east bank of the Tennessee and Fort Donelson on the west bank of the Cumberland. Progress on the forts was pathetically slow, receiving very little attention from either the generals in command or the politicians in seats of government.

The truth was that if these forts fell the Yankees would have again penetrated the Kentucky defense line and in the process would have separated the Confederate forces at Bowling Green and Columbus. Also, the Yankees would have opened a supply line deep into the heart of the Confederacy. By the first weeks of 1862, the Federal navy had developed to a point that it presented a formidable weapon to the Confederates whose naval force was almost non-existent. Compared to the potential dangers of this situation, Mill Springs meant very little.

At the points where Fort Henry and Fort Donelson were built, only twelve miles of hilly, swampy land intervened. Although it was, as of yet, unknown how effective these forts would be against naval power, the Confederates had few alternatives available — so they waited.

The prospects of a successful defense of Fort Henry seemed unlikely to the Confederate officers in charge. It was the same story that seemed to plague all military operations in the region. The men were poorly trained, poorly armed, and poorly situated. Captain Jesse Taylor had assumed command of the fort during the fall of 1861, and upon his arrival, immediately detected its inherent weaknesses. The installation was so situated that it was dominated by high ground on both sides of the river. Through conversations with local residents, Taylor learned that the ground on which the fort was placed often disappeared under two or more feet of water when the river was high. Taylor reported this information to his superiors but was told that the site had been selected by competent engineers and that no change would be made. Taylor was told by state officials to henceforth send his suggestions to General Leonidas Polk and not to Nashville. Polk in turn told Taylor to contact General Albert Sidney Johnston, the overall Commander. [22] Johnston dispatched Major Jeremy Gilmer, an engineer, to the scene, but by the time he arrived it was too late to take action.

In the meantime, Fort Henry received a new commander, General Lloyd Tilghman, a native of Kentucky. Tilghman was a graduate of West Point, who had spent much of his life as a railroad engineer. Upon his arrival at Fort Henry, Tilghman and Gilmer inspected the installation and found it woefully inadequate, but the time for significant changes had already passed — the Union forces were on the move.

During the first week of February 1862, Grant's army, in concert with Flag Officer Andrew Foote's navy, started toward Fort Henry. Foote's gunboats were followed by "countless transports", whose role it was to deliver Grant's troops as close to the fort as possible. Jesse Taylor watched from inside the fort as the Yankees approached. He later wrote, "Far as the eye could see, the course of the river could be traced by the dense volumes of smoke issuing from the flotilla — indicating that the long-threatened attempt to break our lines was to be made in earnest." [23]

The worst fears Jesse Taylor had came to pass. Several days of incessant rain had flooded the river and the backwater from that flood had seeped onto the low ground upon which the fort was built. Much of the area inside and surrounding the fort was under water, but there was nothing the Rebs could do except await the inevitable.

Grant's army landed three miles north of the fort and began moving toward their objective. Upon reaching the outer limits of the fortifications, they halted while the navy continued its journey up the river.

February 6th had dawned "mild and cheering, with a light breeze . . ." At 10:20 A.M., an order was passed aboard the Union flagship to prepare for battle, and thirty minutes later, the fleet steamed toward the fort. According to a Yankee sailor:

> . . . not a sound could be heard nor a moving object seen in the dense woods which overhung the dark and swollen river. The gun crews of the CARONDELET stood silent at their posts, impressed with the serious and important character of the service before them. About noon the fort and the Confederate flag came suddenly

*into view, the barracks, the new earth-works, and the
great guns well manned.* [24]

While the Yankees approached, General Tilghman made
some decisions of his own. Realizing that Grant's infantry
would move upon him immediately following the naval
bombardment, and believing that his small force of less than
3000 men of whom "only one third . . . had been at all
disciplined or well armed" would be totally ineffective,
Tilghman ordered his own infantry away from the scene and
toward Fort Donelson. The Confederate commander's primary
objective then became one of providing the retreating infantry
time to escape the clutches of enemy troops. As Tilghman saw
the situation:

> *I had no hope of being able successfully to defend
> the fort against such overwhelming odds, both in point
> of numbers and in caliber of guns. My object was to
> save the main body by delaying matters as long as
> possible, and to this end I bent every effort.* [25]

Thus, with seventy men, Tilghman sought to defend Fort
Henry. Fifteen minutes before noon, the first Yankee shell
came screaming inland and the warships began closing the range
between their positions and the fort. For well over an hour the
battle raged. In the face of unbelievable odds Tilghman and his
men continued to fight for time. At 12:35 P.M., one of the
Confederates' most effective guns burst, wounding every man
assigned to it. Other guns leaped from their carriages as Union
shells came crashing in. Even though Tilghman's men knocked
out the gunship, *Essex*, it was obvious to the Confederate
general that time was the only element he could hope to conquer.
Seeing the hopelessness of the situation, Tilghman ordered
Captain Taylor to strike the colors. Because of the damage
inflicted on the flag-staff it was necessary for Taylor to climb the
pole to release the emblem. According to Taylor:

The view from that elevated position at the time was grand, exciting, and striking. At our feet the fort with her few remaining guns was sullenly hurling her harmless shot against the sides of the gun-boats, which , now apparently within two hundred   yards of the fort, were, in perfect security, and with the coolness and precision   of target practice, sweeping the entire fort; to the north and west, on both sides of the river, were the hosts of "blue coats," anxious and interested spectators, while to the east the feeble forces of the Confederacy could be seen making their weary way toward Donelson . . . The fight was over; the little garrison were prisoners; but our army had been saved. We had been required to hold out an hour; we had held out for over two. [26]

The surviving Confederates at Fort Henry were taken prisoners by the Union Navy. Jesse Taylor, a graduate of the U.S. Naval Academy, knew many of the Union officers, who in turn introduced him to army personnel who arrived later. The greetings were cordial, and even warm, as representatives of each side seemed genuinely impressed with the valor displayed by the other. Taylor wrote:

Here I first saw General Grant, who impressed me, at the time, as a modest, amiable, kind-hearted but resolute man. While we were at headquarters an officer came in to report that he had not as yet found any papers giving information of our forces, and, to save further looking, I informed him that I had destroyed all the papers bearing on the subject, at which he seemed very froth, fussily demanding, "By what authority?" Did I not know that I laid myself open to punishment etc. etc. Before I could reply fully, General Grant quietly broke in with, "I would be very much surprised and mortified if one of my subordinate officers should allow information which he could destroy to fall into the hands of the enemy. [27]

The capture of Fort Henry had been surprisingly easy as far as the Yankees were concerned. So confident was Grant of future developments that he wired his superiors on February 6th, "I shall take and destroy Fort Donelson on the 8th and return to Fort Henry with the forces employed." [28] It was not to be so simple.

3.

The news of Fort Henry's fall quickly reached the Rebel troops at Fort Donelson. Tales concerning the awesome power of Union gunboats had a demoralizing effect upon men who knew that those same gunboats would shortly seek new targets. Meanwhile, General Albert Sidney Johnston began shuffling his army to meet the situation, which grew more desperate with each passing hour.

The Confederate commander faced a situation which could only be met adequately by an ample supply of men and supplies; he had neither. His right wing had already folded at Mill Springs, now Fort Henry was gone and he soon learned that Fort Donelson was next on the Federal agenda. In addition to all this, the Bowling Green contingent faced a hostile force several times its own strength which was under the command of General Don Carlos Buell.

The day following Fort Henry's fall, Johnston met with his generals and discussed the alternatives that remained open. The decision was reached that the garrison at Columbus should withdraw to Humbolt in West Tennessee, while the men at Bowling Green would move to the south bank of the

Cumberland River at Nashville. The troops in the vicinity of Fort Donelson would be placed at the disposal of the commanding general— whoever it might be.

Fort Donelson had assumed very little importance in the minds of Confederate generals prior to the fall of Fort Henry. Scarcely any thought had been given to the possibility that it would need defending from its land approaches since it was viewed primarily as an obstacle to Federal gunboats moving southward. The fort's big guns were dug in facing north, the direction from which an attacking force was sure to come. The position was protected on the northwest by a swamp, on the east by the river itself, but the western and southern approaches had been left unguarded. Johnston immediately sent in troops to protect the latter two approaches.

Prior to the fall of Fort Henry, the Rebs had begun constructing a series of rifle pits behind the big guns inside the fort. These pits were dug along a chain of hills immediately behind the fort and extended far enough south to encompass the little town of Dover where supplies and ammunition were stored. Following the fall of Fort Henry, work on these entrenchments reached a feverish pitch, and while the work progressed, Confederate troops continued to arrive.

The town of Dover had little to recommend it as a tourist attraction. Federal General Lew Wallace later described it as a village,

> ...unknown to fame, meager in population, architecturally poor. There was a courthouse in the place, and a tavern ...unpainted, and with windows which, if the panes may be likened to eyes, were both squint and cataractous ... If there was little of the romantic in Dover itself, there was still less of poetic quality in the country round about it. [29]

The Confederate soldiers arriving at Fort Donelson would probably have agreed with Wallace's evaluation of the community, but just now they had little interest in scenic beauty.

Just how many men eventually made up the Confederate Army at Fort Donelson can never be known but estimates generally agree that approximately 15,000 were within the works. The Federals on the outside totaled approximately 27,000, giving Grant enough men to form a semi-circle around the Rebs — thereby pinning them against the river. Adding to the seriousness of the situation, as far as the Rebs were concerned, was the fact that the Federals could increase their army as the situation demanded.

The fate of Fort Donelson and its garrison now rested chiefly in the hands of three generals: John Floyd, Gideon Pillow, and Simon Bolivar Buckner. All were brigadier generals, but since Floyd possessed seniority in rank, he was the commanding officer. All three men offer an interesting study in Confederate leadership.

John Floyd was a former governor of Virginia, and a former Secretary of War under President Buchanan. He resigned his position as Secretary of War in late 1860, and was subsequently accused of maliciously transferring arms to the southern arsenals. Floyd was held in contempt by Grant and, if Grant's later writings reflected his true feelings, much of the strategy at Fort Donelson was based on an utter disregard for Floyd's competency. At the time of Fort Donelson, Floyd was still being sought by Federal authorities.

Gideon Pillow was a lawyer from Columbia, Tennessee, and had formerly engaged in practice with James K. Polk. Pillow had served as a major-general in the Mexican War, following which, he returned to his home south of Columbia and tended his vast estate. Pillow volunteered his services to the State of Tennessee during the secession crisis and was promptly made a major-general in the state's provisional army. Upon the acceptance of Tennessee troops into the Confederacy the rank was reduced — a fact which was forever resented by the general. Pillow arrived at Fort Donelson on February 9, 1862, and assumed command of the Army. It was he who supervised much of the construction on the earthworks behind which the Rebs now waited. Pillow, like Floyd, was held in low esteem by his enemies. General Lew Wallace wrote, "it is said of him that he was of a jealous nature, insubordinate, and quarrelsome." [30] Few who knew him would have disagreed.

Simon Bolivar Buckner, a native of Kentucky, graduated from West Point in 1844. He too had fought in the war with Mexico. Prior to the Civil War he had served with the independent forces of Kentucky but, although being offered a commission in the Federal Army, chose to serve the Confederacy instead. Buckner and Pillow had known each other during the Mexican War but their relationship had not been pleasant. The feud between the two men had not abated with the passage of time and neither welcomed the presence of the other at Fort Donelson. It was probably well that the ill-equipped men who waited behind the breastworks around Dover knew so little of the men in whose hands their fate now rested.

The big naval guns inside Fort Donelson commanded great attention from the soldiers in the rifle pits. Somehow the conclusion had been reached that if the Yankee navy could be controlled, the ground troops could finish the job. Even though such importance was attached to the big guns, as late as Tuesday, February 11th, some of them remained unmanned. It was into this situation that Captain Reuben Ross and his Maury County artillery arrived.

Reuben Ross was no ordinary captain of artillery. The fact was that all of the captains who commanded the big guns at Fort Donelson were extraordinary men and Reuben Ross probably felt comfortable among them. Ross was a native of Clarksville, Tennessee, having received his early schooling at the feet of his father who taught at the Masonic College in that town. He later attended West Point in the same class with Federal General John M. Schofield and Confederate General John Hood. From the time of his graduation, Ross had taught school until he was commissioned captain of the Maury County Artillery.

Reuben R. Ross

According to Ross' journal:

I arrived at Fort Donelson on the 11th of February, 1862, the day previous to the first attack of the gunboats. General Pillow told me that men were wanted at the river batteries. I told the company what was desired and what was required of them, making a full explanation to them of the circumstances. I told them, as General Pillow had told me, that it was the post of danger, but the post of honor. Every man declared that the post of honor was the one he wanted. [31]

Ross looked upon the success of the artillery as being the crucial factor in the upcoming battle. "Indeed," he wrote, "the whole army, from what I saw and heard, believed that the great danger lay in the gunboats; that the land forces were safe if only the gunboats could be driven back." [32]

The next morning, Wednesday, February 12th, thirty minutes before a Union gunboat appeared on the river to the north, Reuben Ross' company was put through its first drill on the river batteries. When the gunboat was spotted it was driven back and General Pillow came by to congratulate the men from his home county. Their confidence soared as a result. Meanwhile on the hills behind the big guns, Rebel soldiers continued their frantic pace of readying the earthworks to receive the Yankees who moved steadily toward them. According to James D. Porter, a commander of an artillery unit, "The investment of Fort Donelson and the works occupied by the Confederate forces was complete by the afternoon of February 12th . . ." [33]

Thursday morning revealed to the Rebs that their enemy had moved closer during the night. Hills which had been unoccupied at sunset the day before now bristled with Union artillery and soldiers in blue edged ever closer to the Rebel line. During the day Union artillery swept the Confederate entrenchments, but not to be outdone the Rebs answered in kind.

At eleven o'clock on Thursday morning, the Yanks moved against the Confederate line but were driven back. Again at one o'clock the Yanks moved forward, and again the Confederates held — but with greater difficulty. Night found neither army able to claim significant gains. Although the fighting had not been of a decisive nature, it nevertheless introduced the men of both armies to the more ghastly aspects of war. J. P. McGuire, a member of the 32nd Tennessee, told how the enemy "charged right up to our breastworks, so that when driven back their dead and wounded lay thick upon the ground for hundreds of yards back to the woods . . ." During the fighting the ground over which the Yanks had charged was set afire by exploding shells, and the wounded who still lay there became victims of flames that fed upon fallen trees and underbrush. McGuire observed, "The shrieks of wounded were heart-rending. " 34 Neither army made an attempt to rescue the dying men. Thomas Turner of the 42nd Tennessee arrived at the fort while the fighting was in progress and was thrown into the worst of it. He reflected, "It was here that we began to understand the seriousness of war. Here around us lay our brethren, mangled, cold, stiff, dead." 35

Late Thursday afternoon the spring-like weather of the past few days gave way to a chilling rain which turned to sleet and eventually snow. The men of neither army were ready for this abrupt change. Many soldiers had discarded their heavy coats and blankets; it was now too late to retrieve them. In most places along the lines, fires were not allowed and both Yanks and Rebs cursed the impulse that had prompted the disposal of heavy clothing.

Friday morning the temperature dropped to ten degrees, but from the east the sun came up as bright as was ever seen. Where fires were allowed, men made coffee and gathered closely around the puny flames. Seldon Spencer, a Mississippi soldier, told of watching a wounded Yankee crawl up to the Rebel rifle pits and pull himself close to the fire. The Rebs gave him coffee, but the night's horrors had taken their toll and the wounded man soon died. As they drank their coffee the

Confederates could see more and more Yankees taking positions along the opposing line. They could sense that the Yanks were edging southward across the road leading to Nashville — the only way out for the pinned-in Rebs.

But the highlight of the day would not be furnished by land forces. Instead it would involve the Union Navy as it steamed its way up the river to challenge the big guns of Reuben Ross and his fellow artillerymen. The day before, a single Union gunboat had made its appearance, but like the one before it, was driven away. Ross understood that the single boats had been sent forward to discover as much as possible about the Confederate defenses; he also knew the worst was yet to come.

Writing of Friday morning at Fort Donelson, Reuben Ross said:

> *I have seldom seen a more piercing wind than blew that morning. At about nine we discovered a vast number of transports in the river below the bend, visible only by their chimneys; and, looking closer with telescopes, we could see, by the help of the snow, a dark, continuous line of men passing the remote bend of the river. Cavalry and infantry in great numbers, we found, were debarking and marching round to enforce the enemy's line.* [36]

Ross suggested that it might be well to turn the big guns on the transports, but before he received permission for such an action, the troops had disappeared. The Rebel gunners did drop a few shells in the midst of the departing transports, but as they watched the ships scramble for safety, a more ominous sight met their eyes. They saw, among the white puffs of steam given off by the transports, an intermingling of dark, ugly smoke that rose like an angry cloud from the river. The gunboats were on their way.

Captain Ross explained:

We prepared as usual, and did not allow the first boat to half clear the bend without a shot from our rifle, which we kept up unceasingly. Soon another boat came into view, and then another till four were abreast. There was delay till each one came up separately and arranged itself in line of battle. Then they advanced, firing as they came. [37]

In a matter of minutes, two more boats appeared in the rear and slowly, but steadily, all six steamed closer to the river batteries.

The big guns of Fort Donelson poured forth volley after volley of killing metal. As the four leading boats came up the river, Reuben Ross sighted in the left-most vessel and concentrated his fire on it. The boat was hit and pulled out of line, but only for a few minutes. While the other boats waited she veered back into formation and the front four vessels continued their advance. Closer and closer the Yankee Navy came, but as of yet, the Rebel gunners had not fired their most devastating weapons. After a short interval of time the boats came to the "blockade" — a place where trees and other obstructions had been placed the summer before — and at this point the battle reached its most intense moment.

Reuben Ross remembered the moment well.

The first round from the battery was fired at nearly the same time by all guns, and the report was tremendous. The cannonade was then at its utmost, and beyond anything ever seen by any of the parties engaged. Not infrequently did all our guns open nearly together. The air above and around us was full of shot, solid, case, and shell, while the river below was almost a continuous spray. [38]

Admiral Andrew Foote, commanding the Union Navy, was not to be intimidated. He still remembered the victory at

Fort Henry and he still believed in getting his gunboats up close. As they approached to within less than five hundred yards, they were met with a fire so continuous that it must have seemed like one perpetual shot to the men aboard. Reuben Ross noticed that the portholes were open but that no men were firing from them, and that as the boats came closer, their fire became weaker. Confederate gunners handled their assignments as if nature had intended them for the task. As the big guns fired, the infantry on the hills behind sent yell after yell skyward. The deafening roar of the iron monsters sounded like bass-voiced angels to the men who sensed that the fort was not to be taken from the water side.

The coolness of the gunners was dramatically illustrated when one of the big guns jammed during firing. Captain Ross described the incident.

> *One of our balls refused to go down, stopping halfway in the bore; and all efforts to drive it down with rammers had proved unavailing. The boats were advancing, and things were looking serious. Ten or twelve men were ordered to leave the batteries and find a log long and large enough to fit the rifle. This they soon succeeded in doing, and in the midst of the fire they mounted the parapet and drove the ball home.* [39]

The Yankee Navy was absorbing unbelievable punishment. Commander Henry Walke observed, "Before the decks were well sanded there was so much blood on them that our men could not work the guns without slipping." [40] Suddenly, after an hour and a half of bitter fighting, the Rebs noticed that the distance to the boats was steadily increasing; the Yankee Navy was withdrawing. "Then it was that a great shout from our batteries rent the sky," wrote Reuben Ross. "The artillery seemed to halt long enough to finish their shouting, and again resumed with increased fury. We had then no mercy on them." [41] With fifty-four dead and wounded sailors aboard, the Yankee navy drifted out of sight.

On the night following the defeat of the Union Navy, General Floyd met with Generals Pillow and Buckner. They had already met once that day, at which time it was decided to make an attack on the Federal right and open an escape route to Nashville. The night meeting reaffirmed this decision. Pillow was assigned the task of leading the attack.

After the meeting was dismissed, troops were pulled from the center and right of the Rebel line and hurried to the left where the breakout would be attempted. Half frozen soldiers put their shoulders to the wheels of cannons and pushed them along the icy ridges as teamsters shouted and whipped the horses forward.

At five o'clock on Saturday morning, the Rebs struck. Their immediate objective was to push the Yankee line back far enough to clear the road to Nashville, and with a determination of men fighting for physical freedom they threw themselves at the enemy. By early afternoon, the road to freedom was clear. Unfortunately for the weary Rebs their generals chose this particular time to rekindle old feuds.

Pillow and Buckner engaged in a heated argument with Buckner urging that the original plan be followed to evacuate the troops. Pillow argued that the enemy had been routed and that the army should be returned to their rifle pits. Buckner contacted Floyd, who agreed that the evacuation should proceed. Shortly afterward, Floyd talked to Pillow, who convinced him the men should return to the fort. The issue was resolved when Floyd ordered the victorious Rebs to return to their former positions. In a matter of hours the Yankees reoccupied the ground lost during the early morning, and as far as the Rebs were concerned, the door to freedom was closed.

On Saturday night another conference of generals was held, at which it was decided that the Confederate Army must be surrendered. With this decision came the most ludicrous scene of the battle.

The main issue was: Who would surrender the Army? Certainly Floyd could not since he was in ill favor with Federal authorities. Pillow indicated he had rather die than surrender. By a process of elimination the task fell to Buckner, who accepted it with a degree of courage which seemed extraordinary when contrasted with that of Floyd and Pillow.

While Buckner prepared to surrender, Floyd and Pillow prepared to leave the beleaguered army by boarding boats to Nashville. Floyd had with him a brigade of men from Virginia and the 20th Mississippi Regiment.   The former Virginia governor insisted that he be allowed to take his brigade with him and so it was decided. At daylight on Sunday morning Floyd had his brigade at the boat-landing ready to leave. Spotting the steamboat, *GENERAL ANDERSON,* coming downstream, he directed that the four hundred recruits aboard be unloaded — they were later surrendered with the garrison — and that his Virginians be put on board while the Mississippians stood guard. Later the Mississippians prepared to go aboard, but at that moment Floyd came to the lower deck of the boat and ordered the gangplank raised.

Colonel Tom Sykes of the 20th Mississippi drew his pistol and yelled to Floyd, "General, I'll kill you if you attempt to leave my regiment here after standing guard all night." To this Floyd replied, "Colonel, I am surprised at you. You see the boat is now heavily loaded. I am going across the river and put off part of the men, and then will come back for you." Instead, "The gangplank was pulled in and the boat went across the river until it got near the opposite side, when it turned and left up the river toward Clarksville, leaving the 20th Mississippi at the landing." [42]

In his official report of the incident, Major William Brown of the 20th Mississippi said:

> *I sent my adjutant to inform him* [Floyd] *we were ready to come aboard. I did not get a satisfactory answer . . . There seemed to me to be room enough on board for us all . . . I returned to the boat to make every effort to get aboard, but it had shoved off and was making up the river, with very few persons aboard.* [43]

80

J.J. Montgomery, a "half froze" Tennessean, was among those who decided that if evacuation was the proper course for Floyd's Virginians, it might also be a proper course for him. He therefore made his way to the landing with the intention of going along. When Montgomery informed the officers in charge of his intentions, he was told that the boat was already overloaded and there was no room. It was a bewildered Reb who stood and watched "three horses and two negroes with baggage taken on afterwards." [44]

It had been almost midnight on Saturday when a messenger awakened Lt. Colonel Nathan Bedford Forrest and summoned him to Floyd's headquarters. Upon his arrival Forrest was amazed to hear the generals and their staffs discussing surrender. As later events would demonstrate, Forrest was not one to accept defeat gracefully.

Nathan Bedford Forrest was a millionaire slave and cotton trader from Memphis who had already demonstrated extraordinary courage and ingenuity when dealing with the enemy. Throughout the fighting at Fort Donelson, Forrest's men had rendered invaluable service, sometimes fighting as cavalry, and sometimes as infantry.

Forrest was unorthodox in his approach to war. He was scarcely literate but was endowed with an instinctive ability to make correct decisions under stress. One of his subordinates described him as being "transformed" by battle. As Lt. Col. D. C. Kelly remembered his commander:

Around the fireside of his home or at the mess-table in camp he was kind, gentle, and considerate of all. His voice was soft and low in pitch, the words spoken slowly and deliberately . . . When the storm broke, this picture vanished. The man became an intellectual fighting-machine, seemingly intent on expending the great supply of pent-up energy in the destruction of the foe. The color of his face, which ordinarily was olive or sallow, became flushed and red, not unlike that of a painted Indian warrior; the eyes flashed with a look that suggested no mercy for any one who showed a disinclination to do promptly that which was bid. [45]

On Saturday night at Fort Donelson, Forrest repeatedly informed his generals that a gap existed in the Yankee line wide enough for the Confederate Army to pass through. When the generals ignored his advice, the Rebel cavalryman announced to the group that he was taking his command south toward Nashville. At four o'clock on Sunday morning Forrest's column began their move, and as they were marching away, the faint sound of the surrender bugle could be heard in the distant, early morning air.

With his brother Jeffery riding beside him, Forrest rode at the head of his escaping column. The road to freedom was carefully probed. When an ice-covered stream was reached, volunteers were sought to test the depth of the water, and when none came forward, Forrest plunged his horse through the ice and led his men to safety. Not a man was lost.

By daylight Sunday morning, Floyd and Pillow were on their way to Nashville. Simon Bolivar Buckner had assumed command of the Confederate Army and was in the process of seeking a conference with Grant. When Buckner inquired as to possible terms of surrender, Grant replied bluntly, "No terms except unconditional and immediate surrender can be accepted. I propose to move immediately upon your works." [46] Buckner had little choice but to accept and a meeting was arranged with Grant in the village of Dover.

Federal General Lew Wallace rode into Dover before Grant arrived and announced himself at Buckner's headquarters — the reception was cordial. According to Wallace:

I found General Buckner and his staff at breakfast. He met me with politeness and dignity. Turning to the officers at the table, he remarked: "General Wallace, it is not necessary to introduce you to these gentlemen; you are acquainted with them all." They arose, came forward one by one, and gave their hands in salutation. I was then invited to eat breakfast, which consisted of corn bread and coffee, the best the gallant host had in his kitchen. [47]

Shortly thereafter Grant arrived and Fort Donelson was officially surrendered.

Postlude

Battles in the Civil War, like all battles, did not end with the firing of the last gun, and since Fort Donelson represented the first experience in battle for most of the men involved, it offers an interesting glimpse into the ongoing events which compose the lives of human beings. Few of the men at Fort Donelson, whether Rebels or Yankees, had ever seen death in such an ugly form. Certainly, few of them had ever before been an instrument of death. Perhaps it was because they could view themselves as "instruments" that they were able to perform the tragic demands of war, for certainly it was not the nature of most of them to do what they had just done.

All around them were silent reminders of human agony, men long dead with their eyes wide open, men frozen in grotesque configurations, men whose bodies were scattered over wide areas, and men who awaited the moment of death to relieve their torment. War was not, in its ultimate form, giant armies battling for the high ground and strategic routes of communication. War was not, in its ultimate form, imaginative generals who planned brilliant strategy. Instead, war was one inexperienced and frightened soldier shouldering a gun, aiming down its barrel at another human being, then pulling the trigger with the hope that during the process the chances of his own survival would be enhanced. The political orators of 1861 had not developed this aspect of war in their speeches.

If **war** provided its victims an outlet for their most inhumane tendencies, it also furnished an opportunity for the sensitivities of such individuals to assert themselves. The surrender scene in the village of Dover and the debarkation of Confederate prisoners from Fort Donelson offer dramatic evidence that the consciousness of man does not isolate itself entirely to the immediate present, but rather is projected and conditioned by previous events. General Simon Bolivar Buckner did not, at the time, record the thoughts which entered his mind as he awaited the arrival of General Grant in the inn at Dover. It was, nevertheless, quite probable that he remembered a day back in 1853.

The scene was New York City, and the chief character besides Buckner himself was Captain Ulysses S. Grant. Buckner later wrote:

> We were schoolmates together, though not classmates, at West Point and were very good friends. We served together in Worth's Division in the Mexican War. About 1853 he [Grant] resigned from the army, his regiment being in California. He landed in New York. He stopped at the old Astor House, and, being without friends, was ejected from the hotel and his baggage seized for the payment of his bill. I was then stationed in New York, and, knowing the proprietor of the Astor, Mr. Stetson, I accompanied Captain Grant to the hotel, introduced him to Mr. Stetson as my friend, and requested him to restore Captain Grant to his room, assuring him that his brother would soon be in New York and would pay the bill, also that I would be responsible for its payment. Mr. Stetson complied with my request.
>
> My next meeting with Grant was as his prisoner at Fort Donelson. After the surrender I called at General Grant's headquarters on his boat, and after transacting some business in connection with the surrender he

*accompanied me to the bow of the boat as I was leaving
and in a very quiet and modest way tendered me the use
of his purse. I was touched by his generous offer; but
as I had announced my purpose to share the fate of my
men, I felt that I could not accept a favor that could not
be extended to them; therefore . . . I declined to accept
the generous proffer of his aid.* [48]

Captain Reuben Ross who performed so well during the naval bombardment on Friday had a similar experience. Ross had been a classmate of General John Schofield at West Point, and on the trip to prison following the surrender at Fort Donelson met Schofield at St. Louis. Schofield was moved by the plight of the Confederate prisoners and took the gloves from his hands, giving them to Captain Ross.[49]

The future held varied fortunes for the men who fought at Forts Henry and Donelson. Grant was to become President of the United States. He would also be the only general in the Civil War to accept the surrender of three armies: Fort Donelson, Vicksburg, and Appomattox Court House. Simon Bolivar Buckner was to become Governor of Kentucky as well as a candidate for the vice-presidency of the United States.

Nathan Bedford Forrest would become what many believe to be the greatest cavalryman of the Civil War. After the conflict he would assume the presidency of an unsuccessful railroad, but perhaps much more significantly, he would become the most controversial personality produced by the war. It is probably safe to assume that Forrest, in the last half of the twentieth century, would command more attention from newspapers and the general public in Tennessee than all other Civil War generals combined. The events that would fuel this attention were still ahead as he led his men from Fort Donelson.

General Lew Wallace's military career would be overshadowed by his authorship of the famous novel *Ben Hur*, — something that he might have wondered about.

Unfortunately for others, the future was either short or unpleasant. General John Floyd would die of natural causes before the war ended. General Gideon Pillow would never recover from the shadow that was cast on his career as a result of Fort Donelson, and following the war, he was forced into bankruptcy. General Lloyd Tilghman, who surrendered Fort Henry, would die in the Battle of Champion's Hill in 1863.

Following the Battle of Fort Donelson, Reuben Ross would remain in prison for many months, longer than most of the men taken prisoner at the same time. Later during the war, according to some sources, he was promoted to brigadier general, but this fact is not firmly established. In any event, he was taken prisoner again, but while being conveyed north to prison, jumped from a train and made his way to the command of General H. B. Lyon of the Confederate army. Lyon persuaded Ross to accompany a cavalry raid into Kentucky, and during that raid Ross was killed. [50]

The Battle of Fort Donelson would remain fresh in the minds of most Confederate soldiers who fought there. They looked upon it with bitterness, a sense of betrayal, and humiliation . For as long as they lived most believed their generals had sold them out. Few forgot — almost none forgave.

The fall of Fort Donelson would not stop the war and would, eventually, become a minor reference point in its history. Even before the battle, Albert Sidney Johnston started his main army at Bowling Green toward Nashville. The Confederate force at Columbus, Kentucky would retreat south into West Tennessee. Worst of all for the Confederacy, the door to Tennessee was now open from any point, and the people, who less than a year before, enthusiastically prepared to "go to " war, were about to be visited by that very war.

Chapter III

The situation did look gloomy

The city of Nashville became a focal point following the fall of Fort Donelson. Nashville newspapers had reported the encouraging results of Saturday's action at Dover, and although Albert Sidney Johnston's army was retreating through the city, there was a general belief that all was well. The people of the city made their way to church with the same self-confidence that had buoyed them throughout the summer and fall of the previous year.

Before noon, the news of the surrender spread throughout Nashville and the calm of the early morning disrupted into panic. William G. Stevenson, a Union sympathizer who had been forced into the Confederate army, wrote:

> Never was there greater commotion than Nashville exhibited that Sabbath morning. Churches were closed, Sabbath schools failed to assemble, citizens gathered in groups, consulted hastily, and then rushed to their homes to carry out their plans. Bank directors were speedily in council, and Confederate officials were everywhere engrossed in the plan of evacuation. A general stampede commenced. Specie was sent off to Columbia and Chattanooga, plate was removed, and

valuables huddled promiscuously into all kinds of
vehicles. Hack-hire rose to twenty-five dollars an hour,
and personal service to fabulous prices. [1]

Wild rumors spread where ever people gathered. Nashvillians imagined themselves about to be attacked by the victorious Union Army moving south from Bowling Green, or shelled by the Yankee Navy that was reported on its way up the Cumberland River. Other rumors had General Buell's army already on the outskirts of the city, and that by late afternoon, the "city would be shelled, without notice, and laid in ashes."[2]

An eye-witness wrote, "Men and women were to be seen running to and fro in every portion of the city, and large numbers were hastening with their valuables to the several railroad depots, or escaping in private conveyances to some place of fancied security in the country."[3]

Albert Sidney Johnston then announced that his army would not defend the city and a new wave of panic swept the residents. Instead of welcoming the retreating soldiers, insults were hurled from all sides. John M. Taylor, a member of the 27th Tennessee, wrote,

> *Never will it be effaced from the memory of many*
> *gallant Tennesseans who yet survive — the taunt that*
> *was thrown out by by-standers on the streets, that we*
> *were leaving the people and our capital city to the mercy*
> *of the Federals. Many who indulged in this were young*
> *and vigorous, and ought to have been with us, with*
> *muskets on their shoulders, but they were not — they*
> *would have swelled our ranks considerably.*[4]

The greeting received by the retreating army was far different from that many of its members received in the same city only a few months before. Nashville had become an index of Southern sentiment. During the preceding spring, thousands of young men had marched down its main street on their way to war. Enthusiastic crowds had lined their paths and bands played martial music and colorful decorations rose and fell with the gentle breezes of early spring. Raw recruits with idealistic dreams had marched in step to the music that sounded like a prelude to a glorious future. Those dreams had soured; the anticipated future of April and May of 1861, had become the reality of February in 1862, and to the minds of Nashvillians, it was a discordant blend.

John Miller McKee, a local newspaperman, witnessed the panic that seized Nashville and wrote:

> *Many who were wealthy removed themselves and what property they could take with them out of town, while the thousands of poor had no alternative but to remain and make the best disposition of themselves they could. . .[5]*

Wealthy residents of Nashville loaded their possessions into wagons and departed the city. It was written:

> *Neither private nor public property nor human life was safe . . . Wagon loads of material were being carted away to the country without authority and for private use. The government officials had gone. The president of one of the largest railroads, with more discretion than valor or patriotism, appropriating an engine and a great train of cars for the removal of his personal property, had steamed away for the far South.[6]*

On Monday morning, General John Floyd arrived at Nashville with the men he had evacuated from Fort Donelson and the general assumed command of the city. Meantime Johnston had hurried his army across the river and disappeared toward Murfreesboro. Floyd wrote that upon his arrival:

... I beheld a sight which is worthy of notice. The rabble on the wharf were in possession of boats loaded with Government bacon, and were pitching it from these boats to the shore, and carrying what did not fall into the water by hand and carts away to various places in the city.[7]

Floyd dispatched the 1st Missouri regiment to restore order, but finding that additional help was needed, impressed labor from the streets to load trains going south. At 10:00 A.M. on Tuesday, Nathan Bedford Forrest and his command entered the city, and with characteristic skill took immediate action.

According to John Allan Wyeth, Forrest's chief biographer:

The rabble refused at first to disperse as ordered. When this was reported to Forrest he rode with his troops directly into the plundering crowd, belaboring the more obstinate members over the heads and shoulders with their sabres until they yielded. In one instance a fire engine was brought up and a stream of cold water played upon the mob with great and immediate success.[8]

Even as Forrest and his men fought the angry mob, supplies were being loaded and moved south from the city. Meat, clothing, and ammunition were carried to railroad stations where crowds of stampeding people fought for room on the overcrowded cars.

One of the more pathetic episodes of the chaos was the removal of the sick. Prior to leaving Bowling Green the health of the soldiers had been excellent, but the march to Nashville had taken its toll. The severe winter weather had decimated the ranks as the army moved toward Nashville. "Many froze to death as they camped by night on the way; thousands more were overcome by exhaustion or disease . . ."[9] Roughly one third of the army was under medical care by the time they crossed the Cumberland River.

In view of the great number of sick from Bowling Green it was decided to forward them all to Chattanooga. The crisis such a decision created can be better appreciated when it is considered that, even before the movement began, "The seats and aisles of all cars arriving at Chattanooga were literally 'packed' with refugees; the platforms were crowded also, and numbers were seated on the steps, clinging to the hand rails for safety."[10] The weather continued cold and railway cars arriving at Chattanooga were covered with frozen snow.

Amid such scenes, Major Charles Anderson, a quarter master of transportation in Chattanooga, received a telegram stating, "Prepare as best you can for the reception of some thousand or twelve hundred sick and convalescent soldiers from this Army and from hospitals at Nashville. They will be sent forward as fast as cars can be supplied."[11]

Anderson faced an almost impossible situation. There was no organized body of troops in Chattanooga at the time and not a dollar of government funds was available. Moving as swiftly as possible, Anderson called together prominent citizens of the community and asked for help. According to Major Anderson:

Three large buildings were taken possession of and a force of negro men and women put to work cleaning them up. Two bakeries were contracted with for bread, and coffee, sugar and other supplies were purchased. Fuel was provided at all the buildings, and arrangements made for conveying to the hospitals all soldiers unable to walk, and a special contract was made with a reliable man to put up temporary stands at the depot and serve each soldier with hot coffee and fresh bread as the trains arrived.[12]

Although Anderson was prepared both mentally and physically for a bad situation, he was appalled once the trains began arriving. In describing the scene he wrote:

When the first train arrived with some three hundred on board, they were in a most pitiable condition. They had been stowed away in box and cattle cars for eighteen hours, without fire, and without any attention other than such as they were able to render each other. Tears filled the eyes of many at the depot when these poor fellows were taken from the cars, so chilled and benumbed that a majority of them were helpless. Two other trains came the following day with men in the same condition. Three soldiers were found dead in the cars, one died in the depot before removal, and another died on the way to the hospital.[13]

The Confederate authorities had sent no physicians with the sick, and while soldiers continued to die each day, Anderson made out as best he could. Seriously sick soldiers were forced to lie on bare floors without proper cover, while carpenters worked frantically to build the necessary cots. Although he had no money, Anderson obtained enough cotton for quilts and while the afflicted men waited helplessly every sewing machine available was put to work. How the cots were to be covered and bed sacks made were problems that "greatly troubled" the quarter master, but it was at this stage of the operation that Anderson received unexpected help in the person of Mrs. Ben Hardin Helm.

Mrs. Helm was the sister of Mrs. Abraham Lincoln. Her husband was the colonel of the 1st Kentucky Cavalry, a part of the Confederate Army then retreating south from Nashville. Mrs. Helm had been at Nashville when the panic hit and later wrote of her experiences in trying to locate her husband as the Army moved south. She had resisted the flow of the retreating Army for over two hours, but her husband's unit had moved when she arrived at its former location. Disheartened, she made her way to the railway station, and just as she was boarding the train, Col. Helm appeared to tell her he had made arrangements for her to go to Murfreesboro. She decided instead to ride the train on to Chattanooga where she discovered the plight of Major Anderson.

Mrs. Helm recalled:

> *The refugees came from the trains into the little dingy reception room to wait, sometimes for hours, for a room, looking so worried, with baskets, bundles, and dilapidated valises surrounding them. Sometimes there would be a mother with a sleeping child in her arms, and others on the hard floor, with little or nothing to eat, ennuied to death. As they waited, I would go in, with brass thimbles, needles and thread and cotton sacks on my arm and inquire if there was anyone among them who would sew a little on the cots so much needed for the suffering soldiers. Every fagged woman would brighten up at the idea of being useful, and sew diligently until time for them to continue their journey ... A lady in the hotel helped greatly ... I went to her room one morning to cut out the sacks; the little stove, combined   with the poor food I had tried to eat for breakfast, made me faint. There was no stimulant at hand, but Mr. Brooks ... found a man with a bottle of Hostetter's Bitters, which, without ceremony of adding water, they poured down my throat. It would have resuscitated the dead.[14]*

Eventually the command of General John Floyd arrived at Chattanooga and a better organized attempt was made to relieve the suffering of the sick. Major Anderson later reflected:

> *The removal of these soldiers from the hospitals at Nashville was a military necessity; but why they were sent, unaccompanied or preceded by a proper corps of surgeons, medical supplies, and hospital attendants, I never knew.[15]*

The scenes and encounters experienced by Major Anderson and Mrs. Helm at Chattanooga would seem mild compared to those that lay ahead. Anderson would later join the command of Nathan Bedford Forrest and ride with him into many of the most exciting scenes of the war. Tragedy would punctuate the future of Mrs. Helm whose husband and two brothers were destined to pay with their lives for their efforts in establishing a new nation.

2.

The collapse of the Confederate defense line across Kentucky not only brought panic to the civilians, but prompted indignant responses from many Tennesseans serving in other states. Captain Monroe Bearden, a member of the 8th Tennessee from Lincoln County, wrote his parents from South Carolina:

> That such a fate was necessary for Tennessee to expedite, or make more sure the success of our cause I never shall believe... Johnston and Harris have succeeded in burying the fame and chivalry of Tennessee in utter obscurity from whence it can never vindicate, but being a Tennessean, once a boasted heritage but now a degrading title, I shall ever condemn it ... I think this war has become more fomidable and a great deal nearer home than a great many of our men anticipated—or else they have less courage than they did have when they first tried to secede.[16]

As news of the enemy's advance into Tennessee reached the troops in Virginia, great concern was expressed for the welfare of the families left behind. The war had taken its first unexpected turn as far as the South was concerned. The eager troops who had gone to Virginia in the spring of 1861, had never considered the possibility that they were leaving their families to the mercy of the very enemy they envisioned themselves about to destroy. In view of recent developments, such men desired to return home.

Colonel Robert Hatton of the 7th Tennessee wrote from Virginia:

> *As nothing, so far, has been accomplished toward getting us to Tennessee, I fear we have no longer any chance. I have done my utmost, can do no more . . .*

> *The news from Tennessee, has greatly troubled me. Our arms are seeing sad reverses, indeed; the enemy growing bold and confident. He must be met with "a will to triumph or die," by our men. Thus only, can he be checked, and driven back; <u>that he will be thus met,</u> I shall not permit myself to doubt.*

On March 5, 1862, Colonel Hatton wrote his wife:

> *Now that our homes are invaded, we feel that we should be sent there. That we should feel so, is most natural; that our wishes should be disregarded, just now, I regard as something unfortunate.*[17]

Tennesseans serving in other states had reason to believe they might be sent home. Throughout the preceding year, they had heard speeches about this being a war for States Rights and how no central government should have the power to tell a state what it should do. But Tennesseans in Virginia found that both generals and politicians exhibited great agility in interpreting the theory of States Rights; they also found out what soldiers of all ages have learned: it is much easier to get into an army than to get out of one.

If they could not go home, at least the men could write their families instructions and advice to be followed should the enemy continue its advance into Tennessee. Colonel Hatton wrote his wife:

> *Say to father and mother, that I will expect you all to get together, and either go off, or remain at one house, if the Yankees get into our country . . . You could go to some point in the interior of the State of Alabama, or Mississippi and be out of the reach of annoyance, from the enemy. You must not think of the cost; your comfort, and that of those dear to me, at home, must be the only consideration . . . I trust it may yet appear for the best, to let us go to Tennessee.*[18]

Hatton, like Bearden, had **very** definite opinions regarding the behavior of some people in Tennessee. He wrote:

> *One thing has disgusted me. Men, who were, not long since, most eager, seemingly, for war, most full of their boasts of nerve and spirit, are now the first and most shameless croackers. Poor boasters, poor cowards.*[19]

Of the men in his own brigade who were getting somewhat tired of army life, Hatton said, "[They] should go home and raise corn for those not so easily dispirited."[20]

If it were possible for the more affluent to escape the invading enemy the expense involved prohibited the same luxury for the poorer class. Helplessly, and sometimes bitterly, the wives of poorer soldiers watched from the doorways of their modest homes as the wealthy loaded their finery into slave-driven wagons and headed south. These wives, whose husbands had volunteered in the Rebel Army on a promise that their families would be well cared for, were left to the mercies of the invading Yankees who oftentimes singled them out for the most inconsiderate treatment.

From South Carolina D.C. Spurlock of the 16th Tennessee wrote his sister in McMinnville:

Nothing would give me more pleasure than to be ordered to Tenn that we might be near to those who are dear to us and share with them the dangers which seem to threaten our common homes . . . I think it is nothing but right that Tennesseans should be allowed to defend their own homes.

I hardly know what to advise you all to do in case the enemy continues to advance and our forces to fall back but I would say to keep out of the neighborhood of both armies if possible. I have seen something of life in the vicinity of armies and know that it is by no means pleasant especially for ladies. Soldiers are generally thoughtless and frequently reckless and many of them have little more respect for friend than enemy . . . Would to God that I could offer you some comfort but I must confess that the future of Tennessee is dark uncompromising and forbidding.[21]

It is highly probable that Colonel Hatton, Captain Bearden, and Captain Spurlock never heard of each other, but they shared a common fate: before another year passed they would all be dead.

3.

On the very day that Captain Spurlock wrote the discouraging letter to his sister in Warren County, the army which represented Tennessee's hopes was gathering at Murfreesboro. Albert Sidney Johnston was attempting to assemble the remains of the Kentucky defense line into a single body of troops strong enough to stand against the enemy.

Already the remnants of the Fishing Creek force had arrived at Murfreesboro and these were shortly joined by the troops which had retreated from Bowling Green. Johnston had a total of aproximately 17,000 men.

Johnston's prestige had suffered appreciably since the fall of Fort Donelson, but he did not spend time defending himself. Instead, he formulated plans for the future. He decided to withdraw far enough south to form a juncture with the Southern troops retreating from Columbus, Kentucky, who were already going south through West Tennessee. Corinth, Mississippi, was finally selected as an appropriate meeting place and February 29, 1862, was chosen as the day the troops would leave Murfreesboro.

The day before the army left Murfreesboro, Governor Isham G. Harris and other prominent politicians made patriotic speeches to the men in an effort to lessen the bitterness of leaving homes and families behind. For the most part, the soldiers were unimpressed. A member of the 20th Tennessee remembered:

> At the conclusion of the speeches some one proposed "three cheers," but only a few tried to cheer, they were too sad.
>
> The next morning, however, notwithstanding the sadness and gloom which hung thickly over the army, we formed, and to a man marched out, leaving home and all its endearments in the hands of the enemy.[22]

W.J. Worsham of the 19th Tennessee wrote of this period:

> The sad news of the disaster at Fishing Creek, and the fall of Fort Donelson, the evacuation of Bowling Green, Ky. spread like wildfire over all the South. A great many of the newspapers were full of epithets and denunciations of the direst kind against General Johnson [Johnston]. The situation did look gloomy at this time,

and the newspaper men thought perhaps if they had been at the front things would have gone differently.

They had forgotten that enduring the hardships of camp life, fighting the battles at the front were much more difficult than sitting around the comfortable fireside and fighting them on paper.

Often those who censure most are the ones who do nothing to bring about that for which they condemn others for not doing.[23]

The thought and sight of the retreating army overwhelmed Confederate citizens along its route. Relatives of soldiers lined the streets along which the army passed and, through tear-moistened eyes, watched in silence as the men passed by. Older people were seen to turn their heads in sorrow and walk away from the depressing sight. Others, in an effort to relieve a feeling of helplessness, stepped into the roadway and heaved at wagon wheels that mired into the rain-soaked ground. Throughout the day and night a cold and cutting February wind whipped the loose ends of wagon covers, causing them to pop in a weird monotone which added another dismal ingredient to the already depressing scene.

Mid-winter rains had washed out many of the bridges south of Murfreesboro. Wagons were lashed together and covered with planks, and across these unsteady surfaces Johnston's infantry sullenly made their way toward Shelbyville. The roads were so soft that men sometimes mired to their knees, but by the end of the first day, the advance units had covered twenty miles. Tired and wet soldiers searched for camping sites on which they could build fires, and above the flames they dried their clothing and cooked what food they carried with them.

In describing the retreat William Stevenson wrote:

> *The season of the year was the worst possible in that latitude. Rain fell, sometimes sleet, four days out of the seven. The roads were bad enough at best, but under such a tramping of horses and cutting wheels as the march produced, soon became horrible. About one hundred regiments were numbered in the army. The full complement of wagons to each regiment — twenty four — would give above two thousand wagons. Imagine such a train of heavily loaded wagons, passing along a single mud road, . . . in the midst of rain and sleet, day after day, camping at night in wet fields or dripping woods, without sufficient food adapted to their wants, and often without tents, the men lying down in their wet clothes, and rising chilled through and through; and let this continue for six weeks of incessant retreat, and you get a feeble glimpse of what we endured.*[24]

John Taylor of Lexington, Tennessee, a member of the 27th Tennessee wrote:

> *We had begun one evening to pitch our tents in a low, flat place, when presently the rain began to fall and the valley became inundated. Our camp-fires were put out, and we had to resort to cutting down the underbrush and throwing them together in high piles, that we might keep our blankets out of the water. Half-cooked rations were eaten; and the water was a foot or two deep all through camp. Many soldiers will remember the terribleness of the night as we sat perched upon the brush and discussed the war and its attendant hardships. Songs were sung, stories related, and many a long sigh given when we thought of loved ones at home, until the briny tears traced each other down manly cheeks.*[25]

The retreat was not all gloom and despair. Enterprising Rebs had already discovered that a soldier need not necessarily be controlled by the circumstances in which he found himself. There were always some choices available. Realizing this, some of the men who left Murfreesboro were careful of the contents they placed in their wagons. Among the more unique contents were the wives of some teamsters. Matters progressed well until word reached officers that the female contraband was demanding more stops and better food. The wagon train was halted and inspected, and all the devoted ladies were loaded into separate wagons and returned to Murfreesboro. Some of the drivers had already decided that fighting two wars at once was a bit taxing.

Private John Gumm of the 23rd Tennessee experienced the march to Corinth in all its wetness. He had been at Bowling Green, but when the army reached Murfreesboro he went to the eastern end of the county to pay his wife a visit. Gumm was over forty years old and found the demands of army life quite strenuous but when he heard that his regiment was going south he left home for a second time and cast his lot with the Rebel cause.

Near Huntsville, Alabama, Gumm wrote his wife telling her of a trip filled with hardship. He told of sleeping all night in the rain, of marching all day not knowing where he was headed, of becoming so tired that he fell by the side of the road where the slave who was with him built a fire and cooked him food. He told of wading mud "which was from shoo mout to nee deep," of seeing men and guns plunge into icy streams, of worn out shoes and wet feet, but through it all there was a grim determination to see the job completed and there was no indication of discouragement or discontent.[26]

William Stevenson wrote:

> *This retreat left a good deal of desolation in its track;*
> *for although the officers endeavored to restrain the men,*
> *yet they must have wood; and where the forest was*

101

*sometimes a mile from the camping ground, and fences
were near, the fences suffered; and where sheep and
hogs abounded when we came, bones and bristles were
more abundant after we left. Horses were needed in the
army; and after it left, none were seen on the farms.*[27]

Reflecting his own resentment at being impressed into the
Rebel army Stevenson added:

*And then the impressed soldiers, judging from my
own feelings, were not over-scrupulous in guarding the
property of Rebels. The proud old planters, who had
aided in bringing on the rebellion, were unwillingly
compelled to bear part of its burden.*[28]

By the first of April, Johnston's army was settled at
Corinth. The town itself did not excite the imagination of
Southern soldiers. Thomas Fuller described it by saying it was
located

*...in a swampy place, not much regularity about the
streets, houses scattered over a good portion of land ...
I have no idea what number of inhabitants it contained
before the war, it seems though like a business went on
that is common at R Road stations, the surrounding
country is poor.*[29]

The characterisitic of Corinth that impressed Fuller was the
very thing that impressed his generals the most. In his diary,
Fuller wrote, "this place is at the Junction of the Memphis &
Charleston & Mobile & Ohio Rail Roads, the trains come in
from every direction, it is nearly a constant thing to hear the
whistle of the Locomotive."[30] The railroads into Corinth had
already delivered thousands of troops and much needed supplies
from the east, south, and west. Every locomotive whistle was
music to the ears of Rebel generals who knew that only a few
miles north at Pittsburg Landing a dangerous Federal Army was
leisurely awaiting reenforcements.

4.

While the Confederate Army at Corinth organized itself for the days ahead, Middle and West Tennesseans got their first taste of Yankee occupation. Some strange idea had possessed many of these people that they were to enjoy the glories of war without its attendant hardships. They were to learn that all choices lead to consequences and some of those consequences are less than desirable.

No sooner had the Confederates withdrawn southward than an avalanche of Federal soldiers descended behind them. Instinctively, the rural population wanted to fight them. Militant citizens organized themselves into "home guard" units and foolishly stepped into the path of the invaders. As the advance patrols of the Federals reached Columbia a group of old men and youngsters "50 strong, came galloping up and from behind boulders for an hour wasted many shots from shot guns and hunting rifles."[31] Such efforts served only to annoy the enemy.

The appearance of real live Yankees tested for the first time the fiber of Southern loyalty in occupied areas. In more instances than would have been imagined the year before, that fiber was found wanting. County officials, who the year before, had shouted, "I do not ask you to go, I ask you to follow me to the field of honor," now courted friendship with those they had vowed to destroy and at least a few became informers on those whose rights they had so patriotically promised to defend. A clearer picture of war was beginning to emerge and its form was not attractive.

Not all Yankees proved as bad as Rebel politicians had pictured them. Nelson Rainey explained:

I must do them credit that they were very kind to mother. She never asked the officers to the house, and during their whole occupation none ever forced himself across the threshold. Mother was given a guard of two

*young Kentucky boys. They drew a dead line around
the house and yard and if a soldier dared cross it, he was
arrested and told to do so no more . . . They slept in the
stable and every day mother sent them something nice
from her table. They became attached to mother and the
children; and when they left they went to tell Mrs.
Rainey goodbye. Mother told me one of them fairly
blubbered.*[32]

The two Kentucky soldiers spoken of by Nelson Rainey
were in the army of General Don Carlos Buell, then camped at
Columbia. Following their farewell they began moving toward
the Tennessee River and a little country church called Shiloh.

5.

At Corinth, Albert Sidney Johnston's army had grown
substantially through additions from Florida, Louisiana,
Arkansas, and Kentucky. For the first time, Johnston believed
he could effectively strike his enemy. The Confederate general
was probably aware, also, that his career rested on the result of
that strike.

The South's confidence in Johnston had been replaced by
skepticism, and even some of his subordinate officers doubted
his ability. Francis A. Shoup, chief of artillery to General
William Hardee, and later a general in the Confederate Army,
wrote:

*. . . there was a serious trouble at the start, which I
do not think has been made public. It was the distrust on
the part of the corp commanders of the military capacity
of Sidney Johnston . . . Johnston's loss of all that
region from Bowling Green down to the Mississippi line*

*had set the press howling to such an extent that he
wanted to resign his command. There never was a
grander man, and I love his memory, but his movements
are open to serious criticism. He was not a man of
expedients, and had been so long used to the slow
routine methods of the old army that he did not adapt
himself to the new, extraordinary conditions of things.
He was too magnanimous and modest, and did not know
how to seize authority and knock people over. At any
rate, the corps commanders were nervous about going
into battle with him in command.*[33]

Shoup's criticism ignored some important considerations.
Neither the Confederates, nor the Federals for that matter,
constituted what the old textbooks had referred to as armies.
Neither group represented a body of well disciplined and well
equipped men. Generals on neither side had ever before
experienced a situation in which so many men were involved,
and the Rebels at this particular time represented little more than
a large group of rural boys whose personal spirit of
independence had not yet been conquered by army regulations.
In addition, almost none of the soldiers in this Southern Army
had ever heard a shot fired in anger.

Federal strategy before Shiloh was based on an assumption
that the Confederates would remain behind their entrenchments
at Corinth waiting for the Federals to attack. Pittsburg Landing,
located on the west bank of the Tennessee River, fitted well into
such an assumption. The two roads leading from the riverboat
landing would be avenues of supply over which men and
material could be funneled to the expected battle area.

On the Confederate side, Albert Sidney Johnston had no
intention of waiting to be attacked, instead, according to his son,
"His general plan was very simple in outline. It seems to have
been to march out and attack the Federals... to make the battle a
decisive test, and to crush Grant utterly or lose all in the
attempt."[34] With such a plan in mind, Johnston alerted his
commanders to move toward Pittsburg Landing and Shiloh
Church.

Colonel Joel Battle

Joel Battle, Jr.— killed at Shiloh

Chapter IV

They call it Shiloah

The Confederates began leaving Corinth on the third day of April, 1862. The picture they presented was a mixture of comedy and tragedy. The men were unbelievably young — it has been estimated that half were under twenty — and, with very few exceptions, had never fired a gun in anger. They wore every type apparel known to the rural South, and rare indeed was the man who had a full uniform. Many had no guns, and many of those who did had no ammunition. About the only thing that qualified this motley crew as an army was its number, approximately 35,000.   If there were obvious handicaps faced by the Army they seemed to bother its men very little. After all, there would be plenty of ammunition and guns once the front ranks got through working on the Yankees, and those who now walked toward the enemy unarmed imagined themselves sorting through the enemy's weapons choosing those that suited them best.

Mingled with the enthusiasm of the Rebs was an underlying intent that pushed them forward.   This was especially true for the men from Tennessee. They had been driven from their homes. Messages had reached them that their families had been mistreated by the Yankees and a deep hatred had developed for an enemy they had never seen. A portion of

107

Maney's 1st Tennessee arrived from Virginia just in time to move north with the Army and Sam Watkins of that regiment wrote, ". . . our loved ones are being robbed and insulted, our fields laid waste, our cities sacked, our people slain."[1] While a bit over-dramatized, such ideas gave purpose to the Confederate soldier and he was ready to follow that purpose to its logical conclusion.

The road out of Corinth passed a field in which carpenters were constructing the five hundred coffins ordered by General A.S. Johnston. The sight was no doubt sobering, but the outward reaction was comical. The men marched by as if they knew for sure that the coffins were meant for someone else. It was a little different for the men in the 20th Tennessee who could still remember Fishing Creek, but even these youngsters were light-hearted since many of them now carried new Enfield rifles on their shoulders and wore new "sewed boots" on their feet.

The blue-clad objective of the Rebel Army was leisurely passing the time on the bank of the Tennessee River. The previous days had been spent in drill to be sure, but there had been no special urgency in the routine. The early days of spring afforded more daylight hours for recreation and the warmer weather had greened the grass, blossomed out the peach trees, and warmed the water in the shallow creeks nearby. Union soldiers had reason to feel an element of smugness. Their position was bounded on three sides by water, on the east by the muddy currents of the Tennessee River, on the north by the swampy-banked Owl Creek, and on the south by Lick Creek. The only exposed approach to the position was from the west and that was occupied by the division of General William T. Sherman which was settled around a one-room log church called Shiloh. The Yankees saw little reason for worry.

While the Yankees attended their routine chores, the Rebs laboriously closed in from Corinth. Since Southern soldiers had not yet developed an appreciation for discipline they moved more in accordance with their own wishes than those of the generals. The fact was, the generals were almost as inept as the private soldiers. Communications were miserably fouled; entire divisions stood for hours awaiting orders while frustrated commanders galloped their horses in meaningless circles.

Once the Confederates did begin to move, the progress was painfully slow. A member of John Hunt Morgan's Kentucky cavalry wrote:

> *The roads were narrow and miry, and were not improved by a heavy rain which fell during the march. ...The infantry labored along with mud-clogged feet, casting sour looks and candid curses at the cavalry and couriers who be-spattered them. The artillery often stuck fast, and the struggling horses failed to move pieces until the cannoneers applied themselves and pushed and strained at the heavy wheels.*[2]

While the generals and cavalry sought to control their horses, the infantry sought to guide their own feet through the endless bed of slush that hampered their every step. Even though tents and other bundlesome equipment had been left behind, the accumulation of mud that clung tenaciously to their feet made the soldiers' progress slow, tiring, and uncertain.

As the Rebs approached Shiloh Church some of them found time to record the history they were helping to create. In his diary W.W. Wilson of the 5th Tennessee wrote, "we are fixing varry Fast For a Fite   wea have Received marching orders   5 days Rashings ordered to Be cucked up   in the day to words [towards] twelv A Clock We Started in the Directness of the enme."[3] On the same day, April 3rd, John Gumm wrote " we cooked 5 Days Rations   at 2 O Clock we taken up the Line of march hearing that the Enemy was on Tenn. River 25 miles off."[4] The following day Gumm wrote,

> *...we got packed up by Day Lite   formed a Line and it Commenced raining   after the Rains we Started*

traveled till 1 Ocloc   Stoped to Rest and Sent out our
pickets   about 4 O Clock our pickets was Run in and
the Yankees after them but only 5 of them Came to the
hill   we kiled 4 of them   I did not shoot my Self as I
only Seen one my Self he was Shot in 20 places and his
hors kiled By him   they Both Lay to gether.[5]

During the second day's march W.W. Wilson wrote:

We started this morning at Day lite traveling Tell A
Torge eaving   We begunn to git vearry close to the
enemy   We Was ordered in line of Battle witch was
Dun   our Calvery Retreated Back and two of our
Ridgments Fired on the eneme   But they didnt Cum
Clos A Nuf For us to kill many   one of the offusers
kum up vary Close But He Soon fell.[6]

General Albert Sidney Johnston had planned to have his
army in position to attack by the night of the 4th, but due to
delays caused by muddy roads and inexperienced officers, it
was actually Saturday night April 5th before the desired position
was reached. One of the most valuable days in the history of the
Confederacy had been lost.

According to William Stevenson, who claimed to be
present, a council of war was held at eight o'clock on Saturday
night. All the top Confederate generals were present. Braxton
Bragg had come with the troops from Florida, Pierre Gustave
Toutant Beauregard had recently been transferred from Virginia
following his successful venture at First Manassas, and of
course there were Polk, Hardee, Breckenridge and the host of
lesser commanders who had been with the Army since its early
formation. Stevenson left a dramatic description of the meeting
between these generals. He wrote:

In an open space, with a dim fire in the midst, and
a drum on which to write, you could see grouped around

110

*their "Little Napoleon," as Beauregard was sometimes
fondly called, ten or twelve generals, the flickering light
playing over their eager faces, while they listened to his
plans and made suggestions as to the conduct of the
fight....*

*For two hours the council lasted, and as it broke
up, and the generals were ready to return to their
respective commands, I heard General Beauregard say,
raising his hand and pointing in the direction of the
Federal camps, whose drums we could plainly hear —
"Gentlemen, we sleep in the enemy's camp to-morrow
night.*[7]

General Albert Sidney Johnston, according to Stevenson,
held back and listened. Stevenson wrote:

*General Sidney Johnston stood apart from the rest,
with his tall straight form standing out like a specter
against the dim sky ... His face was pale, but wore a
determined expression, and at times he drew nearer the
center of the ring and said a few words, which were
listened to with great attention.*[8]

There were those in the council who advised withdrawal,
but Johnston would not entertain such suggestions; he had
come to fight and fight he would. In later times he would be
credited with making such statements as "I would fight them if
they were a million," and "We will water our horses tomorrow
night in the Tennessee River." The decision had been made;
there would be a battle.

While their generals discussed strategy, the soldiers in the
Rebel Army, now officially entitled The Army of Mississippi,
tried as best they could to get some rest. "Yet that was a dreary
night to prepare for the dreadful battle of to-morrow," wrote

111

William Stevenson. "The men were already weary, hungry, and cold. No fires were allowed, except in the holes in the ground, over which soldiers bent with their blankets round their shoulders, striving to catch and concentrate the little heat that struggled up through the bleak April air."[9]

On the bank of the Tennessee River the Yankees crawled into their blankets unaware of what was taking place. Sherman, on the 5th of April, sent a message to Grant saying, "I do not apprehend anything like an attack on our position." Grant in turn wired his superiors, "I have scarcely the faintest idea of an attack (general one) being made upon us."[10] Almost unbelievably, a Confederate Army of over 35,000 men had approached within hearing distance of Grant's army and not a Yankee knew it.

During Saturday night, W.W. Wilson's regiment was ordered to lie down and "keep a Wake   But we Had thrown our knapsacks and Blankets a way and Wea was two cold to sleep mutch."[11]   Before daylight Wilson and the tens of thousands of men with him stirred from their uneasy places of rest.   Guns were checked, harness adjusted, sleepy hands fumbled through pockets for decks of cards, whiskey bottles, dice, or any other articles considered inappropriate possessions for one who might suddenly meet his Maker.

Only the faintest light of dawn was needed to set these men in motion against an enemy about whom they knew very little except that they were in a part of the country where they had no business. In the two days to follow, the untrained men of both armies would attempt to decide with their blood what their politicians had been unable to decide with their brains, and in the process they would fight the bloodiest battle that had, as of yet, been fought on the North American continent.

2.

To Confederate generals, the water-bound position of the Union Army called for a special plan of attack. Like a giant sickle they would thrust their Army into the haven of the enemy and sweep the Yankees northward into the swamps along Owl Creek. Such a move, if successful, would deny the enemy any further use of Pittsburg Landing, thereby eliminating the possibility of reinforcements being brought across the river. Once the enemy was pushed into the swamps, there was little they could do but surrender or be annihilated.

Long before daylight on Sunday morning the Rebs formed themselves into three lines facing the enemy. The first line extended along a front of three miles, long enough to close the only route of escape open to the Yankees. Behind the front line, two more moved in support, and still further back, a reserve force brought up the rear.

Through an early morning fog, Johnston's men moved in for the kill. Only a few hundred yards away, the Yankees were about their morning activities unaware that anything unusual was about to happen. Some were cooking breakfast, others were in the process of putting on their clothes, while others were attempting to get a few seconds of additional sleep before responding to the bugle's call. Somewhere in the grayish fog the initial contact between the enemy forces took place. No sooner had the first shots been fired than the battle was underway.

John Taylor of the 27th Tennessee said:

> *Before the gray and silver light began to stretch across the plains on that beautiful, holy Sabbath day, the army was in motion, moving forward ... Pickets were driven in, and we pressed forward. Coming to an old field, and going quickly across it, we discovered a*

113

battery to our left and front. Several of the enemy's pickets were found dead upon the field. Just about the time we were getting fairly through the old field, a heavy line of pickets opened a spirited fire upon us, which drew a response from our regiment. Then the fight began in earnest, and we could plainly see the enemy's tents, and the men rushing here and there falling into line.[12]

Wave after wave of disorganized Rebs broke through the protecting curtain of fog to hit the irregular line presented by Grant's army. Those Rebs who had guns shot at everything that moved. They fell upon the Yankees with a determination born of confidence and the effectiveness of their efforts was immediately apparent.

The initial reaction of the Yankees, many of whom had never before been under fire, was to run, and that is exactly what they did. High-ranking officers threw down their guns and yelled to their men to save themselves from the screaming tide of humanity that was sweeping down upon them.

For the attacking Confederates, it was a glorious moment. About all they had done was yell and, just like the politician had predicted, the terrified blue-coats had deserted the field. Some Confederates, believing the battle won, curbed their aggressiveness long enough to survey the scene around them, and what they saw completely neutralized their war-like tendencies. In the enemy's abandoned camps the hungry Rebs found breakfast cooked and ready to serve and they promptly sat down to enjoy the delicacies prepared by their now departed hosts. Scattered all around were guns, ammunition, money, and other articles which offered much more appeal to undisciplined soldiers than chasing Yanks through the underbrush behind Shiloh Church. The spoils of war had diverted attention from the war itself and soon they filled their arms with Federal loot and headed toward the rear.

But such men were the exception. To the rank and file Confederate soldier this was a battle to the end and he intended being on the firing line when the end came. Men who had marched to Shiloh without guns picked up those discarded by the enemy and fell in with their regiment to pursue the retreating foe. Soon it became a race to see which regiments could stay ahead as the Confederates pushed back the demoralized foe.

General Grant heard the opening shots on Sunday morning as he was eating breakfast nine miles away at Savannah. According to the mistress of Cherry Mansion where Grant was staying, "He [Grant] was at my breakfast-table when he heard the report from a cannon. Holding, untasted, a cup of coffee, he paused in conversation to listen a moment at the report of another cannon. He hastily arose, saying to his staff, 'Gentlemen, the ball is in motion; let us be off.' " Mrs W.H. Cherry, the author of those lines, added, "I believe Gen. Grant was thoroughly sober."[13]

When Grant arrived at the battlefield, he was told of the Confederate onslaught, of how, without warning, Southern soldiers had slipped through the morning fog to deliver their devastating attack, and how the most valiant efforts of some Union regiments had failed to stop the stampede that followed. Grant could see for himself the thousands of demoralized Federal troops wandering about without the faintest semblance of organization. Even as his boat pulled to the shore at Pittsburg Landing he watched hundreds of men cowering against the high bank of the river. It was a disheartening scene for a general who had recently been relieved of his duties on a suspicion of incompetency.

Captain W.S. Hillyer had been eating breakfast with Grant when the cannon shots at Shiloh were heard. He hurried aboard the dispatch boat "Tigress" with the general and started for Pittsburg Landing. Hillyer later wrote his wife that while still on the river the "Tigress" met another boat coming from Pittsburg Landing and that the word was passed that the Federal right and center were folding. In describing the scene shortly after he had gone ashore, Hillyer wrote his wife:

We arrived at Pittsburg Landing about half past eight o'clock, got on our horses and galloped out to the battlefield. Arrived [?] there we found the enemy had attacked and were engaging our right and center in overwhelming force and our troops were falling back. We met hundreds of cowardly renegades fleeing to the river and reporting their regiments cut to pieces. We tried in vain to rally and return them to the front.[14]

In what must have seemed a hopeless situation, Grant was informed of one encouraging development: as the center section of his line was retreating the men came upon an old sunken road bed and here General Benjamin Prentiss had rallied enough men to temporarily stall the Confederate advance. As Grant worked frantically to reorganize his army, only the men in the sunken road stood between him and total disaster.

Meanwhile on the Confederate side, the troops had become almost as disorganized in victory as the Federals had in defeat. Officers no longer attempted to find their own men, but led anybody who would follow. Brigades lost their identity as regiments became mixed, and high ranking officers galloped aimlessly over the field looking for their commands. All the while the battle was heating up.

Robert Gates of the 6th Tennessee wrote:

The regiment was ordered to charge a battery on its right front about 11 o'clock A.M. To do this an open field, or an old orchard, had to be crossed. The regiment went at the work in gallant style, but when about one hundred yards from the battery a terrible fire was opened on it from an ambuscade of infantry that was concealed in the woods around the field in somewhat the shape of the letter V. The regiment charged into the very jaws of the V, and the men fell like grass before the sickle. The dead lay in line of battle, as if on dress-parade. Over two hundred and fifty men were placed <u>hors de combat</u> in less than as many seconds.[15]

Continued assaults by the Confederates failed to dislodge the Union men who held the sunken road. The area was appropriately dubbed "the hornet's nest" by those who were forced back time after time. Shortly after noon, Albert Sidney Johnston galloped his horse toward the crucial point, and upon his arrival, saw the ground dotted with dead and wounded Southerners. Still the enemy showed no sign of retreat. Johnston turned to his staff and remarked, "They are offering stubborn resistance here. I shall have to put the bayonet to them."[16] According to Johnston's son, "It was the crisis of the conflict. The Federal key was in his front. If his assault were successful, their left would be completely turned, and the victory won."[17]

Governor Isham G. Harris of Tennessee was by Johnston's side when the decision to charge the sunken road was made. Harris was asked to lead a Tennessee regiment; without hesitation he accepted the assignment. Johnston rode to the front, and instead of pulling his sword form its scabbard the general held a tin cup above his head and shouted, "Boys, fix bayonets and follow your general."[18]

With officers leading the charge, the Confederates once again started toward the sunken road. The advancing line soon became irregular as portions of it were pushed back by enemy fire. The screams of the wounded were indistinguishable from the threatening yells of those who continued to advance. The Rebel line continued to advance until it had passed a point farther than it had gone all day and pockets of Federals could be seen pulling back. During the charge, Johnston's horse was shot in four places and the General's uniform was pierced in many places, but he seemed uninjured. As a group of enemy soldiers pulled back they turned to fire a final salvo at their pursuers; one of these shots struck Johnston below the right knee. In a few minutes the general bled to death.

Late in the afternoon the Federal soldiers in the sunken road surrendered. General Prentiss and approximately 2500 men were taken prisoners, but they had rendered an invaluable service to the Federal Army. During the time they held out, Grant was successful in consolidating his troops in a small arch which emcompassed Pittsburg Landing and there the Union Army waited for night and the arrival of reinforcements. On the Confederate side, it was up to Beauregard to win or lose the fight. He decided to wait for another day, and shortly after nightfall the fighting tapered off.

By the time darkness covered the field at Shiloh there were no greenhorns in the Confederate Army. All had been tried and most had been found true. There were exceptions. The Colonel of 5th Tennessee reported:

Lt. W.R. Morrow is reported as having left the field Sunday morning under pretense of assisting a wounded brother, and though he was positively forbidden to do so by his captain, and did not again return to his company during the two days' fighting. Private Demon Martin of the same company showed great timidity and had to be repeatedly ordered to fire his gun before he would use it.[19]

Sam Watkins remembered one soldier by the name of Smith "stepping deliberately out of the ranks and shooting his finger off to keep out of the fight."[20]

While some Rebs had proven unequal to the task they had been asked to perform, others possessed the needed qualities in excess. Private Samuel Evans, "after being severely wounded, the ball passing through his cheeks refused to go to the rear, but remained and fought for a considerable length of time, cheering the men and loading and shooting as fast as he could."[21] It had been a day during which green, scared, but determined boys had been transformed into deadly instruments of destruction. Such young men had experienced, for the first time, the sight of a man throwing his gun in the air, his hands flying to his head, and his body quivering in death as a result of enemy fire.

To the politician, war was a technique for deciding political issues. To the generals, it was a game of strategy and tactics. But to the individual soldier, it was a contest between destruction and survival. The men of the 27th Tennessee watched in disbelief as captains and other officers fell before the disorganized fire of the enemy. In their very first charge, the men of the 27th saw their Colonel fall from his horse in a lifeless heap, and as their Lt. Colonel attempted to mount the horse, it fell dead in its tracks. As Captain Isham Hearn fell dead, a soldier nearby "shuddered as I saw his manly form quiver in death."[22] Isham Hearn had been a Methodist minister and one member of his company remembered the sermon he had preached before leaving Corinth.

> *His discourse was earnest and practical, and he warned the boys against the pernicious vice of swearing. He spoke eloquently, feeling in the interest of his Master; perhaps not expecting in one short week he would be in the presence of that God he was serving and advising his comrades to worship.*[23]

The men of the 20th Tennessee entered the fight shortly before noon. No sooner had the Fishing Creek veterans been committed to action than the 54th Tennessee, mistaking them for the enemy, poured a merciless fire into their ranks. While an attempt was being made to stop the fire of the 54th, the men of the 20th Regiment were hit from the front by a segment of the Federal line and were driven from their position. During the fighting, one soldier observed that "the barrel of my new Enfield had become so hot I could only hold it by its wooden stock."[24]

Even the slave body servants had gotten into the fight. The slave of Captain Micajah Griffin, 7th Tennessee Cavalry, who was "in the habit of shouldering his gun and going with the boys whenever a fight was up," fell in with the advancing Rebs and:

managed to get hold of two prisoners, and as he was
bringing them from the field he met two or three
Federals, who made an attempt to rescue their comrades.
The negro, making a bold defense, repulsed his
assailants, with the loss of one killed, and succeeded in
bringing off his two prisoners.[25]

W.W. Wilson carefully recorded the events which
happened during his first day of battle. He wrote in his
diary that the night before the battle opened, his regiment
reached its position and upon

Hearing the eneme Drum Wea all lay down in line
of Battlee and stade there until in the night . . . At Day
lite Wea started our Brigade in Furent Wea stopt in a low
place just on A slant High A Nuf to Shoot over . . . Wea
shot and lay down to lode   Rite there our men sufered I
saw severl of our Boys kild and wounded.[26]

Later in the day when Wilson's regiment was ordered to
charge the enemy's position,

Wea started and Hollerd evy step   just as Wea got
to the top of a slant A Boom struck my Rite shoulder
whitch Stopt me from Fiting   i Fell Back to the
Hospittle and stade tell Night.[27]

John Gumm had also been in the thick of the fighting all
day. Gumm wrote:

...at Day Light the pickets Com fiting   our
Brigade Com advancing a bout Sun up   We Com Fiting
our first attack was to charge a batery   we Lost Severil
of our men   Our Company had four kiled . . . but we
taken the Battery   that was about 7 O Clock in the
Morning   We then pass on formed our Line and Com
Advansing a bout 12 O Clock   we Lay a fiew mindts

they trowed a bomb in our camp   it killed four and
wounded 2 . . . we fought on til Dark   we Lay all night
in the Yanky tents   we got some crackers to Eat to
Night it being the firs Since fridy morning   we Slep
well all though the Dead Lay all a round the Camps.[28]

On the Federal side the situation had improved appreciably. During Sunday night, Buell's army arrived from Middle Tennessee, and during the morning hours, was ferried across the river at Pittsburg Landing. General Lew Wallace's division had, at long last, arrived from Crump's Landing and was ready for action. Grant utilized river gunboats to hold the Rebs at bay as explained by Captain W. S. Hillyer:

Sunday evening the enemy had pushed our lines
back until their batteries almost commanded our
transports; a little further and they would have made it
impossible to land our reinforcements. But, fortunately,
they got within range of our two gunboats, which were
lying anchored in the river, and which opened upon them
with a perfect shower of shells. Night never was more
welcome to any poor mortals than that night to our little
army at Pittsburg [Landing]. [29]

For the Confederates at Shiloh, the night was long, dark, and stormy. The wounded begged for water and the dead lay scattered over the ground in every conceivable form. The soldiers who were able to walk roamed about looking for water or a lost comrade, while others, too stunned to make sense out of the confusion around them, wandered without purpose. Officers continued to search for misplaced commands and, in the midst of it all, a violent storm erupted to add its fury to the already damnable scene. The rain made it impossible for officers to reorganize their troops and still more difficult to move heavy guns. As a substitute for meaningful action the men were forced to stand in the rain with no other consolation than the knowledge that it was just as miserable for their Yankee enemy.

Tired beyond the point to care, the men in the Confederate army sought the nearest place where refuge could be found from the Union gunboats. There was nowhere to hide and the Yankees threw their deadly missiles at the exhausted Southerners throughout the night.

In the pelting rain that saturated the ground at Shiloh, General Grant leaned against a tree and surveyed the situation. The Federal general was forced to use crutches as a result of a fall from his horse a few days before, and now, as he leaned against the tree to lessen the pressure on his injured foot, he heard sounds that made his spirits rise. Buell's troops were crossing the river, and to the north Wallace's men were arriving. According to Captain Hillyer, "Before morning we had received twenty-five thousand reinforcements, and before Monday's battle was over ten thousand more."[30]

Satisfied with the progress about him, Grant made his way to a cabin under the bluff where he intended to spend the night. But, as he later wrote:

>...all night wounded men were brought in, their wounds dressed, a leg or arm amputated as the case might require .... The sight was more unendurable than encountering the enemy's fire, and I returned to my tree in the rain.[31]

Although drenched by the rain and distressed by the horror he had seen, Grant waited confidently for the dawn to break.

On Monday morning, the Confederates pulled themselves up from their muddy resting places just as the darkness was dispelled by the greying dawn. Governor Isham G. Harris spoke to the Tennessee troops urging them to continue the work of the previous day. Harris spoke without full knowledge of the reinforcements Grant had received during the night. It would take more than inspirational speeches to stop the Union Army now poised on the bank of the Tennessee River.

Shortly after sunup, the fighting resumed with the Yankees striking out like suffocating animals fighting for air.

Most of the action on Monday took place between Pittsburg Landing and Shiloh Church with the armies surging back and forth as each strove to push a point of advantage. The result seemed inevitable. Fresh Union troops smashed their way through Confederate lines, and only occasionally did the Rebs regain their balance and strike back. Courage alone was not enough.

During the afternoon, Beauregard ordered his battered army back to Corinth.

The journey from Shiloh was a sad one for the men in the Confederate Army. Those who had been captured were loaded on boats and transported to prisons in the North. Many left the field knowing that their sons or brothers were among the hundreds of unburied dead left in the wake of the bitter struggle. One such prisoner was Colonel Joel Battle of the 20th Tennessee whose two sons lay dead on the battlefield.

Meanwhile, the road to Corinth had become an avenue of misery, fatigue, and death. Those too badly wounded to walk were loaded into wagons and the trip back to Corinth was started through the rain, mud, and hail. Men were piled like sacks of grain in wagons which mired to the hubs under their groaning and cursing cargoes. Teams of mules slipped and heaved and plunged with every outburst of their frustrated drivers, and with every maneuver of the crude ambulances the wounded screamed and yelled to the top of their voices.

All along the route could be found the bodies of the dead who had been removed from the wagons to lighten the load and to give the living a better chance for survival. Soldiers with bloody bandages around their legs, arms, and heads hobbled through the mud on improvised crutches amid a procession of stretcher bearers who carried men whose gaping wounds mutely warned that the trip for them was being made in vain. Those who had escaped injury walked sluggishly, their eyes seeming to see nothing, their faces covered with a mixture of gunpowder and mud; they seldom lifted their eyes from the ground.

When the retreating caravan reached Corinth, the townspeople looked in horror as blood dripped from wagons carrying the wounded. Already over three hundred had died during the journey from Shiloh and many of these were indiscriminately mixed with the wounded who waited helplessly for aid or death. Every available house became a hospital. Physicians from throughout the South were summoned to meet the needs of the unprepared army. Women came by trains, wagons, and horseback to act as nurses, but after every reasonable effort had been exhausted, the terrible death rate did not diminish. So scarce was the supply of physicians that men who picked up medical books and read the technique of amputation were soon performing delicate operations that, in most instances, proved fatal. The wounded had little choice but to submit.

One of the badly wounded at Corinth was Nathan Bedford Forrest. As the infantry retreated from Shiloh, Forrest threw his cavalry between them and the 4th Illinois Cavalry which was in close pursuit. Forrest's men drove the cavalry back over the Federal infantry which "were thrown into a panic, threw down their guns and also broke for the rear."[32]

As Forrest chased the retreating Yankees his horse carried him well inside the enemy ranks and he was immediately surrounded by embittered Federal soldiers. "Shoot him," was shouted from all sides as the Yanks opened fire. One Federal soldier was so close to Forrest that he pushed his musket to the Rebel general's body and fired. The ball entered "just above the left hip … lodging against the spinal column."[33] Not one to surrender easily, Forrest spurred his wounded horse, and with pistol in hand, opened a path of escape toward Corinth. Like thousands of others at Corinth, Forrest found that aid was slow in coming.

The 19th Tennessee was assigned the task of protecting the roads leading to Corinth from the battlefield and W. J. Worsham described the scene.

Reader it is useless to attempt a description of the battle field of Shiloh. Language would fail to portray it as it was. The dead were piled on each other in many places. In the center of the battlefield was a pond in and around which were many dead men and several horses... This could truly be called the "death-pond" of Shiloh. All over the field the dead lay side by side — the brave "Who wore the blue and those who wore the gray" now no longer foes. The wounded of both armies, who yet remained on the field, showed the true manhood and brotherly feeling by helping each other as far as possible, consoling each other and sharing each other's woes . . . Dead horses, broken ambulances and shattered caissons lay thickly strewn over all the field, all of which made up the sad, sad scene.[34]

Tuesday morning, two Federal soldiers, John Lewis and Cliff Ross, wandered among the dead that awaited burial. Their eyes were attracted to the body of a Confederate soldier, probably because the arm of the corpse was held in a sling. A closer view revealed the body to be that of Allen Battle their former room-mate at Miami of Ohio University. Allen was one of the dead sons of Colonel Joel Battle who was already on his way to a northern prison. According to still another classmate of Allen Battle, "The last time I saw Allen alive was in June, 1858, at Miami University the year I graduated. When I saw him next it was on April 8, 1862, dead in the camp of Hurlbert's Division on the battlefield of Shiloh."[35]

The former classmates of the dead Confederate soldier took his body to their camp and prepared it for burial. According to a third classmate, John R. Chamberlain,

A rude coffin made of cracker boxes contained his body when it was let down into a deep grave, where it was buried on sloping ground in the rear of the 31st Indiana Regiment. There was no name put at the head of

125

the grave, and the earth was beaten down flat so that the place could not be recognized by those who had no business to know it. About twenty paces from the grave stood a large black oak tree. I cut with an axe a big chip out of the tree facing the grave, so as to guide us in finding the spot should we ever be required to do so.[36]

At Corinth, amid the suffering and death that surrounded him, John Gumm learned the name of the battle through which he had just passed. Under the protection of a makeshift shelter Gumm wrote:

I have learned the name of the Battel ground they call it Shiloah   it was   the greatest Battle in modern history   its duration and Bravery never his bin Surpassed Either in ancient or modern history   it was one Continel Charge . . . it was a Scarary time to me for it was the first Battel that I Ever was in and Bombs and Grape Shot fell as thick as hail and minnie Balls whising round my Years like Bombel Bees . . .[37]

The conduct of his colonel had greatly impressed Gumm. He wrote, "i will say that Col Nail [Neil] is as Brave as the Bravest and I fear a Litel too Brave for the Safty of his men but he is excitable."[38]

Reminded by the suffering at Corinth of the terrible price paid for what glory had been won at Shiloh, John Gumm was inspired to write a tribute to the battle and to his comrades who fought there. The tribute said:

. . .the Batel field of Shiloah will be memorabel in the annels of our history   it has bin stained by the Blood and illustrated by the gallantry of her heros and Sons that name like the music of Carroll   It will be Sweet yet mournful to hur Sole and when the appointed pin Shall Come to weve the Stands of its Stiring incidents into the Enduring Cord of history   the Laurel and Cypress will

be found Closely blanded   alas that the Shouts of victory and the nobel Exoltations which stirs generous minds to prais and admiration of heroic actions Should be mingled with the wail of bereaved harts over their Love ones   Lest the bright Bloody record stand before us in names as familiar as hous hold words in our comminuty or Engraved uppon it in   Deathless Characters   Mytars and heros Stand Side by Side in Batel as did they in days of old when the Fathers of Revolution was Contending for their Liberty and their Children's independence.[39]

While John Gumm was giving vent to his emotions, W.W. Wilson was getting acquainted with the "Hospittle." Three days after being wounded he wrote, "wond was Drest For the Furst Time." Five days later he wrote from Columbus, Mississippi, "I got Hear and Had my Wond Drest For Second time." The scenes at the hospital proved very depressing to the wounded soldier. He observed,

Now in the Hospittle I cant state How many Dies for Surtain   But there is som Dying Som Howlering and a grate many Things two tegus to menchun.[40]

It was painfully evident to the young Reb that there "is so many that Wea cant be Treated as we art to Be."[41]

3.

While the main Confederate army fought sickness, wounds, and boredom, the 8th and 16th Tennessee Regiments made their way from South Carolina to join it at Corinth. To many of these men, like Monroe Bearden, the trip had great meaning. It would afford an opportunity to face the Yankee invader who so arrogantly made Tennessee "a land paluted by the invasion of a mircenary foe — the vanquishers of our rights, liberties and institutions."[42] To others not so emotionally involved in the issues, the trip was just another unpleasant experience in the ever-mounting list of unpleasant experiences which made up army life. To such men, the trip was endurable mainly because it was expected to be one of the final inconveniences of their soon to be completed one-year enlistment.

At least Resinor Etter of Warren County had reason to be happy. Luckily, he had survived wading the icy, "rump-deep" streams of western Virginia and had recently returned to his regiment from a visit home to see the "little stranger" who had made its appearance in late December. Before Christmas, Etter's wife had written him suggesting they name their new son Jeff Davis, but the Rebel soldier informed his wife emphatically that he "did not want no Jeff Davis at my house."[43]

Etter got his way about the baby's name and arrived home in March to take a look at the youngster. He found his wife "comfortably situated in the bed   beside her lay my two little boys   one was two an a half years old the other I never had seen . . . it was a pleasant looking chap   my oldest child knew me   that was beyond my expectation also his dog that stays with him knew me."[44]

Etter greatly enjoyed his visit home. He delivered letters from soldiers in his regiment to their families, ate dinner with most of his neighbors, and thoroughly basked in the admiring attention of the community.

Other members of the 16th Tennessee arrived in Warren County to find that some of their former secessionist friends "seemed to disrelish the Confederate uniform, and were therefore cool and distant."[45] The visiting Rebs found the home-folk "generally depressed in spirits on account of the near approach of the enemy, many believing the country will soon be overrun by them."[46] Some of the men were successful in wooing and winning for themselves new brides, who were left reluctantly when the furlough ended.

By the middle of April, the 8th and 16th Regiments were in Atlanta, again headed for Corinth. Outside the city "the train run off the track   nine boxes turned over   killed one man by the name of Green wounded 25 more   Killed sever horses   is a wonder it did not kill all in the boxes."[47] Such incidents at least broke the monotony of otherwise boring hours of travel. Occasionally the boys got into a town where a pint of Georgia "pine-top" whiskey could be bought for a reasonable price. One character by the name of Waldo "left his post and got a buggy run all over town," and it took most of the night to land him in the "gard house."[48] Waldo represented that element who found the attractions of city life irresistible and a few of his kind were usually left behind after each stop.

Resinor Etter found the people of Georgia very understanding. At La Grange he:

> .. .went up town and got my dinner   they would not charge me a cent and said they would never make money from a solger   she said that she had a son out and she would think hard of any person that would not give him something to eat when hungry   the ladies came down to the depot with Bokes [bouquets] an give the boys some nice flowers.[49]

The recent visit home and the warm reception they received from the people of Georgia cheered the men up. In a few days, they arrived at Corinth.

Although many of the wounded had already been transferred from Corinth, the newly arrived men found "everything presenting the true aspect of war in its fullest sense." The surrounding countryside was one vast encampment of troops. Tents dotted the hillsides as far as the eye could see. Groups of dust-covered soldiers could be seen making their way wearily from the breastworks north of town;   a general uneasiness was detectable as the Confederates kept a close watch on the roads leading to Shiloh Church. But the main fare at Corinth was boredom, that particular kind of boredom known only to an inactive army whose members know little of the significance of what had happened and even less of what to expect.

Far away, in Richmond, the politicians were thinking. Most of the men in the Confederate Army had enlisted for one year only. That year was almost over and there was reason to believe that thousands would not choose to re-enlist. Such men were about to leave for home just as the war was assuming its momentum and there were few indications that volunteer enlistments would refill the ranks. Indeed, the Yankees were watching the calendar knowing that their enemies might soon go home and hoping there would be no replacements. To Southern politicians, there seemed only one solution, a Conscription Act, which was passed in short order, and which evoked a wave of bitter resentment among the troops at Corinth.

As far back as February, Burton Warfield had written his girlfriend:

> *There is some talk of 12 months volunteers being pressed for 2 years longer. But I can't think they will do that. If they want to press anybody let them press some of the corwardly scramps that are at home who can retire to their feathered couches protected and made secure by us who are undergoing the rigors of winter and the perils of the soldier while they can undisturbed in their repose sleep without a dread upon their minds, dream sweetly of home comforts and ponder in their minds in what maner they can swindle the country and the family's of the volunteers. I say press them.*[50]

In March, Monroe Bearden had written, "I have not reenlisted yet. Neither do I expect to until after I get home. As I have some choice in regard to the maner of serving my country in regard to the locality in which I serve."[51] Under the new

Conscription Act Monroe Bearden was spared the trouble of choosing either the manner or the locality of his service and the denial of choice did not set well at all.

As Sam Watkins saw the situation, "Soldiers had enlisted for twelve months only, and had faithfully complied with their volunteer obligations . . . They wanted to see their families; the war had become a reality and they were tired of it."[52] Soldiers from the hill country raved in anger when they learned that under the Conscription Act a man who owned twenty or more slaves could go home and oversee them. The cry of "Rich man's war, poor man's fight" echoed throughout the scattered camps surrounding Corinth. The element of bitterness became more apparent.

To those Confederates who had volunteered the year before, and would have remained under almost any circumstances, the Conscription Act was regarded as an insult to their patriotism. To those planning to go home, it represented a bit of political trickery which took from them their natural rights. In both groups, the feeling varied from simmering resentment to outright rage.

Companies, regiments, and brigades were reorganized following the enactment of the Conscription Act. Many officers who had organized units the year before suddenly found themselves voted out of rank. When men cast their ballots for officers, they remembered how they had been required to stand picket duty while a friend of an officer rested, how they had been denied a furlough while other soldiers went home, and how some officers had been among the first to leave their posts at Shiloh. In many instances, officers defeated in their bid for re-election took up their guns as privates and remained with their regiment. In other instances, such officers went home and were "so indifferent to the cause as to appear tender-footed on the issues ever afterwards."[53] As one soldier noted, "The patriotism of a few men completely exhausted itself during the first year, and they appeared fully inclined to cancel the contract into which they at first entered with so much enthusiasm."[54]

Resinor Etter had no intention of canceling any contracts, but the whole idea of conscription went against his grain. On May 8, 1862, he wrote:

All is confusion today   we have to elect officers or have them appointed   this was much against our feelings as we did not like to be compeled to do anything of the kind   we wished to return home when the present expected battle was fought and reinlist again as it suited us tho we was not allowed that privileg . . . I never give a vote in the regiment and I never will under no such law.[55]

After the initial resentment against the Conscription Act spent itself, the men resolved to live with it. Actually the alternatives were even less attractive. Soon the conscripts began arriving in camp, but as one veteran observed:

It is true the ranks of the army were apparently considerably swollen, but virtually they were weakened. The hearts of but few of the Conscripts were in the cause, and it took efficient soldiers to look after them. Some few fought as became Southern soldiers, and stayed with us to the end, but a great many deserted at the first opportunity.[56]

While some soldiers were trying to stay out of the army, W.W. Wilson was trying to get out of the "Hospittle". At Columbus, Mississippi, Wilson continued to observe the distressing scenes of death and suffering caused by the fighting at Shiloh. On May 12, he wrote:

. . .theire is on A avredge A Bout four or five Deths Pur Day   They Beary ten men Pur Day . . . I was at the graveyard yeasday and they aire still Buring ten Pur day on A avredge.[57]

Meanwhile, at Corinth, all was not well with the main army. In addition to the unrest caused by the Conscription Act, there were other matters which caused concern. Speaking of the conditions that prevailed at Corinth, Edwin Reynolds, from Henry County wrote:

We finally returned within the fortifications immediately around Corinth. No water was to be had except that in small creeks, which ceased to flow on the approach of summer, and was covered with a green scum. This stagnant water, which was polluted in various ways, produced an epidemic of dysentery and typhoid fever, which debilitated, decimated, and disheartened the army to a serious extent.[58]

Poor living conditions, coupled with resentment, prompted many men to desert. Newly elected officers watched helplessly as their ranks continually dwindled. Colonel C.D. Venable of the 5th Tennessee called his regiment into formation and told them, "I want to say to the Fifth Regiment that if any more of the men intend to leave, I hope they will go tonight."[59] In some instances regiments came close to mutiny. If the army were to survive, strong measures were indicated.

Confederate generals decided to make examples of those who deserted. Public whippings, even brandings with red hot irons were utilized, but the desertions continued. Eventually the ultimate instrument was utilized: the firing squad.

A Lawrence countian by the name of William Rowland had been pressed into a Confederate regiment and, during the months that followed, deserted and became a member of a Union regiment. At Shiloh he was captured by the very Confederate regiment he had deserted. After the battle he was tried and sentenced to death.

Thousands of Tennessee troops were called into formation to watch his execution. A grave was dug and a black pine coffin was placed beside it. The prisoner was led out and placed on the coffin. According to a witness:

After Rowland had ceased to speak, he took off hat, coat, and necktie, and laying his hand on his heart, he said, "Aim here." But the sergeant of the guard advanced to tie his hands and blindfold him. He asked the privilege of standing untied; the request was not granted. His eyes were bandaged, he kneeled upon his coffin, and engaged in prayer for several minutes, and then said he was ready. The lieutenant of the guard then gave the word, "Fire" and twenty-four muskets, half of them loaded with ball, were discharged. When the smoke lifted, the body had fallen backward, and was still.[60]

For other men in the Confederate Army it was a time to take stock. Those who had returned from Virginia had no battle honors to their credit. Those who had remained in Tennessee had seen their defense line across Kentucky crumble. The army had lost over twelve thousand of its number at Fort Donelson and another ten thousand at Shiloh. At both places what appeared to be a victory turned into a heart-breaking defeat and withdrawal. Now at Corinth they faced an enemy that was potentially one hundred thousand strong.

After spending the morning of May 14, 1862, in the rifle pits three miles north of Corinth, Captain Jim Womack came back to camp, took out his diary and wrote his reaction to the situation.

Twelve months ago today, I left my happy & prosperous home in McMinnville, Tenn., to battle for my country's freedom and Independence, which were then denied her, and still are, by a vaunting and insulting enemy. In consequence of the odious and intolerable duplicity beginning to be forced on the people of that, and other states, I felt it to be my duty not only to my country, but also to myself and family, to enlist in the C.S. army . . .

During the year we have undergone many privations & hardships; especially was the fall and winter campaign among the mountains in western Va. severe. Here we were frequently deprived of even the few comforts that the soldier in the field might reasonably expect, having to sleep on the cold, wet and sometimes frozen ground, with no other covering than the canopy of Heaven. Day after day we marched over muddy roads and snow-covered mountains, sometimes barefoot and almost without clothing. Notwithstanding all this, and notwithstanding the clouds of war grow thicker & darker still, yet we have never seen the hour when we would give up the struggle for Southern Independence. And we never will, but by the help of God, Liberty and independence will yet be ours.[61]

If Southern freedom and independence were to be won, it would not be at Corinth. On at least two occasions, Beauregard had sought to isolate portions of the Federal Army and destroy them, but both attempts failed. Confederate generals tended to blame each other for these abortive efforts, but John Gumm had his own theory. Referring to a movement against the Federal General John Pope, Gumm wrote, "the object of the Moove was to attack General Popes Division of the Federal Army and to Cut them off from the main army . . . but for Some cause he Smelt a mice a Littel too quick for us."[62] In any event, when the Yankees came close enough to Corinth to use their big guns, Beauregard decided to pull out, and on May 29th the army headed toward Tupelo.

The trip was difficult and was accented by many hardships. The 16th Tennessee walked all night through mud and camped the next day on a river bank. They had no food and were without water except that in the river. John Gumm and his comrades in the 23rd Regiment stayed behind and felled trees along the way to keep the enemy at bay. Toward night on May 30, 1862, Gumm wrote, "we have packed wood and piled

135

under a Bridge and truselwork   it is now on fier, it is a valuabel piece of work and Seams a pity to be Distroyed."[63]

Resinor Etter worried more about his clothes than Mississippi bridges. During a halt in the march he "pulled off my shirt and washed it , as I had no other in my possession. I have at this time one shirt an old pair of pants, one coat, no blanket."[64] But even to a soldier so destitute of wearing apparel there were some bright spots. On June 4th, after the army was safely away form Corinth, Etter wrote, "Night is here and I am permitted to lay down on my bed of erth without cover   tho I sleep sweetly."[65]

John Gumm

Chapter V

Virginia Interlude

We go to attack the enemy

On the very day that Corinth was being evacuated by the Confederates, three regiments of Tennesseans were preparing to enter battle for the first time in Virginia. The men of the 1st, 7th, and 14th Regiments had walked so many miles they had begun to wonder whether war meant shooting the enemy, or walking him to death. But that was all behind them; the men from Tennessee would soon test the mettle of their enemy.

In length of service, Turney's 1st Tennessee was the senior Tennessee Regiment in Virginia, having arrived even before the Volunteer State had seceded. Colonel Peter Turney was the commander of this anxious group of Rebels. Turney was a Franklin County politician — a hell-raising secessionist — and a man who already had his eye on an expanded political role in the post-war Confederacy. His emotionally charged oratory had convinced the hill boys of his area that there was glory to be found in war, and like hounds responding to the hunter's horn, they followed him to Virginia.

The 7th Tennessee went to Virginia under the command of Colonel Robert Hatton of Lebanon. Before the war, Hatton had been a member of the state legislature, a member of the national congress, and an unsuccessful candidate for governor. While in Congress, Hatton had strongly opposed secession until all hope had vanished for the preservation of the Union. He returned home and organized a regiment and was elected its first colonel. Hatton's efforts to preserve the Union had not been appreciated by some of his fellow-townsmen, especially the students at Cumberland University, who burned him in effigy, knocked windows from his house, and beat tin pans around his home at night. But when convinced that war was inevitable, the thirty-five year-old lawyer was among the first to volunteer his services to the Confederacy — sooner than many of his tormentors.

A schoolteacher, W.A. Forbes, was Colonel of the 14th Tennessee Regiment. Forbes had begun in early 1861 to drill the boys who attended his school at Clarksville. Fired by their teacher's enthusiasm, most of these young men joined the Confederate Army. Although this particular group of boys later joined the 49th Tennessee, they reflected much credit on Forbes during the fighting at Fort Donelson. But the former schoolteacher was no less proud of his present regiment and predicted great success once the enemy was met. Forbes, like Hatton, had been anxious for the Tennessee brigade to return home, but denied that privilege, he was ready and willing to lead his men in Virginia.

Like their leaders, the men in the Tennessee brigade were ready for a fight. The winter months had been trying on the patience and endurance of these soldiers who had been led to believe the war would be over by Christmas. David Phillips, a schoolteacher from Watertown, wrote in his diary during the winter, "Dreadful times for poor soldiers in camps. Our tents are rotten and the gales tear them down."[1] On the 20th of November he wrote,

> *This morning begins the last six months of our service. Day gloomy and rainy. During the past six months we have endured innumerable ills such as soldiers alone are heir to. May the next six be the consummation of peace is doubtless the wish of all.*[2]

On Christmas morning Phillips surveyed the scene presented by his regiment, the 7th Tennessee, and was not pleased. He said:

Christmas morning a fine one. The boys began to take their Christmas last night. A good deal of drunkenness in camp. In the morning the captain gave us a treat of egg nog. One-half the boys very tight by nine o'clock . . . Never saw so many drunk men before. It might be said with propriety that the 7th regiment was drunk on the 25th. 3

The lives of men like David Phillips were not controlled by surface appearances; they looked much deeper into the meaning of things. They converted the common, ordinary experiences into symbols of deeper significance, and while some soldiers escaped the boredom of camp life through intoxication, Phillips anguished over a reality which seemed meaningless. On the last day of 1861, he wrote:

*The last day of 1861 has come. I am still living the life of a soldier. I see no prospect for peace in the incoming year. Oh, how my heart would leap for joy if peace were declared and I permitted to return home again. I look back over my past year and see nothing of profit I have done. May my hour of usefulness soon come. I am tired of doing nothing and gaining nothing. The sky indicates rain, the sun refuses to shine. It seems as if the dying year would weep over the unhappy state of my country. May the bright sun of peace soon light up and enlived our sunny South, making our fire-sides happy and our homes the homes of peace. The year 1861 adieu forever.*4

If John Williams, another member of the 7th Tennessee, had any deep-seated thoughts about the war, he was reluctant to record them in his diary. He did record the incidents and experiences which impressed him. Describing a march in which he participated, he said:

> ...to days march take us to Huntersville a little town in Pocahuntus County its one of the nastyest places out of jail . . . it only noted for filth when we come in sight the head of the column was halted until the rear could come up . . . Col Hatton Formed the Rest in Regular order and right faced it and off for Huntersville we Started with fife and drum going we went on at this lick until we got through Town as I learned afterwards by looking around when I stoped I thought that I had just Commenced entering Town to my great Surprise I was then in the far side from where I had entered it.[5]

The nearest thing to combat Williams had experienced was during the Cheat Mountain campaign. According to him, his regiment was preparing to camp on the side

> ...of one of the lonelies mountains that any of us ever Seen . . . Col Hatton came upon an old citizen as he reported himself hunting his cows Col Hatton arrested him I was detailed to guard him for the night Soon after I took him in my possession it commenced raining The citizen being very sorrowly Clothed I taken him under my Blanket with me for the night We sat lent back against a tree with my Blanket throughn over our selves in this position we remained all night I loaded my gun before we sat down when I sat down I made the old man Sit by my side I lay my gun accross my lap giving him the musel.[6]

Although possessing some element of suspense, such incidents failed to satisfy the fervent desire to fight Yankees and many men had begun to wonder where all the glory was of which Pete Turney had spoken so glowingly the spring before.

The days and weeks following Christmas were spent in drill, small talk around campfires, and the endless chores that constituted army life. In February, the Tennessee brigade had been ordered to Manassas, the scene of the war's first big battle. There, for the first time, many of the men saw the effects of war. David Phillips was surprised to see:

> ...*a great many   skeletons of both men and horses. Saw a great many clothes that had been torn from the bodies of the dead enemy . . . The sight was sickening.*[7]

It was while on this march that the news of Fort Donelson reached the Tennessee brigade and the men were "shocked by the news . . . and every man's heart seemed ready to burst with mingled emotions of regret and indignation."[8]

But now it was spring and the spirits of the men warmed with the weather. They went about their duties with a renewed enthusiasm. The Confederacy's defeats were temporarily forgotten in the hustle and bustle of preparing for battle, and now on the banks of the Chickahominy River outside Richmond, the men in the Tennessee brigade waited eagerly for the enemy to make his appearance. David Phillips mused over those who expressed discouragement with the losses at Fishing Creek and Fort Donelson by saying, "Some are effeminate enough to think we are subjugated. Alas, that such cowardly poltroons should ever have encumbered our righteous cause. My faith is as firm and unshaken as the rock-ribbed hills themselves. We will triumph yet."[9]

The action in which the Tennessee brigade was about to enter would be known to history as a part of the Penunsula Campaign. Union troops had come by boat from Washington D.C. to Fort Monroe located on the tip of a peninsula which led directly to Richmond. After several weeks of maneuvering, the Union Army was poised outside the city to launch what its general, George McClellan, had promised would be a decisive blow to the Confederacy.

On May 29, 1862, while the Tennessee brigade waited under its new commander, Brigadier General Robert Hatton, it is probable that the General's thoughts transcended the scene of which he was a part. As bugles sounded the call for his men to move toward a place called Seven Pines, it can scarcely be doubted that Hatton's thoughts included an event that took place at the St. Cloud Hotel in Nashville the summer before.

During the previous year, the weeks had slipped by rapidly for Robert Hatton. Following his enlistment, Hatton had worked tirelessly in organizing his regiment. Confined to camp by his duties, and knowing that he would soon leave for Virginia, he wrote his wife Sophie to meet him at the St. Cloud Hotel with their children. On the appointed day the Colonel came to the hotel early and waited in the sweltering heat for the stage from Lebanon. Alerted by the sound of the approaching horses, Hatton had climbed to a point which afforded the first possible glimpse of his wife and children. When the stage jerked to a halt, he discovered to his bitter disappointment that his family was not on board.

Saddened and disappointed, Robert Hatton sat down and wrote his wife:

> *I have not, in my life, felt more disappointed, than I was this evening, when the stage drove up to the St. Cloud, and you were not in it . . . Half-an-hour before sunset I went up to the St. Cloud and seated myself on the pavement, to be ready to welcome you . . . Sophie, why didn't you come?*[10]

It had been a busy time for Sophie Hatton and she thought it best not to attempt the trip. She, no doubt, believed there would be plenty of opportunities to see her husband, and besides, the war would probably be over soon. Rather than fixing the children and riding the bumpy stage to Nashville, Sophie Hatton stayed home.

It had been only a short time thereafter when Hatton was ordered to Virginia. There were faint hints in his letters home that Governor Isham G. Harris, against whom he had run for governor in 1858, was having him sent to Virginia to get rid of him. Be that as it may, he left without seeing his family since the day he enlisted.

The gap of loneliness had been bridged by a constant flow of letters between Robert and Sophie Hatton. Even after he reached Virginia, the letters continued, and through them, the young colonel revealed the innermost thoughts of his sensitive mind. From Fredericksburg on March 18, 1862, Hatton wrote his wife:

My Dear Wife,

. . . Many weary, weary months, have passed, since the day we parted. How many are to pass, before we meet? God only knows. That my home — all that is dearest to me, on earth — should be in the hands of the enemy, I can scarcely realize. It is so! How long, oh, how long, shall this be? My blood leaps and boils, at the thought. Providence may have some wise end in so ordering it. May-be, we are never again to meet, at least on earth. If not, shall we, in another and a better world? My earnest prayer to God is, that we may — that "with parents and children, we there shall meet — meet, to part no more." Say this to my dear old father and mother, to sister, and to the children — that, as I sit by my camp fire, on the shores of the Rappahannock, my earnest petition to God, is, that He may be merciful and kind unto you, my wife, and unto them, during your stay in this world, and that you all may then find a home — "a house not made with hands, eternal in the heavens."

Say to the children, that, if I never again write to them, my last and earnest counsel to them, is to "remember their Creator, in the days of their youth" — to be truthful, just, kind. Then, will they certainly have the love and favor of God, if not of the world. May God bless and care for you, sustain you in all trials, and save you in heaven, where there shall be neither pain nor death.

Affectionately, your husband,

Robert Hatton [11]

It had been almost a year since the incident at the St. Cloud Hotel and over two months since the above letter had been written. Now on May 29, 1862, Hatton found himself just outside Richmond facing a Union army determined to capture the Rebel capitol. For five days Hatton had been a brigadier general and, at the moment, commanded the Tennessee brigade which was about to get its baptism of fire.

The preceding night amid the confusion which surrounded him, Hatton wrote his wife:

> *My brigade will move in an hour from its encampment, en route for Meadow Bridge, on the Chickahominy. We go to attack the enemy to-morrow, beyond the river ... The struggle, will, no doubt, be bloody ... Would that I might bind to my heart, before the battle, my wife and children. That pleasure may never be granted me. If so, farewell; and may God of all mercy be to you and ours, a guardian and friend.*[12]

To his mother he wrote, "If I should not return, be a mother to my wife and children," and to his father, "If I never return, let all your affection lavished in the past, upon me, be transferred to Sophie and her children."[13]

After a night of getting men and equipment in order, of checking last minute details and of waiting for orders to move, Hatton's brigade left camp at daylight. The events of the day were carefully recorded in the diary of John Williams.

> *Genl Hatton had his men up before day in readiness to march when the light Should make its appearance when daylight came our Brigade Set off for the Sene of action we knew nothing of where we were going untill near noon when we heard the distant roar of artillery this gave us notice that we might Soon be into it it went on So until the midal afternoon when we had orders to move up to the field of action our Brigade arrived on the ground about the Setting of the Sun after*

Double quicking about 3 miles the Brigade was halted long enough to load and then continued their charge untill they were in a few paces of the enemy.[14]

David Phillips wrote that during the charge "We passed Generals Johnston and Lee and Jeff Davis on the field over a redoubt made by the enemy."[15] Sooner than it was possible to believe, the Tennessee brigade made contact with the enemy and, almost as soon, it became apparent "that the enemy was too strong for us." John Williams wrote, "the fire of the enemy were So distrucked it Seem unreasonable for men to Stand and take it   the Brigade lay and loaded untill they were order to fall back by Genl G. W. Smith which was done in tolerable order considering what was before them."[16]

On the withdrawal, David Phillips fell in with a soldier named Jim Weaver and together they began making their way toward the rear. Just as they appeared safe from the enemy, they "ran suddenly upon a Yankee picket of six men," and were taken prisoners. In a state of disgust and disappointment, the two Rebs were hustled off to a nearby hen house to await their trip to a Northern prison.

Meanwhile, the brigade was making good its withdrawal. But as the retreating soldiers cautiously made their way back, two men, T.J. Hollaway and Wisner Davis, carried a special burden. They carried the dead body of Robert Hatton, killed just after his men were ordered back. John Williams saw the general fall and wrote, "he fell in a few minutes after the Brigade got orders to fall back   his horse was killed first under him   while he was taking his Pistols from his saddle he was shot through the heart."[17]

John Williams pulled back with his regiment, waited three days, and went to Richmond.

General Robert Hatton

David Phillips

Chapter VI

I must demand an unconditional surrender

Any romantic notions Middle Tennesseans might ever have had about war were gone by the summer of 1862. Confederate sympathizers had listened in a state of shock when informed of the early defeats in the area and had watched in silence as the remnants of their disorganized army limped home thoroughly beaten. Less than a month passed before the same citizens watched Albert Sidney Johnston's army gather at Murfreesboro and march southward, leaving homes, farms, and towns to the mercy of an advancing army. Then came Shiloh.

While the first weeks of Yankee occupation were not as bad as the politicians had predicted, the atmosphere changed suddenly following Shiloh. When the Confederate Army refused to collapse and go home, Federal authorities realized fully that they had a war on their hands. The Federal policy toward secessionists changed accordingly. Stating his opinion, General Grant wrote:

> *Up to the battle of Shiloh I, as well as thousands of other citizens, believed that the rebellion against the Government would collapse suddenly and soon, if a decisive victory could be gained over any of its armies. Donelson and Henry were such victories . . . But when*

Confederate armies were collected which not only attempted to hold a line farther south . . . but assumed the offensive and made such a gallant effort to regain what had been lost, then, I gave up all idea of saving the Union except by complete conquest.[1]

Grant's newly adopted attitude was reflected in all areas occupied by the Federal Army in Tennessee. No longer were farmers automatically paid for produce taken by the Army and no longer did Union officers see themselves as missionaries in a foreign land. Much of the "civil" now disappeared from the conflict. Middle and West Tennesseans watched helplessly as Federal soldiers took over their towns, rode arrogantly along their streets and roads, loaded their wagons from the cribs of defenseless farmers, and wantonly destroyed whatever they could not use. It was as if the Yankees had heard themselves described by Southern politicians and were intent in doing all within their power to make the politicians prophets of the time.

In Rutherford County, Charles Anderson, of Forrest's cavalry wrote:

McCook's cavalry formed in front of my house and soon every building as well as my residence was in flames. They took my portraits out of which I had two, smashed the frames, tacked the canvass to trees and jabbed their sabers through the eyes. They drove my negroes out of their houses and fired the buildings.[2]

Such Federal soldiers often subjected the Negro slave to ordeals that further stripped him of dignity and denied him the meager comforts he had formerly enjoyed.

On rare occasions the humanness of the participants penetrated the sectional symbolism of flags, uniforms, and uncomplimentary titles applied to "the enemy." For almost a decade, Mrs. L. Virginia French, a widely recognized writer and editor, had lived in McMinnville, Tennessee. Her husband, John Hopkins French, was a wealthy trader who afforded his wife the opportunity to pursue her talents as she pleased. The war brought a sudden change to Mrs. French's life style — a change which was accompanied by resentment toward the Federals and anxiety for her family. But the basic character of the woman remained unchanged.

During early June, 1862, the Federal Army made an appearance in McMinnville and some of its members had appropriated the French's favorite horse "Black Cloud." Later in the week Mrs. French wrote in her journal:

> *Throughout the day the troops came from the road to get something to eat — they were very respectful to me when they saw me, but a squad of them who sent a stolen negro down after dinner for them, sent word for me to "send their dinner, or they would come and take it whether or no." I sent a quantity of bread, meat and vegetables — which they took and sent the boy back a second time saying "that was not half enough." Two of those who came to the house offered to pay — but I would not receive it . . . Oh! how angry and embittered I felt that day (as I often have before,) to see what trouble this vile thing, "Secession," had brought upon us! One of the men told me that, "the South had brought this army with its consequent troubles upon herself." I said, "If you know anything at all — you know very well that Tennessee never brought this upon us. — She stood firm for the Union that she loved until Lincoln's war proclamation, drove her into exile and rebellion — ... He sighed — for he seemed very weary, and said "he wished to heaven it could be ended — he wanted to go home." He looked worn, as there was home-sickness in his voice as he said it, and I did pity him. I knew he was the enemy of the South — that he stood before me, an enemy, but I felt sorry for him and it did me good to see him drink the cool milk . . . with an evident relish.*[3]

149

Certainly not all Middle and West Tennesseans hated to see the Yankees come. The situation provided a much cherished opportunity for people who nourished resentments against local authorities to "get even", and at the same time gain favor with those people now controlling their communities. Informers were easily come by and the Federal authorities seldom turned them away. Conversations were reported to Federal officers, sermons were analyzed for their Southern leanings, and citizens who had formerly walked the streets in total confidence, now watched their neighbors with suspicion and anxiety.

The first sting of the informer was felt in Murfreesboro in early July, 1862. Federal soldiers had been fired upon in the area and the Yankees ached for revenge. Eager informers were ready with their help. Federal scouting parties swept through the countryside arresting suspects wherever informers pointed them out. Soon the jail was filled. Word went out from Federal headquarters that, for every Union patrol fired on, one hundred hostages would be taken. During the second week of July, this mandate was extended to Cannon County, just east of Murfreesboro.

On July 11, 1862, a Federal patrol went into Woodbury, the County Seat of Cannon County, and arrested most of the men and boys of the community. They were taken to Murfreesboro, where they were confined with other hostages already arrested. On the night of the 12th, six of the men confined at Murfreesboro waited for the hangman's noose at daybreak.

The town square at Murfreesboro presented a disquieting scene that night. Wives, mothers, and children followed their menfolk to prison and begged in vain for their release. The Yankees were in no mood to extend mercy. Toward midnight, the townspeople came to the jail and took the grieving relatives to their homes for the night. The condemned prisoners resigned themselves to their fate as relatives fervently prayed for a miracle, but hope had almost vanished.

Unknown to the people at Murfreesboro, Nathan Bedford Forrest had led his cavalrymen onto the town square of Woodbury at eleven o'clock. Forrest was still suffering from the wound he received at Shiloh, but he had been ordered into Middle Tennessee to disrupt Federal communications along the Nashville and Chattanooga railroad. The Confederate commander had welcomed the opportunity to train his inexperienced command on real live Yankees, and having been informed of the Federal garrison at Murfreesboro, determined at once to make it his first objective. If Forrest and his men needed an incentive to spur them on, they found it on the townsquare at Woodbury.

General Forrest,

> *...found the people in a state of terror and excitement. He was surrounded by the women of Woodbury who related to him that on the evening before a large detachment of Federal soldiers raided the town and carried off almost every man, young and old, and rushed them to prison in Murfreesboro.*[4]

With noticeable agitation, Forrest shifted in his saddle and listened to the tearful accounts of the arrests. Soon the anger which was equally terrible to friend and foe began to stir the energy and imagination of the cavalry leader, and when the women finally concluded their story, he begged them to calm their fears. Without the least pretense of boasting, Forrest promised that they "might confidently look for the restoration of their husbands and kinsmen by the next sunset."[5]

Cheered by the cavalryman's encouraging assurances, the women of Woodbury hurried to their homes and quickly returned with pies, cakes, and other food which was hurriedly served to the hungry horsemen. While the women brought food for the men, the older male citizens brought forage for the horses. For over an hour and a half both men and beasts enjoyed the hospitality of the country village. But Murfreesboro was eighteen miles away and there was no time to waste. At one o'clock in the morning, Forrest's men were ordered to mount up. In short order they were on their way through the darkness toward their unsuspecting foe.

Forrest rode at the head of the column as it threaded its way through the hills between Woodbury and Murfreesboro. Close behind came the Texans, Georgians, Kentuckians, and Tennesseans who composed his command. As of yet, Forrest had seen very few of these men in action and their bravery was an unknown quantity. Of course, the same was true with the men who now fought off sleep as they followed the man whose legend was just beginning to build.

Forrest was described by his men as a "soldier by nature." He was a master horseman having ridden and handled them since his early childhood. He possessed a broad, high forehead, shaggy eye-brows, prominent cheek bones, and a bold, assertive nose which indicated great tenacity. When his six foot, two inch frame was motivated by anger he was the personification of aggressiveness. At his side swung the saber by which many men would die before the war's end, and around his waist were strapped two potent pistols which spelled death as quickly to friend as foe when the occasion demanded.

In describing Forrest, his chief biographer said:

> *He could cut or thrust deeper with a sharp than a dull sword, and if in the melee he should happen to hit one of his own it was all intended for the good of the cause. He spoke not much, but when his thoughts were fashioned into words they came like pistol-shots short, quick, sharp, and sped right to the spot. Who heard them had no thought of answering back, no dream of questioning, no argument, and, above all, no flickering. To his subordinates his order was, "Shoot any man who won't fight! and he set the example.*[6]

It was almost daylight when Forrest and his command reached the outskirts of Murfreesboro. Scouts were sent forward to ascertain the strength and location of the enemy. In a short time, the scouts reported that "all was quiet, and no notice of the impending danger seemed to have been given, and they appeared not to apprehend it."[7]

Through his scouts, Forrest learned that the 3rd Minnesota Regiment with a battery of four guns was west of town near the road leading to Nashville. The 9th Michigan, with a detachment of Pennsylvania cavalry, was northeast of the town, and a provost guard from Michigan was at the courthouse and jail, guarding the hostages. In number, the opposing forces were about equal — 1200.

Forrest planned his attack in such a way that each Federal encampment would find itself thoroughly engaged so none could go to the aid of another. When the plan had been explained, the main column moved in closer to the town, and at the designated spot, the Texans swung off to the right and dashed upon the Michigan camp while the remainder of the force continued toward their assigned objectives. For their part, the Federal soldiers were sleeping the peaceful sleep of the unsuspecting.

In only a matter of minutes the Texans sent up a piercing Rebel Yell and subjected the Michigan Regiment to a savage saber and pistol attack. The encounter was made even more terrible by the fact that the Texans rode their horses through the tents of the sleeping Federals. Although it was evident that the advantage was with the wide-awake Confederates, every passing minute found the Federals becoming better organized. Soon they were returning the Confederate fire, shot for shot.

While the Texans fought the 9th Michigan, the remainder of Forrest's command had reached their objectives. In the center of town where the hostages were held, the Rebs attacked the courthouse but found that the massive walls of the building prevented any real damage. At the jail, the Yankees simply locked the door and set the building on fire with the hostages inside. While Forrest directed the attack on the court-house, others secured battering rams and knocked in the doors to the jail, freeing the hostages from a furnace of death.

Forrest continued his efforts at the courthouse where the Federals fought stubbornly. According to one witness, the air was so full of bullets that "a man could not show his head without danger of having it filled with lead."[8] The situation became a stalemate. There was no approach to the building except across an open space completely dominated by the fire of the barricaded Federals.

Forrest decided on a plan. He would launch simultaneous assaults from the east and west, hoping to divide the fire of the enemy allowing his men to gain the protection of the courthouse porch. From that point, they were to take axes and battering rams and tear down the door. The rest should be routine.

One block north of the courthouse, Forrest set his plan in action. Axes were procured from a nearby store and a Georgia company was ordered forward. The Georgians were lined up alongside a protecting wall and axes were placed in the hands of the men in front. An order was given to:

> *...advance single file toward the courthouse. When the front men fell, the axe was to be picked up by the next man in line and carried forward. This procedure was to be followed until the axes were transported to the courthouse porch. The company attacking from the east had no sooner come into the open than the man bearing the axe fell. It was picked up by the second, who was shot down. And the third. But by this time the column was under the protection of the walls of the courthouse. . . .Both doors were soon down and the Confederates swarmed into the lower halls of the building.*[9]

Just as it had appeared that Forrest's men were becoming discouraged, an important incentive developed. Hearing the noise from the fighting, the wives and children of the hostages came quickly to the town square and soon were "mingling among the men, and cheering them by their smiles and heartfelt, thankful words."[10]

154

Inside the courthouse, the Federals stubbornly refused to surrender. It appeared as if a costly attack would need be made up the narrow, winding stairway. But outside on the street, those observing the attack saw little puffs of smoke begin coming through the windows; the Rebs were smoking the Yankees out. The maneuver worked beautifully and the Yankees, rubbing their eyes and cursing their luck, came sullenly into the yard.

One of the hostages scheduled to die that morning was Lt. William Richardson of Alabama. He and another prisoner had spent the previous night with a minister preparing for what they believed would be certain death. In later years he wrote of hearing the approaching Confederates and how he had stood on a box to watch them launch the attack. He told of the Yankee guard setting the jail afire and how the prisoners were eventually rescued. After the ordeal had ended and he had been freed:

> *General Forrest came to me and said: "They tell me these men treated you inhumanly while in jail. Point them out to me." I told him there was but one man I wished to call his attention to, and that was the one who set fire to the jail in order to burn us up. Forrest asked me to go along the line with him and point that man out. I did so. A few hours later, when the list of the private soldiers was being called, the name of this man was heard and no one answered; Forrest said, "Pass on, it's all right."* [11]

Local legend has it that Forrest took the guard behind a building and personally killed him. Richardson later became a U.S. Representative from Alabama.

While the gloriously happy hostages ran from the jail and courthouse to be reunited with their families, Forrest turned his attention to the two Federal camps still uncaptured. First, going to the Minnesota camp he made three attacks but found the Yanks so firmly entrenched that additional assaults seemed ill-advised. Leaving only enough troops to keep the Federal regiment occupied, he hurried to the Maney Mansion north of town where the Texans were still battling the 9th Michigan. It was now past mid-day and many of Forrest's men were honest in their opinion that the barricaded Federals could not be taken. Forrest called in his most effective weapon, his creativity.

Dispersing his troops to make the best possible show of strength, Forrest began a game of bluff by sending the Federal Colonel, William Duffield, a note demanding immediate surrender. In an effort to create an atmosphere of impending doom, Forrest made the note short, but very much to the point. Ignoring the facts of the situation, the Confederate commander informed Duffield that all other Federal troops had already surrendered and that the entire Confederate force was now concentrated against his position. The note added, in a most sinister manner, that if forced to assault the Federal position no quarter would be offered. Duffield, previously wounded, surrendered his command.

Forrest then returned to the west side of town with reinforcements to operate against the Minnesota Regiment under the command of Colonel Henry C. Lester. For a second time the Rebel raider resorted to note-writing, telling Lester substantially the same thing he had told Duffield. The Confederates waited impatiently for an answer.

Not wishing to make a mistake, Lester asked permission to cross town and consult with Duffield. This request Forrest was pleased to grant since Duffield was already a prisoner. As Lester was escorted to Duffield's position in the Maney house he was greeted with a show of strength that no doubt astounded him. On a side street the Federal Colonel could see a solid mass of cavalry which appeared to be leisurely passing the time during the truce. What Lester did not know was that he was seeing the same troops over and over again. Forrest constantly shifted his men along a parallel street to make them appear several times and what seemed to Lester an imposing force was in fact only a few men who waited until the Minnesota Colonel passed, then galloped ahead by a side street to reappear further on. As a result of this ruse, every Federal soldier in Murfreesboro was a prisoner by mid afternoon.

The day was one of the most exciting in the history of Murfreesboro, and Sally Ives, a young lady who witnessed it all, wrote in her diary:

> *At daylight we were aroused by terrible yelling and firing of guns at Maney's grove where the 9th Mich. Regt. was camped. Before we could collect our senses, the cook came running in crying — "Mars John, de town is full of Rebels." We ran to the door* <u>*Just out of bed*</u> *& sure enough there were "our boys in gray" dashing across the street .... As soon as Papa observed my condition he sent me in the house* <u>*to make myself presentable,*</u> *and Proceeded to do the same for himself ...*
>
> *Forrest and his men had made a forced march from McMinnville Saturday night & dashed in on the Yankees, taking them wholly by surprise. They rushed in wild confusion from their tents undressed, seeking shelter from the terrible "Rebs."*
>
> *Papa was onto gathering in the wounded & dead. Our house was soon full. The downstairs floors of wounded, while the floor of his furniture house was covered with the dead. When the dead were moved a flattened ball fell from the head of one of our soldiers. Papa gave it to me — I will keep it. While Papa was busy on the streets Ma & I were busy with the wounded & feeding all who passed. On Saturday ma had lightbread & boiled ham prepared for Sunday. She soon had this sliced & in a basket with a large bucket of buttermilk with cup for them to drink from, and the cook soon added a large bucket of wheat coffee. I stood on the pavement and as the soldiers passed they were invited to "take a drink & a bite," as long as the refreshments lasted.*

While standing there I realized something of what the soldier feels in battle, for scattering Yankees were firing at us from the corners of fences & vacant houses & balls were whizzing by our heads, and Yet I felt no fear, but stood my ground until the Rebs rode off.[12]

It had been a great day for the Confederates. They had not only freed the hostages, they had captured the entire Federal garrison including General Thomas T. Crittenden who had arrived the night before. The day had been won. The promise made to the citizens of Woodbury had been kept. And the first Confederate success of note had occurred on Tennessee soil.

The event would not prove important militarily as greater and more significant events unfolded, but it would forever be a source of pride and satisfaction to people who later searched through the ruins of defeat for a symbol possessing the elements which characterized their finest hours. Nathan Bedford Forrest would not have wanted a finer present on this, his forty-first birthday.[13]

L. Virginia French

158

Chapter VII

When they fout, I fit

At Tupelo, Mississippi, the Confederates continued to recover from the experience at Shiloh. June and most of July had been spent in obeying the sharp commands of drill sergeants who had developed more than a passing interest in drill manuals. The recent fighting had revealed glaring weaknesses in Confederate discipline, and much of the intervening time had been devoted to preventing similar occurrences in the future.

The health of the men had improved considerably since they left Corinth, but morale had not kept pace. There was still resentment against the Conscription Act and desertions continued during the early summer. Men who had volunteered for the Confederate service at the insistence of political leaders resented the fact that those same leaders had now passed legislation which stripped their service of its dignity and patriotism. Military service was now no more secure than the government's ability to make men fight, and the men conscripted, "hated war. To their minds the South was a great tyrant, and the Confederacy was a fraud."[1]

In spite of the fact that the army had been forced from Tennessee on two occasions, there were those at home who took an optimistic view. One young lady wrote her aunt, "Well it is said that the 'Old Boy' rote to Beauregard a note and told him not to kill any more Yankees that hell was so full now that he did not have room for any more — that he would have to wait until he stiewed them down."[2]

John Gumm was not quite so unrealistic. To say the least, he saw much room for improvement. During its duty at Tupelo, Gumm's company had often been caught away from supply wagons and been forced to exist for three or four days on one day's rations. In June he wrote,

> *I would be glad if we leave hear . . . Every things Seams to be quiet at this time as Regards fiting though there is a mity bustel getting away provisions and I think we will go South though the Tennesseans ar getting tired of going South   we all have to Slep in the open air with only one blanket Rain or Shine our quarter Master Does not provide well for us   we ar Scarce of Wagons   not a nough for our Comfort and wel fare.*[3]

Picket duty was not something men sought, but it did have some advantages. The tiring hours of being restricted to one locality at least afforded the mind an opportunity to wander, even if the body could not. On a Sunday morning in mid-June, 1862, a young soldier by the name of Wiley Noblett, a member of the 44th Confederate Infantry, utilized some of his time on picket duty to record the images which occupied his mind. Noblett was from Fayetteville, Tennessee, and had been in the army since March 20th. He had missed the fighting at Shiloh because of illness, but had witnessed its terrible aftermath as he watched the retreating Confederate Army.

On the second day of the battle Noblett had been on his way to the field, but before he had arrived, he met the army coming back. He observed:

> *...still meeting the poor soldiers almost dead of their wounds, going to Corinth with nothing but a blanket under them, and in a jolting wagon. No one can imagine*

160

the horrors and miseries the war can inflict until they see it with their own eyes. They can read of war and hear it talked of by the most eloquent of our men, but still have no conception of its horrors . . .[4]

The intervening weeks dimmed Noblett's aversion to the brutalities of war and replaced them with a determined, if not a more optimistic, attitude. In a somewhat poetic stance he wrote:

Today is Sunday and I am again on picket . . . Oh, if I could once more be in Tennessee and visit my friends and people in that most noble state, I could then die almost satisfied, but I can never be nor will I ever be satisfied until the last foot of her noble soil is redeemed from the hands of those ruthless invaders who now hold and try to rule over her with despotic power. I do hope that the day is not far distant when she will straighten her bound neck and with one tremendous serge rend herself from a tyrant's grasp.

I can imagine I see her beautiful daughters as they sit in the door of their solitary dwelling — sitting as though they were in a deep study, and looking for some loved and absent one. Often in my dreams when sleeping in the pleasant shade, I can see them wandering slowly and sadly around as the yellow rays of the setting sun are disappearing in the distant west — and as they walk lonesomely along, you can see occasionally the silent tear of sympathy trickling down their rosy cheeks which gives to them the appearance of the opening rose all sprinkled with the morning dew.[5]

Not all young Noblett's thoughts were so poetic. In early June he wrote:

It has become so that a soldier is thought no more of than a horse or hog. As an evidence of that there was some dead men at Booneville who had been dead two days, and no preparations whatever were made to bury them, and they were still there when I left late this evening. They bury a horse to keep him from stinking, and just so it is with a soldier, he is buried only to keep him from smelling.[6]

Confederate generals had more problems than burying their dead. Vicksburg remained the only strong point along the Mississippi River not controlled by the Yankees, and President Davis, no great admirer of General Beauregard, had replaced him with Braxton Bragg, who would never gain either the love or respect of the Army.

Both the Confederate and Federal armies were broken up during the early summer. The Federals sent General Don Carlos Buell toward Chattanooga, leaving Grant and Sherman in Mississippi. The Confederates left a portion of their men to operate against Grant while sending the other part to check on Buell.

The private soldier in the Confederate Army knew little of the overall picture in which he seemed a very insignificant part. Rather than interpreting reality in terms of grand strategy, the soldiers viewed it in terms of the immediate situation in which they found themselves. The men under Braxton Bragg did not like what they saw. Through methods considered barbaric by many private soldiers, Bragg quickly tightened the discipline of his civilian army. Sam Watkins remembered:

When men were to be shot or whipped, the whole army was marched to the horrid scene to see a poor wretch tied to a post and a platoon of twelve men drawn up in a line to put him to death . . . And when some miserable wretch was to be whipped or branded for being absent without leave, we had to see him kneel down and have his head shaved smooth and slick as a peeled onion, and then stripped to the naked skin. Then a strapping fellow with a big raw hide would make the blood flow and spurt at every lick, the wretch begging and howling like a hound, and then he was branded with a red hot iron with the letter D on both hips.[7]

Soldiering under Braxton Bragg took on new meaning, and although there was much suffering among the troops, the net result was a military bearing which previously had not existed. By the middle of July, the Army was ready to move, but when it moved, memories and impressions of Mississippi went with its men. Wiley Noblett wrote down a few of his.

The greater portion of the people in this northern part are in a disgraceful state of ignorance — some of them do not know what county they live in: I will commence with our third days march from Corinth. By this time I had got so I could ride very well, and that morning brother Jasper [an officer in Wiley's company] gave me permission to ride off the road and procure myself something to eat, as we had nothing that I could eat, and nothing that was suitable to my feeble condition . . . after awhile I came to a house where I saw several chickens scattered around the yard, and heard others cackling at the crib and stables. I was now in high hopes of getting what I wanted when I came near enough. I called at the gate, and it was not long till an old woman who was very dark and wrinkley made her ghostly appearance. After speaking to her as people usually do on such occasions I asked her if she would sell me a chicken or some butter or milk. I then told her my condition but it did no good. She said she had no chickens, only those that were setting or had young chickens — all of which I knew was not so, and then I thought that her mother neglected teaching her when she was young that it was wrong to lie, and perhaps she never thought but what it was alright in telling such a lie. She was old, and looked as if she might be standing over her grave on a rotten stick. And she said she did not get more than enough milk and butter for her own use, and also made very strange of two soldiers that were sick, staying all night with her the night before. I

*offered her large pieces for her things, but the stingy old
creature would let me have nothing . . . I think she must
have been raised in a rude wilderness, and when women
wore dresses only wide enough for them to step, went
barefooted, and bareheaded . . . and in her raising she
did not know that there was any people in the world —
only just a few miles around to where it looked like the
sky dropped down to the earth, and there she thought
was the jumping off place as I have often heard it called.
I suppose I have said enough about the stingy old
woman, and here I will drop her without looking to see
where she falls.* [8]

Such memories would seem old in a week or so as each
new day gave rise to its own. Events moved rapidly during the
last two weeks of July as Bragg placed in motion that portion of
his army that would operate against Buell. On the 21st, the
Confederates boarded trains at Tupelo and headed toward
Mobile, from there they would go to Chattanooga and thence to
Kentucky.

No sooner was the army on its way, than some of its
members were up to their old tricks. As the train creaked its
way through the countryside, Resinor Etter noticed the fields of
grain which stretched before him in all their "lovelyness." The
fields:

*. . .was beautiful covered with corn in ful roasting ear
in the even the car made a halt by a fine peach orchard
its fruits was tempting   I could not bare the temptation I
mounted the fence and quietly filling my hat returned to
the car.*[9]

Marcus Toney's company spied a watermelon patch, and
in a few minutes the entire crop, green and ripe, disappeared.
The men had the misfortune of getting caught and were forced to
pay the farmer for his crop.

164

The trip to Mobile and on to Chattanooga was "tolerable tegus" to the men. At Mobile they got off the train and boarded boats which took them across the bay. Riding on water was a new experience for most soldiers and they found the journey less than enjoyable. On the boats they "Lay wher we Could find Rume," and the idea of being so far from land was anything but satisfying.

Once across the bay, the troops again boarded trains and the journey to Chattanooga continued. During the train ride, Resinor Etter got very little rest. The trains went so slowly up the mountains that oftentimes the boys got off and walked beside them, but when the tracks led downhill it was a different story. Etter said the train he was riding:

> ...came down a mountain and dont think I ever saw a car run so fast   I think she run at the rate of sixty mils and hour   I was frightful to see the wheels jump   I felt uneasy   the most of the rest of the boys knew nothing about it as they were sound asleep.[10]

Spencer Talley said that after his regiment left the boats at Mobile they:

> ...found a long train of cars waiting our arrival. They were . . . freight boxes of every kind and not a few flat or coal cars . . . We piled them full, top and bottom. We were hurried on our long journey and only stopped night or day no longer than to cook and eat . . . We slept on the train and those of us who were on top of the train would tie our selves to the walk way on top with our gun slips to keep from falling off.[11]

After nine days of bouncing over uneven railroad tracks, the Army arrived at Chattanooga. For many Tennesseans it was a joyous occasion. Almost as soon as the trains stopped, the city was swarming with relatives and friends who were well supplied with food, clothing, brandy, and assorted supplies. The attitude of the soldiers was well represented in Wiley Noblett's reaction to leaving Tupelo. On that occasion he wrote:

The long closed mouths of exiled Tennesseans were widely opened, and a noise was bellowed forth as deafening as the falling of some terrible catarack. We are now on our return to that lovely land [Tennessee] and the day is not far distant when yankees must either flee from the land of Tennessee or disappear before our gallant army as the morning mist before the summer sun.[12]

The days at Chattanooga were spent in reunion, and at night, the ardent speeches of politicians literally echoed from the mountainsides. The air became charged with a rebirth of Southern patriotism as past defeats were forgotten and past hardships were suppressed. A new confidence gave rise to a belief that the Confederate Army would go forward and forge its way into the heartland of the Yankees, and there abide in the untold glories of victory.

Any future glories won by the Confederate Army would need be won without the help of John Gumm. Finding it impossible to endure the hardships of army life, the old volunteer asked for and received permission to return home. Unfortunately, his last days in the army were not pleasant. When he arrived at Chattanooga he "Went to the Crutchfield House ... But could not get to Sleep there   the Supper was the Commonest that I ever Eat any where to be called a tavern   the Beef was a vearry Small   Busiscuit Cold and Butter old a nuf to Stand A Lone."[13] If a tired soldier needed encouragement to go home, surely such a meal furnished it. After a difficult night spent on the floor of a railway car-house, Gumm wrote, "I am anxious to get home   I will Stay in town untill I get a Chance to go." Later in the week he said, "I am vearry weak and I fear I will get so weak that I will not be abel to Walk home."[14] When at last the weary trooper was given permission to leave, he began walking to Murfreesboro and, after nine days, arrived home barely able to stand.

Even before John Gumm left Chattanooga, W. W. Wilson rejoined his regiment. The experience in the "Hospittle" had been interesting, but he was more than glad to get away. Upon reaching his regiment, Wilson "Fond the Boys is all Purty Near gon that I First caim out with." But soon the young soldier had made new friends and was about the business of soldiering with all the enthusiasm of an 1861 volunteer.

Once or twice on the way to Chattanooga it had looked as if fate were determined to keep Wilson on the inactive list. As he was riding across Mobile Bay the boat "Sprung a Leak and we Run A shore or Near A Nuf [for] A Part of us to Wade out." When the boat started again it sprang another leak and Wilson noted in his diary, "Hit keeps them Bisy to keep the Water out." Later, as the train was approaching Atlanta, it rammed another, and all night, the troops unpiled themselves from the wreck. After a series of such experiences the young soldier dreaded nothing the army had to offer.[15]

Wiley Noblett was almost hypnotized by the natural beauty of the Chattanooga landscape. In describing it he wrote:

> *Besides the many other accomodations* [of Chattanooga] *it is delightful to behold the high hills that stretch themselves beyond our sight, and seem to connect ours and another world together. The rays of the morning sun fall first on this range of hills whose tops are clothed in verdant, and makes it appear most beautiful in the sight of those who are not accustomed to the mountain.*
>
> *On our left at about four miles distance stands the hugh column of earth and stone known as Lookout Mountain. On our right and front we see a long range of hanging rocks and trees . . . and between these two piles of earth rolls majestically the crystalline waters of Tennessee.*[16]

As the scenes offered by nature held Noblett in awe, some offered by his fellow human beings were less than inspiring. In disgust he wrote:

I have seen today what I hope I may never see again. It was an old woman and her two daughters under guard. I understand she was a lewd woman, and had lived a life of wretched wickedness, and her two daughters are leading the same life. The old woman was palsied, and could not walk at all. Her daughters carried her everywhere they went. The yankees brought them here and left them when they went away.. . . . This was wretchedness plainly pictured.[17]

There were no Yankees to fight at Chattanooga and the Confederate Army moved on. Buell pulled his men toward the west, extending all the way to McMinnville. After spending three delightful weeks in relaxation, Bragg started his army northward over Walden's Ridge. Sustained by an inherent cockiness and needled by a suppressed suspicion that past defeats might reflect negatively on Southern manhood, the men were anxious and ready for a fight. The men in Bragg's Army left Chattanooga with a firmer conviction of success than they had possessed in months. The war was back in focus, the issues were clear again, and the Confederates marched confidently toward what they believed was their inevitable destiny.

2.

As Bragg's Army had prepared to march northward from Chattanooga, one of the isolated bits of drama that compose the total face of war was taking place in Gallatin, Tennessee. On August 12, Colonel John Hunt Morgan and his command swept into the town and created pandemonium among the enemy. One of Morgan's most valuable assets was a nimble-fingered telegraph operator named George Ellsworth who could make the key speak any language he desired.

Following the capture of Gallatin without a shot being fired, Ellsworth telegraphed the Federal authorities at Nashville that a band of Indians was on its way, determined to secure for themselves a sack of scalps. After confusing all the trains in the area by giving them bogus instructions, Ellsworth and the command retired eastward to Hartsville on the north bank of the Cumberland River.

The Federals at Nashville were outraged when they learned the truth. Being unable to catch Morgan, the Yankees pointed their wrath toward the people of Gallatin. On August 19th most of the men and boys of the area were arrested and started on foot to Nashville where they were to be held hostages against future raids.

For some mysterious reason, John Hunt Morgan sensed that something had gone wrong at Gallatin and returned on the morning of August 20. Some weeks later, Morgan visited with authoress L. Virginia French in McMinnville and related the incident. According to Mrs. French the Kentucky cavalryman said,

> *"Does it not seem strange, Mrs. French? ...when I tell you that on the next morning at Hartsville I felt that I must go to Gallatin? I knew nothing of what was going on there ... but I had a strange and strong presentiment that I ought to return. I had no business there — but gathering a portion of my men I mounted my horse and set forward. It was a grey morning when we reached the place — instantly we were surrounded by a whole lady population — crying, sobbing entreating us to save their friends — beautiful girls with dishevelled hair— in their night robes, with bare feet upon the damp streets — just as they rushed from their homes — wives weeping, mothers beseeching us to save their boys — oh! Madame it was heart-breaking. I do not believe there was a dry eye in my whole command. It seems that after we left Gallatin a party of Federals came up*

from Nashville and took every male in the place —
shamefully — carrying off everything they could, tearing
earrings from the ladies, the rings from their hands —
the breast pins from their bosoms. The men old and
young were marched off down the R.R., at the entrance
of a bridge two of my young men had been murdered —
I called my men up to me — pointed them to the blood
and told them whose it was. "We take no prisoners
today" was their reply, and we dashed forward. The
first Yankee I came up to had an old man nearly
exhausted — driving him forward. at the point of a
bayonet — he was perhaps 80 years of age — I think
that was the only time in my life that I felt all humanity
leave my heart —(he here described how the Yankee ran
down an embankment, and he forced his horse after him
sliding down the precipice as it were, and shot him
though he begged hard for his life.) Then he described
their following on — relieving men and killing Yankees
as they went until they came up with the last — 300 —
near Nashville — these they took prisoners. There were
so many of them said he that when they threw down
their arms we couldn't shoot them all. Then he
described their evening entrance into Gallatin — such a
contrast as it was with the morning— ladies in carriages
come after their friends the prisoners — it was a perfect
oration, joyful — overwhelming.[19]

3.

It was August 28, 1862, when Braxton Bragg's army
began leaving Chattanooga. Just where it was headed, the
private soldier had no idea, and there is much evidence that even
Bragg was not sure. Two days after the Confederates left

Chattanooga another Rebel force under the command of General E. Kirby Smith attacked Richmond, Kentucky, achieving a stunning victory. Probably realizing Bragg's indecisiveness, Smith urged him to come to Kentucky where the two Confederate forces could be united and deal Buell's forces a fatal blow. And so it was decided.

There was a great gulf between the concerns of the generals and the privates. The privates almost never knew anything of the "big picture", which was constantly developing or constantly breaking apart. "Immediate survival" occupied the men in the ranks, and sometimes it seemed as if nature was an ally of the enemy.

The weather was dry, the roads were dusty, water was scarce, and officers as repulsive as ever, but since there was no way for such matters to be controlled by the enlisted men, they got along as best they could. Even in the face of these circumstances, the men seemed cheerful. Some had salvaged a little brandy from the happier days in Chattanooga, and when they quenched their thirst with this most potent fluid, the weather seemed to moderate, and even the officers were more easily tolerated.

The army had traveled only a short distance before it entered an area of Tennessee which was intensely loyal to the Union. Instead of being greeted by flag-waving admirers, the men met with sullen, resentful stares from mountaineers who peered uneasily from their cabin doors.

Hunger knew no political bounds, and when Resinor Etter became victim of this common ailment, he began searching for food. Sighting a cabin not far from the line of march he made his way in that direction. He found the cabin:

> ...inhabited by one woman   4 little children   one old man that was crippled   they was very poor tho of Union Centiments. I was sorry for them all tho they was against us   I wanted something to eat   they said if they had it they would give it to me.[20]

171

Later Etter stopped at another cabin and encountered a woman whose:

> ...husban had went to the Yanky army   she said he
> was ded   she said that she was in favor of the South
> and done all she could to keep him with her tho her
> influence prevailed not. I could not help feeling sorry
> for this lone woman. She had 5 little children none able
> to help her.[21]

As the army moved along its mountainous journey it was joined by a constant flow of relatives anxious to see their sons and husbands before another battle. To the men, it was a strange sight to see an army on its way to battle accompanied by mothers, fathers, wives and children riding or walking in the ranks with dust-covered soldiers who plodded their way up and down the hills of eastern Tennessee.

The wide open spaces offered an opportunity for many of the rugged individualists in Bragg's Army to exercise their unique talents. Thomas Head of the 16th Tennessee observed:

> There was one peculiar characteristic of many of
> the men ... and that was a harmless insubordination at
> times when there was no danger. The men would
> forage, and no guard could be placed so strong, and with
> instructions so strenuous and rigid, as to withstand the
> sagacity and cunning of a member of the Eighth or
> Sixteenth Tennessee Regiments. They acquainted
> themselves with the country for miles on either side of
> the line of march, and were always up with their
> commands at night, laden with the fruits of the tramp in
> the way of chickens, vegetables, and not infrequently a
> few canteens of whiskey ... In each regiment there were
> a few men who could find a still-house if it was within
> twenty miles of the line of march, and could go to it and
> be in camp at night against supper time. When any of
> the boys procured whiskey, they would divide with their

comrades, and a general jollification would sometimes ensue; but the closest scrutiny of the brigade and regimental officers could seldom, if ever, locate the evil or ascertain who procured, or was in possession of, the whiskey.[22]

On the night of September 4, the army camped eleven miles south of Sparta. That night Resinor Etter wrote in his diary, "the rode has been lined with mothers sisters many prest there son to them a sloger as when he as an infint I have felt for them much."[23] It became almost impossible for officers to keep order as men left their companies to be with relatives they had not seen for over a year. All through the night the celebrations and reunions continued until dawn brought with it a demand that the army continue forward.

The next day at Sparta, the scene was repeated and expanded. Resinor Etter said, "The camps have been full of wimen all day wives here som brothers sisters fathers all have come."[24] Politicians and preachers tried unsuccessfully to be heard above the clamor of conversation which whirled through the night. Fiddles played and couples danced in the streets while others sat around giant campfires and swapped the news of the day. But even amid the joy which prevailed at Sparta on that September night, the more tragic character of war made itself known. Bereaved parents, whose sons had died at Shiloh, roamed among the troops seeking information, while others, not knowing if their sons were dead or alive, sought news to relieve their anxiety.

The night of celebration eventually spent itself and daylight found the Army preparing to move. Men who had "lived it up" the night before pulled themselves slowly off the ground and looked for their equipment, carelessly discarded the night before. Saddened by the thought of leaving their families, the men were slow to move, but by ten o'clock they were headed north toward Kentucky.

The dry weather continued and every step taken by the men raised clouds of choking dust. The trees were coated with a thick layer of brownish dirt and drinking water was so scarce that men sometimes walked for miles in search of a spring. Marcus Toney remembered:

> . . . *sometimes we could not see ten feet ahead. The perspiration caused clots of mud to form in our eyebrows, hair, whiskers, and mustaches. At nightfall, when we went into camp, very little water could be found, and frequently we drank out of ponds in the barn lots.*[25]

The intense need for water sometimes prompted the men to extreme measures. On one occasion Toney's company came upon a man who was hauling a barrel of water to his home in the hills. "We did not ask for a drink, but in a few moments the barrel was empty. The poor fellow said: 'I have not a drop of water at home, and my wife and children are suffering.' We felt sorry for him, but such is war."[26]

At selected places, captains of companies were dispatched home to recruit men for their regiments. Traveling sometimes within the sound of the enemy's voices, these men sought volunteers to fill the ranks depleted at Shiloh or by desertion. Captain Jim Womack wrote:

> *After spending a few days among my fellow citizens at home I am forced to the conclusion that but a few men, now at home, can be induced to volunteer in the service of their country. Many young men with whom I have met ought to be in service, but their patriotism is blank.*[27]

It was September 9, when the Confederate Army finally reached Kentucky. The welcome seemed warm enough. Bands played *Dixie,* beautiful girls showered affection on the dusty Rebs, and through it all, the soldiers suddenly realized what the politicians had meant by "the glorious days ahead." Sam Watkins pretty well summed it up by saying, "All was lovely and the goose hung high."[28]

174

Braxton Bragg was ready with a proclamation whose first sentence was, "I have entered your State with the Confederate Army of the West, and offer you an opportunity to free yourselves from the tyranny of a despotic ruler."[29] The Confederates truly viewed themselves as liberators and they enjoyed a certain dignity that accompanied that role; it was the part of war which came so easily to the imagination of the politician.

While the men in the ranks prospered in the limelight of feminine affection, Confederate officers noticed a disturbing fact in the reception accorded their troops: most of the enthusiasm was radiating from individuals unsuited for military service. The thousands of guns captured at Richmond the month before were going unclaimed.   Like many of their neighbors in Tennessee, the men in Kentucky seemed hesitant to join the Confederate Army.   Without the assistance of the expected recruits, Bragg began a series of marches and counter marches toward the Federal Army on its way north from Tennessee under General Buell.

On September 16th Wiley Noblett wrote in his diary:

This morning we leave Cave City in the direction of Munfordville. I suppose we are going up there to fight a little if it is necessary. They fought there on the 13th, and our boys caught a whipping, but it was not their fault. It was their foolish commander [Gen. James R. Chalmers] to blame for attacking a larger force than his own in their fortifications . . . It is now evening and we have come up close to the yankees, though we are not yet in sight . . . Our lines are now formed, and extend all around them. Our artillery is taking position. I suppose the work of death will commence early in the morning.[30]

But it didn't.   Instead, the entire Federal force under Colonel John T. Wilder surrendered without a shot being fired, and thereby hangs a tale perhaps unequalled in the history of

175

warfare. Wilder found himself isolated from Buell's main army and, as Wiley Noblett pointed out, surrounded by Bragg's main force. Should he fight or should he surrender was the question that no doubt haunted the mind of the Indiana politician. He sought an answer to his dilemma by consulting with the enemy.

As General Simon Bolivar Buckner remembered the incident:

> . . . *about two o'clock in the morning a Federal officer was brought to my bivouac blindfolded. He was in command of the Federal forces. He said . . . "General Buckner, I come to you for advice, though I don't know you personally, sir . . . There are a good many Federal officers who tell me they know you, and you are a gentleman and would not deceive me, and I come to you to find out what I ought to do."* [31]

According to Buckner, the Federal officer was given an honest, professional appraisal of the situation after which he concluded: "I believe I will surrender," which he did.[32]

Wiley Noblett was dumfounded. The day of the surrender, September 17th, he wrote in his diary:

> *This morning, I have witnessed something I did not expect. I have seen the surrender of a part of the proud yankee army; Yesterday they were rejoicing over a great victory over our troops; this morning they surrender to us.*
>
> *They have acted wisely in surrendering, and it is better for both parties.*[33]

Bragg's subordinate officers expected that following the capture of Munfordville the Confederates would turn on Buell's forces. Such was not the case. Instead, Bragg pulled his forces to one side and Buell marched unimpeded to Louisville.

In the days ahead both Bragg and Buell became confused as to the location and strength of their enemy. The end result was that a Confederate force of 16,000 men faced a Federal force of 58,000 men at the little town of Perryville, Kentucky.

On the night of October 6, 1862, the 16,000 Rebs took a position east of the town. The next day they moved toward the village and Wiley Noblett noted, "Skirmishing getting nearer, women and children ordered out of town."[34]

The enemies were separated by a dry creekbed which served as a silent reminder of the terrible heat of the past several weeks. Not knowing what to expect, the Confederates settled and waited for the night to pass. Early the next morning Wiley Noblett wrote in his diary:

The sky is clear and beautiful and the wind is blowing rapidly, and it would be a pleasant day was it not for the awful scene that is probably awaiting us. It was a clear moon-light night last night, and the pickets continued firing all night, and are still skirmishing and getting nearer. Last night we had nothing to eat but parched corn, and broiled meat; our rations have now come, and we are ready for any emergency.[35]

By mid-morning Bragg arrived on the scene and ordered General Ben Cheatham's division forward against the Federals. For many of these men it would be their first experience in battle. They crouched uneasily behind a ridge awaiting the order to charge the open ground on their front.

These Confederate soldiers were in a mood conducive to success. It was their first battle since the Federals adopted a more antagonistic attitude toward Confederate civilians. Recent letters from home had informed the soldiers of the intemperate acts of their enemy, and on the way to Kentucky more stories aroused a deep animosity within those who listened. The incidents at Murfreesboro and Gallatin provoked bitter resentment, and some men, like Resinor Etter, had recently been informed that everything they owned had been destroyed by prowling Yankees. What had been a smouldering resentment suddenly burst into a raging hate. Already during the fighting at Richmond, Kentucky, Colonel A. J. Vaughn of the 13th

Tennessee had been forced to restrain one of his men from killing a wounded Federal officer; in temperament the Confederates were ready.

When the order to advance was received, the men cautiously left their protecting ridge and moved in double-quick time across the open space. They stopped behind another ridge to reform their line. All extra weight was discarded — blankets, knapsacks, anything that might hamper movement was hurled aside. Colonel Ben J. Hill was too drunk to participate, but he wasn't too drunk to give his men expert advice. Calling his troops around him he counseled: "Shoot the bastards in the tail boys, God damn 'em if they've got a heart that's where it is."[36]

The men in Cheatham's division peeped over the hill and saw the enemy securely protected by a wooded area with a battery of artillery at each flank of their line. Above the roar of the enemy's cannon somebody yelled "go", and almost as if they came out of the ground, Cheatham's men leaped to the charge.

The 16th Tennessee was in front and Jim Womack remembered:

> *"Victory" for our motto was shouted all along the line, and fearlessly and gallantly we charged them. The men, from drought and fatigue were almost exhausted at the opening, but they made the charge & received the fire of the enemy, although the first battle in which most of them had ever engaged.*[37]

In short order, the 16th was pushed back, but according to Womack:

> *With our numbers much weakened we rallied and charged them a second time, with about the same success as the first. Again we were compelled to fall back, and again we formed and charged them a third time, but our forces were so diminished by this time that I am not sure we would have been able to drive them from their guns*

had it not been for the timely arrival of reenforcements on our right.[38]

The "timely reenforcements" was the brigade of General George Maney, in whose ranks were Sam Watkins and Marcus Toney. Toney's regiment was assigned the task of capturing the guns at the north end of the Federal line, but before it reached its objective the 16th Tennessee had already accomplished the job. The cost in men was terrible to behold, and lying somewhere among the wounded was Resinor Etter, a casualty in his first hour of battle.

Following the capture of the first battery, the Confederates found themselves faced by a second not far away. Without stopping, they swept forward into an almost solid sheet of lead. At one discharge from the Federal guns, eight color bearers fell dead and two more were dead before the guns were taken. Adding insult to injury, a yellowish dog ran upon the field and snapped at the heels of the Rebs as they advanced toward the enemy!

Shortly after noon, the entire Confederate force was in action. The 5th Confederate Regiment experienced fighting as fierce as any battle had to offer. These Irishmen from Memphis found the Federals braced behind a rock fence pouring volley after volley of deadly fire.

When the Yankees fired, the

...shock was terrific — the line swayed as one body, leaving a track of dead and wounded to mark its former position; then with a yell that burst almost simultaneously from officers and men, it charged over the dead and dying, drove the enemy from the fence, and held it . . . [The Rebs looked around and saw] *all along our front a solid line of dead and wounded . . . in some places three deep.*[39]

While the men in the 5th Confederate hovered behind their newly captured breastworks, the Rebel artillery blasted away at the stubborn Federals a few hundred yards away. One of the shells exploded in an old barn being used as a hospital and immediately the structure was engulfed in flames. The Confederates could "hear the shrieks of the wounded as they burned."[40]

What appeared to be a Confederate success suddenly deteriorated when a body of blue-coats approached from the rear. Confederate officers watched in disbelief as a mass of blue coats advanced toward them. Colonel J. A. Smith turned to Captain C. W. Fraser and asked: "Captain, have you a white handkerchief? I am afraid we will need one." The dismayed captain replied that there was not such a handkerchief in the regiment and suggested ". . . you have the only 'biled shirt' the lower end of which will answer if occasion requires."[41] As the colonel prepared to follow the captain's suggestion, the advancing line of blue let forth a yell that not only prompted the colonel to put his shirt tail in, but brought a responsive yell from the entire Confederate line; the "line of blue" was Pat Cleburne's Rebels dressed in the uniforms captured at Munfordville![42]

In the late afternoon, the Federals were pushed back into a lane running along the top of a ridge in the rear of their last defensive position. Was it to be Shiloh over again? The lane at Perryville proved to be no great obstacle and before dark the Federals yielded. The battle ended for the day.

The twilight hour afforded the Confederates their first opportunity to study the scene around them. To those who had not before experienced a night on the battlefield it was more horrible than the fighting that had produced it. Men, torn apart by the enemy's cannon, lay scattered as far as the eye could see. The dead of both armies lay mingled among the scarred trees and broken equipment which stood in mute testimony to the fierceness of what had happened during the afternoon. Men walking over the field stopped suddenly trying to find the faint whispers of dying soldiers calling for water, and although their own canteens were almost empty, the Rebs knelt to quench the thirst of friend and foe alike.

The moon cast a sickening pallor over the scene. Through the smoke that continued to hover above the field, its ghastly beams were reflected from the unclosed eyes of the dead. Thomas Malone of the 1st Tennessee saw what appeared to be a bundle of rags and leaned over to examine it. The bundle proved to be a body "in which a shell had exploded, leaving no trace of humanity except blood and bones and shattered flesh."[43] In one particular mess of Malone's Regiment seven men had eaten breakfast together the morning of the battle; that night five were dead and another wounded. The day had been a terrible initiation for those who had seen combat for the first time. Some were unable to endure it. Malone saw a fellow-soldier become panicky and throw himself in a ditch where he believed he would be protected. He tried to get the boy to rejoin his company but "a ball, coming from the Lord knows where, struck him and killed him while I was talking to him."[44]

To men who had not seen death before it seemed that a magic command should sound and that those who had so recently marched and fought by their side should rise up and continue in the game of war. As soldiers unacquainted with battle stood among the slain in a dazed state of half-belief they somehow saw in the eyes of the dead what they had never seen before and they understood what they had never understood. It all added up to the same terrible thing: the unbelievable finality of death.

There were several ways death could be viewed. War was supposed to mean killing, but in reality, it was the dead lying around that made war glorious for those who survived. It was death that made the very fact of being alive an achievement and that state of existence carried with it some very practical implications. Some practical-minded Rebs surveyed the Federal dead for boots and other wearing apparel which was scarce in the Confederate Army. When such apparel was discovered it was unceremoniously stripped from its former owner and added to the wardrobe of its new caretaker. Many soldiers searched for new guns and often left the field carrying both the old and new. Everything considered, it was a time for celebration. The enemy had been driven back and nobody seemed to doubt that the battle had been "bravely fought and nobly won."

The Confederates rested as best they could, believing that morning would bring with it a renewal of fighting. But Bragg now knew the situation. During the first day's fighting, Buell had been unable to direct his full potential against the Southerners, a situation that would surely be adjusted before another day. The prudent thing to do was to leave Kentucky. About midnight, Bragg ordered his army south in retreat.

The Battle of Perryville enriched the steadily growing lore of the Southern fighting man, a lore that would entertain generations of the South for many years to come. Like the tale of a drummer boy in the 9th Tennessee. According to one soldier:

> He went forward when the regiment made the charge. His drum was shattered by a fragment of shell, and he threw it away, siezed a gun . . . and gallantly pressed forward with the foremost. When this incident was later reported to General Maney he went out of his way to see the boy. Upon seeing the lad Maney asked him what he had done during the fight. "Why I beat the drum," was the answer. The General then asked, "Well when the men started to charge, what did you do?" "I beat the drum" was again the answer. "But at the last," said the General, "in the desperate fight, what did you do?" Looking at the general with a slight disgust the boy replied, "O, when they fout I fit."[45]

At least one soldier in Bragg's Army was followed to battle by his wife. The other men had no objections since it was handy to have someone around to sew on buttons, mend socks, and the like. During the fighting at Perryville this soldier, John Sullivan from Giles County, received a shot in the head and was left on the field for dead. Learning of her husband's wound, Mrs. Sullivan searched until she found him among the mass of

182

humanity covering the ground. Carefully lifting the wounded soldier to her shoulder, the faithful wife carried him to the nearest hospital. He responded favorably to treatment and in two weeks the couple was on their way home. As they made their way toward Pulaski, they encountered a Union patrol which took them prisoners. Even the fervent appeal of the devoted wife failed to keep them from spending the next few months in a prison.[46]

Among the dead at Perryville was a young man named Robert Hamilton from Nashville. Hamilton had worked as a proofreader for the Methodist Printing Company before the war and had joined the "Rock City Guards" early in the spring of 1861. During the charge at Perryville, the young man was shot through the head and died instantly. Following the withdrawal of the Confederate Army, Marcus Toney, who had been left behind to care for the wounded, found Hamilton's body and carried it to a gulley where it was buried with twenty-six other members of his brigade.

Hamilton's family in Kentucky was just as loyal to the Union as the young proofreader had been to the Confederacy, but throughout the war he had corresponded with his sister-in-law, whose warm, personal feeling for him far outweighed their political differences. It was to this sister-in-law that Toney wrote the news of Hamilton's death. Giving the letter to a Union soldier Toney requested that it be mailed at the first opportunity.

At the end of the third day following the battle, a knock came to the door where Toney was staying and he was informed that a lady wished to speak to him. Upon opening the door, Toney was greeted by Hamilton's brother and sister-in-law, who had brought a casket for the body. Toney guided the couple to the spot where he had buried the body and stopped to uncover the face of the corpse. Neither the brother nor his wife was convinced that the body was that of Robert. Seeking to satisfy them beyond a doubt Toney reached down and pulled from the shallow grave the right hand of the corpse and asked,

"Do you see this?" Robert Hamilton had been a very studious boy and was addicted to biting his fingernails. Seeing the hand Mrs. Hamilton replied, "I am satisfied."[47]

Many other families came to the battlefield in search of their relatives, but since there was little or no way to positively identify many of the dead, relatives sometimes carefully wrapped the remains of a soldier in a blanket with little more than a hope that it was the body for which they had come.

Meanwhile, the army was making its way back in the direction from which it had so recently come. Disappointment and resentment filled the ranks. At Perryville as in most other battles, Confederate officers found it difficult to separate the business of war from the profession of politics. Regimental commanders doubted the wisdom of generals, and generals doubted the wisdom, and sometimes the bravery, of other generals. Those generals whose commands had behaved well were more than willing to take the credit, while those whose commands had encountered difficulty were more than ready to place blame elsewhere.

Tempers were short on the retreat from Perryville. Colonel John Savage accused General Daniel Donelson of playing politics with staff appointments and further accused the general of protecting Donelson's son and son-in-law from dangerous exposure to enemy fire. Generals Maney and Cheatham had argued during the fighting and some soldiers doubted Maney's personal courage. Thomas Malone, an adjutant on Maney's staff, expressed wonderment that the General did not personally lead his men in the charge and was later called to account by the General. In a fit of anger, Maney screamed at Malone, "No man can question my courage and live," whereupon Malone accepted what he thought was a challenge to a duel. Maney explained that it was not toward Malone that his wrath was directed. His conduct at Perryville did become the cause of a duel between the general and Dr. William Nichol, the surgeon of the brigade.[48]

The trip from Kentucky was far from pleasant for the private soldiers. Exhausted and hungry, most of them unable to understand the need for retreat, they looked anything but the conquering heroes that had been predicted by the politicians. Colonel A.J. Vaughn wrote,

The retreat out of Kentucky was one of greater trial and hardship than any march made during the war. Over a rough and barren country, without shoes and thinly clad, with scarcely anything to eat, the suffering was great.[49]

The soldiers began to break rank in search for food, and stray cattle in the line of the march were sure prey to the appetites of the hungry men. Some regiments were fortunate enough to have their own cattle which were driven along with them as they made their way toward Tennessee. Unable to stop and sleep, the men dozed as they walked along. To break the monotony and to help stay awake, they sang familiar songs as they stumbled along the dusty roads. One soldier remembered:

We would usually stop at some branch or other about breakfast time, and all wash our hands and faces and eat breakfast, if we had any, and then commence our weary march again. If we halted for one minute, every soldier would drop down and resting on his knapsack, would go to sleep.[50]

Loss of sleep and lack of food were not the most dangerous obstacles faced by the retreating Rebs. Bushwhackers were far more dangerous than either. "The mountains were alive with bushwhackers," wrote Robert Gates, "and many a brave soldier left behind in some rude hut because of desperate wounds, was killed or murdered by these 'home-guards' or outlaws."[51] East Tennesseans, and many Kentuckians, who had no sympathy for the Confederate cause or the men who fought for it, were ruthless in their treatment of captured Rebel soldiers. Wiley Wood of Co. G., 6th Tennessee was wounded at Perryville, and while being evacuated, fell from a wagon and broke his leg. Wood was left at a mountain village where, "As soon as the army passed the bushwhackers entered the town, and taking the desperately wounded man out hanged him to a tree until he was dead. They then filled his body with bullet-holes, and left it as food for birds of prey."[52]

The Confederates performed some desperate acts of their own. On October 19th, General Marcus Wright recorded in his diary:

> *Left Barboursville and moved through Flat Lick ... I here discharged the most unpleasant duty of my military career. Sixteen Bushwhackers . . . including the notorious Capt. King and his two sons were hung here last night by Chalmer's brigade . . . Under orders from Gen. Cheatham, I took a detachment of 20 mounted men and with Lieut. Mann had them decently buried under the cherry tree on which they were hung . . .[53]*

Wiley Noblett recorded his impressions of the Battle of Perryville and the retreat from Kentucky in his diary. The morning following the battle he wrote:

> *Yesterday we went into the battle with 50 men, we came out last night with about 30; some were killed and wounded; about three others could not stand the racket, and thought it necessary to report to the hospital, immediately. We left four dead at the same time, about twenty others were knocked down, myself one of them, though I was not touched, or my skin even grazed.*

A few days later Wiley's sense of humor had returned and he wrote:

> *Yesterday we traveled hard, passed through London in the evening . . . we traveled till late in the night, and got no rations till after two o'clock, and we have to leave this morning before we got it cooked.*

186

Some of the boys are complaining of their beef kicking them in their haversacks, and want to stop just long enough to kill it.

On October 18, he observed:

This morning dawns upon us in a beautiful level grass lot, or it was a lot when we came here, but now it is only a grass bottom without a fence. It is very cold at night and we have had nothing else to burn.

By October 20, 1862, the scenery had changed and Wiley was prompted to record his impressions.

This cold and first frosty morning finds us in the mountainous region, where it looks as though the sun could never peep over the rough cragged rocks, or cast his sunbeams into the growing plants herein.

It is a region that would appear interesting, and delightful to a person in search of pleasure, but to a broken down, and worn out soldier it is a most horrible sight, and what makes it appear still more gloomy, we have a dead man and fellow soldier lying dead in our ranks at the moment I write this, but poor fellow, I hope he is better off than any of us, his short and troublesome life has come to a close, and I hope his wearied spirit has winged its way to a more delightful region than this unhappy land of war — so drenched with the blood of men.

As the army moved south, Wiley could not help but notice the reaction of the people toward their defeated army. On Oct. 21st he wrote:

We are camped tonight near a very good spring, but the ground is so steep we can hardly lay on it. We are camped on a very poor man's farm, he was wounded at the battle of Richmond, and is not able to get about.

The women are running to dig their potatoes for fear the soldiers will eat them; I cannot see how they keep from starving, anyhow, the land is so poor. Just at dark, I heard a noise among the chickens—I looked that way and saw a long skinny woman running at full speed after the old rooster, I suppose she thought he was in danger too.

The following day he wrote in his diary:

Today we have waded Clinch River, and traveled only ten miles. We took camps early this evening, and I went out to get some wood, and I found two little potatoe pumpkins. I picked them up, and started for camps. Before I got there I learned they were arresting men taking pumpkins, so I set down, and cut up one of them, and put it in my pockets, I put the other one in my bosom, and buttoned up my big coat and walked into camps uninterrupted.

By Sunday, October 26th, the weather had changed radically, but to a perceptive young soldier the situation held both a pathetic and comical interpretation. Wiley observed:

This morning we awoke, and found it snowing down unmercifully upon us. Some without shoes, others nearly naked, and all of us without tents or axes. Oh, who can imagine our horrible situation. We are surrounded on all sides by bares, not bears, and our whole encampment is infested with them. I do not suppose they will hurt us, but this cold weather will hurt them, for they are bare a-s-s-e-s and as a matter of course will suffer from the inclemency of the weather.

It is night again, and our situation is indeed a very gloomy one, for we have only a brush arbor to sleep under, and it is still snowing; the eyes will be few that close themselves in sleep tonight.

On Monday morning Wiley recorded his impressions by saying,

Day has come again at the proper time, and this morning she finds the earth clothed in a different garb; last night she was black and ugly, but now it is white and beautiful; it looks as though it is too good for the dirty feet of men to tread upon. The snow is three inches deep and if I were at home I could enjoy it well, but circumstances will not permit me there.[54]

From his first week in the army, Wiley Noblett had not been well. He had evidently entered the service with a lung disorder, and the circumstances he was forced to endure aggravated the condition. His condition grew steadily worse and a few months later he died at La Grange, Ga.

Meanwhile, the army continued its retreat southward then turned westward toward Murfreesboro. As the men neared their homes they sought furloughs, but Bragg would have none of it. Men like Resinor Etter, wounded too seriously for immediate service, were allowed to walk home, but they were the exception. Efforts were made to recruit, but Tennesseans had learned much about war and what they had learned did not increase their enthusiasm.

In late November, the Confederate Army began to assemble in the vicinity of Murfreesboro. The weather was cold and miserable and many men, weakened by exposure and a shortage of food, became victims to a variety of diseases which plagued the troops. Soon, Bragg's men would be arranging themselves for another battle, subsantially the same men would participate — only the scene, and the casualties, would be new.

4.

The Battle of Perryville eventually became a memory in the minds of the men who were there, and as such, it could be examined leisurely and with less emotion.

Carroll Clark was a member of the 16th Tennessee and was wounded in the initial charge of the battle. Later he thought about the experience and wrote:

> *If you wish to know how a soldier feels in such a battle as that, you must ask some one else. I cannot explain, but I had no hope of getting out alive. Such trials as that has a tendency to temporarily derange the minds of some, at least it was the case with me. If you ask me if I was scared, I answer, I dont know but I do know that I was scared before we got in the thickest of the fight. We were 40 yds of the enemy & they were falling fast . . . Many times when thinking of that bloody battle, the tears roll down my cheeks & I cannot force them back now while writing this article.*[55]

Future historians would speak of the casualties at Perryville in terms of numbers; Carroll Clark spoke of them in terms of men he had known and loved. Writing of the night following the battle Clark said:

> *The moaning & sighing of the wounded & dieing that night was heartrending & enough to make any man oppose war. Lieut. Denny Commings . . . was shot in the mouth breaking his jaw and carrying away 14 or 15 teeth & we thought he would die but he got over it & rejoined our Company . . I would have voted for the war to close then, but Oh Shucks . . .*[56]

Perhaps the most tragic of all observations was that of Colonel David Urquhart of Bragg's staff. Speaking of the Battle of Perryville after many years he said, "The Battle of Perryville, a hard-fought fight against many odds, was merely a favorable incident which decided nothing."[57]

Sam Watkins

Spencer Talley (right)

Chapter VIII

What a scene of confusion, of bloodshed, of war.

The countryside around Murfreesboro was not particularly impressive in late November. Nature had already stripped away her summer attire of lofty green leaves and grass, and little remained but the skeleton props of naked limbs awaiting the passing of winter. At least there was plenty of water, and for this reason, if for no other, the campsites offered a welcomed contrast to the drought-baked regions through which the men had recently traveled. Most of Bragg's army were familiar with the area — they had marched through it the previous spring on their way to Corinth. Since that time, the Confederates had completed a disappointing circle, but now many of them were close to home and morale was good.

With winter approaching, the generals became concerned at the lack of clothing and blankets in their regiments and representatives were dispatched home to seek supplies. Since Spencer Talley was only a few miles from his home in Wilson County, he was selected as the representative from his company to take a wagon to Lebanon in search of food and clothing.

Talley was pleasantly surprised to find that his mother had made him and his brother "a goodly supply of heavy jeans and wool socks that reached well near the knees. Many of our neighbors had clothing ready for their sons and we had a full load of good clothing and other things to bring back to the boys in camp."[1]

The social life around Murfreesboro was above average. Families from nearby counties took advantage of the opportunity to visit their soldiers. Each day found scattered groups of relatives converging from all directions. The orchards of Middle Tennessee had yielded their fruit in abundance, and when converted to its liquid form, the disappointments of the past dimmed into unimportance. One story which emerged concerned a raw recruit who was sent by his more seasoned comrades to invest a dollar in food and drink. When the recruit returned with ten cents worth of bread and ninety cents worth of whiskey he was severely reprimanded for having spent so much for bread.

Although enjoying a brief respite from the bloody carnival in which they were star performers, the Confederates did not forget the enemy at Nashville. Since the Kentucky campaign, Buell had been replaced by General William S. Rosecrans and the new general seemed restless to try his spurs on the Rebel target at Murfreesboro. To guard against any sudden movement by their enemy, the Confederates established an outpost at Lavergne, between Murfreesboro and Nashville, and from there a close watch was maintained on the Yanks.

While matters remained somewhat stable with the main army, Colonel John Hunt Morgan prepared to lead his Kentucky cavalry northeast for a raid on Hartsville, Tennessee. Morgan had been seeking permission for such a raid for several weeks, but the generals had not been impressed with his arguments. The truth was that Morgan was not a popular man with the War Department in Richmond. He exercised far too much independence, his records were often incomplete, his movements a mystery, and he exhibited an obvious scorn for authority.

Basil Duke, Morgan's second in command, wrote:

There were certain officers at Richmond, who, if their souls had been tied up with red tape, indorsed in accordance with the latest orders, stuffed into pigeon holes, would have preferred it to a guarantee of salvation. . . . It was said of a certain Confederate General of high rank that he would rather have his subordinates submit a "neat and formal" report of a defeat, than a slovenly account of a victory.[2]

Morgan left Murfreesboro on the morning of December 7, 1862. The weather was cold and snowy as the cavalry and infantry trudged their way north toward Lebanon. About the only time the silence was broken was when an infantryman cursed a cavalryman who rode by in what the weary foot soldier imagined as the essence of gentlemanly comfort.

It was almost dark when the column reached Lebanon, but not too late for the ladies of the town to treat the half-frozen Kentuckians to all kinds of home-prepared food. The muddy veterans made the most of the situation, but there was little time to linger; if Morgan's plan was to succeed, the troops had to move — and move they did.

As the march toward Hartsville progressed, new problems arose. The infantry had been promised that they could ride part of the way and after passing Lebanon they demanded that the promise be fulfilled. Unenthusiastic cavalrymen dismounted and the muddy foot-soldiers clumsily climbed into the saddles. In a short time, the infantrymen became tired of the swap and yelled to dismount. The procedure, instead of relieving the situation, merely added complications. As one of Morgan's officers wrote:

The infantry had gotten their feet wet in trudging through the snow, and, after riding a short time, were nearly frozen and clamored to dismount. The cavalrymen had gotten their feet saturated with moisture, and when they remounted, they suffered in turn.[3]

The working relationship between the cavalry and infantry, shaky at best, was not improved by this episode.

Hartsville was a small village on the north bank of the Cumberland River and was of little importance to either army. But the surrounding country abounded in cattle and other livestock, and to protect these, the Federals had established garrisons at both Hartsville and Castilian Springs six miles away. It was Morgan's plan to cross the river, attack Hartsville and capture its garrison, and then recross the river before the Federals at Castalian Springs could enter the action.

The infantry was transported across the river in two small boats, but the cavalry encountered all the hardships commensurate with the weather and the undertaking. There was no way for the horsemen to cross except by leaping their mounts into the icy currents and when the riders emerged on the opposite bank many were so chilled it was necessary to leave them shivering against the river bluff while the main column continued on its daring mission.

At daylight on Sunday, December 8, 1862, the Confederates hit hard and fast. After an hour's fighting they had captured over two thousand men and thousands of dollars worth of supplies. The attack was all that Morgan had hoped for. It established the plumed-hat Kentuckian as one of the Confederacy's leading raiders and offered further evidence that, by the end of 1862, the Confederate cavalry had no equal.

If the raid meant a lot to Morgan it also meant a lot to his men. Henry Stone, a member of the 9th Kentucky Regiment, wrote his parents the next day:

> We left camp after sleeping one hour and a half, and got in position in five hundred yards of the enemy at five o'clock in the morning, before it was light. This hour was set by Morgan to begin the attack . . . and well was it carried out . . . The firing soon became general, and of all the fighting ever done that was the hottest for an hour and fifteen minutes. The bombs fell thick and

fast over our heads, while Morgan's men yelled at every step, we all closing in on the Yankees. We took the whole force prisoners, about twenty-two hundred men. ... We took also all their small arms, wagons, etc. I captured a splendid overcoat, lined through and through, a fine black cloth coat, a pair of new woolen socks, a horse muzzle to feed in, and Enfield rifle, a lot of pewter plates, knives and forks, a good supply of smoking tobacco, an extra good cavalry saddle, a halter, and a pair of buckskin gloves, lined with lamb's wool; also a cavalry hat, with a yellow wire cord around it — all of which things I needed.[4]

It is needless to add that the former possessors of these fine items were now as destitute as the Rebs had been the preceding day.

The estimated two thousand prisoners were started toward Murfreesboro where General Bragg waited to greet Morgan with a warm welcome and a brigadier general's commission. Jefferson Davis had arrived in Murfreesboro and graciously added his praise to Bragg's. The entire town turned out to celebrate the victory. Soldiers and citizens alike crowded the icy, wind-swept streets to jeer the frostbitten prisoners, but their pathetic appearance made it difficult to feel anything but pity for them.

2.

Jefferson Davis was accompanied to Murfreesboro by Custis Lee, the son of General Robert E. Lee, and in their behalf Bragg staged a full dress parade of his army. The weather moderated for the occasion and Jim Womack thought it all "an imposing scene, and a time for rejoicing throughout the army and surrounding country. The ladies, old men, children and negroes turning out to see their esteemed president and the army."[5]

The President's visit meant more than the viewers at the parade knew. A unique bit of strategy was taking place in Davis' mind, a strategy that could very well mean defeat for the very men who were now parading in his honor.

With the enemy less than thirty miles away at Nashville, Davis ordered Bragg to send General C.L. Stevenson's division of ten thousand men to Mississippi. Confederate generals rose up in protest and suggested that such a move could result in the loss of both Mississippi and Tennessee, but Davis was not impressed. On the eve of an impending battle, Stevenson and his men marched away from the scene.

While Jefferson Davis planned strategy, "General" John Hunt Morgan planned his weddng to the beautiful Martha Ready of Murfreesboro. The wedding took place on December 14, 1862, and the occasion started a celebration which lasted through Christmas. General Leonidas Polk performed the ceremony and the event was attended by all of the Confederate brass in the area. Some officers viewed the marriage with misgiving, fearing it would impair the efficiency of the Rebel raider, but even these offered their heartiest congratulations to Morgan and his beautiful bride.

To John Hunt Morgan the world no doubt seemed a wonderful dream that night. He was the newest hero of the Confederacy; he had just been made a brigadier general; and he had for his wife, the area's most beautiful belle. But as Morgan stood at the Ready home receiving the congratulations of the most important generals in the Confederacy's Western Army, a Confederate sergeant named Andrew Campbell lay in the fields somewhere around Murfreesboro. Campbell was a trusted member of Pat Cleburne's command, but was on this night indistinguishable among the thousands of men who passed the boring hours as best they could. By an ironic turn of fate, it would be Andrew Campbell who would play a far more prominent role in the ultimate destiny of John Hunt Morgan than any of the people who now seemed so important to him. On a damp, misty morning almost two years later in Greenville,

Tennessee, Andrew Campbell would rest his gun on a rock fence, take careful aim, and kill John Hunt Morgan.

The festivities that began with Morgan's wedding continued as the Christmas season approached. Along a rise west of the railroad depot, the men of the 20th Tennessee had few worries. Officers of the regiment had bought the men a barrel of whiskey to enhance the holidays, but the consequences were not too merry. According to one soldier, "We had many a drunken fight and knock-down before the day closed."

Jim Womack wrote his reaction to the season by saying:

> *How differently spent from that of sixty-one! That I passed in Charleston and Fort Sumpter, where I was delighted and pleased, this I have spent in my tent by the fire in Murfreesboro, attending to many of the daily duties of the soldier. May the coming Christmas in sixty three find our now distracted and unhappy country reposing in the lap of an infantile and glorious peace.*[6]

Later in the week a ball was held in the county courthouse, a new building on the town square. It was the same building Forrest's men had stormed the summer before. On this night the premises were elaborately decorated and the gathering of celebrities gave notice that this would be no ordinary occasion. Only generals and colonels were allowed inside with their ladies, but such a ruling failed to thwart the social inclinations of the more enterprising captains.

Spencer Talley's colonel, P. D. Cunningham, had no desire to attend the ball and graciously offered to lend his uniform to the young captain who definitely had such a desire. To Talley the affair proved to be "a most delightful time   we had the best band of musicians in the army & our table was loaded with the best things that Murfreesboro could offer."[7]

Such a blissful state of existence was doomed to a short duration, for at Nashville, the Federals had begun a move toward Murfreesboro. When this startling news reached the courthouse party, officers and couriers dashed off in all directions. Young ladies found themselves unattended in the confusion and turmoil that followed. A battle was taking shape; there was no time for formalities.

When Bragg and his staff went toward Nashville to select a defense line they found the terrain wet, soggy, and monotonously level. West of town, a small river curled its way north through the level bottoms of Rutherford County, and it was along its banks that the Confederate commander decided to place his army. Almost a hundred years before, Uriah Stone had followed this stream inland and in his honor it had been named Stone's River.[8] The name was about to take on added significance as the fields along its bank would, like a giant vampire, drink the blood of thousands of Northern and Southern soldiers.

Bragg rapidly concentrated his troops along the banks of the little river and because he placed them in a relatively straight line, the meandering waters had troops to its north, south, east, and west.

On the 27th of December General William J. Hardee ordered scouts out to ascertain the exact movement of the Federals. The men chosen were Colonel W. D. Pickett of Hardee's staff and Colonel Tom Harrison of the 8th Texas Regiment. As Pickett later remembered the experience, "The night was dark and stormy, a drizzling rain falling, but altogether it was a favorable night for the work at hand." After riding several miles, the scouts came to the village of Triune. Riding to the top of a prominent hill they saw the faint flicker of the enemy's campfires. Pickett wrote, "The whole valley was lighted by the enemy's campfires. Farmers' fence rails must have been abundant; for though it was ten or eleven o'clock at night, the camp fires were still burning brilliantly. The camp before us was of at least a division of infantry, and down the valley was the reflection of other campfires. The advance of the Federal army had commenced."[9]

When Hardee received the report of his scouts he quickly put his men in motion toward the main army at Mufreesboro.

There was no time to lose for, as Pickett observed, "The vigor and rapidity of their advance showed unmistakable business."[10]

The Federal army moved steadily, relentlessly toward Murfreesboro. It consumed everything in its path. A Confederate soldier wrote, "A portion of them camped around my mother's house that night; the next morning, not a chicken, turkey, hog, horse, or cow could be found on the place, and not a fence rail near the house."[11] By the night of December 30th, the maneuvering was over and the armies faced each other along a three-mile line. In several places, the opposing lines were little over one hundred yards apart. Calmly, almost patiently, the men in both armies waited for daylight.

3.

The men in the Confederate Army always welcomed an opportunity to drive their enemy from Southern soil. But for Bragg's army, now officially called the Army of Tennessee, there was perhaps another reason for meeting the foe. This Confederate Army had not yet won a decisive victory even though the newspapers and politicians had attempted to interpret Shiloh and Perryville in that light. Underneath the facade of confidence that was projected by the men, a gnawing doubt was always present. The Rebs needed a victory, one that left no doubt in anybody's mind. It was a matter not only of sectional advantage, but of personal pride. A decisive win would accomplish everything the Rebs wanted most.

Captain Monroe Bearden had not yet realized his burning desire to drive the Yankees from Tennessee. He still nourished the wish to correct what he considered Albert Sidney Johnston's blunder in allowing the Federal Army to enter the state. It had been almost a year since Bearden had written:

We have tried a government given us by our ancestors, and found it of no value . . . Now to erect one that will stand the test of time we must make great sacrifices — true and noble spirits must perish on the battlefields . . .[12]

On the 28th of December, Jim Womack wrote:

Our troops are all in readiness to meet the coming foe, and confident of success when it is met. That eagerness that pervades the bosom of the army of Tennessee to drive the insulting enemy beyond the limits of this state inspires the belief that they will be able to do so.[13]

Just as the men were preparing to get what little sleep they could, one of the many strange events of war took place. In the stillness of the wintry night, military bands in both armies played their usual serenade, but just as the last notes were drifting off into the darkness a Federal band struck up the strains of "Home Sweet Home." To the soldiers in the line it was a "soul-stirring" experience. W. J. Worsham wrote:

Immediately a Confederate band caught up the strain, then one after another until all the bands of each army were playing "Home Sweet Home." After our bands had ceased playing, we could hear the sweet refrain as it died away on the cool frosty air on the Federal side.[14]

Shortly after the men settled down for the night, Captain D.C. Spurlock of the 16th Tennessee made his way to a hotel on the town square where his mother and father waited to see him. The Spurlocks had lost a son at Perryville and had made the trip to Murfreesboro not knowing that a battle was imminent. After a few hours with his parents, Captain Spurlock returned to his company on the bank of Stone's River. It was only a short time until daylight.

In the cold, damp darkness of pre-dawn the two armies resembled giant serpents sprawled along the river. They were ready to spring at the first signs of light. Only a single command would be needed to change these slumbering giants into screaming, charging monsters whose fangs could cut deeply into what each expected to be a victim caught unaware.

Neither the Yank nor Reb were any longer citizen soldiers. They were schooled by experience in the art of war and the thousands of bodies destined to lie on the rolling fields bordering Stone's River would be dismal proof that they could execute its demands with a high degree of efficiency.

With the first dim grayness of dawn on the last day of 1862, the left flank of the Confederate line crept through the cedar trees, hooked around the right end of the Federal line, and the Battle of Stone's River was on. As the men themselves said, "The ball had started." Without breakfast, the screaming Rebs charged across the frozen ground toward an enemy who thought the battle would begin an hour later and three miles away.

The sleepy-eyed Yanks, who were preparing breakfast, left their fires burning to look for safer ground to the rear. Frantic last-minute efforts to meet the attack were thwarted by the swiftly moving Confederates. It was Shiloh all over; only this time the Confederates were determined to win. Their determination was evident most of all to the Yankees in their immediate path.

Time and again the Federal line folded under the impact of the hard-driving Rebs. Men fought hand to hand using the butts of rifles as clubs. Confederates grabbed the opposing colors from the hands of men who chose to die rather than surrender them. As Federal regiments down the line prepared to meet the advancing Confederates they found themselves hit from the front, rear, and flank. Artillery horses were unhitched and used as means of escape by the Federal soldiers who yelled that their generals had "sold them out."

A Federal officer stationed toward the rear said he saw the approach of "a lot of teamsters, riding their harnessed mules on a keen run to the rear. . . ." Following this spectacle, the officer saw an impromptu parade of "alarmists, crying 'all is lost,' came first the cavalrymen, then teams cut loose from wagons, with each mule bearing from two to three riders, then came the panic-stricken infantrymen."[15]

After all moderate attempts failed to stop the stampede the 9th Michigan Regiment was placed:

>...*in a line of battle across the Nashville Pike, extending its flanks to the utmost limits .... Cavalry, artillery, infantry, sutlers and camp followers came rushing with the force of a cyclone, and the 9th Michigan was ordered to fix bayonets and charge upon this panic-stricken mass of men.*[16]

In the frenzied tumult of close-range fighting the Federal line continued to buckle under the persistent Confederate pressure. One Reb, Lt. J. T. Tunnell from Texas, wrote:

>*Many of the Yanks were either killed or retreated in their nightclothes. We pursued them with the Rebel yell. In advancing we found a caisson with the horses attached lodged against a tree and other evidences of their confusion. The Yanks tried to make a stand whenever they could find shelter of any kind. All along our route we captured prisoners, who would take refuge behind houses, fences, logs, cedar bushes, and in ravines. We drove them helter-skelter . . .*[17]

In some places the Federals rallied and put up stiff resistance, as was the case with General Phil Sheridan's men, but in the process, every brigade commander was killed. The right wing of the Federal Army had been swept away.

Thomas Malone was far enough removed from the initial charge to see its effects upon the enemy. He watched as the fleeing Federals ran for their lives across the open fields south of the Wilkenson turnpike that crossed the battlefield. He saw the Confederate artillery "sending showers of grape through the crowded fugitives."[18]

Confederate soldiers became so enthusiastically unrestrained that they lowered their bayonets and took out after the fleeing enemy, and only after the severe intervention of staff officers, was some degree of order restored. Even after returning to their positions, the Rebs shouted curses to the top of their voices. It was a glorious hour for the victory-starved Confederates; they intended to make the most of it.

In the drifting puffs of artillery smoke, troops lost their bearing and the lines became confused. Color bearers from both armies climbed buildings and trees in an effort to regroup their men; they often met death as a result. Generals, as well as privates, became confused. Confederate Generals George Maney and Ben Cheatham stood and argued on the field as Federal artillery blasted away at their men. Maney argued that the artillery was actually Confederate while Cheatham contended it was Federal and that it should be attacked at once. As it turned out, Cheatham was correct, but even before he gave the order to attack, one of Maney's staff officers had ordered the Confederate artillery to open fire.

A young preacher was ordered to "pint the first gun." He "laid his cheek along the butt of the gun and took deliberate aim, and the gun was fired, he threw himself to one side . . . and looked under the smoke to see the result." The preacher's aim was good; the shell exploded in the middle of the Yankee artillery. After the first shell exploded the captain yelled to the preacher, "Give em hell, God damn em!" and the preacher followed orders.[19]

Even though the morning had brought a sweeping Confederate victory, not all of the bravery had been on the Southern side. The fact was that some Rebs had done some back-peddling of their own and some of it had occurred at a pace which removed it from the realm of gracefulness. After watching a brigade of Federals resist the Confederate advance Colonel A.J. Vaughn of the 13th Tennessee wrote:

I witnessed an exhibition and coolness that I never saw on any other battlefield. We had in our front and opposed to us a brigade of United States Regulars; they were formed in two lines of battle some distance apart. Firing as we advanced, their first line waited until we got within easy range and then cooly delivered their fire; without waiting to reload they faced to the rear and double-quicked through their second line and reformed in line of battle. The second line then awaited our approach, and though their men were falling around them, they cooly delivered their fire and retired through the first line and reformed in line of battle; and thus they continued to fire and fall back until they were driven across the field. Their lines were plainly marked by their dead, who lay thick on the ground.[20]

A Federal soldier by the name of Smith walked up to Lt. Col. Walworth of the 42nd Illinois and said, "Colonel, I come to return my gun to you, for I suppose that I will go on furlough now." The Colonel asked the meaning of the corporal's statement and as the young soldier "moved his hand from his body the intestines followed."[21]

The dramatic bravery of a few Federals was not to stop the Confederate drive that had before noon pushed the battered blue-coats across the Wilkinson Turnpike. The retreating Yankees entered a jungle of prickly cedar trees whose roots were netted among the giant limestone rocks that reared their tops from the shallow soil. Using the trees and rocks for protection the Federals turned to fire as best they could, but as Thomas Malone remembered it, the Yankee fire did " . . . a great deal of damage to the young trees and very little to our pursuing line."[22]

Long before noon the Confederates had bent the Federal right flank back for a distance of three miles until it was at right angles to their left flank. The two wings came together in a grove of trees whose circular shape prompted the name "Round

Forest." Running through the forest was a railroad which afforded the Yanks enough protection to stablize their line and here they took on new life.

During the afternoon, the Confederates began an assault on the Round Forest and the slaughter of the morning resumed. But the tide of battle changed. The Federals now braced themselves and lashed out at their attackers. Now it was the Confederates who watched their lines melt away before the thundering blasts of massed artillery and the stinging reports of muskets.

Early in the assault, the 8th and 16th Tennessee regiments were ordered forward. Now was the time for Monroe Bearden to drive out the Yankees and rid his state of their detested presence; he formed his company and stepped toward the enemy. The 16th Tennessee with Old John Savage in command straddled the railroad track and moved forward. Captain D.C. Spurlock, who had visited his mother and father the night before, led one of the companies on the right; Jim Womack led one on the left. Monroe Bearden was only two hundred yards to their left and on command they all stepped forward. Both regiments were forced to advance across open fields; nature offered no help.

As the crouching Confederate line edged its way toward the Round Forest, Jim Womack noted that the space between the enemies "was now an unobstructed plain of about one hundred yards; we lay shooting, they standing."23 The Yankee artillery was turned loose on the Rebs with a furious accuracy, and in a single blast, ten men in the 8th Tennessee fell to the ground; one of them was Monroe Bearden. A short distance away, the colonel of the regiment, William Moore, was pinned under his slain horse, and as he regained his feet to lead the attack, an enemy ball pierced him in the breast. He died instantly.

To the right of the 8th Tennessee, the 16th faced a blizzard of lead and steel. The regiment advanced to the edge of a cotton patch, and there was pinned down, unable to move. D.C.

Spurlock attempted to lead his company up the railroad, but before he had advanced fifteen yards, he was dead. In fact by the time Spurlock fell there was not an officer living in the entire company and Private Wright Hackett assumed command. Color-bearer J.M. Rice of the 8th Tennessee was shot down but crept on his knee with the flag still aloft until a second bullet killed him instantly. Close by, Jim Womack writhed in a bundled heap amid the carnage that was once the 16th Tennessee. Already Colonel John Savage was accusing his general of putting the 16th in a position to get them all killed. In an almost bitter rage Savage continued to lead his men, not even stopping when he saw his brother fall to the ground mortally wounded.

Just as the Federals had found out during the morning that the gallantry of a *few* men will not win battles, so did the Confederates, in the afternoon, find that the gallantry of *many* men will not always win battles. After the ground was literally covered with Confederate bodies, the attacking regiments withdrew from the field. The 16th Tennessee had sent four hundred men into the charge, of which two hundred seven were casualties. The 8th Tennessee sent four hundred twenty-five men, of which three hundred six were casualties. In Co. D of the 8th, out of twelve officers and sixty-two men engaged, only one corporal and twenty men escaped unhurt.[24]

Late in the afternoon Bragg decided to send in reinforcements to crack the stubborn Federal defense and called for troops from across the river. Instead of sending a concentrated force against the enemy he sent his brigades in one at a time and each in its turn became food for the unerring fire of Yankee cannon.

The 20th Tennessee was one of the regiments brought from across the river. After wading through the icy water, the men entered a cotton field and cautiously moved toward the Round Forest. After being pinned down with nothing but dead cotton stalks for protection the regiment was ordered to fall back. One soldier wrote, "Colonel Smith having ordered us to fall back, and every man for himself, if you ever saw a lot of men get out of a place in quick time the Twentieth Tennessee Regiment did it."[25]

A short time later, Spence Talley's regiment was ordered to join "the ball." The men crossed the river where the water was from two to three feet deep and as he remembered it:

> *We made no halt but plunged right through & soon after crossing our pants were frozen & rattled like a rawhide. The sun had been down for some bit and darkness was fast coming on us. So much so, that it made the sheets of fire from the enemy's cannon look hideous & dazzling . . . When it became evident that no further infantry charge would be made, we were relieved and permitted to retire to a position where we could build fires & dry our clothes.*[26]

The morning had presented the Confederates with a spectacular victory; the afternoon had witnessed a tragic Confederate defeat. Some of Bragg's junior officers wondered where the Confederate general had been all day. They contrasted his absence from the field with the heroic behavior of Rosecrans who was conspicuous in the fight on several different occasions. Many Confederates believed the Rebel generals were drunk, although Bragg was not included in this number. Sam Watkins wrote, "John Barleycorn was general-in-chief. Our generals, and colonels, and captains, had kissed John a little too often. They couldn't see straight. It was said to be buckeye whiskey."[27] Thomas Malone said he saw Generals "manifestly somewhat excited by drink," and that he was unable to depend on their judgement. Both Bragg and General Leonidas Polk later indicated that whiskey had influenced the battle at least to some degree.

Night at Murfreesboro brought with it all the misery that the savagery of war could produce. The ground froze to a depth of two inches, and in the cedar thickets dotting the fields, men froze to the ground by their own blood.

Under cover of darkness the survivors of D.C. Spurlock's company crept alongside the railroad and retrieved the body of their young captain. They wrapped him in a blanket and carried the body to the town square where it was delivered to his parents.

After darkness had settled over the field, a soldier from the 20th Tennessee found "the ground strewn with the dead and wounded." While making his rounds, the Rebel picket heard the whines of a wounded soldier, and making his way to where the soldier lay, asked to what command he belonged. "Eighteenth Regular," came the answer along with the information that he was badly wounded and almost frozen. According to the picket:

> I told him I was a Confederate and on picket just in front of him, and by making a fire would draw the picket fire from the Yankee pickets. He begged me so pitifully, and as he was down in a ravine, I took the chance, and searched around among the rocks and got some cedar limbs and made him a fire and gave him some water, placed his head on his knapsack and made him as comfortable as possible . . . When I left I told him if my line was not attacked or ordered away, that I would come back before day and look after him. I went back in about two hours, but he had crossed over and was sleeping the soldier's sleep and I could do no more for him.[28]

Most of the Confederate soldiers who survived the day's fighting spent the night along the banks of Stone's River. In the gloom about them there was at least some effort made to relieve the strain of the day's experience and the tormenting effects of the winter weather. Spencer Talley's commanding officer ordered a barrel of whiskey for the men. According to Talley,

> A detail of one commissioned officer from each company was sent to this barrel for whiskey for his men. I was sent from our company and having gathered a

dozen or more canteens started for the barrel which was 3 or 4 hundred yards away. When I got there I found the barrel setting on its end with the head out and a crowd around it on the same mission as myself. When my time came to fill up I would take a canteen in each hand & sink them in the liquor & they would say good, good, good till they were full. With the canteens swinging around my neck I started back, & found it was all I could do to walk, bending over the barrel and enhaling the fumes had made me drunk.[29]

Bragg thought the Federals would withdraw during the night, but daylight revealed them standing firm. Due either to the determination of a few officers or a simple mistake in distinguishing Confederate troops from their own, the Union High Command had decided to stay put.

There was little action at Stone's River on New Year's Day. The Confederates gathered their wounded and placed them in schools, churches, private homes or any place that would protect them from the weather. Jim Womack and Monroe Bearden were placed in the same hospital. Womack was attended by his brothers, while Bearden's needs were looked after by the ladies of the community. It is doubtful that many people around Murfreesboro realized that this was the day Lincoln's Emancipation Proclamation went into effect.

The relative quiet of New Year's Day continued through the night that followed. The next morning found the armies still in place with little sign of movement. Only occasional and sporadic firing disrupted the silence during the morning hours. Behind the lines, hospital attendants continued about the business of caring for the wounded while relatives searched for sons and husbands.

One lady who came into town in search of her son wrote:

On entering town what a sight met my eyes! Prisoners entering every street, ambulances bringing in the wounded, every place crowded with the dying, the

Federal General Sill lying dead in the courthouse —
killed Wednesday — Frank Crostwaite's lifeless corpse
stretched out on a counter. He had been visiting my
house, and was killed on Wednesday. The churches
were full of wounded, where the doctors were
amputating legs and arms. I found my own safe, and,
on being informed that another battle was expected to
begin, I set off on my way home, and passed through
our cavalry all drawn up in line. I had gone only a mile
when the first cannon boomed, but I was safe.[30]

The cannon heard by this lady set in motion the last act of
the hideous drama of Stone's River — an act that would feature
one of the war's more notable charges, and one of its bloodiest
massacres.

Bragg had ordered General John C. Breckinridge to leave
his position east of the river and charge the Federals who
occupied a low ridge between him and the river. Bragg's plan
called for the Federals to be driven off just before sundown
when not enough daylight would remain for a well-organized
counter-attack. Breckinridge did not like the idea, but Bragg
was uncompromising in his order and promptly at four o'clock
the Rebs moved forward.

Gervis Grainger, a Kentucky soldier, wrote:

Every soldier seemed to realize that the conflict was
before him. Attention was called by Breckinridge,
repeated by General Hanson and other officers along the
line, all splendidly mounted. "Forward, march!" was
repeated by more than a hundred voices. The colors
went up, the pickets and videttes closed in, and we
stepped forward.[31]

Just before the men moved forward, Breckinridge, a
former vice-president of the United States, called a subordinate
to him and stated his opposition to the charge. He added:

If it should result in a disaster, and I be among the slain, I want you to do justice to my memory, and tell the people that I believed this attack to be very unwise and tried to prevent it.[32]

The attacking Rebs moved forward in two parallel lines, but before they had gone two hundred yards, the two columns had formed a single line to face the Federals who stretched much farther to the right than was first believed. The first Yanks encountered were lying behind a rail fence. When the Confederates got within range, the Federals fired a volley which made the attackers "stagger and waver like a drunken man." Pushing forward, the Rebs knelt behind the fence which put the opposing lines only forty yards apart. By this time the Federals were standing, while the Confederates fired between the rails of the protecting fence.

In a few moments the Rebs were ordered to charge. A member of the 20th Tennessee said:

The Regiment did not take time to climb the fence, but caught the fence about the third rail from the bottom, and the fence, line and all went over together. The first line of Yankees fell back to their second, we pressed them so closely, in twenty minutes the whole mass was going back to the river.[33]

As his regiment passed the original position of the enemy this Reb observed "the straightest and prettiest line of dead Yankees I ever saw."[34]

A Federal officer, standing on a bluff across the river, wrote:

What a scene of disorderd retreat and pursuit . . . What a scene of confusion, of bloodshed, of war was revealed to the eyes! 'Standing near one of the batteries one could see blue-coated men running with all their might, closely followed by a dense mob of butternut — clothed troops, who were cheering and yelling, and crazy almost with delight.[35]

As the Yankee line retreated it seemed to the Southerners that a glorious victory was at hand. But what seemed a forerunner to victory was actually a prelude to disaster. As the Yankees were pushed toward the river they pulled the pursuing Rebs within range of some fifty-eight cannons which were masked on a hill west of the river. In a moment's time it was as if the Rebs had opened the door of hell to be greeted by the devil himself. The soggy river bottom became a death trap to the Confederates who had advanced within range of the hidden cannon, and like hunters shooting trapped animals the Yankee gunners blazed away.

Spencer Talley was hit and as he lay on the ground he felt "the blood running down my side but could not tell whether the ball had lodged in me or passed through." Stumbling toward the rear, the young captain passed a mutilated body which he instinctively stopped to examine. Only a momentary glance was needed to reveal the body as that of his Colonel, P.D. Cunningham. Talley could not help but notice the coat he had so recently worn to the courthouse ball, now torn to shreds and saturated by the blood of the man who had been kind enough to lend it.[36]

W. J. McMurray of the 20th Tennessee wrote:

> *If a soldier ever saw the lightning and heard the thunder bolts of a tornado, at the same time the heavens opened and the stars of destruction were sweeping everything from the face of the earth, if he was in this battle he saw it.*[37]

All around the terrible slaughter continued. A Kentucky soldier said:

> *A shell exploded right in the middle of the company, almost literally tearing it to pieces. When I recovered from the shock the sight I witnessed was appalling. Some eighteen men hurled in every direction ...*[38]

In slightly over an hour, over 1800 Confederate soldiers fell before the awesome power of the Federal cannon. This crushing blow meant that Bragg's army had little chance to penetrate the Yankee defense although it took some time for the Confederate commander to admit this fact. For all practical purposes, the Battle of Stone's River ended when the last Rebel soldier dragged himself from under the fire of the enemy's guns.

4.

The sun mercifully disappeared and night came on, imposing its authority on the chaos along the river. Spencer Talley reported to the hospital in the courthouse. As he waited for the overworked doctors to examine his wounds, the body of his colonel was brought from the battlefield. Talley wrote:

> *When his body was brought to the Hospital my heart was full of sorrow, and regardless of my wound I secured a vessel of water and washed his blood stained face, and hands. The coat which I had worn a few nights before to the grand ball & festival was now spotted & saturated with his life's blood. I removed the stains from his coat as best I could with the cold water and a rag, combed his unkempt hair & whiskers and laid his body with many others in the Court House at Murfreesboro.*[39]

While the families of the dead and wounded poured into Murfreesboro, Bragg's army began moving south in retreat. The day was January 3, 1863. It was another chapter in the story of an army that almost won all its battles, but didn't quite win any. A cold, misty rain cast a melancholy silence over the town.   The men were muddy, cold, hungry, disappointed, angry at their generals and, probably worst of all, overcome by the damaged pride commensurate with retreat.   They scarcely noticed the relatives who walked among them inquiring of loved ones.   The men spoke in low tones and often their sentences were nothing but a string of curse words designed to relieve the bitterness toward what had happened.

To the residents of Murfreesboro, the departure of Bragg's army meant utter defeat.   A young lady who watched later wrote:

> *The retreat!   Who of us that were here does not remember it . . . It was the grandest, saddest sight we ever saw . . .*
>
> *No other sound broke the stillness . . . only the ceaseless foot-steps of the retreating heroes, that followed each other in rapid succession, disturbed the breathless silence . . . Not a word was spoken.*
>
> *The author of these lines saw amid the dreary, falling rain, the dim out lines of a gallant army that was passing away!   and leaving their homes to the mercy of a bloodthirsty enemy — and dropped bitter, burning tears.*[40]

Many Murfreesboro citizens hurried to the train depot in the hope of getting passage on a train going south.   Boxcars were crowded with people willing to leave their homes and possessions to the enemy rather than endure the indignities they believed would follow.   Still clinging to a way of life they were determined to perpetuate, some refugees came to the depot with one, and sometimes more, slaves to wait on them during their "unselfish sacrifice" for the Southern cause.

The Federal Army offered no pursuit.   It seemed content to leave the Confederates alone as long as it could enjoy the same luxury.

5.

The father of Captain Monroe Bearden first heard of his son's being wounded when he rode to the town square in Fayetteville, Tennessee, two days following the event. Although Fayetteville was some sixty miles south of Murfreesboro, the father sent word to his wife concerning the tragedy and immediately left for the scene of the battle. Accompanied by a friend, the frantic father rode throughout the freezing night, reaching the village of Fosterville just before daylight. After obtaining breakfast at the home of a friend, Bearden continued the remaining few miles to Murfreesboro.

When the elder Bearden arrived at Murfreesboro, he immediately began a search for his son and eventually found him in "Soule Female College which was made use of for Cheatham Division Hospital at which place hundreds of our poor boys lay wounded in every conceivable manner."[41] That night Monroe's mother and sister arrived in a wagon accompanied by two neighbors who wished to do what they could for the troubled family. Wishing to remove Monroe from the crowded hospital the Beardens rented a room nearby and the wounded soldier was moved to it. Soldiers from Monroe's regiment cut enough wood to keep a fire going day and night, and as Bragg's army prepared to move south, it appeared as if the captain was improving nicely.

By January 20th, the plight of Monroe had worsened. The careful nursing given him by his family had failed to have the desired effect. Monroe's father had brought with him to Murfreesboro a small, black book in which he had previously kept farm records: when fields were planted, when mares were bred and the like. The little book suddenly took on added significance as the father began to record his thoughts on his son's condition.

On January 20th the father wrote:

Monroe much worse — I lost all hope of recovery. O God who could describe my feelings just to think of giving up my dear boy, the very one on whose manly form I expected to lean on in old age. About 11 or 12 OC [o'clock] PM I told my dear Boy that he was doomed to die, he said that he was not aware of it. Asked how long he had to live — I told him I did not know that death was not on him at that time — he seemed perfectly resigned to his fate. O God this is the hardest trial of my life.[42]

The following day Monroe's father wrote:

But little change in Monroe. Dr. Hatcher visited him this morning and examined his wound — Monroe remarked that we had given him out too soon — Went to work in earnest to try to save him — he seemed to be in but little pain. Monroe called for Father about 11OC PM — being asked what he wanted He said Morphine, I gave him morphine he went to sleep — was conchious and in but little pain — took some coffy after.[43]

On January 22, 1863, the diary of Monroe Bearden's father told a story of war in words that seared and burned their way into the very soul of a man who had paid a price for secession far beyond anything he had ever imagined. The diary reads:

4OC PM 20 mi. died in the north room of Dr. Tompkins residence Murfreesboro, Tennessee Capt. Napoleon Monroe Bearden Capt. of Co. E 8th Regiment Tenn. Volunteers . . . Bot [bought] a Burial Case of Lewis Brown placed and sealed him up late in afternoon.[44]

It had been ten months since Monroe had written:

We must make many sacrifices — true and noble spirits must perish on the battlefield till every heart within Tennessee's boundaries is bound by the same cord and urged to the same loyalties by the same bitter incentive.[45]

Monroe Bearden had made a supreme sacrifice toward that end.

It was early March before the parents of Monroe Bearden were ready to bury his body. Family legend had it that the Yankees would not permit the parents to take the body from Murfreesboro and that it was only after the remains were hidden under a cargo of clocks that the body was smuggled past the sentries. If this is true the elder Bearden did not record it in his diary. He did record, on the 12th day of March:

. . . about 2 OC PM deposited the case containing the remains of my dear son, N.M. Bearden in a vault prepared for its reception in my garden. A large crowd of our friends and neighbors being present. He was in a wonderful state of preservation taking into consideration the length of time since his death — O how natural that manly Brave and pleasant features did look to an almost heart broken Parent. Brothers and sisters the recollections of the day are burned in my feelings.[46]

Monroe Bearden

Chapter IX

The women sit in the hall and chew tobacco

The inaction following the Battle of Stone's River afforded the Federals an opportunity to look around and examine the society they had come to fight. The farms, homes, towns, and cities from which the enemy at Shiloh, Perryville, and Stone's River had come were plainly visible, but a knowledge of the people was harder to come by. Like all people who compose a group, each was an individual and reflected different characteristics, but underneath the uniqueness of individuals, Northern writers believed they saw a social and cultural pattern that explained the "Rebel society."

By the winter of 1863, one thing was firmly established in the minds of Northern soldiers: their Confederate opponents from all Southern states were worthy adversaries. Poor equipment, poor leadership, poor training, and even continuous defeat had failed to dampen the ardor of the Southern soldier in battle. The fact was that the men in each army had developed an appreciation for the soldierly qualities of their enemy and it was a respect that would endure to the war's end — and beyond.

Although the Northern soldier respected the fighting qualities of his Southern adversary he was not so sure about the culture that produced and sustained him. Most Northern leaders considered the Reb an individual who had been talked into

221

fighting the war by an arrogant aristocracy. In most cases, the rich land owner was blamed for the war, while the private soldier was excused on the grounds of ignorance.

One Northern writer, in an article pertaining to the 14th Tennessee Regiment, wrote:

> *Wiley statesmen appealed to the chivalry of Southern hearts to break the bonds of Union, throw off despotism, and strike for liberty, independence, and the firesides of home. Ambitious fathers pointed to future glories of a Confederacy, and by acts, if not words, urged their sons to go in defence of the Southern cause .*
>
> *Wildly, enthusiastically, they left their homes without one solid thought as to the true responsibilities of the undertaking. Their march to camp was more like going to the transient joys of a ball-room or festival, than to the cold realities of the battlefield . . .[1]*

Displaying his contempt for those on whom he blamed the war, the writer continued:

> *Ah! what a terrible responsibility rests upon those that inaugurated this unholy war, and who have sacrificed so many lives for the accomplishment of their desires. May the pale shadows of their victims haunt their day dreams, and appear in ghostly form in all their night visions. May the cold stare of their accusing eyes haunt them continually, stagger their brain with wild fancies, and demons ever howl their guilt in their ears.[2]*

From the very first week the Federals set foot on Tennessee soil, they realized what war meant to a people caught in its path. They saw livestock confiscated, fence rails burned, and people forced to flee their homes. Following the fall of Fort Donelson, a regiment of Grant's soldiers rode toward Clarksville and watched "the people, en masse . . . men, women, and children, leaving their homes, and fleeing in every

direction, seeming only to go somewhere."[3]   Upon entering
Tennessee, one Federal soldier observed that :

> . . . the first acre of Tennessee soil betrayed the
> ruthless track of war. Fallow fields were spread out
> before the vision, and the voice of the planter was not
> needed to prove that the peaceful plowshare had been
> transformed into the biting sword. Fences had been
> absorbed in campfires; the click of the old mill wheel
> had ceased; broken windows and shattered frames
> stared from deserted homesteads; and charred chimneys
> begrimed with smoke stain stood in stark solitude in the
> bosom of deflowered gardens and blistered groves.[4]

The city of Nashville- afforded the victorious Union men
an even better opportunity to study Southerners and their
culture. Of the city itself one soldier wrote:

> There was little social enjoyment . . . The women
> got together to kiss each other, to cry together . . .but
> their glee was more mournful than their sorrow. Public
> entertainment there was none. The theater was open,
> truly, but the drama was public tragedy, at a dead rebel's
> funeral . . . Here and there a gambling den, but no
> gamblers . . . A few loyal residents, and the wives of
> Union officers devised trifling schemes of enjoyment,
> but the baleful shadow of war interposed.[5]

Federal soldiers found that their presence in Nashville was
deeply resented by most people, especially the ladies. A Union
cavalryman reported that "the ladies in the wealthy and
aristocratic portions of the city" were indulging in a new past-
time of spitting in the faces of Federal officers. Relating a
specific incident the trooper wrote:

> . . . as a group of Federal officers walked down
> the street a young lady stepped from the piazza, and
> timing her pace to that of the officers, reached the gate in

front of her house just as they were passing, and
deliberately spat in the face of the lieutenant.[6]

Such displays of contempt greatly annoyed the Yankees
who brought the situation under control by informing the fathers
of such young ladies that it would mean a trip to jail for the
fathers should the incident be repeated.

The occupation of Nashville allowed many journalists their
first opportunity to observe prominent secessionists. Northern
writers selected as special targets the socially prominent and
wealthy citizens on whom they placed the responsibility for the
war. In a book written for Northern readers, Nashville's
leading citizens were taken one by one and introduced. The
introductions were not flattering.

John Weaver, President of the Planter's Bank of
Nashville, was one such citizen. To Weaver was attributed such
statements as:

The true policy of the south is to set up for herself.
At any rate that she has done so, Tennessee must go with
her. As for our city, it will be the making of us . . .
Nashville stands by far the best chance of being the
capitol of the Confederacy, in which case our real estate
will advance two hundred per cent.[7]

Of Weaver it was written, "That such cool, clear, cautious
men as Weaver will entirely escape the calamities which he and
his class have greatly been instrumental in bringing upon the
ruined families of Tennessee, is too monstrous an idea to be
entertained."[8]

The widow of former President James K Polk came in for
her share of attention. The former First Lady was described as
"smart" rather than "tallented," and a true Rebel. Of her it was
written:

She has no children; She took to nursing the
rebellion of the southern aristocracy . . . It is stated upon
good authority that Mrs. Polk was greatly intent upon

*urging the men of Nashville to enter the rebel army, and
that she advised the young ladies of that city to send
petticoats and hooped skirts to young men who proved
backward in volunteering . . .She now reposes amid
comfort and elegance, while desolation sits brooding
around her over the face of a once happy and prosperous
country.*[9]

The Mayor of Nashville, Richard Cheatham, also attracted
the attention of Yankee observers. Of the Mayor it was said:

*Richard Cheatham Esq., Mayor of the rebel city of
Nashville, was a very rabid secessionist . . . The
patriotism, or rebellism, or call it what you will, of such
men, rarely carries them to the cannon's mouth, or to
severe death in the "last ditch." He has taken care of his
individual bacon, while hundreds of poor youth of
Tennessee, goaded on by his kindred efforts, now fill
unknown graves. Since the battle of Stone River and the
abandonment of rebel hopes, Cheatham has become
quite moderate and affable, and has ventured slightly into
Federal contracts, we hear it asserted. Good for
Richard! He will make just as good a Union man as he
did a bad rebel; for circumstances control such men.*[10]

Of special interest to Union writers was General William
G. Harding, one of Middle Tennessee's most prominent
citizens. In almost every respect, Harding typified to the
Northerner the people who brought on the war, and the most
severe editorials were reserved for his kind. Of General
Harding it was written:

*The old Government was quite too oppressive
upon him to be longer content. Let us endeavor to
ascertain the particular oppression under which this man
groaned . . . He had a little farm of some five thousand
acres. His mansion and all its appurtenances would, in
many ways, vie with those of the old manorial estates of*

225

the English baron . . . He was reputed to be worth two and a half million dollars . . . He kept two or three celebrated stallions. A herd of buffalo the genuine article ... bellowed and butted over his great pastures in half civilized mood . . . Added to this, Harding was a man of social note: he was a live general. Happily too, he had acquired this title without wading through any extensive ocean of blood.

Such being the social and pecuniary status of General Harding, the reader will inquire where comes in the unbearable oppression which drove such a man to rebellion. We cannot explain . . . Harding had wealth and family position— which latter mean something among Southern aristocracy— but he was not eminently a man of brains, and has no reputation as a speaker or writer. His ideas hardly rose above the eaves of his stables, and his tastes were upon the level with the roll of his grazing lands.[11]

Although the people of Nashville offered the most accessible source of character study for Unionists, the rural folk demanded their share of attention. General Lew Wallace, testifying before a Congressional Investigating Committee, was asked to relate incidents which might give insights into the people of Tennessee. He answered:

I recollect an instance that occurred out there in Tennessee. I went up to the gate of a secessionist, the owner of a beautiful property between Somerville and Memphis. In order to prevent his property from being injured . . . I had the negroes bring all the tubs and barrels he had on his premises out to the gate and fill them with water, and keep them filled for my troops when they passed. That man was sitting on the porch, and alongside him were two women, the wives of rebel officers then in the army. I knew them to be such, and I knew him to be a secessionist.

Can anybody doubt what my feelings would have prompted me to have done under the circumstances? It was to have said to my troops, "Boys, here are plenty of blackberries; yonder is an orchard full of ripening plums; you can see them on the trees from this distance; now help yourself." Isn't this a damned nice business to protect secesh property as we go along, and we can't even get a plum to eat off those trees.[12]

Wallace's subsequent testimony reflected a mixed perspective on the subject of slavery. When asked of his policy on allowing Federal troops to protect runaway slaves, the General replied that when the slave belonged to a secessionist the slave was assisted in his escape. But when the slave "belongs to a Union man I have no hesitation at all about the matter. I issue a peremptory order to the colonel of the regiment in whose camp the negro is, to give him to his master."[13]

The period of the war referred to in Wallace's comments was before and immediately following Shiloh when Northern leaders believed the rebellion would be short-lived. When subsequent events revealed a stubborn determination on the part of the South, a new and more drastic policy was adopted.

The new attitude was reflected in a letter written by James A. Connelly of Illinois.

I see this war in a different aspect from any in which I saw it before. To some extent I have had a peep behind the rebel curtains, and have been surprised at the very little honesty and very great ignorance to be found behind those curtains.

I have been at their homes and talked with the women while I dangled a dirty faced, half clad infantile rebel on my knee; I have gone dashing through their corn fields, their wheat fields, their cotton fields, meadows and door yards with a hundred good yankee "vandals" sweeping along my train; have eaten at their tables, and slept in their feather beds; have gone in their stables and taken my choice of their horses, to their pastures and taken my choice of their mules, to their granaries and hay stacks and fed my hungry horses, while my men went to their smoke houses, milk houses and the hen's nests gathering material for high living in camp . . .[14]

To the Federals, such practices were in keeping with their efforts to take the war to the people. To Southerners, such practices served to better establish the politician's predictions of the Yank as a thieving, ruthless invader who must be opposed to the very last breath. If the war had little reason in its beginning, the Federals were at least furnishing a reason for its continuance.

As Union soldiers scouted the rural countryside, they noted with amazement what they professed to be scenes foreign to their native North. Colonel Hans Christian Heg of Wisconsin wrote his wife from Humboldt, Tennessee:

Most every body is Secesh around here. They are very ignorant. The women sit in the hall and chew tobacco and eat snuff all day, while the niggers do their work for them. This is a fine country if the people were not lazy, this would be a great State . . . A large majority of them do not know how to spell their own names.[15]

Tennesseans became even more interesting to their Northern observers when viewed in the context of a social structure considered unique to the South. Colonel John Beatty of Ohio observed:

The poor whites are as poor as rot, and the rich are very rich. There is no substantial well-to-do middle class. The slaves are, in fact, the middle class. They are not considered so good, of course, as their masters, but a great deal better than the white trash.[16]

Believing as they evidently did that the illiterate people of the South had been plunged into war by their more educated leaders, the Yankees were sensitive to the educational opportunities afforded the people. Reflecting what seems a general reaction on the part of Northern soldiers, John Beatty wrote from Murfreesboro:

> *On the march hither we passed a little contemptible tumbledown, seven by nine frame schoolhouse. Over the door, in large letters, were the words CENTRAL ACADEMY.*
>
> *The boys laughed and said, "If this school is called an academy, what sort of things must their common schoolhouses be? But Tennessee is a beautiful state. All it lacks is free schools and free men.*[17]

While he felt the superiority which accompanies success, the Northern soldier was not blind to the suffering of those around him. Hans Heg observed:

> *We may talk about being tired of this war, and of suffering from it, but the suffering on our part has no comparison with that of these poor, deluded wretches that live on the lines where the armies are moving. How dearly, and how justly too, many are paying the penalty of their folly . . . The whole vicinity of Rutherford County is completely ruined. Every house is burned and not a fence to be seen. What has become of the poor women and children I do not know . . . I have got so I almost feel indifferent as to how rebels suffer, although many of them no doubt have been forced and fooled into the war.*[18]

Hans Christian Heg's own family would eventually suffer a greater loss than many of those whose plights he now observed. Nine months later the distinguished Colonel would die at Chickamauga.

The occupation of Middle Tennessee proved especially interesting to East Tennesseans serving in the Union Army. When the 13th Tennessee (Union Cavalry) moved to Gallatin they found the people rather cool. As one observer noted, "There were many pretty girls in Gallatin, but they were at first disposed to ignore the 'blue-coats,' but soon became quite friendly, and it was not long before every laddie had his lassie."[19]

The East Tennesseans had their own unique reaction to the institution of slavery. After seeing a "Contraband Camp" in Gallatin, one of them remarked: "It looked as if all the colored people in the world had gathered there." Continuing his observation, the East Tennessean said:

> *The Northern soldiers, who had preceded us at this place, had made the "colored brother" think he was the whole thing. When we first went there our men had to give the pavement to these "Contrabands," who did not seem to think they had anything to do but parade the sidewalks. Our men soon concluded they needed good strong walking sticks. Provided with these the colored gentry soon found it convenient to vacate the walk in ample time when he saw a "Thirteenth" soldier approaching.[20]*

Summing up his reaction, the East Tennessean said,

> *These mountaineers had known the colored man only as a slave and had lost little sleep over him in any way; they were not fighting to free the slave but to restore the Union.[21]*

It was a general practice during the first years of the war for owners of confiscated horses to be given a receipt for animals taken, after which, the owners reported to county seats to receive payment. According to a participant:

On those days the town was thronged with people. Many elderly men visited our camp, some well dressed and sporting "bay windows" and goldheaded canes — momentos of better and happier days. They made all sorts of importunities for the return of their horses, but in vain.[22]

Displaying an entrenched disgust for the wealthier citizens, the Federal soldier continued:

Col. Ingerton [William H Ingerton, Lt. Col. 13th Tenn. Cav. (Union)] *usually dismissed them summarily, telling them they were the class that had brought on all this trouble by their disloyalty . . . Other poor men came, stating that their horses were their only dependence to keep their families from starvation. Col. Ingerton listened to these with patience and often used his influence to have their horses returned. He was always kind to the lower classes and the more ignorant, who were rebels, saying they had been deluded by their richer and more influential men.*

We regret to say this was the exception to the rule with United States officers. They toadied to the wealthy who were responsible for the war, and were wined and dined by them, while they often treated the poor with incivility and needless cruelty.[23]

Of all the scenes experienced by Federal soldiers in Tennessee, the battlefield and its dreadful accumulation of death and misery would be the image burned most deeply in their memory. Two days after the Confederates had left Murfreesboro, Colonel John Beatty rode across the battlefield of Stone's River. That night he wrote his wife:

I ride over the battlefield. In one place a caisson and five horses are lying, the latter killed in harness, and all fallen together. Nationals and Confederates, young, middle-aged, and old, are scattered over the woods and

*fields for miles. Poor Wright, of my old company, lay
at the barricade in the woods which we stormed on the
night of the last day. Many others lay about him.
Farther on we find men with their legs shot off; one
with brains scooped out with a cannon ball; another with
half a face gone; another with entrails protruding;
young Winnegard, of the Third, has one foot off and
both legs pierced by grape at the thighs; another boy lies
with his hands clasped above his head, indicating that his
last words were a prayer. Many Confederate
sharpshooters lay behind stumps, rails, and logs, shot in
the head. A young boy, dressed in the Confederate
uniform, lies with his face turned toward the sky and
looks as if he might be sleeping. Poor boy, what
thoughts of home, mother, death, and eternity
commingled in his brain as the life blood ebbed away!
Many wounded horses are limping over the field. One
mule, I heard of, had a leg blown off on the first day's
battle; next morning it was on the spot where first
wounded; it was still standing there, not having moved
all day, patiently suffering, it knew not why nor for
what. How many poor men moaned through the cold
night in the thick woods, where the first day's battle
occured, calling in vain to man to help, and finally
making their last solemn petition to God.*[24]

If such scenes depressed the Yankees perhaps the
depression was offset by the realization that each such battlefield
would prove another stepping stone toward the final subjugation
of the Rebs.

In any event, when the weather warmed in the spring of
1863, there was little time for men in either army to spend idly.
Urged on by their leaders, the Yankees began devoting their
attention to the Confederates twenty-five miles to the south. The
people who sustained the Confederate Army became secondary
in importance to the Army itself. The Federals would continue

to move among the Rebel population, some of whom aroused pity, others of whom aroused wrath, but it really mattered little in the final analysis. Whether Southerners were motivated by ambitious, selfish desires, or whether they were victims of their own ignorance, they had to be subdued. It was the business of the Federal Army to see that they were subdued.

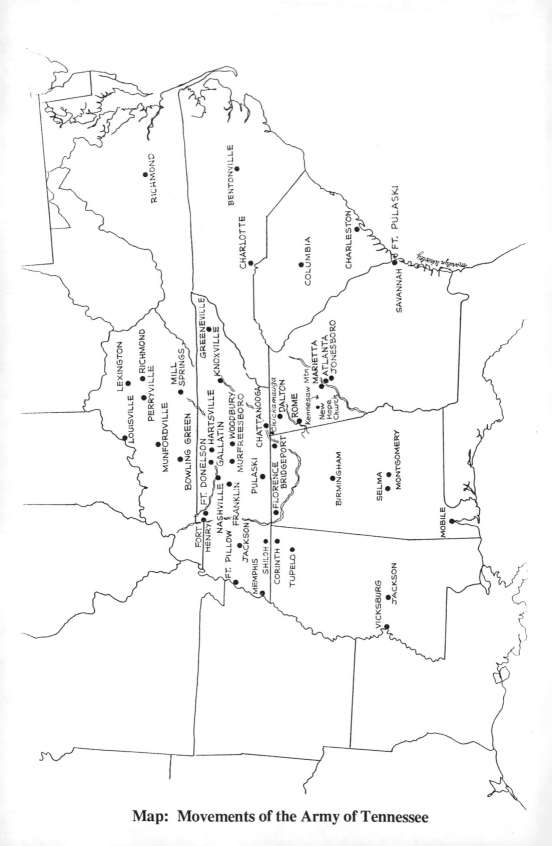

Map: Movements of the Army of Tennessee

Chapter X

The uncertain future
opens out to us

Like all events in which people participate, the Civil War essentially resolved into a series of personal encounters by the participants involved. The individual is the basic fiber of history, and when he becomes indistinguishable, history is denied its most unique ingredient. Major Andrew Jackson Campbell of the 48th Tennessee Infantry represents a basic fiber of this history and his story contributes greatly toward understanding the ultimate meaning of the war in which he participated.[1]

Jack Campbell's home was in the rich farming district of Maury County in Middle Tennessee. The village of Culleoka was near his farm and was listed as his home. The Campbells came to America from Ireland in 1725, migrated to Virginia and then to Tennessee. Andrew Jackson Campbell, the fifth son of John and Sarah Campbell, was born on February 14, 1834. Young Jack attended school near Culleoka until he contracted a case of typhoid fever and was forced to drop out. He later attended a school near Nashville, but the death of his father in 1850 once again forced him to return home. Since his older brothers had by that time left home, Jack became the chief provider for the remaining members of the family.

Like many Southerners, Jack Campbell opposed secession, but when war came he joined a local company. Eventually this company became a part of the 48th Tennessee and was sent to Fort Henry on the Tennessee River. Jack listened to the roar of the heavy guns as the Yankee navy bombarded the flooded fort, but he was not in the action until later in the day when he came under fire from Yankee ground forces. When Fort Henry fell, the 48th Regiment was ordered east to Fort Donelson, where it remained until that position also fell. While inside Fort Donelson Jack began making notes on his experiences, and in the process, wrote the history of his own involvement in the war.

Inside the fort Jack wrote:

> *The night of the 13th [February, 1862] it snowed and rained. We were without tents and bedclothes and had slept scarcely for three nights for watching the trenches. On the night of the 14th it snowed again. A few of us at this time slept, lying upon the ground and covering with what we could borrow . . . For four days I never slept more than six hours. Men were so exhausted that they actually slept in their position while shells were exploding around them and the deadly missils of the sharpshooters flying around their heads. During these four or five days I never had time to get water to wash my face and hands, being glad to get enough to drink. Being without canteens we were compelled to bring water in our cooking pans.*

When the battle re-opened, the 48th Regiment was sent to various positions along the line as the Confederates sought to repel the Union assault. After darkness descended, Jack entered:

> *Night closed on a hard day's fight of twelve hours, from sunup to sundown. The fitful glare of the moon from behind the clouds shone upon the bloody field of*

*Donelson where, lying upon a bed of snow with no
covering, but the blue canopy of heaven, were the dead
and dying Southerners intermingled with the Northmen
who were pressing an invasion upon us. The
beleaguered garrison at Donelson knew that they were
surrounded by a greatly superior force, but the thought
of wife, mother, daughter, sister, and fireside being left
to the mercies of a remorseless foe, caused them to fight
with a desperation scarcely ever witnessed.*

When Sunday came, Jack expected it to bring victory;
instead it brought surrender. He knew of the escape of General
John Floyd and said:

*Floyd, with the greater part of his brigade,
employed a boat until eight o'clock in taking them off,
when word was sent to the wharf that longer delay
would endanger the boat and all on board. Word was
given to shove the boat out, when a rush was made from
the crowded wharf by men in mud and water to their
knees. They were repelled by three or four officers at
the bow of the boat, cutting them with swords.*

Jack, along with thousands of other Confederate soldiers,
was loaded aboard a Union boat and sent north to prison. The
trip was not pleasant. The diet consisted of raw meat and
crackers and, according to Jack,

*The prisoners, huddled up from top to bottom of
the boat with but little means of keeping warm or
cooking, driven about like a herd of swine, of course,
were low spirited. At night we had to pile up like hogs,
scarcely room enough for all on the floor, which was
covered over with mud, slop, and tobacco spittle, well
tamped up through the day.*

As the prison boat made its way along the river, large
crowds gathered to view the captured Rebs. The prisoners,

unwilling to appear subdued, greeted the curious onlookers with Rebel songs and "three cheers for Jeff Davis." At St. Louis, the men disembarked and boarded a train which took them to Camp Chase near Columbus, Ohio. It took only one glance for the men to see that their new home had been designed with neither comfort nor convenience in mind. Jack recorded his impression.

> We were marched into a pen, covering a half acre of ground, surrounded with a plank fence twenty feet high, upon which were placed sentinels. Inside this and an adjoining pen were about a thousand prisoners, with only house room for about a third of the number. Tents were stretched in the mud for those to pile up in who could not get into the shanties. Our clothing was all left outside to be examined and we were tramping around like a herd of swine, so thick we could hardly turn around, nothing to eat but crackers and nothing scarcely to cook with when we drew rations. At this point I must confess I went under deeper than I ever did before. My feelings can better be imagined than described.

Soon after Jack arrived at Camp Chase the snow began falling. There was not enough shelter for the sick, some of whom were forced to lie in the cold. In spite of the discomfort around them, most of the Rebs were sustained by a stubborn determination to survive. They returned insults to those who taunted them and sang Rebel songs to their tormentors. They sometimes brought on confrontations with their guards and sometimes they fought each other. After several weeks in such confinement, the winter months began to give way to warming temperatures, and hope for escape or exchange became prominent among the men.

In May, Jack and his fellow prisoners were transferred to Johnson's Island prison near Lake Erie. On August 9, 1862, the young Tennessean wrote in his diary concerning the death of a fellow prisoner at the hands of the guard. The incident aroused indignation within the prisoners and Jack responded by writing, "Everytime I see a villainous yankee it makes my blood boil to think we are to be shot down like dogs without any provocation whatever and no means of redress."

Witnessing the death of his fellow prisoner prompted Jack to reflect on his situation, and two days later, he wrote:

Lying with my head in my prison window and looking out upon the calm waters of Lake Erie, which presents a striking contrast to the state of our country, where men of the same race are engaged in deadly combat, deluging her fair fields with human blood and strewing her plains with the dead and dying, and where one continual roll of battle in all its fury is raging from one side of her borders to the other, I am led to ask myself the question, When will this cruel and bloody war end? It is bringing suffering and anguish to the hearts of untold thousands. Its progress is traced in the tears of the widow and the orphan. It is shrouding the country in mourning for the untimely death of fathers, brothers, sons, and husbands. The end is hard to divine. In this reflecting mood reminiscences of home and of home's loved ones spring up in my fancy. I see their smiling faces, the inviting groves and the old winding streamlets; the old school house and the familiar church; the smiling faces that once peopled them. I again wonder when will this relentless war end and with it my labors, toils, and dangers as a Confederate soldier in defence of Southern homes. I will look forward to this period with hope and anxiety and with the help of God will strike with a will until this end is attained.

But since I have left home swarms of despoilers have invaded my native heath. The old homesteads are laid in ashes by the Huns, Goths, and Vandals of the North. The seats in the old church are vacant. The

*school boy is no longer seen engaged in innocent sport
around the old school house. His gray-haired father is
dragged off in chains, his brother is murdered and his
mother and sister are no longer secure from the violence
of indignities. Our fathers can no longer worship God
under their own vine and fig tree . . . From my prison
my thoughts wander far away and when I think of the
condition of my country and my own, time drags heavily
and a sigh for freedom escapes my bosom and a fervent
wish springs up for Herculean strength to avenge the
wrongs of my people.*

Rainy days were especially difficult for the prisoners. It
seemed that the chilly dampness reflected a spiritual depression
that was always seeking a means of expression. Days of the
week lost their distinctiveness and, each in its turn, became little
more than a period of daylight set apart by two periods of
darkness. Even Sundays lost their meaning. "Sunday with us
has lost all its joys and attractions," wrote Jack. "It is the same
long, dreary, tiresome day of yesterday."

Throughout August of 1862, rumors circulated constantly
that the prisoners were to be exchanged. Each new day brought
hope, but that hope died in the disappointing silence that came
with sundown. Finally, late in the month, word was received
that the exchange was arranged and on August 31st Jack wrote,
"Today we have all been in a bustle, wearing bright faces,
packing our clothes, rolling our blankets and cooking our
rations and putting them away for the trip; carrying our baggage
to the wharf and giving our surplus plunder to our Southern
brethen who are to remain."

The next morning the men were up well before daylight
and had their meager breakfast by candlelight. Many of them
were already at the gate when daylight came, waiting to begin
the trip to Vicksburg, Mississippi, where the exchange was to
occur. At 2:20 P.M. the trains were loaded and the happy
journey toward freedom began. Jack rejoiced at the prospects

and thoroughly enjoyed the sights as the train followed its course. The corn was still green and the countryside still retained the remnants of the passing summer season. At Cairo, Illinois, on September 8, 1862, the men were transferred to boats, and two days later, arrived at Memphis.

When the prisoners finally reached Vicksburg, Jack found the town disappointing. Freedom was not as glamorous as the thoughts it had inspired. There was no place to sleep, prices were unreasonably high, and it seemed that nobody was especially glad to see the returning captives. Jack's comment was, "This place is nearer played out than any place I ever saw." He was quite happy when he received an order to leave.

Four days later, the 48th Tennessee reorganized, and although Jack was assured of the support necessary to be elected colonel, he refused, and, instead, became the regiment's major. A few days later, a boil developed on his arm and at Water Valley, Mississippi, he wrote,

> Could use only one arm and could scarcely get a citizen to help me with my baggage . . . Soldiers are not a whit more respected in this country than a negro . . . The citizens use all means they can to fleece them of what little money they have. They would see soldiers at the devil before they would let them in private homes.

Dissatisfied with Water Valley, Jack decided to move. The arm continued giving him trouble and on the 21st of October he recorded in his diary, " Had high fever yesterday evening and last night; Suffered dreadfully with my arm; couldn't sleep a wink. Not able to help myself and among entire strangers. I feel the want of friends more than ever before in my life."

Later in the month Jack observed:

> Remain in by myself nursing my arm all day. I think I would like to be at home and I think my being there would be appreciated. Silently suffer . . . suffer with no one to console or try to alleviate the pain. I long

for the golden wings of peace, that I may return to my loved ones.

By November 7, 1862, Jack's arm was much improved, and to add to his pleasure, he was granted a twenty-day furlough. The young soldier arrived home "With what delight no one can tell except one who has experienced a return home after an absence of a year, and seven months of that in prison among semi-civilized people." The days swept by as if on wings. He visited friends, his sister made him a uniform, and in the meantime he crowded in all the enjoyment the hours would accommodate. When his furlough ended he

...bade adieu to home and friends, with a fervent wish that this war would soon terminate in an honorable peace and soldiers be permitted to return from the hardships of camp life and enjoy the comforts of home. The prospects of a speedy peace are anything but flattering.

For Jack Campbell it was a return to duty and a return to a life that had, to this point, brought little but pain and disappointment. On December 14th he rejoined his regiment at Port Hudson, Louisiana, but within a week he was sick again. The illness this time stemmed from a lung disorder Jack had developed in prison, but unlike his previous illnesses he found the people of the community sympathetic and helpful. Of these people Jack said:

...I shall never forget their kindness to me while sick and far away from home and relatives, where there is no kind and loving mother or sister to minister to my wants or to sympathize with me in my affliction.

On Christmas Day, 1862, Jack wrote:

This Christmas day brings with it no joy or swelling of the heart with hope and life. The young ladies send me eggnog and other nice things, but I am

242

too sick to enjoy them. [Three days later he could] *Feel myself slowly improving; need some tonic, but can't get any.*

When the last day of 1862, arrived, Jack turned to his diary and attempted to bring into focus the myriad events that had happened since the war began. He no doubt wrote without the knowledge that at Stone's River a desperate battle had begun. He said:

The Year Eighteen Hundred and Sixty-two comes to a close on this bright, bracing, beautiful day after witnessing many tragic events. To the Confederacy and in fact the American Continent it has been a most eventful year. The destinies of the chivalrous South have hung in the balance. The nation has been covered with the deepest gloom; the stoutest hearts have yielded to despair. Gold worshipping friends of the South have joined the Yankees and have abandoned their people to a ruthless mob. To me it has been a year of suffering, both mentally and physically . . May the next twelve months be fraught with fewer trials and troubles to the Confederacy and to myself is my prayer.

Today our prospects are brighter than at any time during the history of this momentous struggle. Yet I cannot feel rejoiced and light-hearted in view of the many heart-rending scenes occasioned by this clash of arms between the North and South, the many valuable lives lost, the many desolate firesides, the widowed and the orphaned. Truly our Southland is in mourning for the lost whose bones lie bleaching upon a hundred battle fields and around Northern prisons. Oh, how long is this to continue?

Jack's reflective mood continued into the next day, New Year's Day, 1863.

Happy New Year. Would it were a happy one for me. But the bright, smiling faces that were wont to greet us in hope are absent and in mourning. This day to the soldier, has the same monotonous routine as yesterday. The sick and wounded here have no cessation of their pain; languishing perhaps in some filthy hosptial with scarcely the attention deserved by the meanest of God's creatures; dying upon the streets of our most populous cities without moving a chord of sympathy in the breast of his fellow man. The uncertain future opens out to us. The clash of hostile arms still resounds over our land. No one can tell but that the casualities of war will forever separate us from home and home's loved ones. But yet hope, sweet hope, whispers that we shall meet again, and peace shall reign over our desolated fields.

The sickness which drained Jack's body grew steadily worse. The weaker he became, the greater was his desire to return home. "Nightly in my dreams," he wrote, "I am at home attending to the business of the farm, but awake to find it all a bitter mockery." Faced with the fact that his lungs were getting no better, Jack applied for a furlough, but he knew its approval would be slowed by the cumbersome routine of army administration. Throughout most of January he suffered too badly to write in his diary, and on the 31st, he suffered a hemorrhage. The next week, physicians informed him that the upper portion of his lungs were diseased, but they did not indicate the seriousness of the condition.

The news of the infection intensified Jack's desire to return home. On February 9th, he wrote,

Can get no candle to eat supper by and it never comes until an hour after dark. I am completely out of patience about my leave of absence. My condition is worse and I am kept here by the neglect and foolish orders of men who pretend intelligence.

244

Even with his limited knowledge of the human body, Jack knew he must start home soon if he ever expected to make it. Helplessly he wrote:

> *Have almost despaired of getting home . . . No one can tell the anguish I have suffered, waiting for my leave of absence, in my anxiety to get started away from this villainous hole and climate. I pray God to sustain me in this extremity . . . I am constantly tortured with anxiety that I shall be too weak to travel. And perhaps when I hear, if my papers are approved, I can get no one to go with me.*

On February 13th, Jack's diary reads, "With ecstacies of delight I received my furlough this evening after supper." The next day was his 28th birthday and he celebrated it by leaving Port Hudson for his home in Maury County. He sold his horse, bridle, and saddle for $325, got a seat on the train and made himself as comfortable as possible. He noticed that outside the train peach blossoms were already in bloom; hopefully they might be symbolic.

The trip home was anything but easy. Railway bridges were out and schedules meant nothing. Sometimes Jack was forced to wait for days while roads and bridges were repaired and during those periods he found little help or sympathy from citizens who lived nearby.

At Vicksburg he learned that the train might leave early and so "Started to the depot at daylight through the mud, afraid to wait for a hack." The trip was for nothing; the train did not run that day. The next morning:

> *Got up two hours before day and started to the office before it was light, through mud and water shoemouth deep. Went into office to dry my feet. One of the clerks came in and I proposed to move my baggage out of the way. He said that I had better move out myself.*

Wet, cold, and weak from his illness Jack was forced out into the early morning dampness, but finally received permission to sit by a resident's fire. He observed, "The exposure is making me cough a great deal."

By March 1, 1863, Jack had reached Chattanooga and ten days later he arrived at home. He wrote in his diary, "Reached home pretty badly used up."

Two weeks later, Major Andrew Jackson Campbell died.

Chapter XI

God help us in our need

The two columns of the Confederate Army that had left Murfreesboro following the battle of Stone's River arrived at their destinations toward the end of New Year's week, 1863. One column settled in the Tullahoma area — the other near Shelbyville. The morale of the men suffered as a result of their recent experience. Fence rails burned on open fires, furnishing only temporary relief from the wet, cold weather that continued as the winter season progressed. Men who possessed no clothes other than those on their backs shivered in the knowledge that matters would likely get worse.

Food was scarce. In many regiments .the men were responsible for securing their own rations, and often after searching for miles around, they returned to camp with little more to eat than they had before. The countryside was in the grip of winter, nothing was growing, and few citizens were anxious to share their own meager supplies of food with the haggard individuals who now moved among them.

Resentment against Braxton Bragg was rampant. This resentment, when combined with hunger and cold, made for a most unhappy situation. Fayette McDowell wrote his sister Amanda:

I should feel very well if we had anything to eat but our chance is bread without grease and beef that can climb a tree . . . I wish those in favor of carrying on this war had to eat a whole cow horns and all every day one each. I mean until they are ready to quit.[1]

The results of their battles proved disappointing to the Rebs, but at least some of the incidents associated with them provided interesting topics of conversation — like the "preacher election" at Murfreesboro. Before the battle, a character by the name of Mack Luna decided he would contest the application of one Lige Hester for chaplain. Luna challenged Hester to a public demonstration of their respective talents, following which the men of the regiment were to make their selection. Luna swore he could outpreach Hester and to prove it he mounted a stump and belted out a few off-colored songs followed by a discourse on the topic, "Wher de hen scratch, dar de bug also." After delivering his tirade, Luna told his highly amused audience: "Now if you don't think I'm a better preacher than Lige Hester, vote for him, darn you." Luna won the election, but his officers failed to bestow the proper credentials upon him and his ministry came to an inglorious end.[2]

Members of the 20th Tennessee remembered that, on the night before the battle, the men of Company "C" were sitting by a fire when, suddenly, someone heard a rooster crow. "Scouts" were immediately dispatched to investigate. In a few minutes a member of the regiment returned "with his hand on the rooster's throat and the other holding his wings to keep him from fluttering . . ." Not satisfied with the trimmings available, another soldier was sent to a nearby regiment to "steal a piece of bacon and a sack of flour to make dumplings with the rooster for the next day."[3]

Beneath the facade of humor which was so apparent, the men could not help but be aware of the more serious consequences of their recent history. Every casualty at Murfreesboro represented a personal loss to many people and the fact that the loss had occurred in the context of wholesale slaughter in no way lessened its individual impact. Casualties were people, they were relatives and friends, and when such relationships are disrupted suddenly, an emotional injury results that only time can heal. Even grandmothers far removed from the battle scene became victims of its barbarity. Before the Battle of Stone's River, Alben A. Abernathy of the 18th Tennessee, wrote his grandmother:

I was much pleased with the contents of your letter, and with the good council it was filled with. I will strive to come up to it and as you say, if I am slain after obeying the commands of our heavenly Father, I will not be lost in the regions of torment, but will be saved in heaven.

There I hope to meet all my friends and kindred. Should I fall upon the battle field, Oh what could be the feelings of myself, upon the battlefield if I had' not strived to serve God, wretched wretched, I know. But many seldom think of being killed themselves, but only think of killing others. It is not my desire to kill any man nor never has been   But I fear I will be forced to do the like before very long.[4]

Young Abernathy was killed at Stone's River.

The war had a dramatic impact on all the women of Tennessee, but unfortunately, few of them recorded their feelings. One who did was Mrs. L. Virginia French of McMinnville. On the day that the Battle of Stone's River began she wrote in her journal:

This has been a most eventful day. At daylight this morning heavy cannonading was heard in the direction of Murfreesboro. It was a clear cold morning, with a brisk breeze setting from the North. I suppose there was 50 men left town for the scene of the conflict — and everything in the shape of a soldier went . . . All the morning there was a continuous roar of artillery — heaviest from 9 o'clock until noon . . . I commenced writing my book in the morning . . and the sound of the firing came rolling into the quiet of my chamber every few seconds. Every now and then I would pause in my occupation to utter the fervent prayer, "God protect those gallant men who stand between us and the foe!" ... I felt keenly how much depended on the issue of this battle . . . This battle was to decide whether or not we were still to have a home, or be sent forth as refugees to find a sojourning place in a land of strangers.[5]

It was almost dark when Mrs. French received the good news that the day had gone to the Confederates. The message from Murfreesboro was, "We have taken 2 million worth of stores, and given the Yankees hell." Upon receiving this news she wrote:

And when I went to bed as I lay there so comfortable and cosy, I could not go to sleep for thinking of the many poor fellows who were then lying on the battlefield — some cold in death — others shivering with cold and writhing in pain. The cold clear moon looked down upon them, for it was a brilliant, frosty night — but who was there with a warm kind glance to cheer their last agonized hours?[6]

The next day was New Year's Day, 1863, and Mrs. French observed, "A New Year commenced today — heaven grant that ere it ends *peace* may reign among us once more." The Warren County resident did not write in her journal again until January 4th. By that time she had learned the truth, and remembered how she had felt on New Year's Day:

How bright and hopeful I felt that bright morning — how I expected to sit down day after day to write in my book — and to succeed in it — Alas! how was this triumph sullied with blood. After supper we were all sitting in the back room when Cooper [evidently a slave] *came to the door and said "Mas John, Mr. Spurlock has just come from Murfreesboro en he wants you to come up there. Mr. Cap Spurlock is killed and they are bringing his body up now." Great God! I felt as if stunned by a thunderbolt. "Cap" Spurlock* killed! *I could not believe it. I could not realize it. Alas! alas! it was too true . . . We went into the parlor at John's* [Captain D.C. Spurlock's father] *to see poor Cap, as soon as he was laid out. His uniform was very bloody and had to be cut off him — they had dressed him in a fine suit of black cloth such as he used to wear before the war began. How noble and handsome he looked, and how natural . . . On Friday afternoon we attended the funeral . . he looked the Christian hero he was . . . Few looked on him without tears — his family and friends were overwhelmed with grief . . . As Miss Sophia Searcy stood for hours beside his coffin, weeping, I wondered if she remembered the time when she said, "Let the war come! I want it to come! I want these Tennesseans roused — let it come — we are ready.*[7]

As Captain Spurlock was being buried, those at the funeral heard the tremendous roar of the cannon that spelled doom for the advancing Confederate line under Breckinridge. Later, Mrs. French was told that the army was retreating to Shelbyville, but she had doubts.

They say this — but they will retreat to Chattanooga, as sure as you live — and we will be left here at the mercy of those savages, the Yankees. What is to become of us God only knows . . . I feel as though it was no use to try to save anything — for we are ruined let us go or stay. We may as well give it up — I do —

251

and if we save our lives it is all that I expect. God help us in our need![8]

Meanwhile at Shelbyville, the men passed the winter months scratching lice and trying to keep warm. Sometimes the former effort assisted in accomplishing the latter! Spencer Talley found himself inhabited with the pesky little camp followers and "had all my clothes put into boiling water with a view of being rid of them but it was not so." Finding that hot water would not kill the lice the men developed a more effective method. They stretched their garments "by inserting stiff brush & held them over a blazing fire until almost hot enough to burn."[9] This approach to the problem proved so effective that lice as a major nusiance disappeared for a while and all energy could be devoted to keeping warm and seeking food.

The extensive casualties at Murfreesboro necessitated the reorganization of regiments. Depleted regiments were consolidated to create one of near regular size, but officers found out quickly that such an operation was not without its risks. Regimental pride approached fierceness and regimental flags were as sacred a mark of identification as family names. To suggest that one regiment consolidate under the numerical symbol and flag of another was to invite open warfare among men who would just as quickly defend their honor from each other as from Yankees. Realizing the situation, officers accomplished a compromise by allowing each group within a new regiment to retain its original battle flag. Such a practice, no doubt, offered solace to Union generals who would later report they had faced three Confederate regiments, when, in reality, they had faced only one regiment with three battle flags.

While the private soldiers busied themselves meeting the demands of survival, their generals pursued other objectives. Talks of duels between brigade and divisional commanders made the rounds as high ranking officers sought to protect their honor against accusations growing out of the recent battle.

Regardless of their personal differences the subordinate generals agreed on one thing: Braxton Bragg must go.

Old John Savage had already left for home. As at Perryville, Savage believed his 16th Tennessee Regiment had been grossly mishandled at Murfreesboro and he would have no more of it. He also believed that military rank in the Confederate Army depended primarily on pre-war politics, and that many of the generals were cowards. Above all, he professed to believe that the leaders of the South were steering a conscientious, God fearing people down the road to sure destruction.

Of Braxton Bragg, Savage wrote:

> . . . *If General Bragg was a farmer the eagles and the owls would catch all his turkeys, the hawks and the possums would catch all his chickens, the minks and the coons would eat all his ducks, the foxes would catch all his young pigs, the rabbits would bark his apple trees, and he would never know how to set a trap, snare or deadfall to catch one of them.*[10]

Jefferson Davis became so concerned that he sent General Joseph E. Johnston to Middle Tennessee to investigate, but after a three-week study, Johnston recommended that Bragg be retained. Disappointed and somewhat shocked, the men and officers decided to make the best of what they considered an unfortunate state of affairs.

Toward spring, the lot of soldiers improved considerably. Food was brought from the south, new clothing was issued, and permanent camps were erected. In view of the improved situation, soldiers found themselves with little entertainment to occupy their leisure time. In the absence of planned entertainment, the men improvised for themselves, and if such entertainment possessed qualities that made the chaplains frown, it at least served to neutralize the ever-threatening enemy — boredom.

As Marcus Toney put it:

The two great evils attending war are drinking and gambling. Mr. McGrew kept a drugstore on the square in Shelbyville, and by some means it was ascertained that he had some whiskey in the cellar, and one night some soldiers got into it and took the whole stock, consisting of about half a barrel; and the old mill situated on the river, was frequently robbed of its stock; and in unloading commissaries at the depot the soldiers would make <u>mistakes</u> and throw meat under the depot, and at nightfall bring it to camp.[11]

At Shelbyville, the Confederate officers faced a problem which was new to them. They were camping in and around a town predominantly Union in its sympathies. The situation called for the organization of a secret service force to maintain control. So strong was the Union sentiment that local citizens encouraged the soldiers to desert. Squads of Confederate secret police roamed the streets to keep a watch on soldiers and citizens alike. Although few, if any, local people were apprehended, the few soldiers who were caught were subjected to a punishment which soon put a halt to desertion.

Three such deserters were caught in early February and sentenced to die before a firing squad. A soldier who witnessed the execution described it by saying:

On the day of their execution they were handcuffed, placed in an ambulance, and taken to the place where they were to be shot. Strong appeals were made to General Bragg to pardon them, but he sternly refused . . . Arriving at the spot of execution, they faced death bravely. They refused to be blindfolded . . . The condemned men were taken out on the Fairfield Pike to where the command from which they had deserted was encamped, and all three were shot by a platoon of soldiers. They fell dead at the first discharge. They were wrapped in their blankets and buried. The execution cast a shadow of gloom over the army as well as over the citizens.[12]

Realizing that his army was dangerously undermanned, Bragg sought recruits from the surrounding area. Parties were dispatched in all directions to seek new men. So urgent was the need that recruiters were sent through the Yankee lines into upper Middle Tennessee in the hope that replacements could be found. More often than not, the recruiters came back empty handed. In White County, potential recruits hid out even after threats had been made to burn their homes. The appeal was no longer to patriotism, but to fear. Even so, most Tennesseans saw more security in staying at home than in following an army that had never won a battle.

2.

While the main army remained relatively inactive, the same was not true with the cavalry guarding its flanks. General Joe Wheeler guarded the right flank at McMinnville, while Nathan Bedford Forrest occupied a similar role on the left at Columbia. Forrest's command had experienced a busy winter season. During the Battle of Stone's River, Forrest led his men into West Tennessee to operate against the supply lines of General Grant. Thrusting his column deep into Yankee territory, the Rebel horseman went almost to the Mississippi River before turning back. On its return to Columbia the command encountered the enemy at Parker's Cross Roads. Forrest had been forced to retrieve his men from what appeared to be a disaster. When it was found that the Yanks were in his front and rear, Forrest was asked what he proposed to do. He replied, "We'll charge them both ways," and with the timely assistance of two regiments that had been guarding the flanks, that is what he did. A narrow path to safety was cleared, and soon the Confederates were crossing the Tennessee River into friendly territory.

During the latter part of January, Forrest was called to Shelbyville by Bragg and told that Joe Wheeler was on his way to make an attack on Fort Donelson. Forrest was ordered to overtake Wheeler's column which included eight hundred of Forrest's men, and support the attack.

The idea did not appeal to Forrest in the least, but his advice went unheeded. When the column was overtaken, Forrest found his men poorly equipped with food, clothing and ammunition, but he found Wheeler determined to carry through the attack. In the biting cold of early February, 1863, the attack failed and Forrest lost one-fourth of the men engaged. After having two horses shot from under him, the Rebel leader ordered his men away in retreat. Embittered at the results of the expedition, Forrest met Wheeler in a cabin south of Dover and informed him, "I mean no disrespect to you . . but there is one thing I do want you to put in that report to General Bragg — tell him that I will be in my coffin before I will fight again under your command.".[13] Thus two more military leaders were added to the growing list of those whose personal feelings could well become a factor in the prosecution of the war.

For Forrest's men, the winter months were spent in sharp skirmishes with the enemy in the Columbia-Franklin area. The confidence lost during the Fort Donelson attack was quickly restored as the skilled cavalry watched the Yankees give way before their dashing attacks and stubborn resistance. By the first of April, they were razor-sharp and ready for a major assignment. Braxton Bragg could furnish the assignment.

It had long been an objective of the Federal High Command to disrupt the railroad between Chattanooga and Atlanta and during the summer of 1862, a daring raid was planned at Shelbyville, Tennessee, under the direction of Master Sgt. James J. Andrews. After meeting east of the town, the raiders broke up to make their way to the rendezvous point south of Chattanooga, where the Yankee raid would occur. They met at the appointed time and place and the operation began in earnest. A locomotive was captured for the purpose of tearing up the tracks, but unfortunately the Yankee raiders stole the engine of a very determined Rebel who took off after them on foot. After a few hours, during which the indignant engineer utilized hand cars, engines going backward, and a lot of help from north Georgians, the Yankees were captured and the railroad remained unharmed. Andrews and eight of his raiders died on the gallows for a plan they believed would bring them undying glory.[14]

Now in the spring of 1863, it was time for another try. There was much to be gained for the Union cause should the attempt succeed. Federal plans called for either driving or maneuvering Bragg out of Middle Tennessee and it was assumed that he would retreat to Chattanooga. If the railroad from Atlanta could be disrupted, it would force the Army of Tennessee to retreat further south. The prospects of such a situation urged the Yankees to action.

The fortunes of the Federal effort would ride on the shoulders of Colonel Abel D. Streight of Indiana. It was he and James A. Garfield who had blueprinted the plan and its execution would depend on Streight's talents.

Streight's plan was worthy of praise. It called for him to leave Nashville with a highly select group of men and travel by way of the Cumberland River to the Tennessee River on which he would proceed to Eastport, Mississippi. From Eastport he would travel by land across the state of Alabama and into Georgia where his command would strike the railroad at Rome. Streight, with two thousand men, left Nashville on April 10, 1863, and by the 19th he was at Eastport. It was there that his troubles began.

While Streight was camped at Eastport, Rebel cavalrymen in the area slipped in and turned loose the mules which were the expedition's chief source of transportation. Mules scattered throughout the countryside and Yanks had to spend several days rounding them up. While the mule search continued, Forrest left Columbia, Tennessee "like a whirlwind" to give chase to this new threat to the railroad.

The Federal column recaptured its mules and moved leisurely across Alabama unaware that Forrest was in pursuit. By the night of April 29th, only sixteen miles separated the two forces.

When Streight finally learned of Forrest's presence, he became understandably excited and drove his men day and night in an effort to shake free of his pursuer. But each day found Forrest closer than the day before. On the morning of May 2nd, the Yankees crossed a deep creek three miles west of Gadsden and burned the bridge just as Forrest's men came in sight. Forrest asked the occupants of a nearby farmhouse the location of the nearest undamaged bridge, and found that the closest bridge was two miles away. Living in the farmhouse were a widow, Sansom, and her daughter Emma, who informed Forrest that on their land there existed a "lost " ford which could be crossed when the water was low. Emma volunteered to guide the Confederates, and leaping on Forrest's horse behind him, pointed the way. In a matter of minutes, the Rebs were crossing the river and were soon in pursuit of their enemy.

On the morning of May 3, 1863, Forrest's command, which had now dwindled to under five hundred, found Streight's force at Lawrence, Alabama. The Yankees were tired from marching all night, and although they numbered, at this time, some sixteen hundred, their taste for war had vanished.

Forrest lost no time in demanding that Streight surrender. Under a flag of truce Forrest told the Yankee raider, "I have a column of fresh troops at hand, now nearer Rome than you are. You cannot cross the river in your front. I have men enough right here to run over you." John Allan Wyeth, Forrest's biographer, observed, "In all this there was not a word of truth; but this was war, and in war everything is fair."15

After a short meeting with his officers, Streight decided to surrender. One of Forrest's soldiers, J.T. Garretson, was present during the surrender and wrote the folk at home:

> *Gen Forrest bluffed him into surrender. Streight first refused to Surrender and Gen. Forest told him "I have you surrounded   Shoot and you will Smell Hell in about ten minutes," and started off, when they called him back and run up the white flag. We marched them off from their Armes and off to Rome. When Streight found he was bluffed he complained to Gen Forest and cried like a child   Gen Forest told him he was a Prisoner of war and he didn't want to hear another word out of him.*[16]

Forrest and his men rode on to Rome where the citizens feasted them with food and drink. They were hailed as deliverers from the curse of Yankee capture and the town wished to express its appreciation. The chase had been difficult, it had called for extreme sacrifices, but it had been successful. The trains still ran from Chattanooga to Atlanta.

3.

As the star of Nathan Bedford Forrest gained more and more luster in the Confederate sky, that of General Earl Van Dorn fell permanently from the constellation of Rebel raiders which had shined so brightly during the first years of the war.

Earl Van Dorn was a dashing, handsome, Mississippian whose qualities of graciousness endeared him to the people he met, especially the ladies. Van Dorn had graduated from West Point in 1842, and , at the age of forty-two, was a promising commander of cavalry. The preceding fall had been eventful for Van Dorn.   On October 4, 1862, he had attacked firmly entrenched Federals at Corinth, Mississippi, and had been severely repulsed. A Court of Inquiry had been appointed to investigate the matter, but Van Dorn had been found innocent of any misconduct. In December of the same year, after he had been assigned to the cavalry, he swept in behind Grant's main force and destroyed a major supply base at Holly Springs, Mississippi, thereby upsetting the Union general's original attempt to take Vicksburg. For this feat Van Dorn was hailed as another in the illustrious list of Rebel cavalrymen.

While Forrest was away on the Streight raid, Van Dorn was at Spring Hill, Tennessee, guarding the left flank of the Confederate Army. As usual, the duties assigned him were performed with an acceptable degree of efficiency. He was a fighter and the Yankees knew it — they left him alone. Unfortunately for Van Dorn, it was his extra-military activities that would prove his undoing.

In the quiet village of Spring Hill lived a most attractive lady by the name of Jessie Peters. Her physician husband was away much of the time attending his farming interests in Mississippi. In Dr. Peters' absence General Van Dorn became a frequent visitor to the Peters residence, and according to Dr. Peters, " I arrived at my home on 12 April, and was alarmed at the distressing rumors which prevailed in the neighborhood in relation to the attentions paid by General Van Dorn to my wife."[17]

After the rumors became more persistent, Peters set a trap for Van Dorn by feigning a trip to Shelbyville, while actually concealing himself on the premises. According to Peters:

The second night after my supposed and pretended absence, I came upon the creature, about half-past two o'clock at night, where I expected to find him. He readily acknowledged my right to kill him, and I fully intended to do so.[18]

In exchange for the promise of a statement from Van Dorn exonerating his wife, Peters let the matter be. Two days later, May 7, 1863, Peters called on Van Dorn and demanded the statement, but found the general in no mood to accomodate him. Tempers flared; Peters drew his gun and fired. Earl Van Dorn died instantly.

To the Confederates, it was a plain case of a jealous old man murdering an intemperate but attractive Southern General. To the Yankees it was justifiable homicide brought on by the immoral conduct of a fiendish Rebel General. In any event, the Yankees lost a formidable opponent, the Rebels lost a promising General, and Mrs. Peters lost a fond admirer.

4.

Along the main line at Tullahoma and Shelbyville, Bragg's army waited. The first weeks of spring had not aroused the Federals at Murfreesboro and Bragg had done nothing to initiate action with his enemy.

Although recruiting efforts had not progressed well, there were at least a few men who were intent on entering the army. It had been almost two years since Nelse Rainey of Columbia had signed his name to a Rebel roster only to have his father declare he was too young. The aspiring young Reb was eighteen now and , according to Nelse, his father had

> *...for some time promised to let me go when the opportunity occurred to get me in a good company. He had bought a good horse for me. Old Mammy spun the black and white mix to be woven into cloth for my clothes. A neighbor wove the cloth. Mother made me a jacket and trousers, an army coat with caps. Had a pair of good strong boots made ... Pa had a "McClelland" saddletree ... nicely covered, all ready for war when the time should come.*[19]

The time was not long in coming. When General Van Dorn moved into Middle Tennessee one of his brigades, under the command of General William H. (Red) Jackson,[20] camped almost in sight of the Rainey home. When Jackson's cavalry rode away from Columbia, Private Nelson Rainey was in its ranks. He was a Rebel raider sixteen days before his eighteenth birthday.

The first hints of spring prompted increased activity in Bragg's ranks, and as the weather moderated, drills became the order of the day. Officers now cast a critical eye at equipment carelessly handled during the winter months. The warmer weather encouraged the men to strip themselves of clothing they had worn for months and soon Duck River was lined with naked soldiers scrubbing out the dirt that had accumulated during the winter.

In their spare time, the soldiers wrote letters to their families. Sometimes the news was not pleasant. Jim Parrott, a native of Lincoln County, wrote his wife,

I want to see you and the children offul Bad   I think of you oftimes when a Sleep . . . I saw a man shot to death with muskets   he was charge with desertion   the Brigade was all ordered to the field where he was shot and then the prisoner was brought they Sung and Prade for him   he said he was prepared to meet his god in peace   after they prade they tuck him and led him to a stake and tide him and 12 guns was discharged at him 6 was loded with Ball and 6 with Blank lods   he would not let them Blind his eyes Jeneral rite [Wright] said he never saw a gallant a fellow as he was   Jeneral Rite [Wright] shed tears when he shuck hands with him after he had tied him.[21]

The men in the army took special pains to inform the folk at home regarding the situation in camp. Lee Edwards from Coffee County wrote his sister:

. . . I will tell you something about the times here they are very hard about getting anything done   you cant get any washing done any where about here   when you get it done you have to pay twenty five cents a garment and you know that is very extravagent   We bought five gallons of dried apples last Sunday and paid 1 dollar per gallon for them & we paid 6 dollars a pound for soda and 1 dollar a dozen for apples and they was not as large as a big marble.   Small pies is only 50 cts. apiece and scarce at that.   Candles is 50 cts. a piece and none at that.[22]

The spring season was especially trying for farmers whose land lay unattended while they responded to the commands of the drill sergeant.   Men who had wives and children at home trying to till the soil asked for furloughs to plant their crops, but in Bragg's army there were no furloughs for private soldiers. Since they were not allowed to go home, the best alternative was to write instructions and hope a messenger would deliver them.

Corporal William Tripp wrote his wife in early spring, "We have cold weather here at this time not favorable for your planting corn without you aim to plant winter corn   Save your seed beens yet shure."[23]   William Tripp was representative of thousands of men in Bragg's army who had left a rather routine rural life to defend their homes against what the politicians had described as the "oppressive National Government."   Such men had been assured by wealthier neighbors that their families would be well cared for, but, as of yet, the help promised was not in evidence.   As a result, the William Tripps of the Confederate Army found it difficult to worry about the outcomes of battles, the "rightness" of the Confederate cause, or anything else so far removed from their immediate interests.   In spite of his anxieties William Tripp did not lose touch with the humanness of his existence.

On March 29th, 1863, William wrote his wife Martha:

*I hope that you will take good care of your self and
as to you wanting to See me there is no use in talking
You cannot want to See me as bad as I want to see you
and the children and pap and mother.*[24]

The resentment the Confederate soldiers felt against the
war punctuated a loneliness that haunted them night and day.
From Shelbyville, Jim Parrott wrote his wife:

*I all waz love to read as kind letters as you send
mee that lets mee now [know] that you are living a
christian . . . I love you and my children Better than
every thing in the world   you must kiss the boys for
mee and hug the Baby Bless his hart   I want to kiss him
I now [know] he is sweat By his Being so fat   nomore
I remain you husbin until death.*[25]

Some future historians would tend to believe that it was a
fervor for the Southern Cause that sustained the South's fighting
men. With men like Monroe Bearden it was probably true, but
in the letters of men who could barely spell and who were not
hesitant to express their emotions, it was family, not "The
Cause," that dominated their thoughts. In another letter to his
wife, written within a week or so of the one above, Parrott said:

*I want to see you all Sow Bad that I can hardly
keep from running away   they will not furlow anyBody
I dont want to run away   it will Be a dis grace   Besides
punishment of some kind   But I intend to come home
sometime Bewn [between] this and fall furlow or not ...
I dreame of eating dinner with you   and you had a god
dinner   it was ham and cabbage and chicken and
severell other things   O if that could be so it would be a
great pleasure to mee   I long to see the time come when
I can get the pleasure of coming home to stay. if I could
get one kiss from you it would be more pleasure to mee
than every thing here   I remain your trew hus Bin untill
deat.*[26]

Lee Edwards had no wife to write so he directed his letter-writing talents to calming the anxieties of a worried mother. From Tullahoma he wrote:

> *Ma you wanted to know what I done about my washing I have not had any done since I have been here.*
> *. . .You was talking about how we slept   we all sleep very well there is only twelve of us in our mess and that is a plenty I think   dont you   You wanted to know how I stood that cold spell. I done very well   I did not think it was so powerful cold . . . You wanted to know wether I had clothes enough. I have got plenty   I had on a pair of socks when I left that was a little holy about the heels   you may send me a pair of socks by the first chance . . . Tell Pa that he may send me a pair of soles to put on my boots . . . Ma you wanted to know what was the condition of my pants   they are not worn out bad only a little in the seat and I think I can make out a month or two with them.*[27]

Even to an unmarried lad like Lee Edwards, the war had lost any glamor it had ever held. He wrote his sister in March:

> *It is just like you said   if the war last twelve months what will people do. there will not be enough men left to make a support for the women and children.*
> *. . .when you sit down you dont know what moment the Yankees will be there on you all and take all you have got and what they dont take they will destroy. So I think you all will have a hard row to weed as well as myself. Although if the Yankees will let the people make a crop it will not be bad on you all without they turn stock on the wheat and eat it up. I would not be surprised if our own cavalry would not do that themsleves. If they do the people will sufer for something to eat around here.*[28]

The discontent which invariably arises when an army remains inactive for an extended period of time was no stranger to these soldiers. They had become tired of the scenery, the incessant drilling, and the monotony of the routine that filled their lives. They wanted a change. The evils they sometimes identified were not the evils of a locality so much as inherent weaknesses within themselves, but they seemed not to comprehend this fact. From Shelbyville, T.M. Webb, a sharpshooter with the 24th Infantry Battalion, reported to his wife:

> *I don't like to stay here for there is too much devilment carried on for me. A man cannot live well here unless he can steal and lie. There is plenty of preaching here but it does no good, as I can see here a man preaching and there is one swearing and over there is one singing a song to suit himself and right out there is a gang of them playing cards, and in fact everything is doing here at the same time.*[29]

At Wartrace, Tennessee, General Pat Cleburne's command passed the time in drill and matters of a higher importance. In late spring, a religious revival was held and passes were issued to all who expressed a desire to attend. The revival was a great success and chaplains were pleased until it was noted that a sharp increase in hog-stealing had accompanied the event. From that time on, the issuance of passes was greatly restricted and the religious enthusiasm of many soldiers diminished considerably. It was during this time that Sergeant Andrew Campbell deserted Cleburne's ranks and made his way to Nashville. There he joined the 13th Tennessee Cavalry (Federal) and, on the 4th day of September the following year, fired the shot that killed General John Hunt Morgan.

In Washington, the federal authorities were becoming impatient for Rosecrans to move south from Murfreesboro and attack the Rebs. Rosecrans himself had other things on his mind.   He was being considered as a candidate for the Presidency by Horace Greely and others in New York, and a substantial portion of his time was involved with that possibility.   In the meantime, his Chief of Staff, James A. Garfield, drew plans of attack on Shelbyville and Tullahoma, but still Rosecrans hesitated.[30]   It was June 24th, 1863, before the Yankee Army began its advance south from Murfreesboro.

It had been a long and frustrating spring for William Tripp. His home was in an adjoining county, yet he had not been allowed to visit it once. In his letters home he urged his wife to visit him in camp and there are indications that she did so. On April 11th he wrote her from Tullahoma, " I desire very much for you to be here as you would see more than you would in all your life and stay at home." Evidently she responded to this invitation by visiting camps because on the 30th of the month William wrote her from Wartrace, "Martha I want to come home worst than I every did cints you left hear. I suppose that col. fulton [Colonel John S. Fulton] ses all that wants to come home they can come before Christmas   god grant how soon that hit may bee."[31]

From Wartrace on May 20th, 1863, William wrote Martha:

Martha come up A Saturday if you can   if John Smith [a neighbor] *comes up with the waggon fetch the children if you can for I want to see thim   tell Martha Smith to come with you and all the rest that can come fetch mee one pair of pants . . . if you come in a waggon you will haft to start very Soon ar you want make hit in A Day* [32]

Ten days later, William's regiment had moved to Fairfield, Tennessee, and from there he wrote:

I want you all to take care of your Selfs the beste you can and I will too but I have a bad chance to take

care of my Self out hear but I am doing vary well now
... Sum of the boys diting [dieting?] have nothin to eate
all the tim . . . I hope thar is A day coming whin I can
come home and live in peece with you and and the
children   if thay hant I hope to meet you all in heavin
whar thar is no wars nor troubles[33]

On June 22nd, 1863, two days before the Federal Army
began its advance from Murfreesboro, William wrote his wife,
"[I wish?] I culd come home to Stay with you and the children
 hope the time will come whin [I] can come home and Stay and
live in pease and dy in pease."[34]

William's regiment, the 44th Tennessee, followed Bragg's
army to the Chattanooga area, and went on to Virginia with
Longstreet, but what happened to the young soldier after that
time is not clear. It is known that Martha Tripp received a letter
from one J.B. Clark written on June 24th, 1865. The letter said
in part:

> *It is my Painful duty to inform you of the death of*
> *your husband late a member of Co. B 44 Regt Tenn*
> *(Confederate Army) which took place at this hospital last*
> *nite.*
>
> *Mr. Tripp was brought here yesterday on his way*
> *home from point Look Out having been released from*
> *that prison.*
>
> *He was quite low from congestive fever and lived*
> *but a short time after his arrival.*
>
> *Sympathy deeply with you in your bereavement.*[35]

Except for sharp skirmishes in two gaps of the hills which
separated the enemy armies, Bragg did not contest the advance
of the Federal Army from Murfreesboro. Although the
Confederate commander had been afforded six months to
anticipate the movements of his opponent he was in no way
prepared for them when they occurred. Middle Tennessee was
permanently lost as a part of the Confederacy.

Chapter XII

The Confederate soldier
was growing weary

In later years the experts would say that the war should have ended in the late summer of 1863. During the first week in July of that year, Lee's invasion of the North failed at Gettysburg, and Vicksburg was surrendered to Grant. Before the month ended, Bragg was forced out of Middle Tennessee and John Hunt Morgan's command was captured north of the Ohio River. As one veteran put it:

> *It seemed that Confederate history at this time was fast becoming a catalogue of reverses, and the Confederate soldier was growing weary of the many and prominent additions that were being made to the list.*[1]

The objective which had seemed so easy two years before had now become more elusive, while those pursuing that objective were becoming less able to sustain the pursuit. Those people in Tennessee who had encouraged the war had now become its victims and, being unable to pull themselves from the mainstream of events, were being swept along by the currents of disaster which engulfed them. It was a disappointing way to begin the last half of the year.

Many of the soldiers in Bragg's army were obviously demoralized. Hundreds deserted, some making it a point to be picked up by Yankee patrol parties. Still the war went on. Somehow in the face of adverse circumstances, most of the men in the Army of Tennessee marched toward Chattanooga believing that the varied elements of war would yet combine to bring them victory.

The journey out of Middle Tennessee was uncomfortable to say the least. Mid-summer rains made their appearance daily and poured endless amounts of water into the already muddy roads. John Allan Wyeth, a cavalryman, wrote:

> *We followed a road leading south to Tullahoma. The wagon-trains had evidently gone by this route, and how they ever got through was a wonder. The June rains had been pouring down for the last week and were to keep pouring for another. Once or twice every day or night the heavens opened and soaked the earth and us; then the hot sun would do its best to dry us by a process akin to steaming; then another shower, and so on.*[2]

If times were hard for men riding horses it was doubly so for the infantry. W.W. Heartsill, a native of East Tennessee wrote:

> *Hour after hour we march through the mud, so tired we can scarcely put one foot before the other, every few hundred yards may be seen one, two or half a dozen men by the road side too tired to go further without rest . . .*
>
> *We can hear nothing reliable of the whereabouts of the enemy, which is nothing unusual for I tell you a "private" is the most complete "Know Nothing" that ever was, all that he professes to know is how to draw rations, keep his gun in order, "fall in" and fight like "blue blazes" when told to or run like a wild turkey when he knows he is whiped.*[3]

When the Confederate Army reached Chattanooga, there was little time for rest. The sun was hot, the ground dry and dusty, and only rarely did it rain enough to stop work on the fortifications which had begun shortly after the army's arrival. Certainly this period of time did not inspire sonnets on the pleasures of soldiering. Blistered hands and aching backs evidenced the fact that spadework constituted the chief occupational hazard of soldiers who worked in the uneasy knowledge that their Yankee enemy was descending from Middle Tennessee.

Even the urgency of the situation did little to relieve the boredom at Chattanooga. Sam Watkins said,

> *It was the same drudge, drudge day by day.*
> *Occasionally a Sunday would come; but when it did*
> *come, there came inspection of arms, knapsacks and*
> *cartridge boxes. Every soldier had to have his gun*
> *rubbed as bright as a new silver dollar.*[4]

Perhaps the dust and boredom would have seemed more bearable had they been endured on a full stomach, but as far as the men in the ditches could see, little effort was made to keep them fed. In late July, reports reached Chattanooga regarding the way Confederates at Vicksburg had eaten rats to stay alive. Sam Watkins, never one to let a novel idea go untried, wrote:

> *We at once acted on this information, and started*
> *out rat hunting . . . Presently we came to an old*
> *outhouse that seemed a natural harbor for this kind of*
> *vermin. The house was quickly torn down and out*
> *jumped an old residenter . . . After chasing him*
> *backwards and forwards, the rat finally got tired of this*
> *foolishness and started for his hole, and as he went in*
> *we made a grab for his tail. Well, tail hold broke, and*
> *we held the skin of his tail in our hands . . . After hard*
> *work we caught him. We skinned him, washed and*

salted him, buttered and peppered him, and fried him.
..Well, after a while he was said to be done. I got a
piece of cold didger bread, and raised the piece of rat to
my mouth, when I happened to think of how that rat's
tail did slip. I had lost my appetite for dead rat.[5]

While the men at Chattanooga dug fortifications and cursed the war, a lone figure left the mountains south of McMinnville and headed toward the Army of Tennessee. Resinor Etter was on his way back to the 16th Tennessee. The wound in his throat he had received at Perryville was not completely healed, but he had waited as long as he could. He was determined that his regiment would fight no more battles without him. After a three days' journey, Etter crossed the Tennessee River and entered Chattanooga. He found before him a jungle of tents, supply wagons, livestock, artillery, and great mounds of newly piled dirt. Finding his regiment seemed at first a great challenge, but by coincidence it was camping at the exact spot it had used the year before on the way to Kentucky. Soon Etter was settled in. He noted, "It was a happy meeting with me and the boys . . . I felt very proud to meet my old friends again   I had been away from camp life so long that all things seem new to me."[6]

Much had changed since Etter had left the boys at Perryville. Stone's River had exerted a devastating effect on the 16th Regiment and the happiness of rejoining the group was somewhat diminished as the young soldier reflected,

I Seccan time entered upon this painful strugle that
has caus so much sorrow and deth among us   All our
boys is yet in good spirits. Though there is many that is
no more   They have gone by desese and Lord to their
homes to return no more. I think of them often tho they
cannot be brought back again.[7]

The hot days of August dragged by slowly for the Confederates at Chattanooga. They knew that each day would be a dull repetition of the one before, bringing with it more digging, more tiresome drill, and another day's ration of saltless meat. Their only satisfaction was the belief, or at least the hope, that the fortifications they were erecting would withstand any Yankee attack. The thought at least lessened the misery involved.

The cavalry fared better than the infantry. Being less confined they moved about the countryside where food was more abundant. George Guild of the 4th Tennessee said that the quartermasters:

> ...would buy a field of corn, move to it, and remain until it was exhausted, and then move to another purchase. The horses would be fed on corn, stalks and all ... besides grazing them on grass for an hour or two each day . . .The soldiers too, were supplied with an abundance of wholesome rations.[8]

In spite of their better situation, W. R. Dyer, of Forrest's cavalry, entered in his diary, "Times very dull   Soldiers in low spirits."[9]   Dyer's   diary   tells   a   story   of   boredom, discouragement, discontent, and anxiety which was prevalent in many regiments.

While the Rebs fortified Chattanooga, the Yankees leisurely made their way across the Cumberland Mountains from Middle Tennessee. There was no sign of urgency in their pace. The march from Tullahoma was a slow, methodical journey, like that of a hunter who steadily and confidently stalks his prey, believing that only time separates him from conquest.

2.

If the last weeks of August, 1863 held little joy for the Confederates at Chattanooga, such was not the case for East

Tennessee Unionists. The "Old Flag" was about to return. The long months of waiting were coming to an end and if that end was two years later than expected, it made the event even more welcome. In Southern Kentucky a Federal army was poised to enter the mountains, and in it were thousands of East Tennesseans who had been forced from their homes many months before.

The months spent under Confederate occupation had been far from pleasant. Many prominent citizens had been sent south to prisons amid all the humiliation and degradation the Confederates could muster. Untold numbers of people had been brutally murdered by roaming bands of outlaws who posed as loyal Confederates. In truth, a reign of terror had existed for those people whose loyalty to the Union never faltered.

As one witness to the times wrote:

> God only knows what the wives, mothers, and sisters of men who braved the perils and hardships of war did endure. The sufferings and sacrifices of those in East Tennessee were beyond description. A majority of the men were plain farmers, and I knew of instances where wives were left with from three to six children, for whom they not only made bread, but spun and wove the cloth for their clothing, and then cut and made the garment.[10]

In Unionist East Tennessee, as in Confederate Middle and West Tennessee, it was the plain people who became the real victims of war. These people did not lose fortunes of material wealth — they lost the services of breadwinners who meant the difference between a minimum existence and bare survival. When the women of such families wept, their tears were not wiped away by scented handkerchiefs, but were more likely absorbed by the dirt from freshly cultivated fields which represented their only hope to avoid starvation. In East Tennessee this situation was about to end.

When Bragg's army withdrew from Tullahoma, the Confederates in the north eastern portion of the state had little choice but to follow suit. Rebel supplies were concentrated at Knoxville, and every day, train loads were started toward Chattanooga. The departure of supplies was accompanied by the departure of troops and, in a few days, only the "Louisiana Tigers" remained in the area. In the opinion of the Unionists the "Tigers" behaved badly. They spread such terror among the people that, for a short time, East Tennesseans forgot their differences as they sought to protect themselves from what they considered the irresponsible acts of these men.

Meanwhile, the Federal Army was winding its way south under the command of General Ambrose Burnside. This bewhiskered General had failed miserably as a commander in Virginia, but he was about to find his true role in the war as "Savior of East Tennessee."

As news of the army's approach spread throughout the area, a wild enthusiasm exploded. The day of liberation was at hand. On prominent mountain peaks giant fires were started to signal the people that the "old flag" was returning. With every step of the Federal Army the heartbeats of East Tennesseans quickened; it was the grandest day in the lives of the devoted mountaineers.

Oliver Temple, a distinguished judge, wrote:

> As the army advanced into and through East Tennessee, the excitement and enthusiasm among the citizens became wild and tumultous. There was scarcely a family in all the mountain region to be traversed that had not given every able-bodied man to the army. Women and children and old men alone remained at home. All these, as the advance became known, flocked to the roadside to see the army, bringing with them for distribution such food as they had on hand. Shouting and rejoicing, the waving of bonnets and handkerchiefs, weeping and sobbing, and enthusiastic praise to God for the great deliverance, everywhere greeted the army.[11]

All roads led to Knoxville and, by the third day, thousands of people jammed the city's streets. Some had walked all night. Mothers, wives, and children fought through the noisy stampede seeking word or a glimpse of a soldier from whom they had heard nothing for almost two years.

Burnside's main column entered Knoxville on September 3, 1863. At the head of the column was the 8th East Tennessee Cavalry. These Tennesseans were enjoying their finest hour. They rode through the streets of Knoxville at the head of a liberating army and they rode under the admiring stares of relatives who had begun to wonder if they would ever return.

Judge Temple, in describing the scene, wrote:

> *All day the exiles met mothers, fathers, wives, children or sisters, scenes such as these — scenes of wildest rapture could be witnessed nearly every moment on the streets . . . Now and then, as a wife met her husband, or a mother her boy, a wild scream was heard. From morning to night, the people gave themselves up to the most unrestrained demonstrations of rejoicing. The long gloom, doubt, almost despair, which filled their minds were all gone. The exiles had returned, with the old banner waving over them.*[12]

The Confederate withdrawal from East Tennessee had a special significance to Rebel soldiers, especially those who had recently been paroled at Vicksburg. J.J. Blair was such a soldier. As he watched the Rebs withdraw, he wrote, "E Tenn is being left to the mercies of an enraged foe."[13] Blair knew he faced an uncertain future. On one occasion he had paid a substitute $2500 to take his place in the Confederate Army and had hired substitutes for his friends who became tired of war. With such a record he was sure to be reported to Federal authorities.

Still, he was determined to stay at home. "My conscience is clear," he wrote, "I put my trust in God . . . Some of my friends who are Union men advise me to go to the country a few days. I will do so and return with my family."[14]

In early September, Blair had encountered Federal soldiers and found them not too different from other people. He talked to members of the local garrison "all of whom appear to be gentlemen." By the second day, the Reb was entertaining Yankees in his home, and during the following week, he subscribed to the Oath of Allegiance to the Federal Government.

The case of Blair was an exception. In East Tennessee the hunted had become the hunter and, for many years, angry East Tennesseans would seek retribution in the lives and property of fellow Tennesseans.

3.

It was late August when the Confederates at Chattanooga looked across the river and saw what they believed were the approaching Yankees. They were correct, and while the Confederates braced themselves for an attack, the Federals pulled their big guns and sent screaming projectiles toward the Confederate trenches. Although the shells did little harm, they served to screen the real intent of the Federal Army. While the Confederates watched for an attack on Chattanooga, the main Yankee force went south of the city to operate against Bragg's supply line from Atlanta. The Yankees would now attempt to accomplish with an army what the Streight and Andrews raids had failed to do. Should they succeed, they would isolate the Rebs in Chattanooga from their supplies in Atlanta as well as their reinforcements from Virginia and Mississippi. Bragg had but one wise choice: leave Chattanooga and pursue the enemy.

Of all the "cussin" done by Confederate soldiers during the war, none surpassed in quality or quantity that delivered when the men received word to leave Chattanooga. They were ordered to walk off and leave the fortifications they had dug in the sweltering heat of July and August, and it didn't set well. Some men were so disgusted that they left their equipment atop the mounds of dirt that served as little more than reminders of useless effort and, so many privates thought, the stupidity of their officers.

General William Stark Rosecrans, the Federal commander, divided the Union Army into three sections and crossed the mountains south and west of Chattanooga. Bragg devised plans to strike the separate sections, but the plan was never executed and by the middle of September the enemy armies faced each other across a deep and winding creek called Chickamauga, an Indian name meaning "River of Death."

Throughout the preceding days there had been contact between the enemies, but no general battle. Men had been killed but not in numbers sufficient to arouse the imagination of the press or even the general officers. Such a situation prompted one soldier, W.W. Heartsill, to consider the plight of the individual soldier. Men like Heartsill did not wish to be considered only as a part of a massive army; they wanted to be thought of as valuable, significant, individual human beings. This attitude is reflected in Heartsill's fictional description of an "occasional shot," written in the last week of August of 1863, in north Georgia. He said,

> *The enemy is very quiet over the way, nothing but an occasional shot. How often has that same remark been made or written "NOTHING BUT AN OCCASIONAL SHOT," of what little importance it appears to be, but trace up, in your imagination this "occasional shot" and its effect. Oh! says the News paper reporter, "only one of the privates killed," a blanket is his winding sheet, burried [sic], and in the camp soon forgotten. a thousand miles away; out on the western frontier of Texas in an humble unpretending cottage do you see that care worn face; as a fond mother gently tries to sooth the sufferings of her darling child,*

she knows that ere the dawn of an other day the little
sweet baby will be with the Angels in the Glory World;
but oh could He come to see our darling and quiet its
lisping supplications . . . The night passes, another day
dawns;   with all the beauty and lovliness that
characterizes the work of the Great Creator;   in that
mothers heart there is a "void this world can never fill."
her JEWEL is gone . . . she turns away from the new
made grave and with dispair depicted in every lineament
of her face; she retraces her steps to her desolate home,
a gleam of joy! yes of joy is seen to dance in her eyes;
for now she remembers the promised return of her
husband . . . yes this is the day that he wrote he would
be home. A letter is on the table, she seizes it alas! a
strange hand-write, with trembling hands and fainting
heart she breaks the seal, look at the first line; "Your
husband was killed to day by a stray shot."   Thus it is
we might trace the sorrow occasioned by these
"occasional shots." "No general engagement; only one
of the men killed." [15]

By Friday night September 18, 1863, the individuals had
combined to form two armies stretching along a line six miles in
length. They would fight for the next two days in a battle that
would attract the attention of the nation. During Friday night,
Bragg crossed most of his army to the west side of
Chickamauga Creek, and among the scrubby undergrowth
which covered the area, they waited for the chilling hours of
darkness to pass.

George Guild

Chapter XIII

Soldiers...
You must seek the contest

Soldiers in the ranks were uninformed about the overall plans and movements of the army; they knew only to march forward when the command was given. The attitude of the Confederates at Chickamauga was grim as they pushed through the undergrowth to take their positions on line. One soldier noticed that there was "no guying of each other and no frivolous flings at passing horsemen. The rapid step toward the scene of conflict indicated the determination that was written on every brow and remarks to each other such as 'Boys, we have retreated far enough; we will whip 'em this time or die,' figured in every tongue."[1]

The Rebs had already received an annointment of verbal inspiration. In an attempt to prepare his men for the fight ahead, Bragg issued a statement saying,

> *Soldiers, you are largely reinforced; you must seek the contest. In so doing I know you will be content to suffer privations and encounter hardships . . . Our cause is in your keeping. Your enemy boasts that you are demoralized and retreating before him . . . Your generals will lead you. You have but to respond to insure a glorious victory over an insolent foe. I know*

what your response will be. Trusting God and in the justice of our cause, and nerved by the love of the dear ones at home, failure is impossible and victory must be ours.[2]

Saturday morning, September 19, 1863, dawned under an overcast sky, but soon the sun broke through to light up the valley of the Chickamauga. There had been little sleep in either army and the final preparations for battle continued during the early morning hours.

Regimental and brigade commanders rode up and down the line shouting instructions and inspirational challenges. As he galloped by the 1st Tennessee, General George Maney yelled, "We shall soon have the opportunity of striking for our homes and firesides, and to acquit ourselves like men worthy of the old Volunteer State." Colonels walked restlessly among their companies, checking the little details which experience had proved so important. The men stared at the underbrush wondering when and where the fight would begin. Almost all of them had seen battle before and what they had seen did not prompt the joyous outbursts which had preceded their previous engagements.

On the extreme right of the Confederate line Forrest's cavalry, dismounted as infantry and bolstered by two hundred of John Hunt Morgan's men who had escaped capture in Ohio, moved in the direction of the enemy. Cautiously probing the thick underbrush they slowly narrowed the distance between themselves and a Federal unit following a similar course. Without warning, the two groups met and "hell broke loose in Georgia."

Expertly developing the opposition in his front, Forrest soon discovered he had aroused a hornet's nest of Yankees. In the face of what seemed a solid stream of fire, Forrest's men instinctively pulled their hats low over their eyes and fought back tenaciously. Even after additional regiments were thrown into the fight, the cavalrymen were overmatched and were forced to withdraw. Along the Confederate line to the left, other brigades and divisions entered the fighting and, before nightfall, over thirty thousand Rebs had engaged forty thousand Yankees.

As the battle spread south, Confederate soldiers discarded bundlesome equipment, checked their guns for a final time, and made ready to enter the fight. Orders were shouted above the incessant roar of bursting artillery shells, and amid the whizzing of musket balls, the men cleared paths through the brush in their front.

Even in the tenseness of situations like this there was usually a Reb ready with a wisecrack. As the 1st Tennessee moved out, a "fire eatin" chaplain stepped before the men armed with words of inspiration. After telling the Tennesseans of their noble ancestry he pointed out that all Yankees were the offsprings of the "crop-eared Puritans and witch burners." He pledged himself to fight Yankees in this world and, if necessary, to chase their ghosts in the next. Raising his voice above the din of battle, the parson shouted instructions to aim low and kill the enemy as if they were wild beasts, adding that, if only he had a gun, he would go with them. In one final outburst of evangelical enthusiasm he yelled, "Remember, boys, that he who is killed will sup tonight in Paradise." The last declaration was too much for one soldier who yelled back, "Well,parson, you come along and take supper with us," and as the preacher galloped away the soldier observed, "The parson isn't hungry, and never eats supper."[3]

As they pushed forward, the Confederates met what Marcus Toney believed was "more wounded coming out than there was of us going in,"but there was no turning back. Toney said his company moved "in line through the thick wood of oak and pine, we struck the enemy, who were posted on a hill much higher than our position . . . A shell exploded in front of us, a piece striking the shoulder of Lieut. W.H. Webster, of the Maury Grays, from which, he soon bled to death." Toney's company continued its advance and finally reached the top of a ridge. The men were ordered to lie flat. Ensign Joe Campbell raised himself up on one arm "and a shot from the enemy pierced his brain, and he was instantly killed."[4]

Before he entered the fight, Bob Stout of Mt. Pleasant, Tennessee, refused rations saying he had a premonition of death. After a charge on the enemy was completed a comrade yelled to Stout, "Bob you weren't killed, as you expected," but Bob Stout did not answer. At that moment "a solid shot from the Federal guns struck him between the waist and the hip, tearing off one leg and scattering his bowels over the ground."[5]

As Colonel A. J. Vaughn led the 13th Tennessee through the underbrush, a Yankee soldier jumped from behind a bush and, supposing Vaughn to be a Federal officer, inquired, "Where is the enemy?" Discovering his mistake the Yank jerked his gun up and fired. The shot passed just in front of Vaughn and into the body of Captain R. S. Donaldson who fell to the ground dead.[6] For miles up and down the line, the armies stood toe to toe and slugged it out. Neither could gain more than a temporary advantage. Generals waved their hats and urged the men forward with colorful appeals to manhood and patriotism, but perhaps Old Ben Cheatham's was as good as any. According to W. J. Worsham, the hard drinking Tennessean yelled "Give 'em hell boys, give 'em hell."[7]

Throughout the day, isolated bits of drama passed unnoticed except by those directly involved. In one such incident, Drew Brock of Cheatham's division was taken prisoner and escorted to the rear by an officer in whose custody he was placed. As they made their way toward the rear the officer expressed a desire for water and asked Brock if he knew of any. The captured Reb willingly guided his captor to a spring nearby and as the Yank knelt to drink the water Brock seized a rock and hit him in the head killing him instantly. Even before Brock could leave the spring, the Confederates reappeared and he fell in line to charge the enemy one more time.

The bitter fighting on Saturday lasted until darkness imposed its merciful silence along the battle line. Neither side had made substantial gains. It had been Bragg's intention to turn the Federal left and interpose his own army between the Yankees and Chattanooga. The next move in Bragg's plan called for driving the Federal Army into a mountainous cove where it could be either destroyed or forced to surrender. But the Confederates fought an enemy that would not be moved. Little had been gained; much had been lost.

Resinor Etter wrote in his diary on Saturday night, "Night has come and the Battle has sesed. We lay down, the wounded to die and the wery to rest." Bromfield Ridley looked about him and observed:

> *No fires allowed; the night cold and chilly; the moon, although shining, sends a meager light through the dense woodland. Dead and wounded all around us, friend and foe writhing in pain; litterbearers worked to exhaustion for their comfort; cries for water from the wounded rending the air, and yet a threatened night battle.*[8]

The ringing sound of axes from the Federal side indicated what the morning would bring. The Confederates were too tired to worry and most of them took advantage of the darkness to gain what rest they could. Other men roamed the battlefield in search of food or a wounded comrade while still others wandered aimlessly for the most gruesome of reasons. Bromfield Ridley watched as a smoke-covered Reb walked slowly among the dead and wounded. He watched as the man leaned over a wounded comrade and gave him a drink of water. And then, after the wounded man died, the Reb reached into the dead man's pocket and removed a gold watch. Hungry men searched through the haversacks of the dead for food which was often stained with blood. The stained portion was chipped off and what remained became supper for the half-starved wanderer.

In some instances the horror of the battlefield became a backdrop for sacrifice between enemies. W. C. Brown, a Yankee soldier of the 93rd Ohio, was wounded just before dark. His regiment was falling back at the time and soon the young soldier was left lying in a no-man's land between the armies. After dark Brown heard a squad of Rebel pickets approaching.

I called to them. They halted, and asked who I was and what I wanted. I replied that I was a wounded Federal soldier, and wanted to be helped into an easier position, as I was suffering from a broken leg. They came to me promptly and assisted me as gently as if I had been one of their own men, first taking off my woolen blanket and spreading it down for me to lie on, placing my cartridge box under my head for a pillow and spreading my oilcloth over me.[9]

When the wounded soldier awoke the next morning he found "that one of them had spread half of a homemade calico quilt over me, saying nothing about it, and doubtless keeping the other half to shelter him in his nightlong watch on picket duty."[10]

Amid the suffering around them, Confederate generals planned strategy for the following day. During the night, General James Longstreet arrived at Bragg's headquarters. Longstreet had come from Virginia with the divisions of John Hood and Lafayette McLaws, approximately 5000 men in all. A portion of these men had been present for the first day's fighting, but the presence of Longstreet himself and the remainder of his men bolstered Rebel hopes for a crushing victory come Sunday morning.

Ever-so-carefully, Bragg explained the plan for Sunday: turn the Federal left, drive it into the mountain, and wait for victory. To accomplish this objective, Bragg divided his army into two wings with the right under Leonidas Polk and the left under Longstreet. Plans called for the battle to begin with

Polk's wing. General D.H. Hill's corps would open the fighting at daylight whereupon each unit to his left would take it up in turn. Immediately a courier was sent to Hill's headquarters to inform him of his important role in the next day's battle.

The private soldier knew none of this. The reality of his situation extended no further than what he could see or hear, but that was enough. The 32nd Tennessee was assigned to picket duty and one of its members wrote:

That night was one never to be forgotten . . . We stood at the muzzle of the enemy's muskets, so to speak, and they stood at the muzzle of ours; so that the least noise never failed to provoke a shot . . . We happened to occupy a portion of the field near a farmhouse, in and around which large numbers of Federal wounded had been gathered during the day, and near which a very large number of animals in harness were left. . . As the night grew old the monotony was heavy, and the stillness intense and painful; yet often, in the midst of this, wounded soldiers about the house could be heard begging piteously for water; another and another would shriek with pain as if a dagger was at his heart; then the groaning of the wounded animals, or neighing of a sound horse, would appear to be the signal for the rest of the animals to make complaints and efforts to be released from their confinements; yet no one dared to offer relief.[11]

Sunday morning at Chickamauga dawned "crisp but clear," but no Confederate attack came with it. Somewhere in the confusion of the preceding night, the courier from Bragg's headquarters had failed to reach D.H. Hill — the battle plan was uncommunicated. While the Yankees frantically closed gaping holes in their line, the Rebs sat and waited for their Generals to clear the confusion. Bragg raved in his disappointment, but it was almost 10 o'clock before the attack was under way.

George Guild's cavalry regiment was held in reserve on the left of the Rebel line and he watched and listened impatiently from a position near the front. When the attack began he noted:

> *Commencing on the right, the deafening thunder would roll along the line toward the left, when it would be taken up and swept to where it had started. The sound indicated with accuracy the result in different parts of the field; for as a column would advance to the charge you would first hear the rapid and quick discharge of the batteries, indicating that their position was threatened, then would come a crash of musketry as if every tree in the forest had fallen, and high above all this the shouts of the Confederates.*[12]

The initial action on Sunday morning found the Confederates charging the breastworks built by the enemy the night before. As one Confederate officer said, ". . . it is a charge of breastworks for four long miles. The din of musketry is like the unintermitted sounds of firecrackers, the terrific cannonading so deafening that the eyewitness stands aghast at the idea that he is living through it."[13]

Trying desperately to follow Bragg's plan of battle, the Rebs hammered relentlessly at the Federal left. General George Thomas' men refused to give ground. Time after time, Thomas called for reinforcements to throw against the attacking Confederates who, during each successive attempt, threatened to push his men into the mountain. On each occasion, Rosecrans pulled men from other sections of his line, and throughout the day Thomas held his position. Enemy soldiers stood in each other's faces and delivered deadly shots which left the ground covered with dead and wounded. The fire became so intense that men sought the protection of the scrubbiest pine or the smallest rock as they delivered their missiles of death into the enemy line.

The incessant pounding of the Federal left paid dividends, but not in the way Bragg expected. Throughout the morning and early afternoon Rosecrans continued to send Thomas reinforcements, but in so doing the center of the Yankee line was substantially weakened. During the process of shifting troops toward the left, a gap developed in the Federal line facing the command of Longstreet. The Rebs needed no invitation to enter. Pouring into the gap, Longstreet's brigades caught the Federals by surprise and pushed them around like men "closing a barn door." The right end of the Yankee line was completely routed, and in the wake of screaming Rebs and flying bullets, the Yanks threw down their guns and started toward Chattanooga. General William Starke Rosecrans, their commanding general, went with them.

The scene presented by the routed Yankees was one of indescribable beauty to the men in General Bushrod Johnson's brigade. In his report Johnson said,

> The scene now presented was unspeakably grand. The resolute and impetuous charge, the rush of our heavy column sweeping out from the shadow and gloom of the forest into the open fields flooded with sunlight, the glitter of arms, the onward dash of artillery and mounted men, the retreat of the foe, the shouts of the hosts of our army, the dust, the smoke, the noise of fire-arms — of whistling balls and grape-shot and bursting shell — made up a battle scene of unsurpassed grandeur.[14]

The collapse of the Federal right was not without cost. All along its front, the Rebs had been forced to charge, withdraw, reform, and charge again. Each time a new charge was made the dead and wounded increased as the lines wavered back and forth.

As the men who constituted the right end of the Federal line retreated toward Chattanooga, only George Thomas' Corps stood between the Yankees and total disaster. Pulling his men around the crown of a hill inhabited by the Snodgrass family, Thomas braced for the attacks he knew would come.

During the afternoon the Rebs charged Thomas' position time and again and, on each occasion, left hundreds of their men on the sloping terrain. But the victory-hungry Rebs were not to be denied, and in the waning hours of daylight, after sixteen successive attacks had failed, they reformed for a last time. Screaming and yelling like wild men, the Rebs started up the hill shoulder to shoulder never noticing those who dropped around them, but keeping their eyes fixed on the Yankees at the top. The charging line passed the farthest point reached before, and in a holocaust of smoke and flying lead, they watched with unrestrained satisfaction as George Thomas' men pulled back to join their retreating comrades who were already on their way to Chattanooga.

It was the happiest moment of the war for the Army of Tennessee. As W. J. McMurray said,

> *When the great blue mass was seen sliding down the north slope of the hill, leaving behind them their killed, wounded, and artillery, there was a rebel yell that went up from Bragg's army that echoed and reechoed until it filled the valleys and shook the mountains, the like of which has never been heard since Josua encompassed the city of Jerico.*[15]

Tired, smoke-covered, and blood-bespattered Rebs stood triumphantly on the hills and hurled indignant insults at their departing foes. Some Confederates insisted on following the enemy and finishing them off for good, but others, tired beyond the point to care, "fell down with the dead and wounded of the enemy inside their former breastworks, and went to sleep."[16] Captain James Lytle of the 23rd Tennessee led his company in pursuit of Yankee stragglers and succeeded in capturing a few. Such Yankees "would surrender in a cheerful maner," and the captain said he "caused them to be treated with kindness . . . I honestly believe all Prisoners should be treated with respect the Boys would swap Canteens and share rations with them."[17]

The trails and roads leading from the battlefield were jammed with Yankees doing a "two-forty" gait toward safety. Every available vehicle was utilized as an ambulance but still thousands were left behind. An East Tennessean in the Union Army, W.R. Carter of the 1st Tennessee Cavalry, was among the Yankee horsemen who "began to dismount and place a wounded soldier in his stead, and in this way hundreds could have been brought from the red field of Chickamauga." But the plan was vetoed by officers of the regiment. The wounded men were made to dismount and return to the hospital. It was explained to the cavalrymen that should an attack be made on the withdrawing army "the wounded would be greatly in the way" since some could scarcely sit on the horses. Furthermore, the dismounted cavalry would be of no service without their mounts.[18]

In their attempt to escape the prowling Rebs, Yankee soldiers muffled their artillery wheels by "wrapping blankets around them," and in the cavalry "each man was required to carry his saber in hand to avoid noise."[19] No one was allowed to speak above a whisper.

Meanwhile, night had settled on the battlefield itself. The ground over which the armies had fought offered a study in war which taught the dramatic lesson that there are no real winners — only many losers. Spencer Talley noticed that "Trees as large as my body were severed in twain. The trees were shattered into splinters & dead and wounded men [were] covered with fragments of torn trees which almost covered the ground . . ."[20] Captain James Lytle saw a tree which had received "87 Rifle Balls, one cannon Ball and Ramrod as its share of the battle."[21]

The pathetic victims of the battle were not the trees; they could generate new growth. The real victims were the men who had fought among the trees. Men with their insides exposed led other men who had lost their sight and, together, they stumbled along searching for relief they knew could not be found.

George Guild was ordered by General Joe Wheeler to follow the Yankees and to determine their plans. Moving toward Chattanooga, Guild spotted a small white house and rode near it. He remembered:

> As I approached I noticed a hog running through the woods with a soldier's amputated leg in his mouth. This was one of our field hospitals, the windows of which was some three or four feet from the ground. The surgeons within as they amputated a limb would throw it out the window. The pile outside was so high that they would have to brush away the topmost limbs.[22]

Mothers and wives walked half-stunned through the fallen timber searching for a particular soldier. With mixed emotions they examined each successive body hoping on the one hand to quickly end their morbid search, but on the other, wishing not to erase the faint hope that by some miracle their loved one was yet alive. Soldiers with lanterns walked about searching out the cries of the wounded and administering aid as best they could. Often the women asked that lanterns be brought to a pile of dead soldiers so that identification could made. On one such occasion a young lady held the lantern close to the body of a dead Confederate and screamed, "O, there he is! Poor fellow! Dead, dead dead!" Nearby, a battle weary soldier paused only long enough to observe, "This war is a terrible thing," as he walked on.[23]

The 16th Tennessee stayed on the field most of the night. Some tried to sleep; others could not even try. Resinor Etter leaned against a tree, pulled out his diary and wrote, "The battle has been sevier all day   We have laid our werry frames down to rest to grieve for our friends."[24]   H.H. Dillard, another member of the 16th, told of walking across the field among the wounded, both blue and gray. "The scene was sad indeed and pitiable. . . . Some were praying, some were dying; while the rough stern soldiers, with hands and faces black with powder, pitying, stood in groups about them."[25]

Throughout the chilly night, soldiers wandered about looking for a friend they had seen fall during the day. There was little sound to be heard. The emotional appeals of the officers, the prayers of the chaplains, the screaming yells of advancing troops, the booming roar of artillery, and the vicious whine of minnie balls had drifted into eternity. These more heroic sounds of war had been replaced by a sinister silence broken only by soldiers stepping on fallen tree limbs or the gutteral sounds of dying men whose defiant yell was now nothing more than a humble plea for water.

Monday morning dawned on a victorious Confederate Army and the spirits of the men were in tempo with the event's significance. It was assumed by most of Bragg's Generals that he would send his victorious army against the disorganized Federals now cluttered together inside Chattanooga. While his generals urged him to move, Bragg stubbornly hesitated, and while he hesitated, the Yankees placed themselves in the earthworks dug by the Rebs the summer before.

The Confederate commander settled on a plan that, to him, seemed logical: he would bottle the Yanks up inside Chattanooga and starve them into submission. On the east, Confederate troops occupied Missionary Ridge which formed a towering obstacle to the Federals. On the west, Bragg's men stationed themselves on Lookout Mountain from which they could see every move the enemy made. To the north, the Tennessee River formed a deep and muddy barrier, and to the south, enough Confederates were deployed to make the encirclement complete. Or so it was thought.

Market Street, Chattanooga, 1863

Chapter XIV

The very air smelt of battle

Despite the abundance of evidence around him, it was difficult for Braxton Bragg to realize that his army had just won a great victory. Oddly enough, the commanding general's mind seemed more intent on finding fault with his subordinate generals than taking decisive action against a defeated foe. Although Bragg had reason to be displeased with the conduct of some generals prior to the battle, those who had performed well lamented the fact that he allowed his displeasure to dominate his thinking.

In fairness, it must be admitted that Bragg received conflicting reports concerning the enemy's intentions following the battle. Longstreet advised Bragg to move a part of the army north of the Tennessee River to force the Federals out of Chattanooga, but from Forrest, Bragg received information that the Yankees were leaving on their own. For whatever reasons, Bragg did nothing.

When the men in Bragg's army finally realized that no pursuit of the enemy was to be made, the enthusiasm which follows victory gave way to a sullen resentment. As the men saw the situation, the dead had died in vain and the living had risked their lives in a victory left unclaimed. The triumph had no kick — it did not inspire — it seemed meaningless.

H.H. Dillard looked back on the situation later:

In my opinion there was scarcely a battle ever fought in which men poured out their blood and gave up life more readily and resolutely than upon the field of Chickamauga . . .I must say I believed then, and still more firmly now, that if we had been permitted to pursue the enemy Sunday night after he was routed, on Monday we could without loss have captured the whole Federal army . . . But mere subalterns and the common herd of soldiers have no right to know, much less question, the propriety or reasons for the conduct of those who command them in war, be they right or wrong, good or bad.[1]

Major battles do not compose the total personality of war, nor do they exhaust the possibilities through which final victory can be gained. Starvation of the enemy is an effective weapon if it can be accomplished and, certainly, that possibility existed at Chattanooga. The Federals had only fragile communications with the outside world and Bragg quickly moved to disrupt these.

As a part of this objective, General Joe Wheeler was ordered to leave Chattanooga and operate against the Yankee supply line from Nashville. Leaving almost half his men at Chattanooga, Wheeler crossed the river and launched what would subsequently be known as his Middle Tennessee raid.

The first obstacle Wheeler encountered was the displeasure of Nathan Bedford Forrest. Forrest was on a mission to upper East Tennessee to check on Burnside's forces at Knoxville. On September 28th, Bragg ordered Forrest to turn over his command to Wheeler whose raiding party was admittedly weak. Forrest disliked the idea. To Forrest, the order represented another decision to take from him a group of men he had recruited, equipped, and trained. Most of all he didn't like the order because it came from a man he despised and distrusted.

Forrest sent Bragg a scathing letter and promised to visit him soon.

Up to this time, the discontent of Confederate generals had been expressed in carefully worded statements whose gentlemanly phrases cushioned the urgency of their contents. But just as Forrest had taught these refined gentlemen something of warfare, he was now about to provide them new insights into expressing discontent.

Accompanied by his chief surgeon, Dr. J. B. Cowan, Forrest made his way straight to Bragg's headquarters, entered the general's tent and, after refusing to shake hands, said:

> *You commenced your cowardly and contemptible persecution of me soon after the Battle of Shiloh, and you have kept it up ever since. You did it because I reported to Richmond facts while you reported damn lies ... You have played the part of a damned scoundrel, and are a coward, and if you were any part of a man I would slap your jaws and make you resent it ... I say to you that if you ever again try to interfere with me or cross my path it will be at the peril of your life.*[2]

What the unlearned and rough-edged Forrest really said would, in all probability, be much more interesting than the refined version related above by Dr. Cowan. In any event, the word of Forrest's blast spread throughout what was left of his command and the men at once began to speculate as to what might follow. Rumors flew thick and fast. One day's rumor had Forrest leaving the service, another had him transferring to Virginia, and, at least for a while, his men believed he was about to assume command of a privateer ship and begin raiding Yankee shipping.[3]

Nathan Bedford Forrest was far from the only general who wanted something done about Braxton Bragg. So intense was the resentment against Bragg that his subordinate generals signed a "round robin" to Richmond calling for his relief from

297

command. The situation became so volatile that President Davis soon arrived in Chattanooga to soothe the troubled waters.

2.

While many of his fellow generals sulked and pouted at Chattanooga, Joe Wheeler searched for Yankees in the mountains to the north and west. The physical condition of Wheeler's force left much to be desired. Many of the men, especially those acquired from Forrest,were poorly clad, underfed, weary from too much riding, and mounted on horses that scarcely could move along. Slowly and laboriously the column limped its way toward Jasper with little promise for success.

John Allan Wyeth was riding in this column. He later observed:

> *I often wonder now how our poor animals lived through the privation and punishment of this expedition. We scattered in small companies and turned off on sideroads and byways looking for forage and food. The old men and women and children, all that were left at home, had been preyed upon by friend and foe alike until they had learned to hide away the little that was left. My company came on a dilapidated lone cabin, in the garden of which were half a dozen rows of cabbage-stalks from which the heads had been cut. We broke ranks and made a rush for them, pulled the stalks up, root and all, and devoured them.*[4]

George Guild rode near the front of the column of horsemen as they approached Jasper and was among the first to see "hundreds of Federal wagons . . .standing, with their big white covers on them . . . solemn in their stately grandeur."[5] Since the main purpose of Wheeler's expedition was to cut off supplies to the beleagured Yankees at Chattanooga, he immediately prepared to attack. Sorefooted horses were reined up, weariness among the men gave way to excitement, "close-up" was yelled to the rear, and anxious eyes gazed in amazement at the raider's dream of cumbersome wagons clumsily climbing the mountain side.

Wheeler's raiders struck fast and decisively. For two hours the Rebel horsemen delivered stinging blows in the face of determined resistance. The fight eventually resolved itself into a deadly game wherein men on horses ran down infantrymen who had exhausted their ammunition and sought to escape in the mountains. Wheeler's men had won the prize, and like an impatient child opening Christmas packages, they began looking inside the canvass-covered wagons to determine their contents. Indeed it was Christmas come early. It was as if the Yankees had delivered canvass-covered packages, inside which, the Rebs found everything from underwear to artillery shells. For eight hours Wheeler's men joyously sorted through the captured goods keeping what they wanted, sending back to the main army the things that couldn't be carried along, and destroying what could not be utilized.

Before the attack, Wheeler informed his men that no plunder would be taken, but the men had other ideas. The ragged Rebs saw no sense in burning good clothes, and many who went into the raid clad in garments that would hardly stay on came out wearing the very latest in Yankee blue. Unfortunately for Wheeler the attitude of the men toward their general's orders in this incident would prevail throughout the raid in Middle Tennessee.

When the looting finally subsided, what little remained of the Yankee supply train was burned. Most spectacular of all was the destruction of over three hundred wagons of ordinance. So great was the noise that the armies at Chattanooga believed another battle had begun. Less spectacular, but more pathetic, was the destruction of thousands of mules which were sabered or shot. The destruction of the wagon train was complete, but as George Guild observed, "If it ever created a ripple of discomfort anywhere , we never had the satisfaction of knowing it."[6]

With their spirits, confidence, and bodily comforts boosted by the capture of the Yankee train, Wheeler's men continued their journey toward Middle Tennessee. On October 3, 1863, the column arrived at McMinnville where it captured the Federal garrison intact, destroyed another wagon train, and captured a locomotive engine and a long line of cars attempting to escape. From McMinnville the column traveled west and struck the railroad at Murfreesboro. Cars were burned, tracks were wrecked, bridges and supplies destroyed, and prisoners were taken daily as the men moved south toward Wartrace.

From Wartrace the raiders continued west to Shelbyville whose garrison of Yankee troops had evacuated the previous night. By the time Wheeler's men reached the town they barely resembled a military command. Discipline had almost vanished and the men behaved as though they were a plundering band of guerillas. Everything not nailed down became subject to confiscation or destruction by men who had stopped listening to their officers and had become victims of their own uncontrolled desires.

George Guild explained that at Shelbyville the Rebs "found a great many shops, sutler's stores, etc. in the town, well supplied with goods of every description.. . . .Such plunder was considered legitimate for capture as a United States mule or wagon, and to many it was more acceptable."[7] Guild wrote that the officers attempted to restrain their men, "but efforts were generally futile."[8]

Not all the looting was done by soldiers. According to J. L. Hudson, a citizen of the community:

> All stores were thrown open to loot not only by soldiers, but by the citizens of the surrounding country. And we must say to the discredit of the said citizenry, that they rushed into the town, in every conceivable way, afoot, horseback, and in wagons, and proceeded to help themselves to the loot . . .it was a common sight to see the roads crowded with returning looters, well loaded

*with their ill-gained treasures . . The writer remembers
distinctly to have seen squadrons of cavalry passing the
road most grotesquely laden. Belts and bundles of all
kinds of cloth, domestic, calico, linsey and Jeans,
strapped before and behind, boots and shoes dangling
from the saddles, two or three hats piled on each head,
strips and sides of bacon hanging from throat latches, the
whole appearing to be a hugh comic pantomime.*[9]

To Hudson the Confederate raid on Shelbyville was
"perhaps the most shameful deed perpetrated by Confederates
during the war."[10]

As busy as Wheeler's men were in looting for themselves
they did not forget the fairer sex. According to George Guild,

*. . . a couple of ladies had come to town that
morning to make some purchases. When they saw what
had happened, they waved their handkerchiefs and
cheered lustily for Jeff Davis. The soldiers gathered
around them, filled their buggy full of goods, and then
escorted them out of town.*[11]

Despite the lack of discipline in Wheeler's command, his
raid, so far, had been successful. Even though much of a non-
military nature had been plundered, much of a military nature
had been destroyed. The charred ruins of railroad cars, bridges,
warehouses, and wagon-trains along the route offered
convincing evidence as to the raids' effectiveness. But the road
ahead would prove rough and dangerous. The Federals had
Wheeler's column in their sights and a death blow was aimed at
its heart.

In due time, the Confederate column headed for
Lewisburg, twenty miles to the southwest. Midway between
Shelbyville and Lewisburg, at the little village of Farmington,
Wheeler encountered a Yankee force and for two hours his men
fought for their lives. Battered and outmaneuvered, and in

many instances outfought, Wheeler finally managed to withdraw, and on October 9, 1863, the raiders crossed the Tennessee River. In his report Wheeler said:

> *Most of the troops fought nobly; others acted shamefully . . . Many men were allowed by their officers to throw away their arms to enable them to bring out private plunder . . .*
>
> *If we could have one brigadier-general for every five or six regiments, who will obey orders, and make his officers and men do so also, we can get along.*[12]

Wheeler's men had hit the Yankee supply line whenever and wherever they could, they had destroyed more than a million dollars worth of material and had demonstrated to the enemy that anywhere a horse could go was subject to Rebel attack. But on the other hand, the raid had revealed that Wheeler was not an effective commander when put on his own. St. John Liddell, an aide-de-camp to General William Hardee, referred to such events as "one of those miserable, useless, plundering raids."[13]

3.

On the very day that Wheeler crossed the Tennessee River, October 9, 1863, Jeff Davis arrived at Chattanooga to soothe the fevered tempers of his generals. In a series of interviews, at which Bragg was present, Davis probed from subordinate generals an admission that they doubted Bragg's ability to command and believed he should be relieved. Instead of relieving Bragg, Davis gave him a vote of confidence and retained him as head of the army.

Davis at least settled the Forrest-Bragg controversy. Even those who could not get along with Forrest realized his potential to the Confederate cause and nobody, as far as is known, suggested that disciplinary action be taken against him. Davis and Forrest met and the two decided that the Rebel raider should have an independent command. Forrest was assigned to West Tennessee, and for the third time, the incredible leader set out with little more than an order of authority to raise, equip, and train a band of fighters. As in all the times before, Forrest would perform with a degree of excellence that astounded both friend and foe.[14]

During his visit to Chattanooga, Davis decided to favor the private soldiers with the presence of his person. Mounting a spirited horse he gathered his staff around him and galloped along the top of Missionary Ridge. Sam Watkins was among those who viewed the scene, but Sam was unimpressed. Rations were not too plentiful and the overall condition of the Rebel soldier was not conducive to celebration. The men were described as "starved and almost naked, and covered all over with lice and camp itch and filth and dirt. The men looked sick, hollowed eyed, and heart broken, living principally on parched corn."[15]

President Davis and his reviewing party met no fanfare; there were no hats tossed in the air. Instead, according to Sam Watkins, Davis and his party met with shouts of "Send us something to eat, Massa Jeff. Give us something to eat Massa Jeff. I'm hungry! I'm hungry!"[16] Davis did not stop; he rode down the line and out of sight — but he'd be back. It seemed he had a way of turning up just before disaster struck the Army of Tennessee.

The Rebs had no monopoly on troubles at Chattanooga — the Yankees had more. In addition to fighting starvation, they were seeking a new commander. Although Rosecrans had won the Battle of Stone's River and had maneuvered Bragg out of Middle Tennessee he was in trouble because of the rout at Chickamauga. Charles A. Dana, the Assistant Secretary of War, had been on the scene at Chickamauga and his report of the affair was not flattering to Rosecrans. He said:

. . . I have never seen a public man possessing
talent with less administrative power, less clearness and
steadiness in difficulty, and greater practical incapacity
than Geneal Rosecrans.[17]

Such criticism, added to the fact that he had just lost a major battle, spelled the end for the Federal commander.

Finding a replacement was easy. The U.S. Secretary of War, Edwin Stanton, informed Ulysses S. Grant that a new department had been created which included Chattanooga and that Grant had been chosen for command. The hero of Fort Donelson, Shiloh, and Vicksburg left straightway for Chattanooga. Six days later, Grant arrived at Chattanooga, and from that moment, trouble gathered rapidly for the Rebs on the heights above.

Two corps from the Army of the Potomac had already arrived under the command of "Fighting Joe" Hooker and were awaiting orders at Bridgeport, Alabama. From Mississippi, General William T. Sherman was on his way with the Army of the Tennessee. Rosecrans was relieved from duty and George Thomas appointed in his place. If Braxton Bragg appreciated the significance of what was happening it was not reflected in his actions. In the face of this gathering mass of manpower he sent Longstreet and Wheeler to operate against Burnside at Knoxville. Forrest was already gone. The men who had helped make the difference at Chickamauga were sent from the Army of Tennessee which was about to face the largest and most dangerous opponent in its history.

4.

High atop the mountains above Chattanooga the Rebs were taking life easy. There was little to do except watch the Yankees below. Monotony was a constant companion — the same could be said of the Yankees. They looked at the formidable barriers surrounding them and wondered if it would be possible to break through. When Grant first examined the situation he observed, "It looked, indeed, as if but two courses were open: one to starve, the other to surrender or be captured."[18]

At some points, the enemy pickets were so close that soldiers saw fit to declare impromptu truces, during which, they met to exchange small talk and trade camp articles. Tobacco was traded for coffee, crap games sprung up between pickets, and news from the outside was freely exchanged. Where water was scarce, enemy pickets shared the same spring, and on at least one occasion, Grant himself talked leisurely with Rebel soldiers. The Federal general had ridden up to a Confederate outpost where he was greeted by the command,"Turn out the guard for the commanding general," whereupon the Rebs lined up, faced the general and saluted. A member of Grant's staff observed, "We knew that we were engaged in a civil war, but such civility exceeded our expectations."[19]

Resinor Etter was a Rebel soldier whose curiosity constantly prodded him to explore the surrounding environment. He remembered well the peach pies he had made when on the way to Kentucky and again sought to supplement his scant diet with the more appetizing products of his own cooking. It was October, and too late for peaches, but Etter had better luck in finding relatives. On one search, he found an aunt he had never seen, but he was favorably impressed with the "live old coon," and while visiting her, he availed himself of the opportunity to view the Yankees in Chattanooga. He noted in his diary, "I go upon Lookout Mountain to see Aunt Polly and to take a look at the Yankees   I have had an interesting view of them   I have seen all off their breastworks I find them strongly fortified."[20]

Marcus Toney was a little more elaborate in his description of the scene from the mountain top. He wrote:

From the top of Lookout Mountain it was a grand sight at night to see campfires of this large army, at nine o'clock at night the many bugles would blow taps after the music from the bands had floated upwards.[21]

W. J. Worsham was impressed with the proximity of the enemy armies. He observed:

A peculiar scene is here presented in the two encampments of supposed hostile foes; both armies were under the range of a single shot; the bands of each played for the entertainment of the other . . . Another uncommon feature of these two encampments was while the enemy could plainly see the men and officers moving around Bragg's headquarters, we in turn from the top of Lookout Mountain and the ridge with glasses could see what the Yankees had for dinner.[22]

Such a blissful existence was suddenly blurred when on November 20th, Sherman's column arrived north of the Tennessee River above Chattanooga. By the 23rd, Grant had gathered the forces needed to break through the Rebel lines. Already "Fighting Joe" Hooker had pushed close to the west side of Lookout Mountain and Grant was eager to begin the work at hand. Within five days of his arrival, the Federal commander had opened a supply line into the city. The importance of this development can better be appreciated after hearing Joseph Fullerton, a brigadier general under Grant, explain the situation as it had previously existed.

The fall rains were beginning, and hauling was becoming each day more difficult. Ten thousand dead mules walled the sides of the road from Bridgeport to Chattanooga. In Chattanooga the men were on less than half rations. Guards stood at the troughs of artillery horses to keep the soldiers from taking the scant supply of corn allowed these animals. Many horses died of starvation, and most of those that survived grew too weak for use in pulling the lightest guns. Men followed wagons as they came over the river, picking up the grains of corn and bits of crackers that fell to the ground.[23]

Now that George Thomas's men were well fed and newly supplied with equipment inside Chattanooga, and Sherman and Hooker were poised on the outside, Grant was ready to move against the Confederates. Besides, President Lincoln was anxious that the affair at Chattanooga be ended so more attention could be given the situation in upper East Tennessee where Burnside's position seemed to be worsening.

Grant had a plan to fit the situation. In Grant's plan, the inside army — George Thomas' Army of the Cumberland — would operate against the Confederate center while the outside armies — Hooker's Army of the Potomac (two corps) and Sherman's Army of the Tennessee — operated against the Confederate flanks. The first matter of importance for Grant was getting his outside armies into position.

Between Hooker and Chattanooga loomed Lookout Mountain which rose defiantly in his face. It would be a substantial task to cross this rugged obstacle unopposed, but with Rebel soldiers on its summit the possibility seemed even less likely.

Sherman had problems also, both personal and military. The General's family had visited him in Mississippi, and during the trip to Chattanooga, one of his sons had died. The child's name was Willie and according to Sherman, "Of all my children, he seemed the most precious."[24] There had been only time enough to put the child's body on a steamer at Memphis before Sherman proceeded with his army.

At Chattanooga, the General had military problems. Because the Tennessee River bent back upon itself north of the city, Sherman would have to cross the river twice before gaining his desired position. But what lesser men might have considered an obstacle, Grant turned to his advantage. He would have Sherman make his first crossing at a point indicating an attack on the Confederate center. Instead of following through, Sherman would slip behind a chain of hills and emerge for the second crossing at a point where he could hit the Rebel right flank at the northern end of Missionary Ridge.

By Monday morning November 23, 1863, the Yankees were ready to begin the Battle of Chattanooga. Sherman had completed his first crossing of the river and was poised for the second. Hooker was ready to move against Lookout Mountain and Thomas waited for the order to move against the Confederate center.

And what of the Rebs? High atop the natural amphitheater that almost completely encircled the Yankees, Braxton Bragg was evidently depending upon his intuition to guide him through the troubling hours ahead. If so, his intuition failed him. On Sunday the 22nd, with the Federals edging ever closer to his lines, Bragg dispatched Simon Bolivar Buckner's division to Longstreet below Knoxville. On Monday, the very day the fighting at Chattanooga was to begin, he ordered Pat Cleburne's division to entrain for upper East Tennessee. Fortunately the latter movement was retrievable and Cleburne's men were recalled in time to face Sherman at the northern end of Missionary Ridge.

The first move by the Federals involved George Thomas' men. During Monday afternoon, these men moved against a Rebel outpost on a prominent rise known as Orchard Knob which was one mile from the base of Missionary Ridge. By late afternoon, the Rebs had been driven away; the Yanks had won the first round.

Early Tuesday morning, shortly after midnight, the Federals made their second move. Under the cover of a foggy darkness, Sherman loaded his men in shallow boats and started them drifting to the south side of the river. By noon they had succeeded in building a pontoon bridge over which the remainder of the army crossed. At 1 P.M., November 24, Sherman's men hit a rise, only to find that it was not Missionary Ridge proper, but a spur separated from the ridge by a deep ravine. Sherman ordered his men to dig in.

Meanwhile Hooker's men had already launched an attack on Lookout Mountain. The pickets in the area had visited freely and had agreed that if either army made a move to open battle that a prearranged signal be given. The Yankees, true to their word, gave the appropriate signal and H.M. Woodson in a Rebel company said that everybody understood that "friendly relations had ceased."25

Hooker took advantage of a heavy fog that shrouded the mountain and pointed his army up the steep and rugged incline. He soon struck a weak line of Rebs and forthwith entered the finest hour of his military career.

J.J. Turner of the 30th Tennessee was in a position to watch Hooker's men as they climbed the mountain. He later wrote:

> *Foot by foot the Federals fought up that steep and rugged mountain, facing death at every step. The day was wet and murkey, and the smoke and the clouds obscured a view of the troops; but the firing and yelling above the clouds soon indicated that our forces were slowly retiring before superior numbers.*26

The fighting had not taken place atop Lookout Mountain, but on a shelf about half way down. Northern newspapers dubbed the action "The Battle above the Clouds," but the greatly outnumbered Rebs present thought it only a "lightening bug" affair. In any event, Hooker now controlled the mountain and Grant's drama was on script. The Confederates driven from Lookout Mountain hastened to join their comrades on Missionary Ridge.

Tuesday night a strange thing happened in the sky above. Suddenly the moon became obscured from view, the heavens turned a sickening black and cast a weird, unnatural spell over men whose humble faith led them to believe God was about to intervene in the events below. Speaking of the moon's eclipse one Reb said,

> . . *from our side the effect was anything but inspiring, every one seemed impressed with impending doom. No amount of reasoning would throw off the gloom."* [27]

Throughout the night, conversations drifted naturally to the moon's disappearance and what it meant. There were those in both armies who would have welcomed the continuation of night until their political leaders could have regained their reason, but such was beyond their power. As in the unvarying past, nature eventually lifted her restricting hand of darkness and raised the curtain on another act of the Battle of Chattanooga.

Wednesday morning dawned bright and clear, the hovering fog was gone and each army was in plain view of the other. Grant walked along the center of his line on Orchard Knob where "the whole field was in plain view . . ." If Grant could indeed see the Rebel army he was no doubt encouraged by what he saw. A member of the 20th Tennessee looked around him and saw what he believed were additional signs of doom about which the moon had warned. The soldier wrote,

> *The artillery was parked behind the ridge, the horses poor and weak. We watched them trying to get guns up the hill, but the horses would not, or could not, pull them up even with double teams.* [28]

Rebel morale was at rock bottom, but in spite of this fact the men of Pat Cleburne were ready to give it all they had. The opportunity would soon be present.

The victory which Grant anticipated meant more to the unkempt commander than a mere conquest of arms. In writing of this battle he said:

310

There was no time during the rebellion when I did not think, and often say, that the South was more to be benefited by its defeat than the North. The latter had the people, the institutions, and the territory to make a great and prosperous nation. The former were burdened with an institution abhorrent to all civilized people not brought up under it, and one which degraded labor, kept it in ignorance, and enervated the governing class. With the outside world at war with this institution, they could not have extended their territory. The labor of the country was not skilled, nor allowed to become so. The whites could not toil without becoming degraded, and those who did were denominated "poor white trash." The system of labor would have soon exhausted the soil and left the people poor. The non-slaveholders would have left the country, and the small slaveholder must have sold out to his more fortunate neighbor. Soon the slaves would have outnumbered the masters, and, not being in sympathy with them, would have risen in their might and exterminated them. The war was expensive to the South as well as to the North, both in blood and treasure, but it was worth all it cost.[29]

That cost would, very shortly, be increased. Early Wednesday morning, Sherman sent his men against the northern end of Missionary Ridge. Pat Cleburne's Confederates fought them with a fierceness that had already established this band of Rebs as among the best fighters in either army. Time and again the Yankees attempted to dislodge the Rebs, but on each occasion the effort failed. When the Confederates gave out of ammunition they rolled boulders at their enemy and, according to some accounts, when Sherman's men succeeded in capturing the entrance of a railroad tunnel, Cleburne's troops slipped to the other end, charged through, and routed them down the ridge.

Sherman found the task assigned him very taxing; he needed help. Where was Hooker? Why hadn't he made his appearance on the Rebel left as he had been instructed? The fact was that Grant too wondered about Hooker. Why didn't he enter the scene to relieve the pressure against Sherman?

Hooker had his own problems. Between him and the section of the Rebel line he was supposed to have attacked ran Chattanooga Creek. When the Rebs had retreated from Lookout Mountain they had burned the bridge, leaving Hooker no way to get to the battle. While Sherman played his role as best he could, Hooker fumbled and struggled in the wings.

For almost two days, the army of George Thomas sat idly by playing the role of understudy to the men of Sherman and Hooker. Had they regained the confidence lost at Chickamauga? Would they carry through an attack? The truth was that Grant had little choice; they must enter the battle. In a move designed to take pressure from Sherman, Grant ordered Thomas forward against the center of Missionary Ridge.

High above, on top of the ridge, the Rebs watched in understandable awe. It appeared as if the whole world had put on Yankee uniforms and was marching toward them. They watched as thousands upon thousands of Yankees marched shoulder to shoulder "three columns deep," marching as if on parade. W. J. Worsham said, "The very air smelt of battle, and the winds as they came sweeping the crest of Mission Ridge, made sad music as if the precursor of the coming storm."[30]

The approaching Yankee mass became even more impressive to the Rebs when they examined their own line. Actually the Southerners had three lines on Missionary Ridge, one at the bottom, another half way up, and the main line at the top. Even though the top line was still the strongest, so many men had been pulled away to strengthen Cleburne that those remaining could reach out with both arms and not touch anybody.

Closer and closer the Yankees came. From the Ridge the Rebs poured shot after shot into the advancing columns. W. J.

Worsham observed that after the Federals had advanced between Orchard Knob and the base of the Ridge, "there were left on the field men dead and wounded seemingly as thick as stumps in new ground."[31] W. J. McMurray wrote, "It was a grand spectacle.... We could plainly see every movement. When about half way across the valley our artillery opened on them and they could not very well reply."[32] But the Federals did not falter. Soon they were so close that the Rebs could see "the glittering steel and flash of the officers' swords in the sunlight," and still the advancing columns came closer and closer.

With hardly enough impact to be noticeable, the Yankees struck the shallow line of Rebs at the base of the Ridge. There was no contest as the Southerners discharged their weapons and began climbing the steep slope in their rear. To remain in their rifle pits meant sure death or capture and neither of these choices appealed to the men at the base of Missionary Ridge.

A Union soldier who made the advance on Missionary Ridge wrote:

> *Suddenly twenty thousand men rushed forward.... The enemy's rifle-pits were ablaze, and the whole ridge in our front had broken out like another AEtne. Not many minutes afterward our men were seen working through the felled trees and other obstructions. Though exposed to such terrific fire, they neither fell back nor halted. By a bold and desperate push they broke through the works in several places and opened flank and reverse fires. The enemy was thrown into confusion, and took precipitate flight up the ridge.*[33]

Instead of halting at the base of the Ridge as they had been ordered to do, George Thomas' men stopped only long enough to get their breath and, as if prompted by a spontaneous impulse, took off after the fleeing Rebs. Stumbling, sliding, pulling up by saplings and protruding rocks, and firing as they could, the men of both armies continued their undignified ascent of Missionary Ridge.

The second line of Rebs scarcely waited for the first to reach their position before they too joined in the race toward the top. Private William K. Poston of the 4th Tennessee was in the second line and said that after the Confederates from the base of the Ridge had passed his position, his Colonel,

> . . . gave the order, "Ready, aim, fire!" and we opened on the foe.
>
> Those in our front quickly shifted, under the stress of our fires, . . . We maintained our position against great odds — probably ten to one — for about half an hour, when the Confederates to our right gave way, and the Federals were on our flank about as high up as we were. Col. Finlay then gave the order, "Men, fall back to the top of the ridge, but face the Yankees and fire as you fall back," which order those seasoned veterans of the Fourth and Fifth Tennessee, with some exceptions, forthwith proceeded to disregard, and ran up that steep ridge as fast as their legs could carry them ....
>
> Our Lieutenant Colonel hovered in the rear of our rabbit-footed boys, trying his level best to get them to face the Yankees and fire as they fell back, without avail.[34]

Poston joined in the retreat as enthusiastically as the next man, but midway up the mountain he was shot through the shoulder and knocked down. Knowing he could go no further, the young private hid behind a log and was soon taken prisoner.

On Orchard Knob, Grant stood dumfounded as he watched the Federal soldiers climb Missionary Ridge. Turning to those around him, he sought an answer to who gave the order for the pursuit. In a low voice he threatened disaster to the person if things did not go well.

Perhaps the most confused of all were the Rebs on top of the mountain. Coming toward them were their own men pursued by an entire army of unorganized Yankees. The men at the top dared not fire lest they hit their own troops and, in reality, the retreating Rebs from the ineffective lines below became the best shield imaginable for the pursuing Yanks.

When the retreating Confederates from the bottom and middle lines finally reached the top of Missionary Ridge, they turned and joined their comrades in an attempt to knock their attackers back. In the confusion which followed, the Rebel line broke, and through the resulting gap Union soldiers poured through and struck out in every direction.

Before the Rebs on either side of the breakthrough knew what was happening, their artillery was captured and turned against them. Luckily, the Yankee infantrymen knew little about firing artillery and most of the shots went wild. But from below Yankees kept coming. Sixty Federal battle flags came up the mountain; the thing about which the moon had warned had become reality.

W. J. Worsham said, "The ridge where we were was quite steep but the enemy came on, crawling up the steep ascent like bugs, and were so thick they were almost in each other's way."[35] When General A. P. Stewart finally ordered his men to retreat, a Private Goodloe was so intent in his duties that he did not hear the order. Seeing the other men withdrawing, Goodloe called to them, "Here is the way to gain your independence," as he continued to fire his gun. Being informed of the order to retreat, Goodloe replied, "I'll gain my independence that way too," and immediately joined his fleeing comrades![36]

What at first seemed only a Yankee penetration, soon became a rout. In only a few minutes, the center of Bragg's line was in a panic-stricken run to the rear. So swiftly was the Confederate line swept from its position that Bragg and his headquarters were almost captured. The Confederate commander attempted to rally his men who answered his pleas with biting, personal insults. A captain of the 20th Tennessee got a group of musicians together and struck up "Dixie" in the hope that the song would inspire the men to turn and fight, but the effort was in vain and before the song was concluded the musicians themselves had joined the rout.[37]

Not all of the troops in the Confederate center and left ran before the enemy. A few regiments of Cheatham's division turned at right angles to their original position and fought bravely. But such incidents were only temporary in nature, the Confederate center and left were gone. Hooker was at last ready to bring in his fresh troops, and the Rebs who had continued to fight had little choice but join their army in retreat.

Mercifully, night covered the arena with darkness and the troops of Pat Cleburne, who had fought off every assault thrown at them, were forced to retreat across Chickamauga Creek. The Battle of Chattanooga was over and, in Richmond, Jefferson Davis would mourn the first Confederate defeat that had resulted from the "misconduct" by Southern soldiers. On the battlefield, a humiliated Braxton Bragg blamed the defeat, in part at least, on the effect that the sight of Grant's massive army had on "weak-minded" Rebs. This, plus the fact that Breckinridge had been drunk for three days.

To the Confederate soldiers making their way across Chickamauga Creek it mattered little what Jefferson Davis or Braxton Bragg thought. Those who had turned and run didn't care what anybody thought, and those who had fought bravely were so humiliated and discouraged that nothing made sense. Together the brave and unbrave made their way toward Dalton, Georgia, where, for no apparent reason, their army ended its retreat.

5.

On Friday, while the Confederate Army was still retreating from Missionary Ridge, a little noted event took place at the town of Pulaski, Tennessee. It was one of the events which occurred as a rippling effect of the major campaign. But for the people directly involved, it was one of the war's more tragic episodes, one they would talk and write about for as long as they lived. The event centered around a twenty-one year old Confederate soldier named Sam Davis. (photo on frontispiece.)

Following the Battle of Chickamauga, the Confederate High Command wished to know the activities of the Federal Army in Middle Tennessee. A company of scouts was organized and sent into the area to report on both the strength and movements of the enemy. Sam Davis was one of those scouts.

Sam Davis was assigned to "Coleman's Scouts," under the command of Captain H. B. Shaw. Shaw was a former riverboat captain who, disguised as an herb doctor, traveled throughout Middle Tennessee in search of pertinent information. Only those people directly associated with the scouts knew that "Coleman" and "Shaw" were one and the same.

Young Davis possessed the characteristics common to the more intelligent Southern soldier. He had been reared on a farm near Smyrna, Tennessee, in Rutherford County, and had attended a military school in Nashville. People who knew him described the young soldier by saying he "had a peculiarly bright and winning way about him, an utterly fearless eye, a frank and gentle speech, and the self-poise of a great soul."[38] Of the military unit to which he belonged, it was written, "These scouts slept in thickets, where devoted friends, mainly ladies, underwent the peril of going to them by night to feed and inform them of all they could learn about the status and movements of the Federal forces."[39]

At the time Sam was ordered into Middle Tennessee, General Grenville M. Dodge was at Pulaski, having been ordered toward Chattanooga from Mississippi to assist in lifting the siege of Chattanooga. According to a fellow scout, Joshua Brown:

General Bragg had sent us , a few men who knew the country, into Middle Tennessee to get all the information possible concerning the movements of the Federal army, to find out if it was moving from Nashville and Corinth to reenforce Chattanooga ....

We were told that the duty was very dangerous, and that but few of us might return.... After we had been in Tennessee about ten days, we watched the 16th Corps, commanded by General Dodge, move up from Corinth to Pulaski. We agreed that we should leave for the South on Friday, the 19th of November, 1863 .... Late in the afternoon we started, and ran into the 7th Kansas Cavalry, known as the "Kansas Jayhawkers;" and when we learned who had captured us, we thought our time had come. We were taken to Pulaski ... and put in jail. Davis was one of the number. I talked to him over our prospects of imprisonment and escape, which were very gloomy. Davis said they had searched him that day and found some important papers on him, and that he had been taken to General Dodge's headquarters. They had also found in his saddle seat maps and descriptions of the fortifications at Nashville and other points, together with a report of the Federal army in Tennessee.[40]

Two aspects of the papers found on Sam Davis greatly interested General Dodge. The first was their accuracy, the second being that Davis was a member of the Coleman's Scouts. From Dodge's own statement there is reason to believe he thought the accuracy of the information was assured through the cooperation of persons within his own ranks. This attitude made him doubly anxious to get his hands on "Captain Coleman."

Of an interview with Sam, General Dodge said:

I took him into my private office and told him that it was a very serious charge brought against him; that he was a spy, and from what I found upon his person he had accurate information in regard to my army, and I must know where he obtained it. I told him that he was a young man and did not seem to realize the danger he was in. Up to that time he had said nothing, but then he replied in the most respectful and dignified manner: "General Dodge, I know the danger of my situation, and I am willing to take the consequences." I asked him then to give me the name of the person from whom he got the information; that I knew it must be some one near my headquarters or who had the confidence of the officers of my staff, and repeated that I must know the source from which it came. I insisted that he should tell me, but he firmly declined to do so. I told him that I should have to call a court-martial and have him tried for his life, and, from the proofs we had, they would be compelled to condemn him; that there was no chance for him unless he gave the source of his information. He replied: "I know that I will have to die; but I will not tell where I got the information, and there is no power on earth that can make me tell . . ." He thanked me for the interest I had taken in him, and I sent him back to prison. I immediately called a court martial to try him.[41]

Consistent with General Dodge's prediction the court martial found Sam guilty of spying and sentenced him to hang. "The sentence will be carried into effect on Friday, November 27, 1863, between the hours of 10 AM and 2 PM."[42]

The plight of Sam Davis aroused great admiration and concern among his enemies as well as his friends. Yankee soldiers beat a path to his cell door imploring the young Reb to name his informer. Sam steadfastly refused. A Federal scout called "Chickasaw" took it as his personal objective to get Sam to reveal the name, but all such efforts were in vain. Later developments revealed that Captain Shaw, alias Captain Coleman, the real object of the Yankee search was actually in the Pulaski jail with Sam, but their captors never discovered this fact.

Joshua Brown did not see Sam again until Thursday morning, the day before his scheduled execution. According to Brown:

> *We were ordered to get ready to be removed to the courthouse, in the public square, from the jail. Davis was handcuffed and brought in just as we were eating breakfast, I gave him a piece of meat that I had been cooking, and he, being handcuffed, was compelled to eat it with both hands. He thanked me, and we all bade him goodbye. The guard was doubled around the jail."* [43]

That night Sam wrote his mother a note. In it he said:

> *Dear Mother:*
>
> *O, how painful it is to write you! I have got to die tomorrow morning — to be hanged by the Federals. Mother, do not grieve for me. I must bid you good-bye for evermore. Mother I do not fear to die. Give my love to all.*
>
> *Your son,*
>
> *Samuel Davis*
>
>
> *Mother, tell the children all to be good. I wish I could see you all once more, but I never will any more. Mother and father, do not forget me. Think of me when I am dead, but do not grieve for me. It will do no good. Father, you can send after my remains if you want to do so ...*
>
> *S. D.* [44]

Joshua Brown wrote:

The next morning Friday November 27, at ten o'clock we heard the drums, and a regiment of infantry marched down to the jail, and a wagon with a coffin in it was driven up, and the provost marshal went into the jail and brought Davis out. He got into the wagon, stood up, and looked around at the courthouse, and, seeing us at the windows, bowed to us his last farewell . . .[45]

Behind a corp of drummers the procession started toward a hill on the east side of town where a scaffold stood. A member of the Federal band said, "I never witnessed such bravery as was portrayed by him at the time of his killing."[46]

When the procession reached the scaffold, Sam stepped down from the wagon and took a seat on a bench nearby. He asked a captain how long he had to live. "Fifteen minutes," came the answer. Sam then asked for news from the front and was informed of the Confederate defeat at Missionary Ridge. He expressed regret and added, "The boys will have to fight the battles without me." In a moment the executioner walked up and said, "I regret very much having to do this. I feel that I would almost rather die myself than do what I have to do." Sam replied, "I do not think hard of you; you are doing your duty."[47]

While Sam continued to sit on the bench a galloping horse approached from General Dodge's headquarters; it was "Chickasaw." By the time the Yankee dismounted Sam was ascending the scaffold steps. "Chickasaw" ran to him, put his arm around him and offered a reprieve if he would name his informant. According to L.W. Forgaves, a member of the drum corp, "As I could hear, he [Davis] told them he would die a thousands deaths first."[48]

Sam then requested that General Dodge be thanked for all his kindnesses. He turned to the chaplain and gave him a few personal items to be sent to his mother. Then, turning to the provost marshall he said, "I am ready," and the trap was sprung.

<h2 style="text-align:center">6.</h2>

On the following Sunday morning, General James Longstreet massed his Confederate force at Knoxville for a daylight attack on Fort Sanders, which stood north of the Holston River and northwest of the town. In a cold, misty rain, the Rebels attacked, only to be repelled by the Federals who had stretched telegraph wire between a network of stumps which dotted the ground. Those Confederates who somehow survived soon found themselves trapped in a watery ditch into which the Yankees threw lighted artillery shells and a ceaseless stream of small arms fire. Momentarily, the dead, dying, and the living were piled on top of each other in the moat, an "indiscriminate and helpless mass."[49]

While Longstreet pondered the situation word reached him of Bragg's defeat at Chattanooga. Another attack was useless. Even if it were successful the victory would mean nothing, for Sherman was already on his way to Burnside's aid.

It had been only a week since the Yankees began the Battle of Chattanooga, but it had been a fateful week for the Confederacy. Tennessee was lost and Georgia was the new northern boundary of the western Confederacy. Longstreet would stay in East Tennessee throughout the winter, but his presence there meant nothing. Bragg's army at Dalton was in a desperate condition. It was defeated, demoralized, some of its best regiments were with Longstreet, unable to return, and most lamentable of all, it had no leadership capable of rebuilding its confidence.

Perhaps it was well that Nov. 28th had passed unnoticed as Thanksgiving Day.[50]

Chapter XV

No armistice on sea or land

By 1864, Tennessee was under Federal control, and few people in the state, regardless of their sectional affiliation, had escaped the hardships accompanying invasion and occupation by a hostile army. On every hand were the ugly scars of war that told of murderous battles, roaming bands of outlaws, efforts of marching armies to live off the land, and the inability of Tennesseans to stop the monstrous struggle many of them had so enthusiastically endorsed two years before.

For many, only memories remained. While the Confederate Army was retreating to Chattanooga in the summer of 1863, Monroe Bearden's father stopped his wagon west of Murfreesboro at the place where his son had fallen during the battle. As he paused at the spot, he wrote in his diary, "Examined part of the Battle ground where Monroe fell. felt cast down & melancholy. oh but this is a sad place for me, still I like to linger near it."[1]

To men like Monroe Bearden's father, the war had already taken from life much of its meaning. Such men were no longer bothered by national or sectional issues. The high price they had paid for secession made them lose sight of any advantages they had ever believed it might bring. When the bereaved father left Murfreesboro, he drove to Nashville and sold his cotton to the Yankees. Thousands of men like Monroe Bearden had died in the various battles to date, and as tragic as those deaths were, they at least possessed a modicum of meaning. Early recruits in both armies had enlisted voluntarily, supposedly to defend an ideal in which they believed. They had chosen to join an army which symbolized an attitude toward sectional disputes, and in so doing, had accepted the risks involved. This was, of course, not true in the case of those who were forced into service; they died for someone else's convictions, therein magnifying the tragedy of their deaths. But there were still others who died as innocent victims of the turmoil which follows in the wake of war; perhaps these were the most tragic of all.

No part of Tennessee was immune from "the demon of border war." In every section of the state there were those who were ready at the slightest provocation to assert an animal superiority over helpless victims. Such people left a trail of blood from one end of the state to the other and, in all probability, contributed more to the lingering hate which survived the war than any other one factor. Such culprits were not predominately Confederates or Federals in their thinking; they were people who had not yet reached the status of civilized human beings. The war to them was little more than an excuse to exercise their natural inclinations.

The eastern section of Tennessee was the first area to feel the special brutality of border war. One East Tennessean found that during the war "an aggregate of 2,500 to 3,000 non-combatants [were] massacred for their Union sentiment."[2] Another author gave a specific incident.

> Guerilla bands claiming to belong to the Rebel army, were engaged generally in the plunder of Union families. One of these bands was commanded by one William Owens. His company was a band of cut-throats, marauding around, seeking to shed blood. They found a lad of sixteen years, whose name was Lizemore.

*His father was a Union man and quite aged. This gang
of desperadoes arrested the old man, took the boy into
the woods and deliberately murdered him.*[3]

To fully depict the tragedies which occurred in East
Tennessee would be to present an almost endless recital of
needless murders, tortures, and atrocities. So intense was the
bitterness between the pro-Union and pro-Confederate groups
that, following the war, when a record of Confederate atrocities
was published it was necessary to collect the books and destroy
them to prevent further hostility.[4]

Following Burnside's entrance into East Tennessee,
Unionist leaders turned the tables on their Confederate
tormentors. Spurred by memories of Confederate intolerance
they immediately began following a similar course and the reign
of terror continued. William G. "Parson" Brownlow, editor of
the *Knoxville Whig*, wrote in his paper:

*The mediation we shall advocate is that of the
Cannon and the sword: and our motto is — no armistice
on sea or land — until all, all, All the rebels, both front
and rear, in arms and in ambush, are subjugated or
exterminated! And then we are for visiting condign
punishment upon the leaders of the rebellion.*[5]

In Middle Tennessee, L. Virginia French wrote of her
feelings toward the Yankees who now occupied her county. In
her diary on December 7, 1862, she described how Union
soldiers invaded private gardens, drank milk from
springhouses, killed cows and stole chickens. She ended by
saying:

*I abominate the very sight of the miserable
wretches — they are so brutal looking — so impertinent
— and so insufferable in every way.*

*We have no pleasures to look forward to now —
but only duties — hence forth we are not to enjoy, but to*

labor, and endure. We shall belong to that class of the world's drudges, who "work that they may eat that they may be enabled to work." It is a cold and gloomy future — how different from that my imagination pictured two years ago! Yet it must be met, and met with stout hearts too, or we shall faint and fall by the wayside. May Heaven help us, and our children.[6]

In West Tennessee, the Unionists had taken over completely and the secessionists lived in a constant state of uneasiness. Poorly disciplined troops from Illinois, Missouri, and Kansas swept through the area robbing the people of watches, silverware, livestock, and anything else that met their fancy. Bands of "home-made" Yankees joined the regulars and together they looted and plundered towns, many times leaving them in ashes. Colonel Fielding Hurst, a home-made Yankee, entered the town of Jackson and demanded a five thousand dollar ransom to spare it from flames. Prominent citizens made up the money and gave it to Hurst who then promptly reduced much of the town to ashes. On another occasion he set a church on fire and then proceeded to sing and pray loudly to the accompaniment of the crackling flames.[7]

To the keen eye of Amanda McDowell in White County the transition from Rebel to Yankee occupation offered an interesting study. Since Amanda had a brother in each army her observations are perhaps even more significant. As Union troops approached Sparta in July of 1863, Amanda wrote:

The roads, woods, and everywhere are full of men getting themselves, their negroes, horses, mules, cattle, sheep, and everything that is movable out of the way. I guess the Yankees would be amused if they could see the simpletons frightened half to death, and running as if the plague was behind them. I am neither glad nor sorry that they have come. If I was sure that it would be a real injury to the country, I should be very sorry, but I

*cannot think they will be any worse than our own men
have been . . . Some men may suffer, that is my belief,
for they had no business to force the war upon us
whether we wanted it or not. And they know they have
trodden Union men under their feet unmercifully and
those who would not stand to be trodden down they
have abused, persecuted, and compelled to leave the
country and some of them to return with arms in their
hands determined to revenge the wrongs that have been
heaped against them. I do not pretend to justify them for
"vengeance is mine, saith the Lord," but just as long as
men are common humanity, they will take vengeance
upon themselves, and if the hot-headed simpletons of
this country had any sense, they might have known that
the other party might get the upper hand some time. I do
not wish any of them harm, but do hope they will tend to
their own business hereafter.*[8]

With the waning fortunes of war went all pretense of civil
law in most parts of Tennessee. In areas near strategic towns
and cities, the Yankees maintained marital law, but in the remote
counties the people were left to survive by their own efforts.
Even where martial law existed, it often was little more than an
extension of the commanding officer's personality.

In rural counties in Middle and West Tennessee, as it was
earlier in East Tennessee, the people who had formerly run the
courts had lost their authority. Instead of courts, bands of
bushwhackers and guerillas roamed the countryside taking the
law into their own hands. The composition of such groups
varied. They sometimes consisted of deserters from both armies
who banded together to plunder for their own gain. Other
groups were composed of men from a single locality who
organized, originally, to protect their community, but later,
became outlaws and terrorized the countryside. So intense was
the hatred generated by these groups that "a difference in
politics appeared to be sufficient cause for murder."[9]

The defenseless people who lived in areas where these outlaws operated, lived in terror. Their chief hope was that they and what they owned were too insignificant to attract attention. A barking dog in the night sent families scurrying into the woods, horses were hidden in caves to conceal them from robbers, and men dared not be over an arm's length from their loaded guns. It was the unholiest part of war, a part that no one seemed to have anticipated, and a part that no one could control.

2.

Pomp Kersey joined the 16th Tennessee Regiment before he was fifteen years old. It was a sad day for his widowed mother, but the boy was reacting to the temperament of the time and she knew it would be useless to counsel him. The Kersey home was located near Short Mountain in Cannon County and since the prevailing sentiment in the community was Confederate, it was natural that Pomp followed.

For two years Pomp fought with the Rebels, having been cited for bravery when, at Stone's River, he risked his life to rescue an officer. Following the retreat of the Confederates, Pomp grew depressed at the ever-growing list of Southern reverses and decided to return home. He had heard reports that prowling bands of Yankees were robbing, stealing, and killing at will in Cannon County. It seemed to him that he could best serve his community by organizing a company of home guards to protect the people. The tales of atrocities committed against their neighbors were all the incentive Pomp and the dozen or so men who followed him needed. Both the leader and the followers possessed the natural instincts to follow such incentives to their bitter end.

Shortly after he organized his band, word reached Pomp that a neighbor, James Higgins, had piloted some Yankees to another neighbor's home where everything of value had been carried off. The Pomp Kersey band rode to Higgins' home where they found him busily engaged in hog-killing. Without formality or hesitation Higgins was killed on the spot and his body left lying in the mud. Satisfied with their first mission, Pomp and his men rode away to find others suspected of assisting the Yankees.

In a few days the Rebel guerillas swept down on the village of Liberty and attacked a group of citizens believed to be sympathetic to the Union. After a brisk shootout Pomp and his men withdrew, but not before they had left several Unionists "fixed for the coffin."

For several months Kersey's company rendered what Rebel sympathizers accepted as a valuable service. But like others of their kind, the little band of home-defenders lost sight of their avowed objective and succumbed to the temptation of plundering for their own benefit. By the spring of 1864, they were roaming throughout the countryside robbing former friends as quickly as they did their enemies.

On the evening of July 23, 1864, a dance was held at the home of Mr. Melton, seven miles from Liberty. It was an unusual affair inasmuch as the guests included both Rebels and Yankees who happened to be in the vicinity. According to a Cannon Countain who believed the story "should be wrote as it happened," the following took place.

> All the boys happened to be in on furloughs at the same time. Being uncles, brothers, and nephews they concluded to have a dance . . . They invited a few friends on the sly, both yankee and rebel . . . All agreed to be friends and keep everything a secret. Somehow Pomp Kersey and Jack Neely got news of the fondang. They came also. They hid in the bluff across the creek from the house. The frolicsom dance went merrily on til near daylight. Pomp and the boys sliped up near the

upper door . . . They could have shot everyone dead but seeing it was a mixed crowd they shot above the door to run the yanks out. They run hury scury down the creek.[10]

During the attack, Pomp's men killed only one Yankee, but the affair was not to end there. The Yanks went to Liberty and recruited their ranks and returned with blood in their eyes. By this time, both Yanks and Rebs had visited the same whiskey-maker and both groups were thoroughly stimulated by his pleasing merchandise. The Yankees were determined to track down Pomp and his men and the next morning the search began.

Shortly after daylight, the Yankees found the Kersey gang asleep in a thicket near a place called Half Acre. Cautiously slipping as close as they could, the Yanks pulled their guns and fired two volleys into the sleeping home-guards, killing most of those present. Pomp himself was not killed and, as rapidly as possible, raced for his horse tied to a nearby tree. Shots from the Yankee guns hit him full blast and he fell to the ground dead. Seven men had died in less than two minutes.

In such incidents the death of opponents seldom satisfied the participants. As told by someone sympathetic to Pomp, the Yankees;

> *...stripped off all the boys clothes. Then went to Bob Jones place, and took aunt Betty's oxen and cart without asking. The cart had no bed, so they threw some planks across the cart and piled the naked dead bodies of seven boys on the cart.*[11]

The citizens of the village of Liberty watched in horror as the corpses were brought in. "They rudely placed them on an open cart frame, their legs and arms swinging to and fro."[12] The bodies were later deposited in an empty store room, an inglorious end to Pomp Kersey's company of home-guards.

The saga of Pomp Kersey followed a plot which was enacted in most rural communities of Tennessee. Unfortunately the people involved were well equipped in both temperament and firearms to push their point of view. In many instances the participants, unwilling to join either army, killed without apparent cause, burned without reason, stole property when and where they found it, and seldom were curbed by the intervention of common decency. Their moral code seemed to be that justice rode with the group which survived.

Representative of such men were "Champ" Ferguson's Rebel band and "Tinker Dave" Beatty's Yankee group. Ferguson was a rugged mountaineer who had migrated to White County a few months before the war began. His counterpart, "Tinker Dave," was an equally rugged and crude individual whose center of operations was a secluded mountain cove in Fentress County. The careers of both men depict the state of affairs in rural Tennessee during the war.

Champ Ferguson was uniquely qualified to take full advantage of the absence of civil law. His own family divided on the question of secession and both Champ and his brother understood it would be a fight to death should they ever meet. Champ had already killed one man before the war began and the act seemed to trigger an impulse that dominated his existence.

Basil Duke, John Hunt Morgan's second in command, once used Champ as a guide. Years later he wrote:

> *He had a reputation of never giving quarter, and, no doubt, deserved it . . . This redoubted personage was a native of Clinton county, Kentucky, and was a fair specimen of the kind of characters which the wild mountain country produces. He was a man of strong sense, although totally uneducated, and of the intense will and energy which, in men of his stamp and mode of*

life, have such a tendency to develop into ferocity, when
they are the least injured or opposed . . . He was known
as a desperate man before the war, and ill-treatment of
his wife and daughter, by some soldiers and Home-
guards enlisted in his own neighborhood, made him
relentless in his hatred of all Union men; he killed all
parties concerned in the outrage upon his family, and,
becoming then an outlaw, kept up that style of
warfare.[13]

Although Champ himself never verified Duke's story of the Yankees mistreating his family, those who sought to explain his actions told how a company of "home-made" Yankees came by his home while he was away, forced his wife and daughter to disrobe and parade up and down before the howling taunts of the men. According to this version, when Champ heard of the incident, he raised the "black flag" on all Yankees and vowed to kill at least one hundred of them. Legend would have it that he exceeded this number by twenty or thirty.

Ferguson's initial efforts in 1861, were in Kentucky, where his first victim was a man named William Frogg. Frogg had aroused Champ's displeasure by visiting Camp Dick Robinson, a Yankee Camp of Instruction, in southeastern Kentucky. According to the victim's wife, Ferguson came to her home and asked to see her husband. Upon being informed that Frogg was sick, Ferguson forced his way into the bedroom and asked the sick man, "How are you Mr. Frogg?" After receiving the reply that he was feeling badly Ferguson said, "I reckon you caught the measles at Camp Dick Robinson." Ferguson then pulled his pistol and shot Frogg twice. The five-month old child of the victim was lying in its crib by Frogg's bed when the shooting took place. In the light of Ferguson's subsequent activities the killing of William Frogg would seem meek and mild.

At a later time, Ferguson and his gang met a boy by the name of Fount Zachery as the lad rode down a remote rural road. A member of the gang described the incident by saying:

[A]boy came out of an ive thicket toward our company with a gun on his shoulder and said, "Boys, you need not go this way; you won't find them here." From the way he talked, I suppose he took us for a Federal company.

George Murphy demanded him to surrender his gun and the lad handed it to him . . . Ferguson, I think, asked him his name and he replied, "Fount Zachery." As soon as he said this, Ferguson shot him. He fell from his horse, and Ferguson then got off his horse and stabbed him. I was within ten or fifteen feet of them at the time, and when Ferguson stabbed him I heard a sort of rough, grating sound that I hardly know how to describe.[14]

Other and more bloody killings marked the path of Champ Ferguson. Three more members of Fount Zachery's family were killed; David Delk was chopped to pieces; John Williams was tortured with knives and sharp sticks; and literally dozens of wounded Federal soldiers were killed as they lay wounded on the battlefield.

Ferguson's activities became of such concern to the Federal Army that the 5th Tennessee Cavalry [Union] was detached to White County to break up the gang.

According to the Adjutant General's Report of The State of Tennessee:

A detachment of the regiment was attacked on Calfkiller Creek on the 22nd of February, 1864, by a large force of guerillas and a severe engagement followed. Three or four [Federal] soldiers were killed in action, and nineteen others were taken prisoners, and deliberately murdered after they had surrendered and given up their arms. The heads of some of the unfortunate prisoners were riddled with balls, one man receiving seven bullets.[15]

General Basil Duke once asked Ferguson,

Champ, how many men have you killed? Champ responded with some feeling, as a man who thinks he has been slandered: "I ain't killed nigh as many men as they say I have; folks has lied about me powerful. I ain't killed but thirty-two men since the war commenced.[16]

While Champ Ferguson went through the hills killing in the name of the Confederacy, "Tinker Dave" Beatty was doing likewise in the name of the Union.

David Beatty, better known as "Tinker Dave," was a scourge to Southern sympathizers who lived in the area of Fentress County. On one occasion, his band of guerillas rode up to the front of a farmhouse where a small boy was playing with his dog. Before a word was spoken, the dog was shot. The boy was then told to have his mother come from the inside of the house. When the mother appeared she was ordered to cook supper for Beatty and his forty men; meantime the guerillas busied themselves plundering her livestock and feed.

Amp Poor was the lad whose dog was shot. "I remember it well," Amp wrote later. "They filled their wagons with our corn, and they took all our horses, and all our cattle, except two bulls. Tinker said to mother 'If you will let your boy take the bulls and help us up the mountain, we will send your bulls back, if you don't we'll take them along.' " Left with little choice the frightened mother agreed to let the boy go; soon the bulls were returned safely. But not long afterward, Beatty's men returned, and the bulls, along with all the other livestock, were driven away.[17]

On the same day, the gang visited an elderly man named Robert Richardson who was confined to his bed and almost blind. Richardson was dragged from his bed to the yard and there stomped to death by his drunken assailants. To make the episode complete, the old man's dog was killed and thrown across his body. The crime of Robert Richardson: he had three sons in the Confederate Army.

At another time Beatty's men went to a school house and took the teacher, Reece T. Hildreth, into the yard and shot him. Hildreth was a cripple and could walk only with the aid of crutches. Adding to the ruthlessness of the murder was the fact that Hildreth's daughter was forced to witness the execution.[18]

Both Ferguson and Beatty survived the war, but for Ferguson there would be little time left. Tricked into surrendering to Federal authorities at Nashville, Champ was tried for war crimes, convicted, and sentenced to hang. On October 20, 1865, as Champ stood on the gallows, he was asked if he had a final request. He reportedly replied, pointing to the coffin awaiting his body, "Put me in that box," and further stipulated that he wanted his body turned over to his wife so he might be buried in White County. Champ added, "I do not want to be buried in such soil as this." As the executioner gave the signal to spring the trap, Champ exclaimed, "Good Lord have mercy on my soul!"[19] Champ Ferguson became the only Confederate soldier, other than Captain Henry Wirz of Andersonville Prison, to die for crimes committed during the Civil War.[20]

"Tinker Dave" Beatty was never brought to trial. He lived to be an old man, "got religion," and became a respectable citizen.

4.

Individuals whose former existence had been marked by peacefulness and an evenness of temperament, suddenly were transformed into desperate people who acted on little more than animal impulses. They had watched helplessly as their entire value system was swept away by the bitterness and brutality which dominated the scene. For many, every thought and act seemed centered around either survival or revenge.

Writing of Stewart County, one historian said:

> *Throughout the war the country was overrun with guerillas and jayhawkers, and much loss of life and property was caused thereby. During 1863 James Gray, an aged and well-to-do farmer, was visited by jayhawkers, who supposed he had money secreted about his house, and was taken by them and tortured by placing his feet in the fire . . . but the old man had no money on hand.*[21]

In the same county, dozens of citizens were shot in cold blood for their political sentiments and one, Garrett Crisp, was choked and tortured into giving up every cent of money he possessed.[22]

Even the young ladies of rural counties were not exempt from the wave of bitterness which engulfed their communities. In Putnam County a physician by the name of Sadler was killed by the Confederates because of his loyalty to the Union. Ordinarily, the matter would have ended there, but in this incident, the murderers aroused the wrath of Miss Livernia Webb who was engaged to marry the doctor. Although two of her brothers were in the Confederate Army the bereaved woman had no idea of letting the crime go unpunished.

Knowing the murderers to be three men by the names of Poteet, Gardenshire, and Turner, Livernia Webb vowed to get revenge and little else occupied her mind but the fulfillment of that vow. Before she could confront the killers, Poteet and Gardenshire were dead, but as long as Turner breathed he remained Livernia's main reason for living.

On a Sunday morning Livernia went to Turner's home and called for him. Finding that he was not at home, she went to a neighbor's house and inquired of his whereabouts. Looking out the window she saw Turner in the yard and immediately rushed out to where he was.

In a letter concerning what happened, Livernia wrote:

I then walked out into the yard, and as Turner was starting, called to him to stop. He turned and saw I was preparing to shoot him; he started to run. I fired at the distance of about twelve paces, and missed. I fired again as quickly as possible, and hit him in the back of the head, and he fell on his face and knees. I fired again and hit him in the back, and he fell on his right side. I fired twice more, only one of these shots taking effect.[23]

Livernia Webb concluded her letter by saying, "I got my horse out, and started home, where I shall stay or leave when I choose, going where I please, and saying what I please."[24]

Not even church services were immune to the ever-present terror of attack from guerilla bands. Amanda McDowell was attending church at Cherry Creek in White County when a group of raiders attacked the congregation, killing at least one and wounding others. In Cheatham County a member of a congregation was taken from the church and hanged in the church yard. Hazel Burns, a Union soldier from Putnam County, visited his home to find his mother and father beaten to death by Rebel bushwhackers. His brother and sister were so seriously beaten that both were forced to spend the remainder of their lives in an insane asylum.[25] The taking of human life became commonplace in Tennessee as the inharmonious sounds of border war reached a terrifying crescendo.

5.

Instead of adding an element of stability to the situation in Tennessee, the Union army sometimes added fuel to the unrest which prevailed. Indeed, some units of the Army proved as skilled in the art of butchery and the ability to terrorize the

337

population as were the native guerillas who shot, carved, and burned their way onto the most inglorious pages of the war's history.

The small community of Triune in Williamson County felt the sharp sting of Yankee bitterness as soon as Bragg retreated from Murfreesboro. Triune is located in one of the richest farming districts of Middle Tennessee. Its inhabitants numbered slightly over eighty, most of whom considered themselves among the "upper-crust" of antebellum society. The slave population far outnumbered the white residents since literally hundreds of people were required to cultivate the fertile land which stretched for miles in every direction. Williamson County had a slave population of more than twelve thousand when the war began and of these twelve hundred were owned in the civil district of which Triune was a part.

The village of Triune was composed of five general stores, one tailor shop, a weekly newspaper, a printing shop, a boot and shoemaking shop, four boarding schools, an undertaker, a hat shop, and several fine brick churches. When Tennessee first voted on secession, the people of the district voted against it, but when it became obvious that Federal troops were to invade the South, the sentiment changed quickly, and in the subsequent referendum, Triune went almost unanimously for separation from the Union. The Yankees could not have wished for a better target.

The men of Federal General Phil Sheridan moved into the Triune community on March 5, 1863. The particular command that occupied the area was under General James Steedman, a former member of the Ohio legislature. Steedman's men lost little time in wreaking havoc on the community.

With precision-like skill they burned the Methodist Church, the Masonic Hall, and the Baptist Church. Next came one of the female academies. Many of the finer homes were burned, while countless others were looted of their valuables.

Later, when General David Stanley assumed command, he ordered every house from which a Confederate soldier had come burned to the ground. Giant billows of smoke soon climbed skyward as residence after residence crumbled before the eyes of their owners.

In some mysterious way, the Federals learned that Sam Burke, a Confederate soldier, was visiting in the home of Mrs. Cherry, north of the village. Slipping in and surrounding the Cherry home, a Federal detachment demanded of Mrs. Cherry that her guest be surrendered. The demand was scorned, whereupon, the troops forced their way into the house. By a stroke of good fortune the Rebel soldier climbed out a back window and was soon on his way to safety. Enraged, the Yankees took one of Mrs. Cherry's sons into the yard and murdered him in cold blood. They then returned to the house, arrested the mother, burned the house, and left the woman's four younger children hovering helplessly as she was taken to the penitentiary at Nashville.

In spite of such incidents, the Triune community was yet to experience its most terrifying hour. It came in late August, 1864.

Dee Jobe, like Sam Davis, a member of the Coleman's Scouts, had been assigned to observe the movements of the Federal Army in Middle Tennessee in preparation for a possible re-entry of the Confederates. While in the Triune community, Jobe stopped at the home of William Moss for food. Since the execution of Davis, Jobe knew the consequences of being caught. After eating his supper, the young scout went a mile down the road and concealed himself in a cornfield where he was later captured by a detail of the 115th Ohio Infantry.

Realizing they had captured a scout, the Yankees attempted to make Jobe reveal his business, but the effort was in vain. After all attempts failed, the Yankees

...tied the hands of their prisoner behind him, and put a leather strap around his neck to choke him. Jobe

was beaten over the head with guns, his upper teeth were knocked out, his eyes were put out, and later his tongue was cut out. He was then tied to the tail of a galloping horse and dragged until no life remained in his body. As a final jesture the Ohio Yankees tied him in a tree, head down, and left his body hanging as they rode off.[26]

6.

Of all the incidents where hate drove men to deeds of brutality, none surpassed those which led up to and included the capture of Fort Pillow by Forrest's command in April of 1864. The fort was on the east bank of the Mississippi River approximately seventy miles north of Memphis. It had never played an important role in the war and had it not been for what happened there on April 12, 1864, chances are it would have made little imprint on the history of the war. The Fort Pillow tragedy was a composite of many incidents which had taken place in West Tennessee—incidents which found their culmination in this tragic floodtide of hate.

When Federal forces occupied West Tennessee early in the war, residents of the area learned quickly that the battlefield did not comprise the totality of war. The people of Memphis were among the first to learn. Memphis was a city of thirteen thousand people. It possessed the only five-story building in the state. During the first months of the war, the city buzzed with enthusiasm for the Confederate cause and many of its leaders envisioned a time when it would be the South's leading city. Then came Shiloh.

After the defeat of the Confederate Army at Shiloh, the Yankee forces moved in to occupy Memphis. Things went well at first, but when Sherman replaced Grant as commander, West Tennesseans felt the full blow of the civil war.

Sherman initiated policies that many citizens considered barbaric. Thomas Gailor, later Chancellor of the University of the South, was a young resident of the city at the time, and later wrote, "Then ensued a Reign of Terror. Fires broke out among the residences all over the city; houses were looted; in some instances sick women were taken out of their burning homes, to die on the streets." Gailor wrote that during Sherman's occupation his small sister became seriously ill and a physician was sent for, "but the pickets refused to let him come to the house at night; and my sister died in my mother's arms."[27] He added:

> *I remember seeing my mother in her long black dress, standing over a little coffin, and a guard of Federal soldiers crowding into the room, pushing her out of the way, lifting up the lid of the coffin, to see, they said, whether arms were concealed in it. I was shocked to see my mother fall to the floor in a faint.*[28]

In the dead of winter, Sherman collected the wives and children of Confederate soldiers and banished them from the city.[29] Prisons were packed with citizens who refused to take the Oath of Allegiance to the Federal Government; others were robbed in the streets. Sherman would never be forgiven for his actions by those who endured them, but the hate that at first was reserved for him soon extended to most Unionists who followed.

Throughout West Tennessee there were many people who sincerely opposed secession from the very beginning. This element of the population endured many injustices and hardships as the war progressed. The practice persisted in spite of the fact that the Unionists controlled the area for the last three years of the war. As was the case with Middle and East Tennessee, the remote sections suffered most.

One writer noted:

The years of Federal occupation were years of unrest and lawlessness in West Tennessee. Neighbor turned against neighbor, and gangs of irregulars and cut-throats roamed over the country, terrorizing one and all. The Confederate soldier, home on leave, was a special target of these marauders.[29]

Other writers noted just as emphatically that Federal soldiers home on leave were forced to hide their uniforms to protect themselves against gangs riding under the Confederate banner.[30] It seems reasonable to assume that a general state of lawlessness prevailed with the advantage riding on the shoulders of the strongest gang, whether Confederate or Unionist.

In Obion County there lived a well respected physician by the name of Almon Case. Dr. Case moved to the county from Ohio, and at the beginning of the war, was an enthusiastic Southern sympathizer. Following the Battle of Shiloh his sectional allegiance changed — or so it seemed to his neighbors. He was suspected of informing on Confederate soldiers who were home on furlough. The person to whom he supposedly passed information was "Captain Berry," a noted Yankee guerilla.

Captain Berry was accused of many ruthless murders, each of which tended to be more hideous than the one before. His name struck terror among Confederate sympathizers in the area. So great was the fear of the man that it was difficult, and often impossible, to find enough people to arrange proper funerals for his victims. Men were afraid to dig graves or make coffins for fear of reprisals. At one funeral "so few men dared attend that brave women assisted in lowering the bodies into the graves."[31]

After a particularly brutal slaying by Captain Berry, men of the community resolved to kill Dr. Case for his suspected role in the incident. Two men, Frank Farris and Henry Darnell, waited for the doctor to return from a trip to a nearby community, but what they did not know was that the physician's son was riding the horse which had been recognized. As a result the son was killed as he returned home.

The mistake in identity did not deter Farris and Darnell from seeking the life of Dr. Case.

> *Soon after, Frank Farris was in Wilsonville (Hornbeck) as Dr. Case rode through. Meeting Frank Farris he spoke pleasantly and said; "Frank, come and go home with me." Frank replied, "I'm riding that way." Together they rode to the point near the Burnt Mill Hollow Road where it leaves the Dyersburg road. There Frank left the doctor shot dead.*[32]

Captain Berry was captured by Captain H. W. Harris of the Confederate Army, and though the Federal guerilla had been seriously wounded during his capture, he was loaded into a farm wagon and hauled toward his place of execution. On the way, a country school was passed and the children were invited out to view "Berry in his last days. School at once broke up, the children running outside in excitement to see the dreaded outlaw." Farther down the road a wooded knoll was found and Captain Berry was shot.[33]

The Berry-Case incidents are typical of the atmosphere which reigned in West Tennessee in early 1864. The Confederates believed that the men who rode with Nathan B. Forrest were special targets of the "home-made" Yankees and that the families of Forrest's men suffered disproportionately with other people. Federal Colonel Fielding Hurst of Purdy, Tennessee, was accused of killing six Confederates from McNairy County and leaving their bodies as mile markers along the road.[34] One of Forrest's officers reported that two men, Lt. Joseph Stewart and Private John Wilson, "while on duty under orders from their commanding officer, were captured by Hurst's command, and three days thereafter their bodies were found, they having been shot to death."[35] Many incidents of a similar nature were reported.

Forrest protested the killings to Federal General C.C. Washburn. Forrest condemned the Yankees "who deliberately took out and killed seven Confederate soldiers, one of whom they left to die after cutting off his tongue, punching out his eyes, splitting his mouth on each side to his ears, and inflicting other mutilations."[36]

Washburn answered Forrest's protest with counter-accusations that the Confederates had committed crimes in excess of those mentioned in the note. Washburn offered no encouragement that the situation would improve. This was the climate of hate and unrest into which Forrest moved his command on the first day of April, 1864. His first stop was Jackson, Tennessee.

The town of Jackson had always been an attractive place for the men who rode with Forrest. William Dyer recorded in his diary how the men had ridden in the moonlight with local belles, and how weary troopers had visited the whiskey bars to ease the pains accumulated during tiring raids.[37] But this time it would be different.

During their first week at Jackson, Forrest's command was visited by a constant flow of families who told of being terrorized by the Yankees. Many of the men asked for permission to return home to protect their families and property from the inhumane acts of their former neighbors. Although such requests were denied, Forrest promised "to employ his present resources for the summary   supression of the evil and grievances complained of, by the surprise . . . and capture . . . of Fort Pillow."[38]   To Southern sympathizers, Fort Pillow symbolized the source of their torment.

Inside the fort two units were present: the 13th Tennessee Battalion (Federal) under the command of Major William F. Bradford, and four companies of the 6th U. S. Heavy Artillery under the command of Major Lionel F. Booth who was also in overall command of the fort. Bradford, a native of Bedford County who became a lawyer and moved to West Tennessee, had arrived at Fort Pillow on February 8th; Booth and his men had arrived approximately two weeks before the Confederate attack. The total number of soldiers manning the fort was 580 men, of which 292 were Negroes. All the Negroes were artillerymen.

At 5:30 on the morning of April 12th, Forrest had his command outside Fort Pillow. The enemy pickets were driven in and by mid-morning the Confederates completely surrounded the land side of the fort. Major Booth was killed during the preliminary firing and the command passed to Major Bradford.

By two o'clock in the afternoon, the Confederates had advanced to within fifty yards of the fort and, as he had so often done in the past, Forrest sent in a note under a flag of truce demanding surrender of the fort. It is at this point that the controversy surrounding Fort Pillow begins.

Federal soldiers accused Forrest of violating the flag of truce to move his men into advantageous positions. The Confederates denied the accusation. In any event the Federals inside the fort declined Forrest's demand for surrender, the note bearing the signature of the already dead Booth. It made little difference to Forrest who said "no," he was only interested in its implications.

Only the first note of the bugle which sounded the charge was heard; the others were lost in the fierce yell that came from Forrest's men. They jumped into a wide ditch outside the main works, and in the mud and water, the bigger men leaned down while others climbed their backs to gain a foothold on the walls above. Federal soldiers who showed their heads were promptly shot by a line of sharpshooters who stayed far enough back to perform this important job.

The Rebs leaped across the top wall surrounding the fort and like a band of pirates jumped into the mass of bluecoated soldiers inside. The Confederates "shoved their guns and six-shooters against their blouses, and lead and powder and wadding tore them to instant death."[39]   Terrified, many of the Federals threw down their guns and ran toward the river where they expected support from a ship which was close by. Instead of finding help, the fleeing soldiers ran into a cross-fire from a group of Confederates who had been stationed near the river to keep the boat away. With nowhere to go, the Federals circled aimlessly as the terrible slaughter continued. It seemed that all of Forrest's 1500 man force was now inside the fort, killing its garrison.

To many Federal soldiers it was evident that surrender was the only prudent course. They threw down their guns and held up their hands. Some were taken prisoner, but others were shot down as they stood with their hands raised. Some Federals broke and ran through the Confederate line, but these were soon run down and killed by Rebs who screamed and yelled with every step. Perhaps there was no scene of carnage during the war that approached this one.

In a short time, Forrest came into the fort and ordered the firing stopped. Whether it did or not is still disputed. Federal soldiers later testified under oath that they saw their comrades killed as late as the next morning; women who entered the fort the next day said they saw a man nailed to a board and that he had evidently been burned to death. Others said they heard the screams of the wounded as the Rebs burned them alive and many White soldiers told of seeing Negro troops murdered as they knelt on their knees pleading for mercy.[40]

The Confederates tempered such stories by saying that when they entered the fort they "found water-buckets sitting around in the fort with whiskey and dippers in them, which showed very clearly that the whiskey had been passed around to Federal troops."[41]   The Rebs claimed the Yankees never surrendered, as evidenced by the fact that their flag never left its staff. Few, if any, Confederates ever denied that a massacre occurred at Fort Pillow, their only point of contention being the circumstances under which the massacre had taken place.

More damaging to the Confederate defense of what happened at Fort Pillow than the testimony of Union sympathizers are the recently discovered letters written by Confederate soldiers.

Achilles V. Clark, a former college student from Henry County, wrote his sisters two days after the attack:

> *The slaughter was awful. Words cannot describe the scene. The poor deluded negroes would run up to our men fall upon their knees and with uplifted hands scream for mercy but they were ordered to their feet and then shot down. The white men fared but little better. The fort turned out to be a great slaughter pen. Blood, human blood stood about in pools and brains could have been gathered up in any quantity. I with several others tried to stop the butchery and at one time had partially succeeded. [B]ut Gen. Forrest ordered them shot down like dogs, and the carnage continued . . . We brought away about one hundred and sixty white men and about seventy five negroes.*[42]

Samuel H. Caldwell wrote his wife:

> *We are just from Fort Pillow which fort we attacked on Tuesday the 13th [12th] 1864 & carried by storm. It was garrisoned by 400 white men and 400 negroes & out of the 800 only 168 are now living So you can guess how terrible was the slaughter. It was decidedly the most horrible sight that I have ever witnessed.*
>
> *They refused to surrender — which incensed our men & if General Forrest had not run between our men & the Yanks with his pistol and sabre drawn not a man would have been spared.*[43]

An undetermined number of Union soldiers ran to the Mississippi River and attempted to reach barges anchored nearby. A Confederate soldier who witnessed this incident wrote:

> *The sight of negro soldiers stirred the bosoms of our soldiers with courageous madness . . .*
>
> *The number in the water was so great, that they resembled a drove of hogs swimming across the stream. But not a man escaped in this way. The head above the water was a beautiful mark for the trusty rifle of our unerring marksmen. The Mississippi River was crimsoned with the red blood of the flying foe. Our soldiers grew sick and weary in the work of slaughter, and were glad when the work was done.*[44]

Major William Bradford was captured during the fighting at Fort Pillow. Earlier in the day his younger brother had been killed and the Major was granted permission to care for his body. According to the Confederates, Bradford abused the privileges extended him and made good his escape. He was again captured and his body was later found lying beside an isolated, rural road. The Federals contended that Major Bradford was brutally murdered.

It was left to Lieutenant Mack J. Leaming to write the report of Fort Pillow for his unit, Bradford's Battalion. In part he said:

> *With the capture of Fort Pillow terminates the history of this Battalion. Hardly a nucleus of the command remained after the vengeance of the rebel soldiery had been wreaked upon the brave but overpowered defenders of our flag. For ten long hours they held out against overwhelming numbers of the enemy . . . Finally, at about four o'clock P.M., the enemy through a violation of his flag of truce, succeeded in overpowering the garrison and compelling it to*

surrender. Up to this juncture only three of our officers who participated in the fight had fallen, but after the bloodthirsty barbarity of the rebels had been dealt out to their unarmed and helpless prisoners, only three of our officers were found to be alive.[45]

Dr. John Allan Wyeth, Forrest's biographer, wrote:

Three years of civil war had passed, not without a deplorable effect upon the morals of the rank and file of either army .... They had been neighbors in time of peace, and had taken opposite sides when the war came on .... When they met in single combat, or in scouting parties, or in battles, as far as these individuals were concerned, it was often a duel to the death .... Between the parties to these neighborhood feuds the laws of war did not prevail. Here, in this melee, in the fir and excitement of the assault, they found opportunity and made excuse for bloody vengeance.[46]

The diary of William Dyer, who participated in the battle, told the story of Fort Pillow in a simple straightforward manner. His entry for April 12, 1864, reads:

We arrived at Fort Piller and attacked same early in the day   The Fort was defended by about 450 Blacks and 250 whites   We captured about 40 Blacks & 100 Whites and killed the remainder   We demolished the place.[47]

Viewed as an isolated military engagement Fort Pillow stands as a needless slaughter of human-kind, but viewed in the context of border war it becomes another tragic reference point in the terrible marathon of hate which, by 1864, had engulfed the people of Tennessee.[48]

Dewitt Jobe

John Allan Wyeth

Champ Ferguson

Livernia Webb

Chapter XVI

Everything here
is at present quite dull

Winter in north Georgia can be very unpleasant, especially if the icy blasts of wind and the slow penetrating cold of the season are endured without adequate clothing. The men in the Army of Tennessee were finding this out in the winter of 1864.

Following the rout at Missionary Ridge, the Rebs settled down at Dalton, some twenty miles below Chattanooga. The Georgia village had nothing special to offer in the way of accommodations, either for a soldier's comfort or his defense against a potential enemy. It just happened to be the place where the army got together after Missionary Ridge and, since nobody was doing much thinking, the troops set up camp for the winter.

Soon after they arrived, the men began building makeshift cabins, and by the middle of December, most of the more industrious men were reasonably well housed. By December 10th, Resinor Etter had almost completed his cabin and the next day wrote that he and his friends:

> *Comest the chimney   work all day hard at night we have us a nice hous every thig is complet ever thing looks nice   Our bed is composed of some chestnut lathing that we have made   we have raised it up off of the groun   covered it over with sage grass   We have*

got a big fire   took our seat befour it and feel with great
obligation to our Heavenly father for giving us the
comfortable dweling that I now sit in.[1]

Not all the Rebs who retreated from Missionary Ridge
were at Dalton. Many had waited alongside the roads where
they were picked up by the enemy. Others simply gathered
together what few belongings they owned and, without
apologies, went home. Those men who did go to Dalton
arrived in a very demoralized state of mind. Many regiments
existed in skeleton form only, food was scarce, whiskey was
rationed in such small portions that it did little to ease the pain of
boredom, and enthusiasm for the Confederacy suffered
tremendously.

The cheers of home-town girls and the glorious verbalisms
of politicians had long since ceased their ringing in the ears of
these veterans. The names of the battles they had fought were
mere milestones along the disastrous road that had brought them
to Dalton. W. J. Worsham wrote:

To Tennesseans the future horizon of the young
Confederacy began to look dark and hazy. We had now
been battling for two and a half years, and had been
driven back and back by our foes, until our homes were
now in the hands and at the mercy of the enemy.[2]

Certainly, the men at Dalton had reason to be discouraged.
They had been driven from Tennessee on three occasions;
killing Yankees had not been as easy as the politicians had
predicted and the silver-tongued soothsayers had forgotten to
say that the Yankees would shoot back. The Confederate army
had won only one victory in two years and the commanding
general had let its fruits go unclaimed. Every time a force was
gathered equal to the enemy's, some "high up" came along and
sent part of it away. Some of the army's generals seemed
madder at each other than they were at the Yankees, and
besides, the war had already lasted much longer than had been
promised.

In view of what had happened to the Confederate Army perhaps a dream recorded by a young soldier had been prophetic. Stating that it had been bearing on his mind with great weight, the soldier said of the dream:

> *It appeared to me in a strange public house where ther seemed to be a no of strangers all men of prominence by a symeltanouse consent we all agreed to pray for the Recognition of the Confederacy and in a fiew minutes we wer comingling our prayers a loud together for a recognition of our freedom when suddenly I a rose and cryed a loud I new there was recognition for the Southern confederacy and I intended to go ask for and obtain it rising up to ward heaven I soon found my self rising up by the side of a high rugged mountain and now which I had to climb before winding my way for I found I had a cart and oxen which seemed almost impossible to assend much further, so werying with my team the water gave out with which I had to water myself and oxen so the alter-native was left me after I had almost over come the precipice to return to the foot of the mountain at which a nice clean River ran and into which the oxen plunged head long and but for the utmost exertions of min prevented them from drounding but succeeding in getting them out I started to retrace the steps a new of which I had just rose so fast. The mountain now appeared to me less steep the rocks and clifts had disapeared and as I assended which I did without any obstacles, the mountain grew less steep until the assent became gradual and thus I drove on until I saw the top of the hil then I a woke or was disturbed in my dreams which prevented me from getting the cherished object.*[3]

The "cherished object" of Southern independence was just as elusive in the real world as in the world of dreams. The

Dr. John Farris in later life (above)
and as a young soldier (below, center)

people of the South were learning that the dreams which did not accompany sleep were just as subject to sudden interruption as those which emerged mysteriously in moments of repose. Braxton Bragg, Missionary Ridge, hunger, isolation from families, and the deaths of friends had all interrupted the dream of independence, but interruptions, by nature, are temporary and dreams can always be rekindled.

Just when it appeared as if the last ray of hope had been smothered, something important and exciting happened: Braxton Bragg was relieved of command. Not even the victory at Chickamauga caused more excitement. Bragg had never been a popular commander, a situation which might have been tolerated if he had been victorious, but his vacillating manner had lost him the confidence of soldiers from privates to generals. Fortunately for Bragg, Jefferson Davis still believed in him and while the men at Dalton cheered his departure, their former commander made his way to Richmond to become a top advisor to the President.

In later years, Bragg's men attempted to understand him better. In 1913 George Guild wrote:

> *General Braxton Bragg was seemingly a cold, austere officer and a thorough disciplinarian, but no one ever doubted his bravery and patriotism.... Every soldier knew that when Bragg got ready to fight it was to be a real fight, and some one was sure to be hurt before it was over. He was particularly unfortunate in the failure of his officers in obeying important orders.... But we must add that Bragg seemed to lose his head at the supreme moment after gaining a battle and let its fruits slip out of his grasp....*[4]

General William J. Hardee assumed temporary command of the Army of Tennessee on December 2, 1863, but his tenure would last less than a month. Hardee had accepted the position with the understanding it would be temporary in nature and, probably for that reason, very little change took place as far as the men could see. The Christmas season was anything but joyous.

Resinor Etter observed:

> *This is Christmas   the boys have got some whiskey and some are tite and others feel there liqor   It is a nice day   We have some potatoes for dinner Tho there is much difference in Christmas here and home.*[5]

To some men, Christmas Day was devastating in its implications. The following morning John Farris, a physician in the 41st Tennessee Regiment, wrote his wife:

> *Christmas day is past & I am truly glad it is so; for such a day as we had yesterday is by no means aggreeable. The drunk men in our Regt. & Brig could not be numbered. I had thought that the army —[?] had got over its demoralization witnessed in the retreat from Missionary Ridge & immediately after, but I was badly mistaken. This army is yet disgracefully demoralized. Nothing could have afforded more evidence of that fact than yesterday's events. Our company and one other met a [?] man on the line between the two streets for a company fight & it seems almost miraculous that it was avoided as no guard, officer of the day, Col. or Brigadier Gen. attempted to stop it.*
>
> *The Col. commanding the Brig [ade] was beastly drunk & so was the Col. commanding the Regt. & officer of the day. Some of the guards were drunk [?]. Many men & officers throughout the Brigade were the same. Some of the scenes of yesterday were awful to contemplate . . .guards and officers were cursed & abused by drunken officers & privates alike. No regard was payed to any law or regulation whatever.*
>
> *Before yesterday I had a very faint hope that something might turn up in the course of events to gain*

for us our independence; but now I have no such hope. Our cause is lost certain; & I would just now say that I do not know but it will be as well as otherwise. I am of opinion that should we gain our independence, that we would have a totering & aristocratic government, & many are of this opinion. From what I can learn this whole army was yesterday & night before last in the same condition of our Brig [ade] all drunk . . . I also understand that one Maj. & four privates were killed dead by accident shots of drunken rowdys. God knows [you?] can have no idea of what took place yesterday, last night & night before. Things passed yesterday unnoticed That 6 months ago would almost have been sufficient to have taken the life of [a soldier?] certainly would have been sufficient to have reduced our officers to the ranks in everlasting disgrace. Why is it not now noticed; [The?] army is too much demoralized to hear a court martial — Arrest a [soldier?] & he will desert immediately, others will follow him & so it will not do to tuch so tender a place. I am vexed and troubled . . .

If I had known at the beginning of the war what I now know, I to day would have been in Canida making an [honest?] living. God knows I wish I was there now.

. . . I expect to stay with the army until it gets to be decidedly a mob & in defiance of the [government?] which will not be long if things go on as they have been for some time . . . Then I shall quit, I will stay with no such army. Everything about this army is disheartening & disorderly . . .[6]

The new year brought hope in the form of General Joseph E. Johnston as the new commander. "Uncle Joe" had long been a favorite of the men and he was destined to win a place in their hearts unequalled by any other general. For as long as they lived, the men who fought and marched with Johnston would speak his name in reverence and would regard the day he assumed command as signifying a rebirth of hope for those pledged to the cause of the Confederacy. The dream which had suffered so many interruptions was back in focus.

Johnston's effectiveness in the Confederate Army had been hampered by a personal dislike which existed between him and Jefferson Davis. The fact was that Davis had agreed to the new assignment only after other possibilities had been exhausted. But the private soldier knew nothing of such intimate considerations and cared even less. The private soldier cared little how Johnston got the job; he was just glad he had it.

Sam Watkins described Johnston as :

> Fancy if you please, a man about fifty years old, rather small of stature, but firmly and competently built, an open and honest countenance and a keen but restless black eye, that seemed to read your inmost thoughts. In his dress he was a perfect dandy. He ever wore the finest clothes that could be obtained, carrying out in every point the dress and paraphernalia of the soldier . . . He was the picture of a general.[7]

It was well that Johnston impressed his men favorably, for it would require all the talents at his command to restore order to the army he inherited the day after Christmas in 1863. The men were disorganized, discouraged, and recently humiliated at Missionary Ridge. They had lost interest in the war, lost faith in the Confederacy, and at least some had lost sight of the basic human virtues.

Sam Watkins noted:

> The men were deserting by the tens and hundreds, and I might say thousands. The morale of the army was gone. The spirit of the soldiers was crushed, their hope gone. A feeling of distrust pervaded the whole army.[8]

During Christmas, W. J. Worsham observed, "It seemed there was more fighting and drinking in camp than usual, gambling was again on the rampage."[9]

The lack of hope which had preceded Johnston's arrival had reduced some of the men to little more than common robbers. On one occasion, "A train load of provisions came into Dalton. The soldiers stopped it before it rolled into the station, burst open every car, and carried off all the bacon, meal and flour that was on board. Wild riot was the order of the day; everything was confusion confounded."[10] That was the situation when Joseph E. Johnston arrived at Dalton.

Changes came rapidly. Johnston immediately ordered three days' rations distributed instead of the usual one. He ordered a triple portion of whiskey and tobacco for the men — the distribution of these "essentials" greatly pleased the hardened veterans — and all men absent without leave were offered pardons if they would return to their regiments. A system of furloughs was worked out, clothing was brought in, and the entire atmosphere took on new life.

No one knew better than Joe Johnston that battles could not be won on morale alone and what he found during his first inspection was not likely to inflate the confidence of a trained military man. He discovered;

> ...a great deficiency of blankets; and it was painful to see the number of bare feet in every regiment .... There was a deficiency, in the infantry, of six thousand small-arms. The artillery horses were generally still so feeble from long, hard service and scarcity of forage, that it would have been impossible to maneuver our batteries in action, or to march with them at any ordinary rate on oridnary roads.[11]

Johnston viewed the existing conditions with respect to their possible influences on future campaigns, but the individual soldier viewed the situation differently. The soldier who was enduring the cold without shoes rarely worried about how his individual miseries affected the welfare of the entire army. To the soldier without a blanket, the primary concern was how to survive the coming night, not how the lack of blankets would affect the future. The present was as far into the future as the average soldier cared to gaze.

The worries of some men came to a sudden, tragic conclusion as Thomas H. Davenport, Chaplain of the 3rd Tennessee Regiment observed:

> *Today I witnessed a sight, sad indeed, I saw fourteen men shot for desertion. I visited them twice yesterday and attended them to the place of execution. Most of them met death manfully. Some, poor fellows, I fear were unprepared. I saw them wash and dress themselves for the grave. It was a solumn scene, they were tied to the stake, there was the coffin, there the open grave ready to receive them. I have seen men die at home surrounded by loved ones, I have seen men die on the battlefield among the noble and brave, I have seen him die in prison in an enemy land, but the saddest of all was the death of the deserter, but even there Christ was sufficient. "Tell my wife," said one but a few minutes before the leaden messengers pierced his breast, "not to grieve for me, I have no doubt of reaching a better world." Let me continue to hold up that savior and point sinners to him. I think they were objects of pity, they were ignorant, poor, and had families dependent upon them. War is a cruel thing, it heeds not the widow's tear, the orphan's moan, or the lover's anguish.*[12]

Offenses less serious than desertion carried a variety of punishments. The "buck and gag" was often employed. During this form of punishment the guard "would take a piece of sackcloth, wrap it around a bayonet, open the soldier's mouth and put it in there to stay until the cruelty became brutal. The man's neck would turn black sometimes before he would give up."[13]

Other than death, the most detested form of punishment was the stocks. Originally designed to punish slaves, the stocks were deeply resented by the soldiers. Offenders were placed so that their ankles, wrists, and necks bore the entire weight of their bodies. Besides the pain resulting from the actual confinement, offenders often developed pneumonia after spending a night in these contraptions or were so paralyzed they could hardly stand.

General Frank Cheatham became intrigued with the use of stocks and ordered a row constructed near the center of his Tennessee Division. If the genial general had dangled a member of the men's families from the end of a bayonet, he would not have outraged them more. Shortly before the stocks were completed, the men formed a line, charged through the night, and completely wrecked the first and only attempt of Cheatham to build these unwelcomed symbols of brutality.

But all was not gloom with the Rebs at Dalton. Faced with what seemed like endless hours of unplanned existence, the men searched for entertainment, and even if their findings were crude, they served a good purpose.

"Gander pulling" was a standby sport of the cavalry and infantrymen who could borrow horses. In this activity the riders would

> ...start from a given point under whip and spur, run be-
> tween two trees, along which was stretched a line, and
> from which hung a gander with a greased head and try to
> pull it off. By each tree stood a soldier with a whip to
> strike the horses when the rider was in the act of
> grabbing for the gander's head.[14]

One soldier at Dalton wrote, "To one who has never tried it the difficulty is hard to realize. The gander is tied by his feet, head greased, and his dodging puts your skill to the test."[15] The least enthusiastic supporters of this game were the geese-raisers around Dalton who were continually missing their choice ganders!

The first signs of spring were accompanied by a renewed interest in things spiritual. The men were fully aware of what warm weather would bring; they knew a Federal army was gathering at Chattanooga and they were aware of its purpose. They felt a need for help, and in that need, they asked for divine guidance.

Giant arbors were erected, empty buildings were converted into churches, and a sort of solemn atmosphere settled on the camps as the men were led in worship by dozens of ministers from all faiths. Resinor Etter attended the meetings every chance he got and was encouraged by the number who "perfest" religion. Private Carroll Clark of the 16th Tennessee wrote:

> *We were cut off from home Communication & had not much hope of ever meeting again the loved ones at home. Preachers referred to these facts & had but little trouble in persuading boys to the mourner's bench . . . I thought of earthly home sweet home & cried, but never went to the mourner's bench without thinking it best to whip the Yanks & then go home.*[16]

Ironically, it was the religious revival which furnished the greatest disaster during the army's stay at Dalton. On May 29th, a group of soldiers from George Maney's brigade remained after the sermon and "were praying with the penitent when a dead tree, having burned at the roots, fell across the alter place."[17] Ten men were killed.

Probably no man welcomed the religious revival more than General Pat Cleburne, but he, also, held the idea that the Lord might look more favorably on the Rebs if they learned some military science. He established schools where brigade commanders were taught the art of war and supplemented their classroom learning with practical drill until he brought his command to an enviable state of readiness.

Cleburne realized that the Army of Tennessee was no match for the Federals who could easily be mustered against it. For this reason he advocated freeing all slaves who would enroll in the Confederate Army. The suggestion so shocked the authorities in Richmond that it was thirty-five years before the proposal reached the press.[18] Such an attitude manifested by Confederate leaders prompted Grant to write, "The people, while willing to send their sons to the field, were not willing to part with their Negroes."[19]

In early 1864, the South was still laboring under the burden of traditions few of her soldiers had ever experienced but which still dictated the rules under which they must fight. From the relative comfort of governmental halls, Confederate politicians still expected their soldiers to perform miracles and persistently, if not patiently, they waited for such miracles to become reality.

The Confederate soldier at Dalton from which such miracles were expected had been cut off from home for almost a year, and many had not heard from home in all that time. To such men, anxiety had replaced anticipation, and personal integrity had replaced sectional pride as the primary motivational force in their lives. Morgan Leatherman was representative of this group.

Morgan Leatherman was a member of the 18th Tennessee. His home was in Rutherford County, and from the quality of his writing, he must have come from a very prosperous family. In April he wrote to an uncle of his anxiety for the people at home. He received one letter from Murfreesboro in February and, at that time, all was well at home, "...but there is no telling what changes may have taken place in this time."[20]

To Morgan Leatherman the war had become a cruel, heartless thing which had cut deeply into his life, tearing him away from all the people who really mattered. In a moment of seriousness he wrote:

I thought it very hard indeed for me to be separated from my home and friends, away from the scenes of my earliest childhood, deprived of the blessings of a mother the wise counsel of a Father, not only this is the case but I am deprived the pleasure of correspondence. Launched out in this world a stranger to its ways without almost any friends with whom I could advise, and in a land of strangers; but I think I know my duty and I will endeavor ever to do my whole duty, let what follow will. I hope ever to have a clear conscience and a name free from all stain of dishonor.[21]

Resinor Etter did not write in the polished manner of Morgan Leatherman, but their thoughts were similar. The appearance of spring made the young Warren Countian homesick; it made him "think of being at home planting corn," but as he observed, " I have no chance to git out of this civel ware." Etter's regiment had suffered through the winter for want of warm clothing and shoes. Many of the men had died of pneumonia and it was only after spring was well along that the people of Warren County were able to slip clothing past the Yankees. Etter noted in his diary that April 8, 1864, was set aside for fasting at Dalton and according to him, "most of the boys are keeping the day   we are willing to doo any thing to bring about peace."[22]

Resinor Etter learned that it required the patience of Job to do some of the things that supposedly would help bring peace. During the first weeks in April he was appointed the custodian of a group of mules which seemed determined to explore north Georgia first-hand. So occupied was he with his charges that his diary during the time could well pass as the diary of the mules. Typical entries read, "I left camps this morning to hunt some Mules that strad of from us   I hunted all day tho I found them not." The next day he wrote, "I left camp this morning to hunt mules that have got away from me   I found them in Dalton in the government lot." No sooner did Etter get the ornery beasts in the pen than they left on another unscheduled excursion, and the following day he wrote, "We lost two mules last night   I have hunted all day   I have not been able to find them." Two days later he recorded, "I leeve camps again this mor to serch again for those mules we lost   I have no found or herd of them   I have traveld on some of the poorest Country I most ever seen."[23]

While Resinor Etter chased mules, Morgan Leatherman wrote his uncle:

> ...*every thing here is at present quite dull, but cannot say how long it will remain so, for Spring is now upon us, all nature seems to be clothed in her loviest garb   the trees are in full bud   the flowers throw out their sweetest fragrance; the grass everywhere is putting up, but the birds of the air and the beast of the field can alone enjoy it, for alas! poor unhappy* man   *there is no spring for him, it matters not wither we bend our eyes all nature seems to laugh at our misfortunes....*[24]

If Morgan Leatherman was in a gloomy mood, Sam Watkins certainly did not share it. In fact Sam had taken a new lease on life since Joseph E. Johnston had assumed command of the Army. Sam felt that the entire army was ready to fight or die for the new commander. That irrepressible determination and optimism, based partly on a hatred for Yankees, and partly on maintaining self-respect, which always came forward when a battle was imminent, began to show itself in late April of 1864. Regardless of the conditions under which they were forced to exist, and in spite of the numerical odds against which they were, most of the time, required to fight, the men in the Confederate Army welcomed a fight. A successful fight represented the only honorable route home, a place from which they had been driven and a place to which they hoped to return.

Far away in Richmond, a newspaper editor hoped there was good reason to believe "that the Army of Tennessee, the most ill-starred and successless of all our armies, had seen its worst days."[25]

General A. J. Vaughn

General G. W. Gordon

Chapter XVII

Be aisy men;
old Joe will get them yet

Within a hard day's march of the Rebs at Dalton, the Yankees were readying their army for action. Important changes had taken place in the high-ranking personnel of the Union Army, but , substantially, the men were those who had fought at Missionary Ridge.

In early March, Ulysses S. Grant had been called to command all Federal Armies in the field and William T. Sherman was assigned to replace him at Chattanooga. Up to this time, the war had not been kind to Sherman. He had been accused of mental instability by some Northerners, his troops had won few laurels at Shiloh, his attempt to take Vicksburg was unsuccessful, and certainly he had failed in his assignment at Missionary Ridge. Both Sherman and his men were loathed in the sections of the South where they had operated. Southerners considered his army to be ruthless and undisciplined, a view shared to some extent by his fellow countrymen. But Grant admired Sherman and the unkempt little general was placed at the head of the army whose job it would be to finish off the war in the deep south. Actually, Grant gathered such an array of manpower for Sherman at Chattanooga that much of the sport was removed from the campaign which lay ahead.

Three armies were assembled for Sherman's advance into Georgia. The Army of the Tennessee, now under General James McPherson; the Army of the Ohio under General John Schofield; and the Army of the Cumberland still under the command of General George Thomas. While all these groups were called "armies" there was a great disparity in their sizes. Thomas had approximately 60,000 men, McPherson approximately 25,000, and Schofield approximately 13,000. It was Sherman's plan to use Thomas as the force around which the other two armies would operate. Thomas would hit the Rebs head-on while the two smaller armies would skirt the flanks of the Confederates and force them out of position.

The combined forces of the Federal Armies, numbering in the vicinity of 100,000 men, began moving south the first week in May, 1864. The weather was warm, but not hot; the ground was firm, but not dusty; and the men in the Yankee Army marched with a briskness which gave its leaders reason to believe another Missionary Ridge could be expected when the Rebs were overtaken. As the Yankees marched along, the Alabama cavalry acting as Sherman's couriers dashed between the general and his army commanders to make sure all were acting in concert and, by the night of the second day, the Federal force was well on its way south. The campaign in Georgia would last one hundred days and during that time many of the men in the opposing armies were destined to live the rest of their lives.

2.

The Rebs in Johnston's army were ready for a fight. The winter months had not been without some activity — Hardee's corps had gone as far as Demopolis, Alabama, on its way to assist the Confederates in Mississippi and Thomas had made a superficial move into Georgia — but nothing of substance had happened. A few isolated brushes had occurred between the armies, but they did little else than reveal the fighting mood of men involved. G. W. Waggoner of the 20th Tennessee had been in on one of these brushes with the enemy and wrote a friend, "I am fond of that duty. I fired several rounds at the sons of bitches if I should say such a word. I cant tell whether I hit one or not but I tride like the devil."[1] That pretty well summed up the attitude of the Confederates; they didn't know how well they would do, but they'd try like the devil.

The enemy armies were separated by a long, broken, rough-surfaced mountain known locally as Rocky Face Ridge. Dalton was located on the east side of this ridge which slanted from northeast to southwest. Sherman decided to move the larger portion of his army directly into Johnston's front as if to attack. But at the same time he sent McPherson's men in a flanking movement to the right toward Resaca, eighteen miles south of Dalton. McPherson was then to emerge through a mountain pass and destroy the railroad to Atlanta. If the plan worked, it would cut the Rebs off from Atlanta and from reinforcements on their way from Mississippi. At the time the movement began, Johnston had approximately 45,000 men to face Sherman's 100,000.

Sherman's plan failed. When McPherson got to Resaca he encountered unexpected opposition from a group of Rebs just arrived from Mississippi and, instead of attacking, he withdrew. Sherman was sorely disappointed, saying "Such an opportunity does not occur twice in a single life...."[2] If the Federal commander couldn't get a part of his army around and behind the Rebs he would attempt to get it all around them.

Leaving only enough troops in their front to make the Rebs believe little had changed, Sherman slipped his army behind Rocky Face Ridge and quietly sent it along the same route used previously by McPherson. If this maneuver worked, he could not only cut the railroad, he would be in a position to destroy or severely cripple Johnston's army. Again Sherman's plan failed.

It was difficult to hide tens of thousands of marching men from Joe Wheeler's cavalry, and when Sherman's army peeped from behind Rocky Face Ridge they found the Rebs entrenched and waiting. Not only had Johnston withdrawn from Dalton, he had acquired an additional 14,000 men under Leonidas Polk who had just arrived from Mississippi. The Confederates formed themselves in the shape of a horseshoe and left the next move to Sherman.

When Sherman arrived at Resaca on May 13th, he pushed his army forward in a cautious probing action. Thomas Head of the 16th Tennessee watched as the Federals approached and thought they

> ...*presented a grand and imposing spectacle. Their forces were massed into three columns. As they came up through an open field their ranks closed up into a solid phalanx, and appeared as so many living walls of blue. Their arms glistened in the sunlight, and the columns advanced as steadily as though they were on dress parade.*[3]

Rebel artillery sent shot after shot into the Federal columns until the advance was stalled. Yankee artillery answered with hissing, swirling bits of steel which bit angrily into the newly built Confederate fortifications, but the Rebs were not to be moved. When night came, no real gain had been made by either side.

The next day's action approached the "dignity of a battle," but still there was no substantial gain by either side. But while the main armies were fighting to an indecisive stand-off, Sherman sent a force by the Rebs' left flank toward the railroad to their rear. The only reasonable course open to Johnston was to retreat.

By the light of continuous flashes from Yankee artillery, the Rebs gathered their equipment and crossed the Oostanaula River south of Resaca. Once across the river and away from the bursting shells, the night became unmercifully dark. Men stumbled and cursed in response to their physical discomforts, but of more importance was the knowledge that the pattern of the Georgia campaign had taken form. They were fighting a Yankee octopus which could, while attacking their front, reach far around on either side threatening to snare them in a trap from which there was no escape.

The fighting at Resaca was not of major proportions, but it had answered an important question for both army commanders. It proved that there was plenty of fight left in the Confederate Army. The state of mind of the Rebel soldier seemed to be reflected in a letter written by Morgan Leatherman a few weeks before the engagement. To his parents at Murfreesboro, Morgan wrote:

> *Our army is in better spirits than it ever was before all feel confident of freeing you at home. the Tenns have all enlisted for the war and are determined to repossess their homes with their lives . . . it wounds me deeply whenever I hear of a Tennessean disserting his countrys banner, oh! would it not be much better to die battling for her rights. Should we not be successful I wish to be among the last that leave the cause for which we have been contending so long.*[4]

The Confederate losses at Resaca were not excessive in terms of numbers, but men did die. Colonel Sidney Stanton of the 28th Tennessee was standing on a log directing a line of skirmishers when he was struck by a piece of a Yankee shell. Spencer Talley saw him fall and to Talley "it was a sad and depressing sight to see this good man and gallant soldier drop to his death."[5] Another of the dead was the Rev. J.P. McMullen, a Presbyterian chaplain in Cheatham's command. During one of the charges, McMullen placed himself in front of the brigade "against the entreaties and protests of the general and many others, explaining that he had been with them in camp where there was no danger, and would not forsake them in the hour of trial . . . He went to the front, waving his hat and cheering the men until he was struck down, and he and his son lay dead upon the field within a few feet of each other."[6]

3.

Resaca was history; the important thing was what lay ahead. With the addition of Polk's corps from Mississippi, Johnston's infantry .force had taken form and his line-up of corps commanders was set. Besides Polk there was William J. Hardee and John Bell Hood, and if they lacked brilliance, their bravery and devotion to the cause could not be questioned.

The day following the withdrawal from Resaca, Resinor Etter wrote, "We left Rececker lat in the night   all of us with drew our selves from the breastworks as directed   marched all nigt   We are very worn out   are encamped near calhoun."[7]

As General Johnston viewed the situation, Calhoun offered few advantages for a defensive stand. He ordered his Confederate Army south through Adairsville toward Cassville. At Adairsville the army was joined by the cavalry of General William "Red" Jackson — newly arrived from Mississippi. Riding tall in the saddle and close behind his general was Nelse Rainey, courier extraordinary. Nelse was now eighteen years old and since leaving home had participated in enough action to view himself as a veteran. His duty in Mississippi had not been too bad — the food was adequate and the girls good-looking — but Nelse was glad to get back with the main army. One reason was that he wanted a crack at Sherman's Yankees, but probably more important was the fact that his brother Joe was marching along with the 48th Tennessee. From Nelse's viewpoint, the coming summer looked promising.

Between Adairsville and Cassville, Johnston threw Sherman off his trail by leaving the main road and cutting cross country. Believing an opportunity existed to strike Sherman's flank, Johnston issued a general order telling the men they were about to "meet the advancing columns." No words could have met a more enthusiastic response. The Confederates yelled until they lost their voices, they flung their hats high in the air, and some Tennesseans were persuaded to take liberal swigs of the "pine-top" whiskey they had acquired a few days before.

The morning was bright and clear as the Rebs formed their lines and waited impatiently. Nothing happened. As was so often the case, the wild anticipation of the men was shattered by a confusion in the minds of their generals. Hood had moved his men without Johnston's knowledge and when Johnston discovered the move the whole operation was abandoned. The army fell back to a ridge below Cassville.

Hood and Johnston could never quite agree on what had gone wrong, nor could they agree on what to do next. On the night of May 19, 1864, Johnston met with his corps commanders. After a heated discussion, a decision was made to retreat further toward Atlanta.

The order to leave Cassville was the first issued by Johnston to meet a protest from the troops. They had been in line expecting to meet the enemy and the order to withdraw did not set well. Many men voiced their disapproval for all to hear and "some soldiers dropped out of line, to be picked up by the enemy."[8] General A. P. Stewart, in his official report, referred to men who "unnecessarily and disgracefully surrendered." But most of the men still believed in Johnston. They believed he knew best when to fight and when to retreat and they willingly obeyed his order. Colonel J. N. Wyatt of the 12th Tennessee wrote a friend on August 10th, "There is some dissatisfaction with Gen. Johnston for retreating so much, but still we all repose the greatest confidence in him as a general."[9]

From Cassville, Johnston's army retreated to Allatoona, where it took position along a group of rugged hills known as the Allatoona Range. Johnston fortified a natural pass that penetrated the "mile high" hills around it and here the men settled down for a much needed rest. During the next few days, Sherman thought the situation through. He had been to Allatoona before the war and knew its strengths as a defensive position. Instead of moving against the Confederates at Allatoona he cut across country toward Atlanta.

Whenever Sherman's army made a move, the Rebel cavalry usually knew about it, and when "Red" Jackson's horsemen saw what the Yankees were up to, they hurried to Johnston's headquarters with the news. Quickly executing a change of position Johnston slid his army directly into the path of the advancing Yankees and when the enemy forces came in sight of each other the Rebs were entrenched along a series of hills looking down at the bewildered Yanks. The Confederate right was anchored at New Hope Church with its left extending to the village of Dallas. Once again, the Confederates waited for the Yanks to move.

For a few hours the tempo of the last few weeks lessened and Col. Wyatt wrote:

> *What a change from the booming of cannon, the shrieking and bursting shells, and the rattle of musketry of the past fortnight! The men are taking advantage of the quiet to rest and prepare themselves for the coming fray, for a battle seems inevitable. Praises to God for all his mercies are ascending to his throne from hundreds of warworn veterans.*[10]

The absence of bursting shells was a welcomed change, but it did not necessarily indicate an absence of work. On May 25, 1864, scattered clouds appeared in the sky and the day was showery and humid. The men in Hood's camp spent the day clearing the ground in their front and erecting breastworks along portions of their line. Logs were piled and scotched in place by rocks and sticks. Trenches were dug behind the logs, and in these the troops waited. The weather warmed considerably during the day, but by late afternoon a pleasant coolness prevailed.

The men in A. P. Stewart's division rested behind their breastworks while water boys gathered up canteens to be filled at a near-by spring. Guns were checked and surplus equipment was placed under trees to the rear, and all the while the soldiers talked of the strengths and weaknesses of their position on the line. Men lucky enough to have tobacco roamed around looking for somebody with a dry match and when the two got together they spent a fleeting moment in the lap of luxury.

About five o'clock in the afternoon a courier dashed into Stewart's headquarters at New Hope Church with the startling news that the Yankees were only a few yards away and advancing steadily. The peace and calmness quickly changed to a state of urgency as men grabbed their guns and hurried to their positions in the trenches.

As the fire of the Union artillery came bursting into the Rebel position, General Stewart mounted his horse and rode along the line. He shouted encouragement to the men who responded with enthusiastic yells. All the Rebs needed was a target and they didn't have long to wait for that. Advancing slowly and steadily, the Yankee lines, three deep, walked toward the Confederate position. When they came within range, the Rebs cut loose with all they had. With the first volley the leading line of Yankees reeled and fell back, but as one officer remembered, "As the advancing line would break we could only greet their departure with a yell before another line would come."[11]

In the midst of the fighting, a violent thunderstorm blended its lightning and thunder into the man-made hell below and added its own disrupting influence to the miseries of the men in both armies. Past sundown and into the night the fighting continued, but the Rebs held fast. The soldiers in Stewart's division were fighting a full scale fight for the first time in months and they were fighting with a resolution that did not accept retreat as an acceptable alternative. When the last of the firing had ceased, the ground over which the Federals had charged bore tragic evidence to the steadfastness of that resolution.

Daylight the following day revealed scenes to the Confederate soldier which stripped from him the bitterness that had served him so well the afternoon and night before. An officer wrote of "the seething mass of quivering flesh, the dead piled upon each other and the groans of the dying."[12] A Federal officer wrote that after the fighting had ended, "the nearest house to the field was filled with the wounded. Torchlights and candles lighted up dimly the incoming stretchers and the surgeon's tables and instruments. The very woods seemed to moan and groan with the sufferers not yet brought in."[13]

The Confederates had won a decisive victory. It would not change the subsequent course of events, but it did prove that even against substantial odds the individual Confederate soldier was a match for his counterpart. It felt good to have the fact reestablished. Stewart's men had won for themselves a prominent place in Confederate military history, and more importantly, their accomplishment at New Hope Church gave new hope for things to come. But the Rebs had encountered only a portion of the Yankee octopus; other tenacles had remained untouched.

Even during a battle as dreadful as the one at New Hope Church, Nelse Rainey found that war has its more pleasant moments. As he related:

I was sent with a message to an officer somewhere near New Hope. Message delivered and too far to go back I begged shelter at a farm house with in half a mile of the church. Cannon shot and bullets were flying thick over and about the house. The farmer, his wife and two pretty daughters were much alarmed. One of the girls ran to me and begged me to save her and threw her arms

376

around me. I didn't object to that but it was embarrassing, especially as mammy and pappy were looking on.[14]

Following the repulse at New Hope Church, Sherman moved his line to the east, and by the next morning had flanked the Rebs by a considerable distance. Johnston immediately moved his line to cover that of the enemy's, and by the 27th of May portions of the two armies squared off for another fight near Pickett's Mill.

In a movement designed to turn the Confederate right, the Federals struck the division of Pat Cleburne late in the afternoon. Again the Yanks moved forward "several lines deep" toward the Confederate works. Behind their protected position the Rebs waited until their enemy came within range and then in one death-filled explosion fired point blank into the front rank. As rapidly as they could reload, the Rebs sent volley after volley into the enemy's line and the men in blue piled up into screaming, yelling heaps. When, at last, the fighting died away, the ground was covered with Federal dead and still nothing had been decided.

Commenting on the fighting during this period, C. H. Clark told of the incessant firing between the two armies, of nights so dark you could not see your hand before your face, of a soldier who stepped out of line and deliberately shot his toes off in order to get a discharge, and how

We were getting ragged & never got a chance to wash our rags except to wade a creek, river or pond — pull off, rub & scrub without soap, wrince the best we could wade out, put them on wet &be ready for any order.[15]

During a drenching rain that had become almost continuous, the Confederates, on the 28th of May, attempted to drive back the Federal right, but the effort proved costly and gained nothing. Meanwhile Sherman was edging his army east toward the railroad running to Atlanta, and Johnston, fearful lest he be cut off from his supply base, kept moving with his adversary, trying always to remain in his front.

The infantry was the first to leave the lines around New Hope Church. The 1st and 27th Tennessee regiments got the command to fall in line;

> ...and for twelve miles or more the men trudged through the rain along the road, with the mud shoemouth deep, through the woods, scattering headlong, pell mell, every man for himself it seemed.[16]

When at last daylight came, the men were shocked at what they saw. "We looked at each other in astonishment. Muddy from head to foot, wet to the skin, guns half full of mud in many instances."[17]

Following the infantry's departure, the cavalry moved out as a rear guard. George Guild remembered:

> We left in a dark, rainy night, going to Marietta. The infantry had preceded us, leaving the cavalry in the ditches; later we followed, leaving about ten o'clock at night. It had been raining, and the road which the infantry had passed over was left much torn up. I remember that a cavalryman just ahead of us went down in a mudhole, horse, and rider; and as he scrambled to his feet again, he cried out to the amusement of the boys: "Be aisy, men; old Joe will get them yet." This was the most comforting expression we heard during the long, dark night.[18]

4.

The rain continued to fall until those fortunate enough to have shoes, ran the risk of losing them with every step they took in the bottomless mire. But rain and mud were not to keep the armies inactive. The Rebs hitched extra teams to heavy equipment. Fence rails and pine branches were thrown under stalled wheels which spun defiantly as barebacked soldiers cursed and heaved to move them forward. Only rarely was there an absence of firing guns. W. J. Worsham observed:

> *Not an hour day or night but the sound of musketry and cannon were heard. Changing positions, fighting as we changed, moving here and moving there, fighting as we went, fighting standing, fighting lying down, yes, fighting all the time.*[19]

Resinor Etter wrote, "It is a desperate time. I isued some shoes . . . It still raining at night every thing weet for three days." The following day he wrote, "Still raining very hard Some skirmishing to day. The roads are ver bad allmost impassable."[20]

By the middle of June, the Confederate Army was anchored among a series of small mountains and hills north of Marietta. The Federals were a few hundred yards to the northwest. General Leonidas Polk's corps occupied the Rebel left at Pine Mountain, a substantial swell of ground from which Confederate officers could study the movements of the enemy. On the 14th of June, Resinor Etter noted in his diary "the rains has sesed and the birds are on the wing again," but this sentence prefaced one of the saddest entries in the diary. His next sentence was:

> *This has been a day of Solemn feeling with us our faithful friend General Polk was shot through the hart with shell. He and general Johnston Hardee & Jackson was upon pine mountain viewing the position of the enemy. the enemy fired some shoots at the bunch of men and unfortunately killed Polk.*[21]

The death of Polk cast a pall of gloom over the Confederate Army. Johnston knelt beside the body and wept unashamedly while Hood confined himself to his quarters to mourn. To Johnston and Hood the death of Polk had special meaning: it had been less than a month since he had administered the ritual of baptism to both. Polk's corps would be commanded temporarily by General William Loring. Although Polk's death saddened the army, many competent observers doubted that it suffered militarily from his loss.

If Morgan Leatherman knew of Polk's death, he did not mention it in the letter he wrote the next day. Taking advantage of the respite from rainy weather Morgan wrote:

> *Situated as I now am out here, exposed alike to the storm of angry clouds and the dangers attending the battle field, and as the sun for the first time in nearly two weeks has this morning come out in all its glory, and the gates of Heaven for the time are closed I avail myself of the present opportunity of writing my much beloved but far distant uncle . . . Uncle the present campaign which has been five or six weeks duration . . . has been one continual scene of excitement, full of hardships and perilous adventures, such a campaign has not yet dawned on the pages of our youthful history . . . Our Brig has been in several severe engagements and tho many of my comrades have fallen around me yet through the kindness of a merciful heavin I am yet spaired and am enjoying fine health and high spirits though I am much war worn and fatigued.[22]*

Morgan Leatherman was soon to learn that it was a bad time for any soldier to be "war worn and fatigued." There were no indications that the tempo of activities would lessen. The rains reappeared, soaking the ground to such a depth that it became a standing joke that private "so and so's" hat was found where he sank out of sight under the terrible sea of mud that enveloped everything. There was no place to walk by day nor sleep by night, but still the armies moved.

Every move that Sherman made was expertly parried by Johnston who, unawed by the odds he faced, spread his three small corps ever thinner to obstruct the path of his adversary. Every time the armies came face to face it ended in the same way: Sherman left a strong force in front of the Rebs while he sent another around the end of the line. In every instance Johnston withstood such maneuvers as long as prudence would allow and then withdrew to have the procedure repeated.

By the last week in June, Johnston had concentrated his army immediately northwest of Marietta. Its line included Kennesaw Mountain, an imposing height two and one half miles in length and rising as high as seven hundred feet at one point. The mountain was accented by steep approaches which made it as near impregnable as any position occupied by either army during the campaign. Wishing to take advantage of this natural salient, the Rebs tied ropes to their cannon, and by sheer manpower, pulled them to the top where they were pointed in the direction of the approaching enemy.

When Sherman neared the Confederate line he cautiously explored its strengths while steadily applying pressure to Johnston's left. There were few idle moments for men in either army while the Yankee general pondered his next move. The Rebs dug shallow ditches well in advance of their main line, and in these, the skirmishers lay exposed to the sweltering heat of the Georgia sun. Further back, the main body of Confederates kept watch from breastworks over which blankets and sacks had been stretched to fend off the suffocating heat.

On several occasions, the enemy pickets met between the lines.

In such cases the men would exchange papers, and the Federal would exchange his coffee with the Confederate for tobacco, besides a general trade and traffic in such articles as were possessed by each party respectively. On all such occasions the truce was brief,

*and at its conclusion each party repaired promptly to his
respective position.*[23]

One veteran remembered that "Sometimes the pickets
would engage each other in friendly conversation. At other
times the conversation would commence with taunts and
continue until the truce would be broken by a shot. In such
cases a brisk fight would be the result."[24]

On Saturday and Sunday, the 25th and 26th of June, there
was heavy skirmishing all along the lines. Artillery shells
literally met in the air as each army sought to inflict damage on
the other. Although such firing was a dangerous nuisance, it
was soon apparent that very little damage resulted. The situation
called for more than an artillery duel.

Probably as early as the previous Friday, Sherman decided
to abandon his old routine of flanking the Rebs and for once he
would hit them head on. In keeping with this idea he aimed his
army at the Confederate center. During Sunday night, the
Federal troops were formed into two main columns and made
ready for the attack. Before the sun set again, the ground
around Kennesaw Mountain would be christened into history
with the blood of the men in these columns.

Monday morning dawned without incident. The early
morning hours were punctuated by blasts from nearby artillery,
but this was so commonplace it hardly attracted attention. The
sun was on schedule and promptly began its ascent across a
cloudless sky which seemed to act as a reflector of its torrid
rays. By eight o'clock, the heat sent the Rebs to the shade of
their outstretched blankets and from under these they peered like
a bunch of ragged gypsies.

By nine o'clock, the Federals were on the move and
advancing in plain view. Down came the blankets, and shouts
rang up and down the line alerting those loafing in the rear. A
great frenzy of noise and activity gave the Rebel line an
atmosphere of urgency as men hurried to take their place behind
the solid mound of dirt that had been thrown up. Soon the noise
died away and the Rebs lay still as a suspenseful silence took
command.

Even before the opposing lines collided, it became apparent that the men of Pat Cleburne and Ben Cheatham were to absorb the main shock. Most of the Tennesseans were in Cheatham's division. They were ordered to hold their fire until the enemy got within close range. They waited. The sight of the approaching Yankee columns was soon accompanied by the sound of their footsteps as they moved ever closer. When they came within seventy-five yards, Rebel lead began to fly.

Colonel J. N. Wyatt wrote a friend:

> ...we opened a murderous fire of grape, canister, and musketry, inflicting terrible slaughter upon them, though boldly they moved forward until some of them were within a few paces of our works. Our fire was so terrific and the slaughter so great they were forced to retire, leaving the ground strewn with their killed and wounded... The woods caught fire and many of the wounded perished in the flames. In this engagement I took the gun of Polk Rice, who was killed by my side, and used it until the barrel was so hot I could scarcely hold it in my hands.[25]

Bob Whitaker of Union City, Tennessee wrote his sister:

> We fought them behind breastworks.... The fire was most terrific. On they came until within a few feet of the breastworks. The contest now became doubtful .... The enemy pressed on until they planted their colors on the top of the breastworks; but they did not remain long, the position being too hot for the bluecoats. They tore their colors down and took to their heels in confusion, leaving their dead and wounded on the field.[26]

Robert Gates of the 6th Tennessee watched the Federals as they came

...with a rush, like ocean waves driven by a hurricane, trampling their own dead and wounded, sweeping on as if by an irresistible impulse, to dash and break and reel and die against the Confederate works, and stagger back like drunken men, broken and routed.[27]

The sight and sound of wounded men burning to death was more than some hardened Rebs could endure. Colonel W. H. Martin of the 1st Arkansas regiment, leaped to the top of the breastworks and yelled to the enemy, "We won't fire a gun till you get them away. Be quick."[28] The Yanks did not hesitate and soldiers from both armies jumped into the inferno and dragged the wounded to safety. Following the evacuation, a Yankee officer pulled from his belt a brace of fine pistols and presented them to Colonel Martin with the remark, "Accept them with my appreciation of the nobility of this deed."[29] The truce lasted no longer than was needed to remove the wounded when, once again, the noise from angry guns reached a devastating crescendo of death.

In commenting on the behavior of the Yankees, General A. J. Vaughn said, "Never did men march into the very jaws of death with a firmer tread and with more determination than did the Federals to this attack."[30] On the Confederate side, guns too hot to handle were thrown to the ground and replaced by those from the dead, who themselves were sometimes pushed out of the works like sacks of grain.

The Federal attack was driven back. The fire, the smoke, the riddled trees, the wounded, and the dead covered the ground between the armies. At one critical point in the line, the Rebel works bent at an angle and faced out on open ground. So great was the carnage at this point that the term "Dead Angle" was used to describe it. Sam Watkins was near there and observed:

Talk about other battles, victories, shouts, cheers, triumphs, but in comparison with this day's fight all others dwarf to insignificance. The sun beaming down on our uncovered heads, the thermometer being one hundred and ten degrees in the shade, and a solid line of blazing fire right from the muzzles of the Yankee guns being poured right in our faces, singing our hair and clothes, the hot blood of our dead and wounded spurting on us, the blinding smoke and stifling atmosphere filling our eyes and mouths, and the awful concussion causing the blood to gush out of our noses and ears, and above all, the roar of battle, made it perfect pandemonium.[31]

For three days the dead at Kennesaw Mountain remained unburied. Exposed to the intense heat they soon became "a sickening scene of formenting humanity." Finally, on Wednesday, the Federals sent in a flag of truce asking permission to bury the bloated bodies whose stench could be smelled for hundreds of yards. Permission was granted. During the ordeal, "Long and deep trenches were dug, and hooks made from bayonets crooked for the purpose, and all the dead were dragged and thrown pell mell into these trenches."[32]

During the burial of the dead, men and officers from the enemy armies visited between the lines. One Reb spent the time searching for the Yankee who took his knife from a stump on which the Reb had dressed a sheep shortly before the battle. The search was successful and before the truce ended the Reb had repossessed his property. Bob Whitaker watched Rebs trade tobacco for "canteens, old clothes, coffee, sugar," while others who had nothing to trade sat around conversing freely with the enemy.[33]

When the gruesome job of disposing of the dead was completed, signal guns were fired and an atmosphere of hostility resumed. There were no more general assaults at Kennesaw Mountain, but W.J. Worsham observed, "A hat raised on the end of a stick above the head log, would be filled with bullets in less than a minute."[34]

Like all battles, Kennesaw Mountain ran its course. After a while, only the hovering smoke, the smell of sulphur, and the motionless dead were left to remind the living of war's uncompromising stupidity. The battle, as bitter as it had been, had decided absolutely nothing. Sherman would never miss the number of men he had lost.

The absurdity of the fight was demonstrated in the fact that the Confederates were winning most of the battles in the Georgia campaign, but they were just as surely losing the campaign itself. They were not being defeated by the Yankees they fought, but by those they never saw. On July 2, 1864, Sherman sent McPherson's army wide around the Rebel left flank and once again the movement south by both armies resumed.

Chapter XVIII

Well Johnny,
how many of you are left?

Late one night, before the Confederates left their entrenchments at Kennesaw Mountain, a lone man made his way to the tent of General Joseph E. Johnston. The night was hot and the man was forced to thread his way through hundreds of Rebel soldiers attempting to find relief from the terrible heat which lingered long past sundown. There were thoughts in the mind of this man which transcended the heat, and in determined steps he continued his way toward Johnston's quarters.

The question pondered by this lone figure held great import for the men among whom he walked. Was another retreat necessary? Could anything be done to compensate for the great numerical superiority of the enemy? Would Johnston listen to a plan that might stem the tide of events which had forced the Confederates back from Dalton?

The man who pondered these important questions was General Francis Asbury Shoup, Johnston's chief of artillery. For several weeks Shoup had tried to devise a defense to stop the Yankees and now he believed he had it. The next step was official approval.

Upon his arrival at Johnston's headquarters, the artilleryman was warmly greeted and invited to explain his plan.

The plan centered around the Chattahoochee River south of Marietta, the last geographical obstacle facing the Federals in their conquest of Atlanta. To Shoup the Chattahoochee represented the last hope of the Confederate Army and he advanced the notion that once that river was crossed the Southern cause was lost. Believing this, it seemed imperative to Shoup that a strong defensive line be established north of the river from behind which the Rebs must, once and for all time, stop the Yankee advance.

The defense line was to be unique in design. According to Shoup, "It was not a system of earthworks, but a line of detached log redoubts packed in with earth."[1] Johnston listened attentively while Shoup continued to explain his idea, and as the conversation progressed, both men became more enthusiastic toward its possibilities. Although it was already late in the night Johnston ordered a special engine to take Shoup south in order that work might begin at daylight the next morning.

Over a thousand slaves were brought from surrounding counties and put to work. An abundant supply of timber was readily available and the slaves, accustomed to building log houses, hastily constructed the defense line. Orders were sent to hospitals to send up all men able to stand and hold a musket, and by the first day of July, 1864, all was ready. On the 4th of the month, Shoup received word that the Confederates were falling back and final preparations were made for their arrival.

Except for the usual artillery duel that continued day after day, the withdrawal from Marietta was uneventful. In fact, the eventfulness of the withdrawal depended much upon the individual making it. General "Red" Jackson's men loved excitement and when none was furnished by the enemy they contrived their own. Two fellows named Sykes and Ewing "livened" things up by fighting a duel. Ewing had entered the war as a Yankee, but following a disagreement with his captain he decided life might be more pleasant as a Reb. He looked up General Jackson whom he had known before the war and forthwith became a Confederate.

The converted Reb thought his opponent in the duel too cowardly to inflict any real damage, but when the two squared off, Sykes sent a ball through Ewing's shoulder. The wounded ex-Yank, willing to let well enough alone, walked over to Sykes and admitted, "You are a damned sight braver man than I thought you." Nelse Rainey, who knew both men, noticed that from that time on Ewing was a bit more careful in his appraisal of his comrades' valor.[2]

As the Rebs retreated toward the Chattahoochee they stopped occasionally to throw up breastworks, but no large-scale action took place. On July 4th, General A. J. Vaughn reached the village of Vining Station and was instructed to fortify the place. The spade work went well and during the early afternoon he walked over to a spreading tree, took out his pipe, tobacco, and sunglass — matches were hard to find — and situated himself to catch a ray of sun breaking through the branches above. Just as he focused the sunlight on his unlit pipe, an enemy shell came tearing through the trees and severed one of his legs and severely damaged the other. Vaughn's journey to the hospital was a fitting climax to a 4th of July celebration.

Luckily the general's wound was not accompanied by immediate pain or the loss of blood. According to Vaughn:

In going to the hospital I passed by General Cheatham's headquarters, who, hearing that I was wounded, came out to sympathize with me, and suggested that as I was looking pale he thought that some stimulant would do me good, and gave me a stiff drink. I then began to feel pretty good and proceeded on my way to the hospital. I had not gone very far when I passed General Hardee's headquarters. He had heard of my misfortune and came out to see me. He also said I was looking very pale and that I ought to have some stimulant, and gave me a big drink. I continued to feel better, and again started toward the hospital, and in a

*short time passed Gen. Joseph E. Johnston's
headquarters. He came out to see me and also said that I
was looking very pale, and that some stimulant would do
me good. He happened to have some very fine apple
brandy, and gave me a big drink, and down it went.
From that time on I knew nothing until I awoke on the
platform at Atlanta at sunrise the next morning. Thus I
lost my leg, and I have not seen it since.*[3]

Generals were not the only ones who depended on
whiskey to relieve the unpleasantness of reality. Although the
privates professed to believe that Georgia whiskey would take a
man's head off at twenty paces, they nevertheless chose to shut
their eyes and make up in imagination what the contents of the
bottle lacked in quality. At Marietta, "Henry B", who was
described as "an amicable and lovable fellow," went into town
and promptly absorbed too much of the potent liquid. Soon,
"Henry's condition began to show its consequences. He leaned
against a tree and solilloquised; 'Drunk! Here I am drunk! No
doubt my poor girl is at home now praying for my poor soul
and here I am drunk like a fool on Sunday'."[4]

The day after General Vaughn lost his leg, a portion of
the Confederate Army occupied the defense line prepared by
General Shoup. The men had not been told of the new works
and their first reaction was not flattering. To the uneducated eye
of the private soldier Shoup's redoubts looked like an uneven
row of log cabins with little to recommend them as protection
against the enemy. Almost in a state of amusement the men set
about tearing down the structures and began digging the old-
fashioned trenches that had served them so well in the past. It
was only after such generals as Pat Cleburne and William J.
Hardee explained the advantage of the "Shoupades" that the
men took a more serious view of them and soon their skepticism
turned to admiration.

When finally the Federals arrived in front of Shoup's line
of works, Sherman thought them "one of the strongest pieces of

field-fortifications I ever saw."[5] Believing it would be folly to make a frontal assault against the position, the Yankee commander swung a portion of his army ten miles above Johnston's right flank and crossed to the south of the Chattahoochee River. From there the way to Atlanta was clear. It was the same old story: the Yankee octopus had slithered its way past the Confederate flank. Johnston was faced with a familiar dilemma and on the night of July 9th he pulled his army away from the Shoup redoubts and, much to the disappointment of Shoup himself, crossed the river to interpose his army between the enemy and Atlanta.

When the Rebs crossed to the south of the Chattahoochee, the Yanks moved up to its northern bank and for a few days elements of the two armies camped just across the river from each other. As far as the privates of the two armies were concerned, it was time for another truce.

Things went well until officers became suspicious when hundreds of rounds of ammunition were expended back and forth yet no one seemed to get hurt. On July 11th, Johnston issued a General Order saying:

> *Intercourse between the pickets of the enemy and our own is strictly and positively prohibited.... Yesterday the enemy had a great interest in finding the fords in the Chattahoochee, and easily attained their object, the pickets by mutual agreement bathing in the river together.   The engineers of the enemy most probably mingle with the bathers.*[6]

When the private soldiers persisted in their observance of the unofficial truce, another General Order was issued declaring:

> *It has been reported to these headquarters that, contrary to orders, intercourse between our pickets and those of the enemy is still kept up, and in some instances it has been agreed that they shall not fire at each other*

with intent to kill, but to shoot over each other's heads.
A stop must be put to these proceedings, and anyone
found so offending will be sent to these headquarters.
Artillery officers and men in the trenches are directed to
fire upon any man, or group of men, who are discovered
holding communications with the enemy.[7]

The impromptu truce was short lived for reasons other than the intervention of headquarters. Sherman had his eye on Atlanta and to get there he must cross the remainder of his army to the south side of the river. This he did on the 17th of July. Johnston placed his men on the south side of Peachtree Creek, six miles from Atlanta, and again waited for the Yankee octopus to move. Although the Rebs were camping within sight of their main supply base, food was scarce. Fortunate indeed was the infantryman who had a brother in the cavalry, especially if that brother was Nelse Rainey.

It was seven miles between the place Nelse's cavalry unit was stationed and where his brother Joe's infantry company was located, but notwithstanding the distance and the stray shells that sometimes fell, Nelse rarely missed a day sharing his food with Joe. Nelse's cook "usually fixed up for me a bucket of cooked peas, some biscuits or other food for the poor ill-fed boys in the trenches. We sometimes drew rations of tobacco and whiskey — I always managed to convey mine to Joe."[8]

On one particular visit to his brother Joe's regiment Nelse found him

...issuing rations to his company. On a blanket, a
much soiled one, were several small heaps of bread and
meat, one for each member. A moderate chunk of
cornbread, un shortened, cooked the day before, and a
small piece of boiled lean beef. Joe looked them over; if
one pile had just a little more in it than the average, he'd
pinch off a bit and add to a smaller . . .all this time the
boys looked on with interested, hungry eyes. Then he

picked up a heap in his not too clean hands and gave it to
the owner of the name called. They had not had a
satisfying ration for days. They were tired, badly fed,
dirty with the yellow clay of the trenches, yet not one of
them thought of giving up; if ordered would have
charged Sherman's whole army.[9]

Although the shortage of food was a general complaint
throughout the Rebel Army, the men were not discouraged.
Even the series of retreats had failed to diminish their confidence
in and admiration for Joseph E. Johnston. The individual
soldier seemed to believe that Johnston was looking out for him
and would order a fight only when the right opportunity
presented itself. Bob Whitaker expressed the sentiments of
many soldiers when he wrote his sister on July 16th, "The
soldiers seem to have the utmost confidence in Johnston. They
think it will all be for the best, and all seem confident of
success. I think when the time comes for a regular open field
fight we will whip them very badly."[10]

The next day Joseph E. Johnston was relieved from
command of the Army of Tennessee.

Many people in the South had questioned Johnston's
policy of falling back before the Federal Army. They were
disappointed that a more determined stand had not been made
north of the Chattahoochee and once the river was crossed they
became convinced that Johnston had no real intention of
defending Atlanta. To the War Department and Jefferson Davis
the situation demanded swift and decisive action, and on July
17th Johnston was ordered to step down.

To many of the soldiers in the Army of Tennessee,
Johnston's dismissal was as great a disappointment as the final
surrender the following spring. In fact, to many the two events
were inseparable and the latter was as sure to follow the former
as night was to follow day. "This was the beginning of
disaster," and "From this time disaster followed," are typical
remarks made by veterans who were there.

From his tent south of Peachtree Creek, Colonel J.N. Wyatt wrote a friend;

> *It was very sad news Monday 18th, when we received orders that Gen. Joseph E. Johnston was relieved of the command of the army . . . The War Department perhaps knows best, but the troops are dissatisfied with the change, for Gen. Johnston was the idol of the army and the country reposed in him all confidence. When the order relieving him from command was read the spectacle was touching to see; men who have borne the heat and burden of this war shed tears. But they are determined to do their duty by their country, no matter who commands.*[11]

Perhaps W.J. Worsham's comment some years later was even more pertinent.

> *Johnson's* [Johnston's] *idea of warfare did not consist of butchery or useless sacrifice. With his small army he acted on the defensive, and only fought when he was certain of doing the most good. No one else could have done more than he, with the means at his command.*[12]

Joe Johnston was gone and the Army must have a new commander. Jefferson Davis moved fast to fill the position with John Bell Hood of Texas. Hood had close ties to the powers-that-be in Richmond. He had in fact resorted to some very questionable methods in reporting the activities of Johnston's army to his friends at the Capitol. In his communications with Richmond, Hood had questioned many of Johnston's decisions and, of equal significance, these communications had gone around Johnston's headquarters rather than through them. In any event, Richmond wanted action and John Bell Hood would give it to them.

Hood brought a damaged body and a damaged ego to his new assignment. He lost the use of an arm at Gettysburg, and one of his legs was amputated on the field at Chickamauga. Before he left Richmond he was scorned by the girl he loved. Partly to relieve the pain in his maimed body, Hood drank too much, but nobody doubted the thirty-three year old general's fighting abilities. His courage had been demonstrated time and again, but few of his fellow officers believed Hood capable of commanding an army in the situation now occupied by the Army of Tennessee.

Unfortunately, Hood's ascension to command left its scars among his lieutenants. Hardee deeply resented Hood's appointment and made no effort to hide his dissatisfaction. Hardee was Hood's senior in rank and considered it a personal insult for the younger man to be appointed over him. In a moment of intense bitterness, Hardee submitted his resignation, only to reconsider when President Davis appealed to his patriotism. Hood's former corps was assigned to General Ben Cheatham a man in whom Hood had very little confidence, and Polk's old corps was now under the command of A.P. Stewart.

If Resinor Etter knew of all the confusion which accompanied Johnston's dismissal he did not record it in his diary. Because of the steady strain he had endured during the campaign from Dalton, the young Reb felt tired and weak, and upon his arrival at a hospital in Atlanta, found that he was quite "unwel." But this was no time to give in to mere symptoms and the following day Etter returned and took his place in the trenches.

The temporary lull in fighting gave Morgan Leatherman a chance to write his parents in Murfreesboro. He said:

> . . . I have had quite a heavy time for the last two or three months. We have not the whole time been two or three days out of the hearing of cannon and small arms and the most of the time have been in range of them and I assure you there in no pleasure to be seen when

burnt shells & minnie balls are flying promiscously...
Although I am not very fond of fighting I am anxious to
see the decisive battle of this campaign come off.... I
have no fears as to the results when it does take place
such soldiers as compose our army cannot be whiped no
matter what the odds may be   I do not think there is a
single man in our army but what would be willing to
meet Sherman's leageons on the open field tomorrow.[13]

Morgan Leatherman was a deeply sensitive young man and, as was the case with many of his comrades, there was a disturbing cloud of anxiety which hovered above the "decisive battle" of which he spoke. In the same letter, but on a separate piece of paper, Morgan said to his parents:

Pa though we may never meet no more below can
we not try to meet in a better world   is this matter of
such importance that we pass it by day after day. Oh!
Pa now is the time and let us try and be prepared to meet
dread eternity. Mother I need not ask you to pray for
your eering and wayward son for I know there is not a
night passes but what you remember your son in your
prayers   Should it be my fate to fall on some field of
Battle oh! how sweet it would be to know that we all
would meet in a better world. I hope that I may yet be
spaired to once more clasp to my brest my dear sisters
Bro & Parents and we may once more enjoy our home in
peace & happiness.
My love to you all   I must now for the present bid
you adieu. May a kind and omnipotent God look over
and protect us all and speed the day when we shall meet
at our own peaceful hearthstone oh! will that not be a
happy meeting. Until then I remain your affectionate &
Loving son.[14]

Before these lines could reach his parents, Morgan Leatherman gave his life at Atlanta in Hood's attempt to assume the offensive.

On July 19, Hood learned that General George Thomas was moving his Federal army across Peachtree Creek and that there was a possibility of catching him in the act. Accordingly, Hood ordered an attack for one o'clock the following afternoon. When the attack finally got underway it was four o'clock instead of one, and instead of catching Thomas in the process of crossing Peachtree Creek, the Rebs found him securely lodged on its southern bank. The Confederates suffered five thousand casualties and were unable to dislodge Thomas' men. It was well that Morgan Leatherman never knew the insignificance of the action in which he gave his life.

Resinor Etter came through the fight unhurt although his regiment "lost very heavy in the attact   some were killed there was a great many wounded."[15] Sam Watkins survived untouched and so did Spencer Talley, but for Talley the attack would forever be remembered as his most trying experience of the war. In speaking of it Talley said:

> *They had us outnumbered to say nothing of their fortified position, however when the word was given, there never was a more desperate and determined rush made on their fortified lines. This charge was begun about three or four o'clock in the afternoon, and the battle raged furiously till darkness over shadowed the field, when we withdrew with no victory no gain to cheer us. On our return I found that my brother R.J. Talley was fatally wounded. He had fallen in a field of corn through which we had passed and I was unaware of his fate until after dark; he had been picked up by a litter company and carried to the field hospital where I found him and a great number of others who had fallen in this struggle. I sat by him all night doing what I could for his relief. He fully realized that his wound was fatal and that he could only live a few hours and maintained a calm & rational mood to the end. He talked incessantly, but in no complaining way, he often said, "I am nearing the*

*end, and ready to go." ...It was just at dawn of day
when my Bro breathed his last and when we wiped the
death damp from his face, we set about for his burial.
One of our boys made a rough box such as he could with
only a saw & hammer to work with, but before we could
get the use of tools to dig the grave orders came for us to
fall in line; a hasty move of our position was made, and
we left the lifeless body of my brother lying in the crude
box, not knowing where or if ever buried. This was the
saddest and most trying hour of my war experience.*[16]

The war waited for nothing and those caught in its grip
either moved with it or were destroyed by it. Sherman was
determined to have Atlanta, and Hood was just as determined to
defend it. In keeping with his objective, Hood was giving the
Army of Tennessee a new personality; it was no longer an
army that waited to be attacked, but one that was ready at any
moment to lash out at the enemy.

By July 21, 1864, Sherman's Yankee octopus had
slithered ever nearer to Atlanta and was reaching for its prize
from both the north and east. McPherson had swung his army
to the left after crossing the Chattahoochee and was now in a
line running north and south on the east side of the city. Hood
learned that in his haste, McPherson had allowed his left flank to
become exposed. The Confederate commander decided to strike
the vulnerable spot. Quickly withdrawing Hardee's corps from
the main line, Hood sent it southward through Atlanta then
eastward into position to attack at daylight the next morning.

Throughout the night of July 21st, Hardee's men stumbled
through the darkness on unfamiliar roads in their attempt to gain
McPherson's flank. Sleepy soldiers were urged to "cuss low"
as they passed through the night, bound for what history would
call the Battle of Atlanta. While Hardee's men marched toward
McPherson's army, Hood pulled the remainder of his men back
toward Atlanta in an attempt to guard the city's northern and
eastern approaches. Hood's plan called for Hardee to initiate the

action of the 22nd by pushing back the Yankee left, whereupon the remaining Confederates would join in to push Sherman's army into Peachtree Creek.[17]

The blueprint looked good on paper, but as he had learned on the 20th, Hood found that plans must be executed by men, and men are more complicated than blueprints. Hood had already accused Hardee of timidity in the Peachtree Creek fighting and what had begun as a dislike between the two generals was rapidly developing into contempt.[18]

Instead of the attack on McPherson getting underway at daylight, it was almost noon before the assault began. In the stifling heat of mid-day the Confederates hit the Federal line with all the enthusiasm attending certain victory. Bitterness at Johnston's dismissal was set aside in the desire to whip the Yankees, and every man fought as if he carried the burden of victory on his shoulders. The first hours of fighting indicated a decisive Rebel victory as the lines of blue were rolled back at many points, but the progress being made was coming at a terrible price.

Sam Watkins said he was marching

> ...by the side of a soldier by the name of James Galbreath ... I never heard a man pray and "go on" so before in my life ... Every time that our line would stop for a few minutes he would get down on his knees and clasp his hands and commence praying. He kept saying, "O, my poor wife and children! God pity me and have mercy on my soul! ... A discharge of cannon, and a ball tore through our ranks. I heard Galbreath yell out, "O God, have mercy on my poor soul." The ball had cut his body in two.[19]

Gervis Granger wrote;

> We charged them. Armed as they were, with repeating rifles, our command was almost exterminated.

Balls flew thicker than I ever before experienced. It seemed I was among a swarm of bees. The air was fairly blue.[20]

Spencer Talley's 28th Regiment was faced with a strong Federal position where the enemy had cut down trees between the lines. Talley wrote:

The limbs were backed down and pointed toward us which made it impossible to make any swift movement or rush on them. Regardless of this advantage and their superior numbers, Hood ordered us to charge and take their position. While our men were much fatigued and worn out from the very recent conflict, they raised the old "rebel yell" and rushed like a storm toward them. The thick underbrush they had filled in their front prevented any rush, when we reached it I suppose we had gotten about half way through when I was shot down. A minnie ball having struck me above the hip in my left side, no bones were hit or broken but my left side and leg were paralized.[21]

While Spencer Talley lay exposed in front of the enemy's works, Corporal Bob Coleman of the 5th Confederate Regiment from Memphis was about to fire the battle's most prominent shot. Coleman was a member of Pat Cleburne's division and shortly after noon his regiment was ordered forward with instructions to turn neither right nor left until the enemy's works were reached.

Quick-timing in the direction of the enemy, Coleman's company entered a black-jack forest where they were forced to probe their way through a matted network of underbrush and vines. Luckily the only opposition encountered was a detachment of skirmishers who surrendered without a shot being fired. Coleman, together with Captain Richard Beard[22] and Asher Stovall stepped into an old wagon road that cut its way through the shaded region of the forest.

Within a few seconds, the three Rebs heard the sound of galloping horses coming from the direction of the enemy and looking up they saw a detachment of Federal officers approaching. It was evident to Captain Beard that the enemy officers were dismayed to find themselves inside the Rebel lines, and Beard at once lifted his sword as a signal for them to surrender. Instead of honoring the signal, the distinguished officer nearest Beard lifted his hat in salute, wheeled his horse in the opposite direction and galloped away.

Bob Coleman was ordered to fire at the departing enemy and his sights naturally fell on the officer who had led the detachment down the road. Taking careful aim, Coleman fired; his target hit the ground. Captain Beard ran quickly to the fallen officer and noticed, "There was not a quiver of his body to be seen, not a sign of life perceptible. The fatal bullet had done its work well. He had been killed instantly." Pointing to the dead man Beard asked a Yankee prisoner, "Who is this lying here?" He received the answer, "Sir, it is General McPherson." Unmoved by the event he had witnessed Rebel Captain W.A. Brown reached down and picked up McPherson's hat, put it on and wore it for the remainder of the war.[23]

The Confederates responsible for McPherson's death were captured in a matter of minutes and in a few days were on their way to a northern prison. As Bob Coleman, Richard Beard, and W.A. Brown were enroute to Johnson's Island Prison they reached Clyde, Ohio, the very day that McPherson's body arrived there for burial. According to Captain Beard:

> *We noticed that the flag was at half mast and asked some of the crowd around the depot what it meant and were told that they had just buried General McPherson whom the "damned Rebels had murdered" and that the flag was at half mast for him.*[24]

Quietly slipping back to his seat, W.A. Brown did not volunteer to tell the angry and saddened crowd from whence came the hat he pulled down over his eyes.

The fighting at Atlanta took little note of McPherson's death and, in fact, became much deadlier as the afternoon progressed. Hood's men continued to hammer the Yankees, sweeping their line back far enough to capture several pieces of artillery. Even Sherman admitted that about four o'clock "the expected sally came from Atlanta . . .Sweeping over a small force with two guns, they reached the main line, broke through it, and got possession of De Gresse's battery of four twenty-pound Parrotts, killing every horse, and turning the guns against us."25

But even such courage as exhibited in this charge was not to decide the day. As the Rebs broke through the Yankee line, Sherman was busy making plans to send them reeling in retreat. The Federal commander ordered an intense artillery barrage from twenty guns directed into the advancing Confederates, and after the barrage ended, the Yankee infantry advanced to reclaim the ground previously lost. By nightfall neither army could cite evidence on which a victory could be claimed.

Although the Confederates would not admit defeat, it was obvious they had not accomplished their objective. Instead of the Yankees being pushed back, they still remained close to Atlanta, but the battle should have removed all doubts as to whether the Confederates would fight on open ground. If Hood needed evidence of this fact he had it in the form of over two thousand dead and wounded men who offered themselves in dramatic testimony. Hood was never quite able to admit this fact. Years later he wrote:

> They had . . . been so long habituated to security behind breastworks that they had become wedded to the "timid defensive" policy, and naturally regarded with distrust a commander likely to initiate offensive operations.26

Before the fighting ended, fellow soldiers picked their way through the sharpened tree branches outside the Federal works and helped Spencer Talley to the rear. Slowly and with great care they transported him to the nearest hospital. According to Talley:

> *This was a spot in a shady grove where lay on the ground just hundreds of wounded men. From where I lay I could see the surgeon's tables. Four doctors were busy cutting off shattered limbs. These arms and legs were thrown in a heap which by night was as high as your head, and I doubt if a two horse team could have pulled them on a wagon.*[27]

As soon as trains came from the south the wounded were loaded aboard and "sent to Macon, Georgia and placed in the blind school hospital."[28]

The night following the battle, Resinor Etter wrote in his diary:

> *This has been a day of sorrow to many of the boys We moved in the rear of the enemy attacked 2 oclock we drove them killed and captured a great many of them Tho we lost heavy . . . I have not been well in some time after the fight I went to Macon Ga. the night very coal for this time of year.*[29]

The 16th Tennessee, of which Etter was a member, lost many of its best men during the day, but none was lamented more than Wright Hackett. It had been Hackett who, after all the officers were dead, had led his company against the Round Forest at Stone's River. At Atlanta he was again in the front of his company, but this time fate was not so kind and he fell before the savage fire of the enemy.[30]

Sam Watkins, like Spencer Talley and Resinor Etter, left for the hospital following the battle. During the fighting Sam was hit in the foot by a shell and crawled to a nearby ditch. As he sat crouched low to avoid further injury "a cannon ball came tearing down the works, cutting a soldier's head off, spattering his brains all over my face and bosom, and mangling and tearing four or five others to shreds."[31]   Sam was eventually sent to a hospital in Montgomery, Alabama, where he was greeted by lines of local citizens selling apples, pies, eggs, and other appetizing edibles to the wounded men.   Among the salespersons were those selling whiskey by the dram, and when Sam spotted a one-legged man pouring from a jug, he inquired as to the price of the product.   "A dollar a drink," came the answer, and Sam promptly became the peddler's customer.[32]

A few days before the Battle of Atlanta, J. W. Jackson of the 11th Tennessee wrote his mother:

> *You cannot immagine the pleasure that it gives me of finding an appertunity of sending you a few lines . . .*
>
> *You can not immagine how bad I want to see you all it seems as if an age has past since I last saw you. I want you all to take care of your selves and we will meet again   it is true our polittical future looks gloomy enough at present but dont be despondent for their is a better day coming for it cant be otherwise*
>
> *Mother I dont want you to let the little children forget me for it may be some time be fore I see them. Mother kiss Eula and Alice for me   tell Johnny & Charles to be smart boys and help Papa work   tell Mary Nancy & Pollie to be good girls and mind their mother . . . Papa when you and mother write   write a home letter tell how things are getting along   how Kit & the cows are faring   how the garden and corn looks and all about the family concerns . . .*

> *your devoted son*

> *J. W.*[33]

Following the fighting on the 22nd of July, Willie Jackson, J. W.'s uncle, wrote the parents:

Dear brother and sister.

It is with a heart full of sadness that I have to communicate to you the death of your beloved son. he fell on the 22nd Inst pierced through the head with a minnie ball entering near the corner of the mouth on the left side and comeing out at the back of his head. I dont expect he ever spoke I did not see him until after he was dead   I succeaded in getting a coffin and burying him I buryed him the best I could under the circumstances cut his name on a plank and put it up at his head so that he could be found   Our army had lossed heavily this month . . . Thank God I have come through safely this far and know my dear brother and sister weap not for the lossed   remember Job in his afflictions was enabled to say the Lord gave and the Lord hath taken away blessed be the name of the Lord. remember that he was a good christian and that you know [now] have another angel in heaven. I must quit   do take care of mother and pa and also of your self   prey for me often   my love to all your brother as ever

Willie [34]

Each soldier awaiting death met it in his own unique way. If all other choices had been removed, at least he could choose his attitude toward death.   Most soldiers, fortified by a fundamentalist belief in an after-life, displayed a great dignity which reflected credit on their faith. Others approached death differently and one such was George W. Darden of the 6th Tennessee. Darden's chief claim to fame was that his father was considered by many to be the world's largest man. The father lived in Henderson County and was reported to weigh over seven hundred pounds.

The younger Darden professed no religious faith and "led the life of a wanderer and a waif." In the fighting at Atlanta, Darden had received a mortal wound and according to a fellow soldier:

Near him was a terribly wounded Federal, whose cries were heartrendering. These cries greatly disturbed Darden, who had composed himself to die, as he said, in peace. He appealed to the wounded Federal to keep quiet and die like a man. He said, "You disturb me very much. I am wounded unto death as well as you. An hour at most and both of us will have passed away, and for the sake of a common manhood let us die calmly and like men of courage." But the wails and groans of the desperately wounded Federal in no wise abated. Darden, with great effort, dragged himself to the wounded Federal, and, after examining his wounds carefully, said: "Friend you can't live long; your sufferings are great, and you will not let me die peacefully. Hence, for the sake of both of us, I will end your agonies." And with these words he raised himself as well as he could, placed a loaded rifle to the Federal soldier's breast and fired. The soldier died without a struggle, and Darden laid himself calmly by his side, pillowed his head against a stump, and remarking "Now I can die in peace," passed away without a sound or struggle or a prayer that anyone heard.[35]

During the days immediately following the battle, Sherman massed his artillery against the city of Atlanta. Elevating their guns to fire over the Rebs who were still between them and the city, the Yankees sent hundreds of rounds into the factories, businesses, and homes of Atlanta. The fires which resulted sent up a stifling ceiling of smoke by day and reddened the sky by night for as far as the eye could see. In the meantime the Yankee infantry was not idle.

In an effort to neutralize the railroad leading south from Atlanta, Sherman ordered McPherson's army, now under the command of General O.O. Howard, to move around the northern side of the city from east to west and entrench as near the railroad as possible. Ascertaining the enemy's objective,

Hood ordered his old corps under Stephen D. Lee to march directly west and obstruct the path of the Yankees moving south. The two forces met at Ezra Church early in the afternoon of July 28th.

The Rebs struck the Yanks as the latter were in the process of entrenching, but picks and shovels were quickly replaced by muskets which fired continuous volleys into the oncoming lines of gray. Hood sent Stewart's corps to aid that of Lee and the fight became increasingly more bitter. Most of the men who took part in the fight remembered it as one of the fiercest of the war. Almost literally, the Confederates who survived beat themselves out charging, withdrawing, and charging again from early afternoon until darkness covered the scene. Crippled, discouraged, and physically exhausted, Hood's men limped away from their third disappointment in eight days. It was during the charges at Ezra Church that a Yankee soldier supposedly yelled to the Rebs: "Well Johnny, how many of you are left?" The answer came back, "Oh about enough for another good killing."[36]

Hood would explain the defeat, in part, by questioning the courage of his men. It would be an explanation unsupported by the Federals who repelled the attack. According to one of them;

> *Perhaps in the history of the war was never such persistent and desperate gallantry displayed on the part of the enemy.* [The Confederates] *were rallied again and again, as often as six times, at the same point, and a few of the rebel officers and men reached our lines of railpiles only to be killed or hauled over as prisoners . . . As many as 642 dead were counted and buried, and still others are known to have been buried that were not counted.*[37]

The 19th Tennessee pulled back from the fighting at Ezra Church after dark and, as best they could, selected a camp site in the smoke filled darkness. The chill of the night had already set in, and when the excitement of battle subsided, the men found themselves shivering from a lack of adequate clothing and blankets. Soldiers left camp in search of fence rails with which to build fires and to their astonishment soon realized that they and the Yankees were taking rails from the same fence. Fires sprang up throughout the area and no one knew for sure which fire belonged to which army. Dr. Dulaney, a surgeon with the 19th Tennessee, walked up to a fire and inquired as to the identity of the men gathered there. The answer came back, "the 17th Ohio." On one occasion a Federal soldier walked up to a Confederate fire and unloaded his burden of fence rails. When the Yankee discovered his mistake he quietly walked away leaving the Rebs better prepared for the night ahead.38

Even before the battle had begun, the Rebs had called on their Northern enemies for help. C.W. Heiskell, a soldier from Memphis, told that:

> The pickets were placed, and the Confederates, who had no picks or shovels, seeing the Federals digging their pits from which to fire, hailed them and asked for their picks and shovels to dig their picket-holes. And the Confederates went to the Federal pickets, borrowed their picks and shovels, dug their positions, when both began their work of death.39

Meanwhile at Macon, Spencer Talley was finding hospital life something less than luxurious. He wrote:

> Our fare was not palatable to say the least of it, consisting of corn bread and beef soup & occasional sugar & rice, meted out to us on crochery ware plates and wooden spoons . . . when our meals were brought in, we had to "shoo" and knock for sometime before we could tell   what was on our plates other than flies.40

It didn't excite Talley unduly when the doctor informed him, "Young man you have gangrene in you wound." Actually Spencer knew little about the condition, but upon asking its implications received the reply, "It means there is only one salvation for you and that is to cut it out right now . . ." The surgeon further explained to the young soldier, "We have no ether, chlorform or other narcotic to administer. Can you stand the operation without anything?" "I think I can," replied the Reb who promised, "I'll do the best I can."

Quickly the surgeon gave Spencer a lecture on the importance of the work to be done, impressing upon him the necessity of keeping absolutely still. The surgeon soon returned with a knife and hook and in the meantime Spencer had made up his mind "not to flinch, move or in any way cause him to fail in making his work a success. It only took him two or three minutes to remove the putrid parts and I did not move or grunt until he was through."[41] The morning following the operation, Spencer boarded a train for Hawkinsville hoping to receive help that would enable him to soon rejoin his regiment.

Resinor Etter did not remain at Macon for very long, and by August 2nd was back with the 16th Regiment. Although still pained by the sickness which had sent him to the hospital he took his turn on picket duty. On August 14th, he wrote in his diary, "It is a constant fight all the time day & night."[42]

August 18th was a pleasant day for Jim Parrott and he expressed his appreciation by writing a letter to his wife;

> *Dear wife it is threw the blessing of god that I have the opportunity of riteing you one more letter to let you now [know] that I am in the land of the living and well and I do hope and trust to God that this letter will reach you and find you and my sweet little boys all well and doing well   I am doing verry well I get plenty to eat   I want to see you and all my friends powerful bad   I hope to God that we will get peace soon sow we can meet again in peace . . . I have ben in several hard fits   I can*

*say thank god that I have never bin harmed   when I go
into a fite I say God be my helper and when I come out I
say thank God   I feel like he has bin with mee   Mahala
ann I feel like god has ancered your parerees for you rote
to mee that you asked God to perserve mee and he has
... Hala ann I want you to kiss my sweat children for
mee and Pray to God that we may all meet a gain in this
life.*[43]

On the same day, August 18, 1864, that Jim Parrott wrote
this letter, Resinor Etter's brother was killed south of Atlanta.
Resinor recorded the impact of the death in his diary.

*I must here record one of the most heart rending
seens of all my life. May God protect me from such an
awful fate or seeing another such seen. The only brother
that I had with me was shot by the inhumane enemy   he
was on picket & was shot in the back of the head cutting
his brain out   I could never describe my feelings when I
saw him   he was sensible of every thing   I went with
him to the distributing hospital   I begged the Dr. to let
me go with him down south to hospital   I could not git
to go   I knew he could not live long   I hope he is at
rest with his god.*[44]

On the day that Resinor Etter's brother was killed,
Sherman dispatched his cavalry under General Judson
Kilpatrick to disrupt the railroad at Jonesboro just south of
Atlanta. Kilpatrick had little trouble in reaching his objective
and lost no time in burning the depot. As the depot went up in
flames, Kilpatrick's men worked frantically ripping up the
tracks on each side of the village. The word of what was
happening soon reached "Red' Jackson's cavalry which left
immediately for the scene. Nelson Rainey rode close to the
front of the advancing Confederate column. As Nelse told it:

410

We had gone about 10 miles and diverged toward the railroad when we saw fires along the line. We dismounted and crept through the bushes to within perhaps 200 feet. The Yankees were tearing up the railroad. A hundred of them would line along the road and turn it over, ties and irons. They made great piles of ties and piled the rails on top and set the piles on fire causing the rails to bend and become useless.[45]

Such Yankee behavior provoked the greatest resentment from Nelse and his fellow cavalrymen who finally cornered their enemy at Lovejoy's Station just south of Jonesboro. General Jackson, hoping to make a clean sweep of things, sent word to Atlanta that he could use some infantry. By coincidence, Nelse Rainey's brother Joe was among those hurried to the scene. Nelse had barely taken position,

...when a long train of boxcars came at a fast rate, halted at the station and each car dislodged a load of soldiers . . . One of the first to reach the ground was brother Joe . . . They deployed quickly in line of battle, Joe's position just in front of mine.[46]

When Joe spotted Nelse he yelled at him to come along and follow the infantry into battle, but when Nelse approached General Jackson on the subject, he met a stern "no" that invited no further communication on the matter. Soon the entire force, with infantry in the center and cavalry on each side, lashed out at the Yankees with full steam ahead. Joe Love, a member of the 48th Tennessee observed, "Although they were in force, and had built pens of rails and logs for protection, they seemed paralyzed when they saw they were attacked by infantry."[47]

To Nelse Rainey it seemed as if all hell had broken loose.

In three minutes the battle was on. Such a roar! The musketry was so heavy that for a time except for the explosion of the Federal cannon no individual shot could

411

be distinguished. I saw Milt Voorheis come limping out of the battle shot in the ankle. I asked him as to Joe. "Joe's all right. Last time I saw him he was shootin every jump and yelling." [48]

Joe Love observed:

A perfect panic followed.... Within the space of twenty minutes we killed seventy-four and captured twenty three prisoners. Some of the prisoners were so drunk that we had to lift them on the train. [49]

The skirmish didn't last long before the Yankees began pulling back toward the main Federal line. But they left a scene that was impressive to those who remained behind. The Rebs found "several dead men, mostly wearing blue." Nelse Rainey saw one enemy soldier lying by a log. "He raised himself ON HIS ELBOW AND LOOKED UP AT ME. He was a ghastly sight. He had a hole in this throat I could have put my fist in. One horrible look, and he fell dead."[50] Nelse found his brother Joe and other members of the 48th Tennessee;

...amusing themselves with the actions of a drunken Yankee; he was limber drunk, couldn't stand. He said when they dismounted for the fight he was a horseholder. Another fellow gave him a bottle of whiskey to take his place in the fighting line. [51]

At another place on the field, Nelse was surveying the Yankee dead when he noticed "A gray soldier had one crotched against a small tree endeavoring to pull his boots off."[52]

Following the fighting at Lovejoy's Station, General Jackson led his men north to Jonesboro. While there, two ladies came to camp complaining that during the Yankee raid a squad of soldiers plundered their house, taking many valuable articles, among which, were two rings given them by their soldier-brother, now dead. Joe Rainey heard the ladies' story and remembered seeing a wounded Yankee in a box car who was wearing such rings. He took the ladies to the boxcar where they identified their rings which were promptly taken from the soldier. As far as the wounded soldier was concerned it made little difference; by the following morning he was dead.[53]

Sherman, convinced that cavalry raids would never accomplish his objective of cutting the railroad to the south, sent a strong infantry force to perform the task. The Federal commander had moved so many men in so many different directions that Hood became confused. By the time he discovered what was happening, the Federal troops were almost at Jonesboro. As quickly as he could, Hood sent Hardee with two undermanned corps of the Confederate Army with orders — it was so easy to give the proper orders, but so difficult to execute them — to drive the enemy back into the Flint River to their rear. By the time the Rebs arrived at Jonesboro the Yanks had succeeded in entrenching, and once again it meant a charge against enemy breastworks.

At 2 o'clock on August 31st, Hardee ordered his thinly stretched line of Rebs to charge the enemy. Gervis Grainger was in the charge and wrote later:

> We started in a full run. Their batteries opened on us by the dozen, with grape and canister shot and shell. The face of the earth was literally torn to pieces . . . I saw a deep gulley to my right and obliquing toward it, I did my best running. I leaped into it only to find six or eight of our boys who had preceded me. . . . Others retreated to the works we had left, many were killed on the way, some captured in ditches, and gullies, but we were overlooked.[54]

It was evident to the men and officers in the Confederate Army that Hood had blundered. So greatly had he misjudged the strength of the enemy that he had sent two of his decimated corps against what amounted to a vastly superior Federal force.

413

At the same time, Hood imagined himself at Atlanta about to be attacked by the very Federals then in Jonesboro.

After several hours of bitter fighting, night came and the firing on each side subsided. Hardee decided his best bet was to move against the Yankees. As he attempted to arrange his troops in a formation that would give them a slight chance of survival, he received a message from Hood ordering one of the two Confederate corps back to Atlanta where the misinformed commander still believed himself about to be attacked. In obedience to the order, Stephen D. Lee's corps was sent away.

The morning of September 1st found Hardee with his one corps facing Sherman with six. Lee's men were half way between Jonesboro and Atlanta, unable to get to either place quickly. Shortly after noon, the Federals drove against Hardee's right, and once again, the maddening sound of battle rose to call hundreds to their death.

Gervis Grainger was in the thick of it and wrote:

> *The long roll was ordered and in ten minutes we were in double quick to our right wing. We were placed in line only one column deep with no support. The enemy could be seen one mile away, forming many columns deep. We went into the ground like gophers, and in a short time had improvised breast works, which, though meager, were better than none . . . We heard the bugle call of the enemy sound "Forward" and the great cloud of blue coats were moving down upon us. The blaze of the cannon could be seen all along the line. The Yankees were coming slowly but surely, nor did they break their gait until within two hundred yards of our works. Then the whole body, ten or twelve columns deep, moved down upon us like an avalanche. Ten pieces of our artillery were playing on them, plowing great roads through their ranks.... Bayonets clashed bayonets and swords crossed swords, but over our works they came in spite of the most stubborn resistance I ever saw.*[55]

Almost by a miracle, Hardee's men held on until night, but the loss on both sides was terrible to behold. Gervis Grainger was captured during the late afternoon and was taken to the rear across the trenches where some of the bloodiest fighting had occurred. He described the scene.

> *In some places they were lying three or four deep, and some guns standing on end with bayonets plunged through the bodies of the victims. At one point we passed where a caisson of a battery . . . had been exploded by one of our shells. Only fragments of the pieces could be seen, but hundreds of the victims covered the ground for fifty yards around.*[56]

The next morning Nelse Rainey rode over the area and was shocked by what he found.

> *It was a dreadful and ghastly sight. The dead lay thick on all sides. I believe there was a thousand in sight. Our dead had been collected and deposited in one place for burial; put in piles like railroad ties . . . As the bodies were brought up they were searched and examined and an officer carefully noted any marks of identification in a book . . . On another part of the battlefield squads in blue were performing the same office for their dead and caring for their wounded.*[57]

In Atlanta, the picture was beginning to clear for the frustrated Hood. Realizing that his enemy was actually at Jonesboro, Hood decided to concentrate his army at Lovejoy's Station to the south. He would have his army together again, a possibility that probably caused little concern on the part of the Federals. By this time, the Rebs were so outnumbered that the action was comparable to three cats chasing one under-nourished mouse, but somehow the cats dreaded the mouse. Hood appealed to Richmond for help, but there was none to be had.

While the Confederate Army waited at Lovejoy's Station, Sherman cast a wistful eye toward Atlanta. The moment he heard that the city had been evacuated he lost interest in the Rebel Army and, instead, turned his attention toward Atlanta which symbolized success to his campaign. On September 6th, the Federal commander pulled his army away form the vicinity of Lovejoy's Station leaving the Rebel soldiers overjoyed and their officers bewildered. Sherman was determined to make Atlanta a mirror in which the people of the South could see their crumbling image; he had conquered a domain and he intended to reign supreme. He did.

While Sherman surveyed his prize, the men in Hood's army put aside their weapons and breathed easy for the first time in several weeks. The incessant roar of artillery and the dreaded report of the picket's fire were gone. The men thankfully sat down to write the folks at home.

Jim Parrott wrote his wife:

> *I want to see you all so bad that I cant hardly stand it   I hope and trust to God that the time is not fare distant that I will get to come home and live in peace the remains of hour days   may God spead the time Dear Companion   I can say to you that I have bin in all the battles   sence   the   battle   of   Muffles   Barrow [Murfreesboro] I was in the battle of Chickey Mogey at resacker and at dars ville [Adairsville]   new hope church   kennisaw mounting and at Jones Borough   I have bin in all these battles and thrur the Blessing of God I have never bin tuched with a Ball. I thank God for it God has bin my sheal and I hope that he will be until I dy   what has bin the Cauze of him being my friend I have ask him for his blessing   you rote to me that you prade for mee   I do believe that God has ancered your parers for he has blest me in every thing and I Request you to Continyou to ask god far to extend his blesings to wards us as a family if we shal never sea each other a*

gain in this life I hope that we will meat in heaven where there is no ware. I want you to pray formee and tell all my christian friends to remember mee in there Prarers Pray to god to give us peace and stop the sheding of blud.[58]

Resinor Etter spent the time looking for something to eat. "I left camps and went out to hunt something to eat   I went some 13 mils I found ¹/₂ bushel of potatoes   I paid 5 dollars for them."[59]

The absence of fighting gave all the men an opportunity to focus their attention on problems that might otherwise have gone unnoticed. Their clothing was hanging on by threads; their shoes, if they had any, were almost completely worn out; they had not had a decent bath since they crossed the Chattahoochee; and almost all of them were bothered by the complications of an improper diet. It was indeed well that the Yankees had given this band of weary fighters time to lick their wounds.

Spencer Talley missed the fighting at Jonesboro, but rejoined his regiment at Lovejoy's Station. Spencer had many experiences to tell his comrades who thirsted for news from the outside. He told of being surrounded at Hawkinsville by wondering boys and old men who had never before seen a real live wounded Reb, of how the older citizens argued over which would get the privilege of boarding him, of how the odor from his wound became so offensive that he was ashamed to enter the presence of ladies, and how a slave boy nursed him back to health. Spencer also told of the young ladies who had been solicitous of his health and how they planned events to take his mind off his troubles. Before he was through he had convinced many of those who listened that being wounded might not be so bad after all.

While the men passed the time as best they could, their generals planned for the weeks ahead. It was obvious that the Confederate Army could not remain long at Lovejoy's Station. On September 21st, Hood moved his men to Palmetto twenty five miles west of Atlanta. Here steps toward reorganization were undertaken. The 16th Tennessee had been reduced "to so small a number that the remnant of the ten original companies was scarcely enough to make three good companies by consolidation."[60] The 8th, 10th, and 28th Regiments were consolidated into one regiment that did not equal the strength of any of the original units. The 19th, 24th, and 41st were consolidated into one regiment, but the consolidation merely concerned the number of men assigned to a particular colonel; each regiment retained its flag and its numerical designation. It took a strong imagination on the part of politicians and generals to believe that this skeleton army of underfed, poorly equipped, and badly beaten soldiers could take the offensive against an enemy with such inexhaustible reserves of men and supplies that it could dispatch troops from the very zone of action. The Confederate Army was being looked upon more as a nuisance than a threat.

There was a mutual lack of respect between Hood and the Confederate Army. The men and officers were tired of the army commander's continuing accusation that the soldiers were poor fighters. The action at Jonesboro had invoked Hood's displeasure because of what he considered another feeble effort on the part of both officers and men. As proof of this accusation, Hood cited the casualties at Jonesboro, pointing out that only 1400 were listed as killed and wounded.[61] It was the same old story: when the generals stopped fighting Yankees, they began fighting each other. It was time for Jefferson Davis to make a visit.

The President arrived at Palmetto on September 26, 1864, accompanied by Governor Isham G. Harris of Tennessee and other politicians. Davis met with Hood and listened as the general outlined a plan to recross the Chattahoochee River in order to operate against the Yankee supply line from Chattanooga. Davis liked the plan and requested an opportunity to address the soldiers. During the address he revealed Hood's plan not only to the Rebs, but to the Yanks as well since his remarks were soon reported in local newspapers. Regardless of the plan, W.J. Worsham thought, "The hope of success in the minds of the soldiers had begun to fade and grow dim."[62] Perhaps the entry for that day in Resinor Etter's diary summed up the attitude of many. He wrote, "I stay al day in camps & eat potatoes."[63]

After a brief stay, Davis left from what would be his next to last visit with the Army of Tennessee. If he had accomplished anything, it was little. He accurately suspected that Hood needed help and so improvised a "Military Division of the West" and ordered General P.G.T. Beauregard from Virginia to assist in planning strategy. Davis also agreed to transfer General William Hardee, an action that pleased both Hardee and Hood. When Hardee left, General Ben Cheatham was appointed to replace him.

Confederate generals and politicians agreed that Hood's best alternative was to pursue the plan of disrupting Sherman's supply line from Chattanooga. The Confederate high command could somehow see themselves isolating Sherman in Georgia and starving him into submission. In any event, since no better course of action presented itself, the Rebs prepared two days' rations and on September 30, 1864, started north.

The following day the Army of Tennessee crossed the Chattahoochee River. It had been nearly three months since it had crossed the same river going south. The sojourn below the river had been costly beyond anything the Confederates had expected. Over nine thousand men had been killed, wounded or declared missing. Atlanta, the deep South's most important city, had been lost, and the men had lost Joseph E. Johnston, the only commander they ever loved. But even if the recrossing of the Chattahoochee held out little hope for many of the men in Hood's army, it at least had special meaning for the men from Tennessee: they were headed toward home. Many of them would never get there.

General John Hunt Morgan

Andrew Campbell

Chapter XIX

Bring Morgan out dead or alive

Perhaps the rise and fall of the Confederacy was nowhere better paralleled than in the military career of Kentucky General, John Hunt Morgan. Every stage of his varied career reflected the fortunes of the government he served, and his fate was a forewarning to those who cherished the cause for which he fought.

Morgan entered the war when the South was enjoying its finest hour, and he brought to it those qualities which Southerners believed would insure victory. He was young, physically strong, daring to a point of recklessness, and headstrong to the point of imprudence. He was a skilled fighter, an expert horseman, and was possessed of the personal charm which characterized Southern officers in the minds of the Southerners in 1861. It took Morgan only a short time to establish himself as a prominent member of the plumed-hat school of Rebel raiders. His name soon became a source of pride and admiration to Southerners — and soon a source of dread and fear to Federal commanders charged with keeping him under control.

Shortly before the Battle of Stone's River, within the span of a few days, he married one of Middle Tennessee's fairest ladies before the eyes of the Western Confederacy's most renowned generals. He was promoted to brigadier general and won the plaudits of the entire Confederacy for his brilliant raid on Hartsville. Generals, and politicians, stood in admiration of his accomplishments; the future seemed unbounded.

The men Morgan led were the best Kentucky had to offer. He had been able to pick and choose from the thousands who applied for acceptance, and those he believed to be unfit were waved on to the infantry. Through 1862, Morgan's command had not wanted for supplies. What its own government was unable to provide was acquired from the enemy. His operations were not encumbered by the red tape which was sure to develop once the government he served became more firmly established. But, of more importance than these considerations, was the fact that Morgan was fighting for a country fired by the enthusiasm of a new crusade and people who believed that victory would surely follow in the wake of their inspired efforts. Men like Morgan soared on the tide of optimism which enveloped the South during the first years of the war — an optimism which shielded the people from the more unpleasant realities that lay ahead.

All of Morgan's fame and success occurred before his capture in the summer of 1863. Even before he led his troops on the ill-fated Ohio raid where his command was cut to pieces, there were disturbing signs which told that the future of the Confederacy might not be as glorious as it had appeared. Already the armor of Southern complacency had been penetrated by the defeats from Fort Donelson to Stone's River, and beneath the bravado of Southern politicians were the disturbing indications that the individual Confederate soldier was losing much of the enthusiasm which had accompanied his early service under the "new flag." Nevertheless, John Hunt Morgan entered his Yankee cell confident that the South would yet taste the sweet fruits of victory. His one compelling desire was to rejoin her armies in the field.

Morgan's chance to reenter the service of the Confederacy came in early 1864, when he escaped from the Ohio State Penitentiary. But the raider was to find that the months of his confinement had taken a terrible toll on the South. It was a far different war to which he returned than the one he had left.

When Morgan reached Richmond after his escape, he was warmly welcomed by the citizens who saw in his return reason for new hope. They cheered and wept as he walked among them with the confidence which was his trademark. To people needing a new symbol of hope, his arrival seemed a sign of better things to come. But at the Capitol, there were no cheers. Braxton Bragg was now President Davis' chief military advisor and Bragg was still bitter for what he considered the raider's insubordination in crossing the Ohio River in 1863. Instead of extending Morgan a warm welcome, Bragg suggested that a court-martial might be more appropriate.

Morgan quickly found out that his relationship to the government would not be the same as it had been before his capture. When he attempted to reorganize his old command, he was informed that the men were scattered throughout the army, and that almost no one saw the necessity of getting them together again. Any request he made was usually turned down when Bragg read it, and only after the intervention of influential friends was Morgan able to secure a command in Southwest Virginia.

Above all other evidence he had been able to examine, Morgan's new command indicated the plight of the Confederacy in 1864.

Instead of the dashing cavalier type he had recruited in 1861, Morgan now found himself commanding a group of half-clad, ill-disciplined, and unenthusiastic men. Their main interest in the war seemed to be what they could steal and plunder, and many of them measured the success of a military operation more in terms of the plunder brought away than the damages inflicted upon the enemy. These men were later to be accused of murder, robbery, and various other types of lawlessness. Few of their comrades in other units doubted the accuracy of these charges.

But the restless spirit of John Hunt Morgan was not to be compromised because his men were something less than they should be. With such as he had, he was determined to reenter the conflict. Depending primarily on a small core of well disciplined men, Morgan carried out a raid in Kentucky during the first part of June 1864, but the outlaw element of his command dominated the action. They robbed a bank, broke into stores and took or destroyed their contents, pointed their guns at women along the way and robbed them of their jewelry — and, in general, raised havoc. The conduct of the troops brought much louder repercussions from Richmond than the failure of the raid. When the two were combined, it meant more and deeper trouble for the now pathetic raider.

Throughout the summer of 1864, the tarnished idol of the Confederacy faced accusation after accusation — both from Richmond and from within his own command. Every idea he advanced for the improvement of his situation was either turned down or ignored. Those who knew him best believed they saw the once confident and sometimes brash raider begin to crumble into something that hardly resembled his former self. But somewhere under it all there still burned the intense desire to engage the enemy, and during the last days of August, Morgan began making plans for a raid into East Tennessee.[1]

2.

While John Hunt Morgan waited in Richmond during February for the Confederate authorities to reach an agreement concerning his future, John M. Smith, a recruiting agent from East Tennessee, arrived at Nashville with almost one hundred recruits for the 13th Tennessee Cavalry (Federal). The recruits were sworn into the East Tennessee regiment on February 25, 1864. Among the names added to the roster was that of Andrew

424

Campbell* formerly of General Pat Cleburne's Confederate command. It had been almost a year since the Confederate sergeant had deserted at Wartrace, Tennessee, and now he was entering the service of the army against which he had fought during the early months of the war.

Andrew Campbell represented the element to be found in both armies which cared little about the issues involved — as long as the food and pay were good. Campbell had gone to New Orleans at the beginning of the war, joined the Rebel Army as a soldier of fortune, but later learned that the fortune element was mostly a myth. One of his fellow soldiers explained his switching armies by saying, "Growing tired of hard fighting and poor pay, he quit that service [Confederate] of his own accord and sought service in the Federal army."[2] Actually Campbell had been found loafing about the streets of Nashville and it was from there that John Smith had recruited him.

Shortly after his enlistment, the 13th Tennessee left Nashville in a brigade made up of East Tennesseans and one regiment from Michigan. The brigade was commanded by General A.C. Gillem. Its first stop after leaving Nashville was Gallatin. The short stay in Gallatin was a pleasant interlude. Although, previously, the people of Gallatin had been treated rather harshly by the Yankees, they didn't seem to carry a grudge against their fellow Tennesseans. A neutral observer might have found it difficult to believe that the people of Gallatin and the members of the 13th Tennessee Cavalry were on opposing sides of a brutal war. When the regiment made ready to leave, local citizens lined the streets to see them off and one East Tennessean described Gallatin as a city of "kind hearted, generous and intelligent people." He added, "Many strong attachments were formed, especially between the young officers and the many handsome young ladies."[3]

The scene presented by the Tennessee Unionists as they left Gallatin was far different from that presented by Morgan's command — then moving west from Virginia. The Yankee

*Not to be confused with the Andrew Campbell of Chapter X.

425

column was described by one of its members who wrote, "The horses were in fine condition, the uniforms clean and new, arms glittering in the sunshine, colors fluttering in the breeze, it presented a handsome picture."4

To Lebanon and on through Sparta, the East Tennesseans made their way amid the unsympathetic stares of Middle Tennesseans. At Sparta, officers of the brigade had dinner with Confederate General George Dibrell's sister who asked, as a reward for her hospitality, that should any of her Confederate sons ever fall into the hands of the 13th, that they be treated well.

As the column moved into the mountains, it gradually entered Union territory. Its reception there contrasted sharply from that received in Rebel country. At every village and town, flags were unfurled, ranks were dressed up, and men who had begun to slouch in the saddle straightened up for the benefit of their admirers who cheered thankfully as the "Stars and Stripes" passed by. Even the officers' wives who rode along in buggies were feted with gifts and admiring glances from people happy to see added protection for their homes.

On August 30, 1864, Gillem's brigade crossed the Holston River and camped near the village of Russellville. A scouting party was dispatched and promptly made contact with a Confederate outpost at Bull's Gap, a short distance from the town of Greenville. The Rebs were driven in and Gillem's entire command was moved up to Bull's Gap. There they spent the next few days shoeing horses and repairing wagons — and waiting.

3.

On the same day that Gillem's brigade moved into Bull's Gap, John Hunt Morgan said goodbye to his wife at Abington, Virginia, and left to join his command which was moving west toward Greenville, Tennessee. Basil Duke of Morgan's command saw Morgan shortly before he left Abington. It was the first meeting between the two since their prison days in Ohio. Duke found Morgan

> *...greatly changed. His face wore a weary, care-worn expression, and his manner was totally destitute of its former ardor and enthusiasm. He spoke bitterly, but with no impatience, of the clamor against him, and seemed saddest about the condition of his command.*[5]

Morgan arrived at Greenville on the afternoon of September 3, 1864, a few hours before sundown. The sight presented by his command would have made any general sad. The weather was cold and wet, and Morgan's men were forced to face it half-clothed. Many had no weapons and, although they were supposed to be a raiding party capable of quick mobility, many had no horses.

After posting pickets around the town, which was decidedly Unionist in sympathy, Morgan asked and received permission to stay in the home of Mrs. Catherine Williams. He had stayed there on occasions and felt comfortable there. It was the same house used by Longstreet when he was in town. After dark, a torrential rain began to fall, and following supper with his staff, Morgan withdrew to an upstairs room where he retired for the evening.

When Morgan selected the Williams house for his headquarters, he put himself in a no-man's land. His command was still east of Greenville and there were only scattered pickets between him and Gillem's Federal brigade to the west. Nevertheless, the Rebs settled in for the night. While Morgan slept upstairs, his staff officers gathered around a piano to blend their voices in old familiar Southern songs.

4.

At Bull's Gap, word reached Gillem's headquarters that a Confederate force had moved into Greenville. After a parley of war, it was decided to strike the Rebs a blow before they could organize for action. Colonel W.H. Ingerton was ordered to select his best mounted men and work his way behind the Rebel outpost west of town. After Ingerton's men had gained position, the remainder of the brigade would attack from the front, thus isolating the Rebs and preventing them from giving a warning to their comrades.

The night march of Ingerton's men was miserable in every respect, but a stubborn determination drove the Yankee horsemen forward in the face of their unpleasant surroundings. While John Hunt Morgan slept comfortably in the Williams House, Andrew Campbell and his comrades stumbled and slid along a seldom-used wagon road in their attempt to carry through their assignment. An officer who made the march wrote:

It was about 10 o'clock at night September 3d, and while forming the regiment it was discovered that the clouds and darkness presaged a storm. Col. Ingerton immediately gave orders for the company commanders to get out every well mounted soldier in each company ready to ride . . . The storm had now broken loose, and it would have been impossible to find the way but for the continuous blaze of lightning that enabled the men to see the road. The lightning blinded the horses, however, so that when the column halted they would often run against each other. But the regiment struggled on, men and horses often falling into ditches and others running against each other. The Third Commandment was broken that night more than once, as men cursed the promoters of this night expedition.[6]

428

By daylight, the men of Ingerton's detachment were in position to intercept the Confederates west of town. Driven back by Gillem's main column, the Confederates were so surprised that there was little for the Yankees to do. While the Confederates were being captured, local citizens ran to Ingerton and informed him that Morgan was in the Williams House. Ingerton immediately ordered two of his captains to take their companies, "dash into town, surround the Williams residence and bring Morgan out dead or alive."[7]

Oddly enough, neither Morgan nor members of his staff had become alarmed during the firing which had accompanied Gillem's early morning attack. It was common practice for soldiers to fire their weapons after a rain to check the powder and it is probable that both Morgan and his officers assumed this accounted for the shots clearly audible to the west. In any case, Federal Captains C.C. Wilcox and Samuel Northington readied their men for a charge into Greenville. When the Tennessee Yankees struck, they struck hard, fast, and effectively. While Wilcox' men surrounded the Williams House, Northington's men captured Morgan's horses. Other Federal soldiers ran the Reb guards away from the artillery they had stationed on a nearby hill. Everything went as the Yankees had planned.

5.

Inside the house, Morgan had at last become aware of the true situation. He and his staff quickly prepared to break through the attackers. Taking only enough time to slip on his trousers, Morgan ran down the stairs and out into the yard. When he reached the outside, he found men firing in every direction, but soon found himself to be the main target. Many Federal soldiers could have shot Morgan except for the fact that the rain had made their guns inoperable. For a brief moment, it appeared that the Rebel general might escape unharmed. As he made his way toward the local depot, a soldier on a horse spotted him, took aim and fired. He missed. Quickly dismounting, the soldier ran to a nearby fence, rested his gun and took careful aim. This time he did not miss and John Hunt Morgan was heard to say, "O, God," before he fell on his face and died. Slowly, Andrew Campbell walked over to the man he had killed and asked who he was. A Confederate prisoner looked down at the body and sadly reported, "That is the best man that ever lived, Gen. Morgan."[8]

For his role in the event, Andrew Campbell was promoted to sergeant and later to lieutenant by Governor Andrew Johnson. Colonel Ingerton was warmly congratulated for his direction of the raid as East Tennessee soldiers celebrated one of their finest hours. For Col. Ingerton, the glory would be short-lived. One month later, as he sat in the lobby of a Knoxville hotel with the infant daughter of General Gillem on his knee, he was assassinated by a former member of his command who harbored a grudge concerning the Colonel's handling of his regiment.

John Hunt Morgan was dead, but of far more importance, the things he had so ably represented were also dying. With the exception of General Forrest, the dash was gone from the Rebel cavalry in Tennessee; men imbued with a fervent desire for Southern independence had too frequently been reduced to, or replaced by, men more interested in when the war would end, than its implications. With Morgan's death went another symbol of confidence which had sustained the Southern people in the face of defeat.

In the Confederacy's western army, again with the exception of Forrest, there was not a man whose name radiated the enthusiasm and hope which accompanied the first years of the war. The individual Rebel soldier had stopped writing about victory in his letters, but instead expressed concern over surviving the final, tragic efforts of a government too beaten to hope for victory, but too proud to admit defeat.[9]

Chapter XX

I begin now
to look forward to the worst

The first day of October, 1864 found Hood's army on the north bank of the Chattahoochee River outside Atlanta. Most of the men were ragged, many had no shoes, and all were commanded by a general of questionable merits. The fighting around Atlanta had taken a terrible toll from the army. Regiments had been torn apart by the savage fire of Federal artillery. Some of the best officers had died leading their men against enemy breastworks, and the physical and mental strain of the campaign was dramatically apparent in the emaciated appearance of the soldiers who had recently been trampled by the overwhelming might of the Yankee Army. On their way south, the men had a flickering of hope — however unrealistic that hope might have been. Now, on their way north, that hope was no longer existent — there was no base of evidence upon which it could rest.

Even the people at home lacked hope. In McMinnville, L. Virginia French wrote:

I begin now to look forward to the worst — to hope for nothing — to expect only disaster — and endeavor to meet it when it comes, not so much with fortitude and courage, as with a sullen and stolid indifference. I have wished a thousand times that I had never married — that I had no family pressing on me — no little children over whose present and future welfare to vex and worry — if I had no one but myself — it would be a small matter — I should not then care for all this trouble I should get out of it. There are some who always seem to ride the top wave — even in times like these I see people who seem always to have plenty — to be in need of nothing — even to be making profits out of the times. Such is not our case — we make nothing save by the hardest of "hard-licks."

We are preyed upon on all sides — we get forward with no work — we gain nothing, in short as Mrs. Myers says of her family — "When it rains soup our plate is always bottom upwards." I have tried to "turn an honest penny" by selling off the surplus of housekeeping articles which I brought from Bersheba [A resort area on a nearby mountain]*— but although such things are scarce and high, I cannot sell anything. No one seems to want them when they have to pay out money, or provisions for them . . .*

I dread this coming winter. In it we shall learn many a stern and stormy lesson and many a sorrowful one! . . . I suppose I am beginning to become embittered by years of hardship, privation and sorrow. Verily, this world is a hard one, would to God I had never come into it! . . . Great Heaven! when shall we have rest and peace? Will it ever come in our day? I am becoming a sadsouled woman — full of secret sorrows — full of heart-burnings, full of longings for the great and good — full of impatience and repining at the chains, the iron chains of everyday circumstances which bind me back from all that my better nature aspires to! How sad a thing it is to feel how powerless, how insignificant, how incapable we are! When the heart is fired for great deeds, when the eye is fixed on some high standard — when the whole nature is straining and struggling forward to have the petty chains of everyday wound about you, a perpetual hindrance and stumbling block — oh! it is hard![1]

Many soldiers in Hood's army would have given a strong Amen to Mrs. French's observation. But if the army's journey north was without hope, it was not without enthusiasm. There was a special kind of enthusiasm that accompanied a north-bound march. Perhaps its nature was nothing more than symbolic, but it was always there. This was especially true for the soldiers from Tennessee. These men were homesick and their homes lay north through the battle-scarred country over which they had battled the previous summer. Tennesseans had not been on their native soil since the rout at Missionary Ridge, and regardless of the price they might pay for the privilege, it was good to be started toward home.

The first days' marches were slow and tiresome. Preparations for the campaign had, of necessity, been scant and, according to Spence Talley, fifteen or twenty miles were considered a good day's march. While the ultimate objective of Hood's northward thrust was still somewhat a mystery, its first undertaking was evident to all. Marching alongside the railroad leading to Chattanooga it would veer off periodically and strike the track. By following this plan, Hood hoped that Sherman could be drawn out of Atlanta and lured into the mountains where he envisioned a defeat of the massive, well-fed, well-equipped, and victorious Federal Army. No fiction writer would have dared such a plot, but since the authorities at Richmond insisted that the war continue, its last tragic act was opened in the West.

On the 4th of October, General A.P. Stewart's corps left the main army and struck the railroad at Big Shanty. As one Reb described the event:

Here was the property belonging to our friends, but this was no concern of ours. The orders were to tear up the tracks, and at once the work was begun. Huge fires of ties were built, rails laid across them, the center heated to a red heat, until the ends met. In some cases the rails were twisted around the trunks of trees, forming a ring, and in every way possible destroying their usefulness.[2]

The next day the Rebs hit a Yankee supply base at Allatoona. It proved to be well fortified and the going was rough. According to a member of the 16th Tennessee, "As our boys swarmed over the parapet the bayonet was freely used by both sides, officers firing their pistols, and many throwing rocks and stones . . ."[3] Just when victory appeared certain to the Confederates, they received a message warning that a Federal column was approaching from the rear. The Rebs immediately withdrew.[4]

By this time, Sherman had left Atlanta and was on the trail of the northbound Rebs. The idea of chasing Hood's army through the pine trees of north Georgia never appealed to Sherman, who suggested his talents might better be used to create havoc in the undefended portions of the state, while George Thomas, who was already in Tennessee, challenged the advance of the Confederate Army. Neither Grant nor Thomas liked his proposal, so Sherman began his half-hearted chase which amounted to nothing.

Continuing their journey northward, Hood's men arrived at Dalton on October 13, 1864. They found the town defended by a garrison of Negro troops who occupied a series of blockhouses on the outskirts of the town. Spencer Talley was a member of the force sent to capture the blockhouses and according to him:

We approached the garrison of negroes, who were commanded by white officers in a manner that they could have a plain view and estimate of our strength. A messenger was sent in under flag of truce demanding that they make an unconditional surrender under the penalty that if they fired a gun at us no quarter would be shown them when captured.[5]

Seeing the futility of resisting, the town and its fortification were surrendered without a shot being fired.

Although void of bloodshed, the surrender of Dalton made a deep impression on Spencer Talley. Nothing infuriated Confederate soldiers as much as the sight of Negro troops. Confederate officers in Northern prisons were known to refuse freedom when they learned that they were to be exchanged for Federal officers who had commanded Negro troops. Fort Pillow would not prove to be the last incident in which this hatred manifested itself in useless killing.

Although he showed no outward emotion, Spencer Talley experienced the distaste which Negro troops aroused in Tennesseans as he watched them surrender. Talley wrote:

They immediately surrendered and my company was sent in to have them stack their arms and march them out. We took the white men as prisoners but the negroes were taken as livestock or other property. The separation of these white officers from their negro commands was an interesting as well as a sickening scene to our southern boys. The white officers in bidding farewell with their colored men showed in no uncertain way their love and devotion to the colored race. Their hearty handshakes and expressions of sorrow over their separation will never be forgotten.[6]

From Dalton, Hood turned west across northern Alabama. Following the southern bank of the Tennessee River, the Confederate commander planned to cross the river at Guntersville, join Forrest on the other side, and strike the

Yankees as he came to them. Meanwhile, Sherman gave up the chase, leaving Hood to the attention of George Thomas. Sherman returned to Atlanta from where he would shortly begin his famous march to the sea.

Hood's plan to cross theTennessee River met unexpected obstacles. High water kept Forrest from meeting him at Guntersville and he was forced to continue his march westward. At every place the Confederates attempted to cross the river, something prevented it, and after each failure he was forced to march farther west until, by November 13th, he was at Florence, Alabama. Although his plans were upset time after time, Hood adjusted as best he could to the situation; he would cross at Florence, join forces with Forrest, and make a direct thrust against the Yankees in Middle Tennessee with Nashville as his chief objective.

While the Confederates waited at Florence for supplies, Resinor Etter sat down and wrote of his trip across northern Alabama:

> We have been on a verry active campaihn   I have under went many hard ships   my trip has been quiet interesting   came over a verity of Country   Some fine lands   Some very poore   the people allso very poore they are in destute circumstances   I dont see how they live espeshly thoes who are so very poor . . . You can cast your eyes around you as fare as you can see   lands lying uncultivated   Houses burned up   Negroes all gon   Have some poor old decripped ones who could not get away or the enemy would not have   Not enough corne growing on these level and rich soils to bred what few wimen and Children from suffering   It is a sorrowful looking sene   I hope the people may soon be at peace & cultivate thoes land again.[7]

G.W. Gordon, a member of the 11th Tennessee, remembered Blountsville, Alabama, for a different reason.

According to Gordon:

> *An unusual supply of "John Barleycorn" had found its way into camp, and one of the Colonels commanding a regiment had imbided a little too freely, and while passing the road near the camp lost his equilibrium and staggered into a small mud-hole, perhaps two feet wide and six inches deep. Whereupon the generous effect of the fluid seemed to culminate and to render the Colonel exceedingly careful of the lives of his men, and he thereupon ordered a guard placed at the little mud-hole to prevent the soldiers who chanced to pass that way from falling into it. To men who had been accustomed to plunge through swollen streams and deep morasses when emergency required, this circumstance was extremely amusing, and often caused a hearty laugh as it was recalled around the camp-fire.[8]*

The incident related above became even more ridiculous when the hardships of the journey were recalled. In speaking of moving the wagon trains toward Florence, Gordon said:

> *Most of the teams in this train were poor, jaded, and apparently half-starved; but after several days of hard marching, the men often pulling and pushing the wagons through creeks and bogs, over hills and the mountains, we successfully rejoined the army near Courtland, and on time.[9]*

A spirit of restlessness pervaded the Rebel troops at Florence. They were anxious to cross the river and head north. It was the first time they had been a part of an offensive movement since the ill-fated Kentucky campaign in '62 and they liked the feeling. Even amid the disturbing evidence of the army's inadequacy, the old boasts of 1861 surfaced. Men around campfires were heard to predict what would happen when the Yankees were met on Tennessee soil. It was as if the familiar hills would somehow become silent allies radiating a perceptible warmth as the ragged and hungry Rebs walked once more among them. Tales of how families of Confederate soldiers had been mistreated were recalled and embroidered until an atmosphere of impatience prevailed. Hood, too, was impatient. He had ordered supplies and a pontoon bridge to be ready when the army reached Florence, but neither was in evidence. As the first rain-drenched weeks of November passed, he hobbled on his crutch in an almost complete state of frustration. His choice was to wait.

2.

While the Army of Tennessee waited at Florence, Alabama, George Guild and the 4th Tennessee Cavalry were on the move. October had been an eventful month for this regiment and November would be even more so. Early in August, Wheeler's cavalry, of which the 4th Tennessee was a part, had been ordered into Tennessee to disrupt communications and inflict all of the damage possible to Federal forces in the area. As the fall weeks progressed, George Guild's regiment drifted toward East Tennessee and in October participated in the Battle of Saltville, Virginia.

At Saltville the fighting began when the Yankees attempted to capture the South's main source of salt. It ended to the satisfaction of the Southerners when the attackers were driven away. But it was probably the events following the battle which would remain the longest in the memories of those who were there.

After the firing ended, and the Yanks had withdrawn, George Mosgrove of Kentucky "heard a shot, then another and another, until the firing swelled to the volume of that of a skirmish line." After mounting his horse and riding in the direction of the firing, the Kentuckian realized he was in front of two Tennessee regiments and that

. . . the Tennesseans were killing negroes . . .
They were shooting every wounded negro they could
find . . . Robertson's and Dibrell's brigades had lost
many good men and officers . . . and they were so
exasperated that they could not be deterred from their
murderous work. Very many negroes standing about in
groups were only slightly wounded, but they soon went
down before the unerring pistols and rifles of the
enraged Tennesseans.[10]

George Guild said of the fight, "The cry was raised that
we were fighting negroes. They were the first we ever met.
Many of them were killed and wounded . . . This field presented
a scene never witnessed before."[11]   Benjamin Rogers, a
member of the 4th Tennessee Cavalry, wrote:

On the night after the battle, the Federals withdrew,
leaving many of their wounded, mostly Negro soldiers,
on the battlefield, and a few white prisoners . . . On that
night as I lay in hearing of the battlefield, I thought the
battle had reopened. It proved to be our own men, who,
disliking the idea of having to fight their former slaves,
went out after the battle was over and killed 500
wounded Negroes.[12]

A few hours later, while lying in a hospital, Rogers
observed soldiers "amusing themselves by shooting Negroes in
the hospital."[13]

George Mosgrove witnessed the same scene and later
wrote:

I pitied them from the bottom of my heart and
would have interposed in their behalf had I not known
that any effort to save them would be futile. Some of
them were so slightly wounded that they could even run,
but when they ran from the muzzle of one pistol it was
only to be confronted by another. Entering a little log

cabin, I passed at the threshold when I saw seven or eight slightly wounded negroes standing with their backs against the walls. I had scarcely been there a minute when a pistol-shot from the door caused me to turn and observe a boy, not more than sixteen years old, with a pistol in each hand. I stepped back, telling him to hold on until I could get out of the way. In less time than I can write it, the boy had shot every negro in the room. Every time he pulled a trigger a negro fell.[14]

Not all who were murdered were Negroes. Champ Ferguson and his men were among those doing the shooting and according to Benjamin Rogers:

I was sent to the hospital at Emory & Henry [A college near the battle site]. I observed from my third story window a score of Ferguson's men, who were easily recognized by their picturesque garb. A few minutes later I heard a gun discharged in the building adjoining the one I was in and soon afterward a number of shots. This first gun was in the hands of Capt. Ferguson. He had learned of the capture of Col. Hanson and Capt. Smith and of their being sent to Emory & Henry hospital. A guard was set, but Ferguson had ignored him and boldly marched into the main ward. One of the first men he saw was Capt. Smith. Without a word he killed him as he lay on his cot. Col. Hanson who had always worn a flowing beard had shaved his head and cut his beard off the night before. On seeing Smith killed, he shuddered and covered his face with a sheet. Ferguson walked to his bed, pulled the sheet from his face, and examined him carefully without recognition . . .[15]

Champ Ferguson's rampage was stopped by Dr. L. B. Murfree of Murfreesboro, Tennessee. After a confrontation in which Ferguson told Murfree, "I don't care who you are, damn you, I will kill you," the physician was successful in having Champ and his gang removed from the premises. Champ was arrested for the murder and tried by court-martial, but according to Dr. Murfree, ". . . it was so near the close of the war that nothing more than this was done to him."[16]

George Guild points out that the death of John Hunt Morgan and other reported atrocities had the Confederates on edge, and that actually three Confederate privates and a lieutenant were hanged by their own army for crimes during this period. Guild comments:

> *Federal bushwhackers were thick along our line of march and occasionally killed some of our men. This, with the killing of General Morgan, caused our men to retaliate, and they were guilty of some outrageous conduct.*[17]

Immediately following the fighting at Saltville, George Guild and the 4th Tennessee Cavalry left Virginia and joined General Joe Wheeler's command outside Atlanta. Their assignment was to keep an eye on Sherman and to report on his movements. Sherman's troops had already burned a good portion of Marietta as they returned from their token chase of Hood, and as soon as they entered Atlanta, everything in sight became a target for their torches. On November 15, 1864, a member of Sherman's staff wrote from Atlanta:

> *A grand and awful spectacle is presented to the beholder in this beautiful city, now in flames. By order, the chief engineer has destroyed by powder and fire all the store-houses, depot buildings, and machine shops. The heaven is one expanse of lurid fire; the air is filled with flying, burning cinders; buildings covering two hundred acres in ruins or in flames; every instant there is the sharp detonation or the smothered booming sound of*

exploding shells and powder concealed in the buildings,
and then the sparks and flame shoot away up into the
black and red roof, scattering cinders far and wide.
These are the machine-shops where have been forged
and cast the rebel cannon. Shot and shell that have
carried death to many brave defender of our nation's
honor.[18]

After Atlanta had been reduced to ruins, Sherman's army began its march to the sea. Certainly, Joe Wheeler's cavalry was no match for the Yanks, but at every opportunity the Rebs made themselves known. At Macon, Wheeler's men drove off the Yankee cavalry and at Waynesboro they held their own against the enemy. But such efforts did nothing to retard the fiery crusade of Sherman.

At Waynesboro, George Guild had an opportunity to observe, first hand, the bitterness which existed between the enemy armies. On a dense and foggy morning, Wheeler's men sighted a Federal column and immediately prepared to strike it. The attack occurred in a large field near the town and resulted in a mixed-up, confused affair in which many men were killed and wounded on both sides. Guild remembered:

In the midst of the battle with balls whizzing in
every direction, I came across a squad of our men who
had taken as prisoners four of the enemy. They were
threatening to kill them, when I remonstrated and told
them to turn them over to the rear guard near by. Just
then an officer of higher rank rode up. I appealed to
him, telling him that the soldiers proposed killing them.
His only reply was: "They know best what to do with
them." As I rode off into the fight, I heard the popping
of the pistols, and I could see the prisoners tumbling
over into the sage.[19]

There was little for Wheeler's cavalry to do but look on as Sherman ruined the country through which he passed. Slowly, leisurely, and brutally the Yankee Army moved toward the sea like a destructive lake of lava, capable of being stopped only by the conscience of its general or the sea itself. The former was unresponsive — the sea could only wait.

Gen. Hiram Granbury

Gen. Pat Cleburne

Gen. O. F. Strahl

Gen. States Rights Gist

Gen. John Adams

Killed at Franklin.

Chapter XXI

The desperate venture
of a desperate man

Shortly after Sherman left Atlanta going south, Hood's Army of Tennessee left Florence, Alabama, going north. While still in Georgia, Thomas H. Davenport, a chaplain in Hood's army, wrote:

A new campaign has been inaugurated, how it will end God only knows. We have been compelled to give up much of our country at this point. It has cost the enemy very much. At other points we have been successful. I am not discouraged, though there is some discontent in the army. Oh God, how long will this cruel war last? My heart yearns for the society of home. I count each day and ask when the last will come? Poor weak human nature is ready to complain and say my burden is too heavy. Cease thy murmuring, God is wise and good... Through many dangers I have been led, have escaped death time and again. It seems that I have led a charmed life. God be praised for his goodness. I see around me much distress and my heart sickens at the destruction of life and property on every hand, in the army and out of it. I see grey hairs and helpless infancy driven from home, penniless almost friendless. I see

strong men cut down without a moment's warning, or
left a cripple for life. I see the poor soldier as he toils
on, sustained by the hope of better days and by the love
he bears to those far away. I saw but yesterday the
Captain commanding this regiment barefoot. Such men
will not be conquered. I cannot give the history of this
campaign language to describe its suffering. It has been
long and bloody, many of our noblest have fallen.[1]

After reaching Florence, Alabama, Davenport observed:

It has been a long, weary march of nearly five
hundred miles, still the soldiers have stood it nobly.
Many of them are barefoot, both officers and men.
Where we will go next is uncertain, and great is the
anxiety. Every eye is turned toward Tennessee. Oh,
may she soon be free. God of hosts be with us and give
us success.[2]

Continuing rains delayed the Tennessee campaign.
Officers and men waited impatiently for the arrival of supplies
and Forrest's cavalry, both of which were blocked by flooded
rivers and muddy roads. General Beauregard was at Florence,
but the show was definitely Hood's. Beauregard was little more
than an interested spectator, watching what would prove to be
the dying gasp of the Confederacy's efforts in Tennessee.

It is probable that after Beauregard looked at Hood's band
of ragged fighters, he was not anxious to be too closely
associated with their ultimate fate. As Thomas Head of the 16th
Tennessee wrote, "Winter was now setting in with its severest
rigor, and many of the men were barefooted and destitute of
many other articles of clothing."[3] Resinor Etter noted in his
diary, "We are looking for some clothing. They are much
needed. The men are in destute circumstances   many
barefooted & have no Pants."[4] Such a situation could not have
boosted the hope or expectation of a general like Beauregard.

During the first week in November, a few blankets and socks were distributed, but the supply had not met the demand. Overhead, the November skies continued to empty their drenching rains into the already muddy roads and the drainage from the water-soaked fields flooded every river and creek in the area. When bridges were built, they washed away; when rails were placed across the roads they sank out of sight; and when the Rebs viewed the situation they were inclined to "cuss a blue streak" and hunt a dry spot.

By November 12, 1864, a pontoon bridge was almost completed across the Tennessee River. From the south, Hood's scattered commands began converging. The next day the troops began filing across the improvised structure as it danced and jumped dangerously on the muddy, swirling water. Spencer Talley saw the bridge as "a shaky, crazy, affair and crossing over it was an uneasy and ticklish tramp, and especially so with teamsters who had heavy loaded wagons."[5] Once, during the crossing, a herd of cattle became frightened, and when those in front balked, those behind were thrown into the swollen river and swept to a watery death.

While Hood's men deployed north of the river, Forrest arrived at Florence. So impassable were the roads over which he had come that on one particular day only two and a half miles were covered. Unable to get fresh horses, Forrest's men increased teams from six to eight, and when these bogged down, local oxen were pressed into service.

Upon reaching Florence, Forrest's men found the town filled with "general officers and their staff, soldiers, baggage-wagons, ambulances, and ordinance trains, and all betokened an early march."[6] Every road leading to Florence was thickly strewn with broken-down wagons and mules that had literally died in harness. The overall scene inspired one observer to evaluate Hood's Tennessee campaign as "the desperate venture of a desperate man."[7]

There was no let-up in the rainy weather. Throughout the days and nights, the elements of nature combined to keep the army inactive. It was as if nature in some kind of infinite wisdom was providing the leaders of the Confederacy a last chance to reconsider, a last chance to face the truth.

The individual Confederate soldier who now cursed the rain and mud did so knowing that a break in the weather would be the signal that would likely send him and hundreds of his comrades to a useless death. But such thoughts were not long entertained by men vitally concerned with the source of their next meal. Resinor Etter wrote:

> *We have not got anything to eat   I cross Cypress [Creek] on a raft and go to hunt something to eat   I went some 5 miles from camps... I visited one mans turnip patch. One a mong the finest I ever saw   they was turnips that would weight som 12 pounds... I got one sack of them   came back to the creek & cross on a raft after night   I got very wet in the rain   I eat a piece of liver & small piece of cracker   I lay myself down to rest.*[8]

Even in the face of the food shortage and dismal weather, there was an almost enthusiastic desire to get at the enemy. The men had never been more determined. As one observer noted, "...there was no faint-heartedness, but on the contrary, an evident desire to go forth and fight it out."

Go forth they did.

2.

Early on the morning of November 21, 1864, the Army of Tennessee began its advance toward Nashville. It was Monday and it was miserable. Sometime during the previous night, the rain stopped and the temperature fell rapidly. In a few hours, the rain was replaced by the year's first snow. Under a general in whom they had little confidence and who, in turn, lacked confidence in them, the men in Hood's army plodded their way toward the enemy. Many would record this march as one of the most uncomfortable of the war. All day the wind blew icy blasts of snow into the face of men whose bodies were barely covered with rags of clothing. All day and all night the frozen ruts cut their way through the thin soles of those lucky enough to have shoes.

Spencer Talley said, "Many of the boys were barefooted... At night when our poor cattle were being slaughtered barefooted boys were thick around the carcase for the skins which they would wrap around their feet with the hairy side next to the barefoot and ankle."[9] The morning after the advance had begun, Resinor Etter wrote, "Last night was excesetive cold. The ground froze some 5 inches in the night   we had to ly in the open are [air]   We left camps at daylight   my beard froze on my face."[10]

The cavalry rode two days ahead of the infantry and pushed back enemy outposts when and where they found them. As usual, Nelse Rainey and his comrades experienced exciting times. The night before his regiment left Florence, somebody stole Nelse's saber and revolvers leaving the anxious warrior to face the enemy virtually unarmed. In this condition Nelse flushed a Yankee picket who lost no time scurring off in the opposite direction. Notwithstanding the fact he was unarmed, Nelse took off in pursuit yelling at the top of his voice, "Halt! Halt!" The Yankee, assuming his pursuer was amply armed turned, rode meekly back , and offered his gun to his shaky captor. Not wishing to "rub it in," but unable to let such a situation remain unexplained Nelse said, "You're a nice fellow to surrender to me, for I have no arms!" To this the bewildered Yank replied, "If I'd er knowed it you wouldn't er got me."[11]

While the half-frozen Rebs trudged through the bitter cold, the actual strategy of the campaign was taking place in the mind of their general. Hood knew the Yankees had a force at Nashville under General George Thomas and another at Pulaski, seventy miles south of Nashville, under General John M. Schofield. Hood's objective appeared obvious: he would go to Columbia, midway between Nashville and Pulaski, seize the bridge over Duck River leading north, and then turn to destroy Schofield while he was isolated from Thomas. With this dream in mind, the Rebs were pushed along by anxious commanders who saw a chance to strike a significant blow for Southern independence.[12]

When at last the Rebs reached Columbia, they found Schofield already there. By forced marches, the Federal commander had arrived in time to erect strong fortifications around the southern part of town. Behind these, his army stood squarely in the path of Hood's troops. Hood's plan to isolate Schofield was off track; he needed time to think.

Resinor Etter and Spencer Talley did not know why the army stopped and probably didn't care. The most that Etter knew was that he was hungry and, while Hood planned strategy, he went to the place where cattle were being slaughtered and gathered up the feet which he boiled in water to make soup.[13] Spencer Talley spent his first afternoon at Columbia sitting on a rail fence watching "the hundreds and thousands of poorly clad and many barefooted soldiers splashing through mud & slush which was now from four to six inches deep."[14]

In his headquarters mansion south of Columbia, Hood considered the alternatives to a frontal attack. The situation was clear: the Yankees in his front were backed up against a river with only one bridge over which they could withdraw toward Nashville. If Hood could get a portion of his army in the rear of the Federals he would have them helplessly cut off — a glorious victory should be forthcoming. And so a flanking movement it would be. He would leave one of his corps at Columbia to demonstrate against Schofield while the other troops slipped to the right from where they could gain the enemy's rear. This was a maneuver every general dreamed of, but few ever had the opportunity to execute.

During the night of November 28th, Hood's engineers prepared pontoon bridges across the river and by the next morning all was ready to begin the secret mission around the enemy. Everything went well. The Rebs crossed the river and in the afternoon were near the village of Spring Hill, twelve miles in Schofield's rear. They were stationed along the only road leading north to Nashville. The weather had cleared and all indications pointed to a memorable day for the Confederacy.

On the same night that the Confederates laid the pontoon bridges, Schofield crossed his army to the north side of Duck River. This move made it easy for Hood's troops south of Columbia to move up, seize the bridge, and control the Yankees from the south. No general could have wished for a more ideal situation. A classic in planning had been accomplished and the Rebs who had doubted Hood's competency began having second thoughts.

What happened next has been almost unbelievable for over one hundred and twenty years. Schofield left Columbia and, during the late afternoon and night, marched through Spring Hill under the very eyes of the Rebel Army without being seriously challenged. What actually happened remains open to debate. Generals in their anger and embarrassment blamed each other. Hood said he ordered Cheatham to attack, Cheatham said he didn't; some said Hood was drunk and failed to comprehend the situation; still others were so dumbfounded by what happened that they projected no theories as to why it happened. Thus, a century and a quarter later, one of the great mysteries of the Civil War is why the Yankee Army was able to pass from Columbia to Franklin on the night of November 29, 1864.

One Yankee soldier said that as his regiment neared Spring Hill an officer approached and cautioned "with his finger to his lips not to speak above a whisper, and pointed to the camp fires within sight of the road. We could plainly see the soldiers standing there were Johnnies, and in the quiet of the night could hear their voices."[15]

Sergeant E. Shepard, a member of a Tennessee regiment, wrote:

> When my regiment reached the vicinity of the Columbia and Franklin Turnpike at Spring Hill, it was at once hastened forward to within two hundred and fifty yards of the pike on the east side and there halted. There was not even a skirmish line between us and the fleeing Federals on the pike . . .
>
> Our command was surprised at being halted, believed it to be only temporary, and was eager, impatient to make the charge. They only wanted permission to do so . . .
>
> We stood there in line until night came and darkness shut from our sight the fleeing Federals, but did not then despair of an order to charge. And when at last we knew there was to be none, the deep mortification and shame for the blunder could be seen in the bowed head of every one, for this is the only instance coming under my observation in the war where a false movement was so apparent as to be recognized by every soldier of the line, from private up, and that at the very instant.[16]

Late in the night of the 29th, Resinor Etter made an entry in his diary that could at least clarify the situation as concerned his regiment, the 16th Tennessee.

> Mooved at daylight up Duck River some 2 mils and crossed   Marched a very hard all day over hilles & hollows   marched around the enemy   We came nigh cuting off the enemy. Tho we was one hour late   we

did not git posesions of the Nashville pike in time . . . I
dont think I ever seen a harder march than we made
today. We marched 17 mils over rough Country with
out any rod to march in   none of the boys was hurt
today I lay myself down at midnight to rest a little.[17]

Hood's dream and the chance for a stunning Confederate victory at Spring Hill had vanished in the cold air of that fateful November night. Morning brought with it the empty feeling of failure, punctuated with bitterness, resentment, and the discomforting thought that Schofield was again in the path of the advancing Rebs.

It was difficult for Hood to accept what had happened. In an attempt to relieve himself of responsibility he asked Richmond to dismiss Cheatham from command — a move which was never made. Later Hood wrote:

The best move in my career as a soldier, I was thus
to behold come to naught. The discovery that the Army,
after a forward march of one hundred and eighty miles,
was still, seemingly, unwilling to accept battle unless
under the protection of breastworks, caused me to
experience grave concern. In my utmost heart I
questioned whether or not I would ever succeed in
eradicating this evil. It seemed to me I had exhausted
every means in the power of one man to remove this
stumbling block to the Army of Tennessee.[18]

Perhaps no equally unjustified criticism was ever leveled at an army.

Early on the morning of November 30, the Confederate Army picked itself up from the fields east of Spring Hill and did what respectable armies are supposed to do; it followed in the direction the Federals had gone. Hood had decided that the best he could do was to overtake the enemy "and rout him, and drive him in the Big Harpeth river at Franklin . . ."[19] In less than eight hours, the full significance of the Spring Hill blunder would make itself abundantly clear.

As his regiment marched northward toward Franklin, Spencer Talley noticed that "The road was strewn everywhere with the wreck of thrown away stuff that they were unable to carry in their flight. Many wagons just set on fire and abandoned were saved from destruction."[20] Resinor Etter said of the Yankees, "They burnt up wagons killed mules & destroyed much property."[21] Another Reb said he saw "thirty-four wagons that had been abandoned . . . In some instances whole teams of mules had been killed to prevent their capture."[22]

The hurried pace of the Federal Army ended at Franklin, where Schofield turned his men to face the approaching Rebs. According to Schofield, the strategy of the Federal Army "was not by any means to secure a safe retreat of the troops under my command and their junction with the forces of Gen. Thomas at Nashville . . . But the all important object was to retard the advance of Gen. Hood's army until Gen. Thomas could concentrate his troops at Nashville."[23]

In keeping with this idea, Schofield deployed his men on the southern border of Franklin, meantime getting all unneeded supplies across the Harpeth River toward Nashville. There were no idle moments for the Yankees who knew that at any hour the Rebs would come into sight from Spring Hill.

H.P. Figuers was a boy of twelve when the Battle of Franklin took place and watched every move the Yankees made from the time they entered town until they left. He watched as they feverishly built fortifications

> *...entirely around the south margin of the town. They worked like beavers, using houses, fences, timber, and dirt in their works . . . These breastworks were high enough to protect the soldiers and had head logs on top, so that the Federals could be reached only when the Confederate bullets entered the cracks between the head logs and the breastworks.[24]*

General Jacob Cox, who would actually command the Federal troops at Franklin during the battle, wrote that after the breastworks were completed,

> *There was now a period of rest and refreshment for the officers and men of the main line. Quiet followed the rattling of wheels and the clatter of arms that had made a continuous din in front of the Carter house all the morning. Our camp dinner was over, the tents at my headquarters were struck, the baggage packed, and the wagons sent into town to fall in at the rear of the trains when the rest should be over the river. The day had proved to be a bright and warm one, a good sample of Indian summer weather coming after the first sharp frosts and snows of opening winter. The air was hazy, and, except an occasional straggler following his command in, nothing was to be seen between us and Winstead Hill, two miles away.[25]*

Whatever relaxation the Federals hoped for was interrupted when "about 2 o'clock" the Confederates appeared on Winstead Hill two miles to the south. The head of the Rebel column halted on the crest of the hill while a lone figure, hobbling on his wooden leg, edged one hundred yards nearer Franklin. Over a gradually sloping plain, John Bell Hood could see the Federal breastworks; he could see a well-constructed fort bristling with cannon. And he could see that, should his army attack, the men would have absolutely no natural protection. He also knew that Stephen D. Lee's corps, with the exception of one division, was too far away to get to Franklin before dark, and therefore, Lee's artillery would not be available. In the face of these considerations, he turned and climbed the hill where his staff impatiently waited and said, "General, we will make the fight here."[26]

As soon as Hood's decision was relayed along the line the air became electric with excitement. Couriers dashed from place to place with orders to and from brigade and regimental commanders; a military band was brought up to add its inspiration to an occasion already alive with anticipation; and weary soldiers forgot their weariness as they prepared their guns for the battle ahead. Men hoisted their guns above their heads and shouted in unrestrained satisfaction at the chance to get at the enemy, and above it all, officers screamed orders which were, more often than not, lost in the noise and confusion.

There was no time to lose — in less than an hour the sun would be hidden by the hills to the west. In a matter of minutes, the Confederate Army was aligning itself for battle. As regiments, brigades and divisions took their positions on either end of the line, Hood's army resembled a giant animal extending its arms to receive a prey. Generals galloped along the line shouting encouraging words to men whose eyes remained fixed on the enemy two miles away. Even through the noise and confusion, there seemed a kind of mysterious silence which swallowed the sounds and made everything seem empty and surreal. Men talked for no other reason than to shatter its sinister effects.

Almost every man seemed to realize the terrible event which was about to happen. The men in General O.F. Strahl's brigade noticed a somewhat pathetic look on his face as he awaited the order to advance. Earlier in the day, Strahl had presented his beautiful black mare to Charles T. Quintard, Chaplain of the 1st Tennessee; the chaplain sensed something very strange in the young general's manner — as if he were possessed of a premonition. One soldier said of Strahl, "A sadder face I have never seen."[27] The only thing anybody remembered the general saying was, "Boys, this will be short but desperate." Before the sun set, General Strahl was dead.

At another point along the line, General John Adams checked his brigade in a final effort to insure its readiness. Adams was only a few miles from his Pulaski home where his wife, four sons, and two daughters resided. Adams had been a roommate of George Pickett at West Point and had listened with great satisfaction to the stories of his friend's role at Gettysburg, but no charge in the war would surpass, in any respect, the one Adams himself was about to make. It would be his last.

Somewhere in the confusion and excitement among the hills south of Franklin, General Pat Cleburne waited at the head of his division. It had been an upsetting day for the young Irishman who had learned during the morning that Hood blamed him, at least in part, for what had happened at Spring Hill. As he had ridden to Franklin, Cleburne expressed his concern to fellow officers who attempted to calm his concern over the matter. When he reached the top of the hill below Franklin, he "ascended to the top summit, rested his field-glasses upon a stump, and gazed long at the enemy's entrenchments."[28] During the moments following, Cleburne took a little black book from his pocket and hurriedly wrote an entry; it would be his final written observation.

The Rebel Army was ready to move. With its bands playing, flags flying, and in parade-ground formation the Confederates stepped toward the enemy. The sun was still shining and its rays were caught in the satin finish of tattered regimental flags and in the polished surfaces of musical instruments which provided a spectacular setting for the unfolding drama. Across the unobstructed plain toward Franklin the Rebs went; it was the greatest moment of the war in Tennessee; it was the moment above all others that would be spoken of by those who lived to tell the story; it was war at its glorious best.

From behind their breastworks, the Yankees watched in awe. One Federal soldier wrote, "At a little past three o'clock we could see Hood's lines begin to move forward. We stacked knapsacks and stripped to guns, cartridge belts, and canteens and 'stood to arms' awaiting the approach of the assaulting columns."[29] Yankee bands struck up "Hail Columbia," and thousands of voices were raised in a defiant yell as the Union soldiers let it be known that they were ready.

Calmly, and in measured steps, the Confederate line continued its way toward the Yankee breastworks. To the rear on Winstead Hill, Hood watched. It would be interesting to know the thoughts which must have occupied his mind. Did he feel the pounding of a repentant conscience for the unjustified times he had accused these men of being afraid to charge enemy breastworks?

A Yank remembered:

> *It was a grand sight. Such as would make a lifelong impression on the mind of any man to see such a charge. As forerunners, well in advance, could be seen a line of jack rabbits, bounding along for a few leaps, and then they would stop, and look, and listen, but scamper off again as though convinced that this was the most impenetrable line of beaters — that had ever given them chase; and quails by the thousands, in coveys here and there, would rise and settle, and rise and turn again to the sunlight that called them back.*[30]

Another Federal soldier wrote, "It looked to me as though the whole South had come up there and were determined to walk over us."[31]

Well in advance of the main Federal works, the Confederates struck an outpost manned by two brigades of Yankees. They were forthwith put to rout. The fleeing Yanks became a shield for the attackers who followed them closely until the main works were reached. "One hour by the sun," the armies clashed head-on and the terrible Battle of Franklin raged.

G.W. Gordon of the 11th Tennessee was immediately behind the retreating Yankees who had manned the outpost. When the Federal soldiers reached their breastworks Gordon's general shouted, "Go into the works with them!" and the Rebs responded with enthusiasm. According to Gordon:

So that when perhaps within less than a hundred paces of their main line, Federals and Confederates promiscuously rushing toward it, the enemy opened a deadly fire that indiscriminately slew friend and foe. It then seemed as if the air was literally filled with rifle-balls, grapeshot, shrieking shells, solid shot, bursting shrapnel, and every conceivable missle used in modern warfare. It seemed that if a hand had been thrown out it might have been caught full of the mad messengers of death.[32]

The gap caused by the retreating Federal regiments threatened the entire Union line. At this moment Colonel Arthur MacArthur*, who had won the Congressional Medal of Honor at Missionary Ridge, rushed his men to close the opening. The nineteen year-old commander was in the lead. Captain Edwin Parsons of the 24th Wisconsin said:

We were posted as a reserve near the Carter House ... At about four o'clock, the Confederates, Cheatham's division of Tennesseans, suddenly hit and broke through immediately in front of us. . . . The whole army was imperilled unless the breach could be closed . . . We just rushed pell mell to meet the enemy in a desperate hand to hand melee. I saw the Colonel sabering his way toward the leading Confederate flag. His horse was shot from under him, a bullet ripped open his right shoulder, but on foot he fought his way forward trying to bring down those Stars and Bars. A Confederate Major now had the flag and shot the Colonel through the breast. I thought he was done for but he staggered up and drove his sword through his adversary's body, but even as the Confederate fell he shot our Colonel down for good with a bullet through the knees.[33]

* Father of General Douglas MacArthur.

459

Elsewhere along the line, the Rebs met a solid sheet of fire. At the first discharge from enemy guns, the Confederate line staggered and the ground became dotted with fallen men. But charging through and over their own dead, other Rebs came up, climbed the Federal works and planted their flags on top, only to have them tumble and fall on the bodies of those who had planted them. Some Federal soldiers reached over the works and grabbed the Confederates by the hair and pulled them over the works where they were clubbed or bayoneted to death. Any instrument that could kill or cripple was brought into service as the men in both armies fought with a savagery never before seen in the Western theater of war.

Screams of agony were heard through the hovering smoke which soon covered the field. The dead piled up in the ditch outside the Federal works and the ground over which the Confederates were charging became covered with bodies. The Rebs were repeatedly thrown back by the protracted fire of their enemy, and Sam Watkins thought that maybe nature tried to hasten darkness in order to end the monstrous event. The fighting was so close that a Confederate soldier ran up to a Federal cannon and rammed a fence rail down its barrel to stop its work of destruction.[34] Sergeant Arthur Fulkerson of the 19th Tennessee fell with sixteen bullet holes in his body.[35]

Spencer Talley charged the Yankee works through a locust thicket and watched as "our men were mowed down like grain before the sycle." In the course of the fighting, Talley was stunned by a wound in the head. He fell to the ground unable to rise. But in the confusion of the moment, there was no time to attend to the wounded and Spencer had little choice but to wait in the hope that after darkness someone would find him.[36]

The appearance of darkness failed to halt the fighting. Using the flashes from guns as indicators of the enemy's position, men in both armies blazed away with uninterrupted fury. It was after nine o'clock before the firing began to diminish. Although the moon was shining, its beams were clouded by the hovering smoke which hung like a heavy black fog over everything. The absence of firing accented the painful moaning of men to whom death had become a hope rather than a fear.

Somewhere in the mass of bodies in front of the Federal works, General Pat Cleburne lay dead. Although he had never received a promotion after suggesting to Jefferson Davis that slaves be freed and enlisted as soldiers, he had remained steadfast in his loyalty to the Southern cause. If the politicians held a grudge, they could forget it; that was all past now. Cleburne's horse was killed from under him as he led his men forward and, as he attempted to mount another, it too was killed. Not wishing to lose more time, the Arkansas general started on foot, waving his hat above his head and urging his men into the smoky hell before them. Shortly before he fell, Cleburne said to Captain D.C. Govan, "Well, Govan, if we are to die let us die like men."[37]

Not far from where Cleburne fell, General O.F. Strahl died handing guns to his men atop the Yankee breastworks. According to Sumner A. Cunningham, a member of the 41st Tennessee,

It happened that General Strahl . . . got a position in the intrenchment, where he stood for a long, long time and passed up guns to the men firing from the embankment. I could get no place in the intrenchment, and, as did many others, I lay as close to the ground as possible . . . loaded the short Ensfield rifle that I had been permitted to carry on account of my size, and had passed it to General Strahl the fourth or fifth time.... The man on the embankment had cocked it and was taking careful aim, when he was shot dead and fell on the heap below him.

Night was on now, so that every soldier's gun by the flash of powder made him a target; and as the entrenchment was practically leveled up with our dead, *volunteers ceased, when General Strahl persuaded others. He said to one man: "have you shot any?" To another: "Have you?" Then he simply pointed to me. I arose, stepped on to the pile of dead, resting one foot on the man killed while aiming my gun and the other on the embankment . . . I felt there was no rule of warfare whereby all the men should be killed, and said to General Strahl suggestively: "What had we better do?" His reply was instant: "Keep firing." It became more and more difficult to get the loaded guns, and eventually the soldier who had been firing by my side was shot and fell against me with agonizing groans. Utterly unable to do anything for him, I simply asked him how he was wounded; but he sank to the pile of comrades back of him, and, I presume, was soon dead. At the same instant this soldier was shot General Strahl was struck; and throwing both hands above his head . . . he fell limber on his face, and I thought he was dead. Not so, however. When I asked the soldier how he was wounded, the General thought I spoke to him, and he said he was wounded in the neck, he didn't know how badly, and then he called to Colonel Stafford . . . to turn over the command to him. He crawled away, his sword dangling against dead soldiers, in search of Colonel Stafford. Members of his staff started to carry him to the rear, when two bullets struck him, either of which, it is said, would have been fatal.*[38]

Daylight revealed "Col. Stafford a little in the rear of the entrenchment almost standing packed around by soldiers, all dead."[39]

Besides Cleburne and Strahl three other Confederate Generals lay dead on the field. They were Generals John Adams, Hiram Granbury and States Rights Gist. A Federal soldier who saw Adams die wrote:

He rode along his line and became conspicuous while he was quite a little distance out. We could see that he was very intent on doing something and he was the one of all others that we were to do business with.... He was riding forward through such a rain of bullets that no one had any reason to believe he could escape them all, but he seemed to be in the hands of the Unseen.[40]

Another Federal soldier who saw Adams die said:

General Adams rode up to our works and, cheering his men, made an attempt to leap his horse over them. The horse fell upon the top of the embankment and the general was caught under him, pierced by bullets. As soon as the charge was repulsed, our men sprang over the works and lifted the horse, while others dragged the general from under him. He was perfectly conscious and knew his fate. He asked for water, as all dying men do in battle as the life-blood drips from the body. One of my men gave him a canteen of water, while another brought an armful of cotton from an old gin near by and made him a pillow. The general gallantly thanked them, and in answer to our expressions of sorrow at his sad fate, he said, "It is the duty of a soldier to die for his country," and expired.[41]

After the firing ceased, every house in the vicinity of the battle quickly filled with wounded and dying soldiers. Townspeople helped those who needed help, regardless of the color uniform they wore. Mrs. John C. Gaut wrote:

One poor fellow ran by my gate with his arm shot and holding the broken part in his other hand. I hastily cut off a part of a window curtain and called to him to let me help him. He stopped, and I placed his arm in a sling. Another just behind him was wounded also, and was so weak and exhausted that I gave him water and whiskey. I did for them what I would have wished their people to do for our boys.[42]

Throughout the night, the women of Franklin tended the wounded as they were brought from the battlefield. Every spare piece of cloth was converted to a bandage, giant fires were kindled under kettles in which soup was made for men who had not tasted hot food in three days. Most important of all, words of encouragement were spoken to men whose last hopes were rapidly fading.

On the battlefield:

Men were going about with such lights as they could procure hunting for the dead and wounded comrades and friends. Men, shot and wounded in every part of the body, were crying out for help, telling their names and calling for friends to help them. It was a weird and gruesome sight.[43]

It was past midnight when Spencer Talley was found lying unconscious in front of the Yankee breastworks. After regaining his senses, Spencer

. . . realized that I was wounded in the head, and I made efforts to rise up on my feet, but in every attempt I would fall back to the ground. My vision was impaired and it seemed that I must climb a very steep hill, the ground and everything I could see was right up in front of me.[44]

After recovering enough to stand, Spence held on to the bullet shattered locust trees which surrounded him and staggered out. By this time, the smoke of battle had drifted upward and, according to the wounded soldier, "The moon shown brightly and I could see the ground covered with the dead and dying, over which I had to pass in making my way out."[45]

Sometime before midnight, the Federals left Franklin and moved toward Nashville. Hood, not aware of this fact, expected the fighting to resume at daylight. Calling on his artillery which had arrived during the night, the Confederate commander sent shells crashing into the Yankee works, but there was no response. The Battle of Franklin had ended.

Daylight revealed more than the absence of Yankees; it revealed the terrible cost of the blunder made at Spring Hill. "O, my God! what did we see!" wrote Sam Watkins. "It was a grand holocaust of death."[46] W. J. Worsham watched as General Cheatham walked across the field and looked into "the hundred of faces, silent in death... and upon thousands of wounded covered with blood, appealing for water and help, he wept, the great big tears ran down his cheeks and he sobbed like a child."[47]

During the morning hours, General William Bate called the survivors of his brigade together and attempted to restore in them some semblance of confidence. He mounted a stump and spoke words of encouragement, but there was no response. As one soldier explained, "With Atlanta, Jonesboro, Spring Hill, and Franklin in mind, any troops would be discouraged. . ."[48]

To the half-clad veterans of Hood's army, the dead at Franklin had special meaning. Winter had made its appearance, and if the march from Florence, Alabama, was an indication of weather to come, much suffering lay ahead. Thinly clad soldiers surveyed the dead for articles of clothing that might be the difference between life and death in the weeks ahead. When such apparel was found, it was removed without ceremony — whether from Blue or Grey; it was no time for sentiment. When Pat Cleburne's body was found, his shoes had been removed and everything of value taken from his pockets. Such incidents were commonplace.

Burial details were formed and the bodies of the Confederate dead were collected and laid in long rows. There were six brothers dead in one Mississippi regiment. By mid-afternoon the bodies of the five generals killed during the battle were lying side by side on the back porch of the John McGavock home. Inside the house, Mrs. McGavock had worked all night with wounded and dying soldiers. In a letter to his wife, Colonel W.D. Gale of Stewart's staff wrote of the scene at the McGavock home.

> . . . the wounded in hundreds were brought to it during the battle, and all night after. Every room was filled, every bed had two poor bleeding fellows, every spare space, niche and corner, under the stairs, in the halls everywhere but one room for her own family.... Our doctors were deficient in bandages, and she began by giving her old linen, then her towels and napkins, then her sheets and table cloths, then her husband's shirts and her own undergarments. During all this time the surgeons plied their dreadful work amid the sighs and moans and death-rattle.[49]

Among the dead at Franklin was Captain Theo Carter whose home was on the battlefield. His family had huddled in the basement of their home during the fighting, but during the night a brother went out and brought the wounded soldier inside where he died in a short while. The Federal dead were left unburied for several days. For the most part, "They were buried generally just as they had fallen by pulling dirt from the breastworks down on them. Many had been stripped of their clothing by living soldiers who were almost naked."[50]

The Battle of Franklin was over. Resinor Etter had been in the thickest of it and the following day wrote:

> Daylight has come   there is no enemy near us & we now look for ded & wounded which ar many   Oh how bad I feel to look at my comrades torn to peaces by those missels of deth   one of my old company was killed ded   they are all buried Side by side and ech grave was marked   It is a horable thought to think of the many friends we leeve on the battle field   the enemys

*loss was very heavy we killed a great many   the ground
was covered with blew coats   We have got our men all
buried   We now take a little rest as we have not taken
any in two days & nights.*[51]

If Resinor Etter found time to rest that day, December 1st,
he was lucky. Even before the burial details were finished,
Hood ordered the army toward Nashville. He would leave
behind, among the dead, many of the best men who had
survived the Georgia campaign. Hood estimated his army,
upon leaving Franklin, as numbering "23,053, which would
show a total loss from all causes of 7,547 since leaving
Florence, and most of this must have been suffered at
Franklin."[52] With what he had, the crippled commander was
determined to go forward. It was nearing nine o'clock in the
morning when Hood made his way along the streets of
Franklin. H.P. Figuers watched the general "with his one
wooden leg and his long tawny mustache and whiskers. I as a
boy," wrote Figuers, "was much disappointed in his
appearance."[53]

The town they were leaving presented a sad spectacle to the
soldiers as they headed north. Every school, church and most
private homes had become hospitals. There was scarcely
enough food available to feed the townspeople, much less the
wounded, and all along the streets could be seen the bodies of
the dead awaiting burial. There was little in such scenes to give
an advancing army the confidence which often meant the
difference between victory and defeat. Lieutenant James L.
Cooper who fought at Franklin said, "The result of the battle of
Franklin was a bootless victory and a demoralized army. The
men were so disheartened by gazing on that scene of slaughter
that they had not the nerve for the work before them."[54]

Hood realized the deplorable condition of his army but
believed it would be better to continue north than to retreat
south. He hoped for help from beyond the Mississippi River,
and by nightfall of December 3rd, his army was camped south of

Nashville. A brief respite from the freezing weather disappeared as rain gave way to sleet, and by the 7th of the month, it was miserably cold. On that day, Resinor Etter wrote in his diary, "Comest raining & turn in to sleet and snow   I am barefooted."[55]   The following day the snow was two inches deep and the temperature continued to drop. Confederate soldiers appropriated anything available to erect temporary shelters. They stole straw from nearby barns and hovered together like animals. In this condition, they waited for the well-fed, well-clothed, and efficiently-commanded Yankee Army of over twice their number to come forward and offer battle.

3.

The remnants of the once proud and confident Confederate Army of Tennessee hovered in the hills south of Nashville expecting daily to be attacked by Federal General George Thomas. Hood's appeal for additional troops had gone unheeded so if there was to be a fight it would of necessity be made with the survivors of Franklin. Since Hood seemed determined to fight, he and his men continued to wait.

W.J. Worsham, in describing the situation, said:

> *From our position we could plainly see the capitol and the guns that stood sentinel in the eastern yard. The morning of December 8th rolled around, bringing one of the coldest days we had experienced in a long time. There were sleet, and snow, and ice, and rain; and the driving wind rendered it the more uncomfortable. We were in the open fields on an elevation, without protection from the wintry blasts, and were thinly clad — many of us without shoes — with nothing whatever to keep our sore and bleeding feet from the cold and freezing ground.*

We were without tents, and with but one old worn blanket to each man, with which to cover at night, and our only bed the frozen ground, and that covered with ice and snow. For days we stood watching the enemy in this uncomfortable plight.[56]

Inside the city, the Yankees were in turmoil. Every minute was occupied in preparing the city against attack. Dr. John Berrien Lindsley, one of Nashville's most prominent citizens, noted in his journal, "Much excitement — army movements to and fro. A very large force of government employees threw up entrenchments from the reservoir through the University grounds . . ."[57] In some instances houses were destroyed or rolled back, and the Federal breastworks made ready for use. It would, no doubt, have given the shivering Rebs great satisfaction to have seen the hustle which their presence was causing.

The Federal General, George Thomas, had his problems. In Washington, as well as at Grant's headquarters in Virginia, the politicians and generals were anxious that the battle be fought. They could not understand why Thomas hesitated to engage Hood's army, and as the days passed without a battle, their anxiety turned to disgust.

Henry Stone, a Colonel of Thomas' staff, wrote:

Probably no commander ever underwent two weeks of greater anxiety and distress of mind than General Thomas during the interval between Hood's arrival and his precipitate departure from the vicinity of Nashville.[58]

Thomas regretted the attitude of his superiors toward him and sent them word that if they thought he should be relieved he would step down without a murmur, but he steadfastly refused to make what he considered an intemperate move. Amid a flurry of critical telegrams calling on him for action, Thomas steadily prepared for the battle ahead.

The weather remained the major factor to Thomas. The ground was frozen. Men and horses fell as they attempted to move from place to place; it simply was not a time to begin a battle. In Washington it was decided that Thomas must be replaced and General John Logan started for Nashville — then the ground began to thaw. During the afternoon of December 14, the Federal commander laid his plans of battle before his generals and that night wired his superiors: "The ice having melted away today, the enemy will be attacked to-morrow morning."[59] General Logan never arrived at Nashville.

·On December 15, the Yankee Army moved southward from Nashville and struck both flanks of Hood's thinly manned line. By nightfall the Confederate left had been swept away and Hood was forced to withdraw to a chain of hills two miles further south. The Federals found him the next morning and the story of the previous day was repeated as fully manned divisions — there were over 10,000 cavalry — poured through, over, and around the sparsely-spaced Confederates. "We could only sting them," wrote one Reb and they stung them hard and often, but stinging alone failed to check the massive lines of blue that seemed to flow from the ravines and hollows south of Nashville. By four o'clock on the 16th, the Battle of Nashville was over and the Rebs were in full retreat.

As far as the Confederate soldier was concerned, the battle was a story of a brave little man fighting a brave giant and the outcome was no surprise. If there was a surprise at all, it was that the Rebs held out as long as they did.

The Battle of Nashville symbolized to the Confederate soldier the absolute absurdity of further resistance, he needed no political interpreter to clarify the picture at hand. The individual Rebel knew there was no hope. Many of the better generals had died at Franklin where regiments literally melted before the withering fire of the enemy. Even before that, the affair at Spring Hill accented a breakdown in command that was pathetically obvious. In the light of these circumstances, the

Battle of Nashville could be considered little beyond an exercise in symbolism and futility.

Hood himself was a dramatic symbol of the army he commanded. During the first day's battle, Sam Watkins saw Hood and noticed, ". . . how feeble and decrepit he looked, with an arm in a sling, and a crutch in the other hand, and trying to control his horse." In writing of this scene, Sam said:

> *And, reader, I was not a Christian then, and am but little better today; but, as God sees my heart tonight, I prayed in my heart that day for General Hood. Poor fellow, I loved him, not as a General, but as a man . . . Every impulse of his nature was but to do good, and to serve his country as best he could.*[60]

Hood's personal appearance reflected the plight of his army at the end of the first day's fighting. Lt. James Cooper, speaking of the late afternoon hours of December 15, said:

> *Late in the evening we received information that our position on the left had been forced, and our division (Bate's) commenced moving by our left flank. We moved across the Franklin Pike and soon received occular demonstration that the battle was going against us. On every side were to be seen the straggling and wounded men, while the artilleries and horses without guns told that more than one battery had been taken. It was now nearly night and the enemy did not seem inclined to press their advantage, but halted at our works. With sad and heavy hearts, forewarning us of the day to come, we took position and made preparations for the dreaded morrow.*[61]

The Confederate line on the second day was two and a half miles long. It extended from Peach Orchard Hill on the east to what was to become known as Shy's Hill on the west. The latter position would obtain its name before the day's end. In the afternoon, the Federals launched an attack on Peach Orchard Hill but were repulsed with terrible losses. But at the other end of the line it was a different story. Through an oversight, the Confederates placed their guns too far back from the crest of the hill, making it possible for the enemy to approach within a few dozen yards before becoming susceptible to Rebel fire. The Confederates on top of the hill waited in the knowledge that down below, out of sight, the Yankees were preparing to charge them. Shortly after four o'clock, the Yanks came, not from just one direction, but from three.

Colonel William Shy commanded a portion of the men on the hill and had taken literally his order to maintain the position as long as possible. Fired by Shy's example, his men stood and fought long after hope was gone. The Federals broke the line and poured through at will. As one Reb said:

> When the Confederate lines gave way all was confusion and disorder. The boys up and down the line stood in the ditches, adjusted their accouterments and prepared for the race before them. The officers urged the men to remain in the ditches and wait orders to leave. If the orders were given I never heard them. I could see our lines giving way on the left, and all at once the entire line jumped out of the ditches and started on a disorderly though rapid run for the Franklin Pike, a mile away.[62]

Lt. James Cooper wrote:

> I was just below the crest of the hill, when I knew by the increased firing and the cheering, that the Yankees were charging. I heard someone say, "look up yonder," and on looking I saw the Yankees and our men so mixed that it was scarcely possible to tell one party from the other. I did not look long enough to confuse them, but mounting my horse, made arrangements to go to Corinth. By the time I was on my horse, all the men

who were left came rushing down the hill, and now commenced one of the liveliest chases of the war. Our men had to cross a ploughed field where the mud was knee deep, and the vile Yankees were right after them, shooting as fast as the devil would let them, and he seemed to have little objection to their shooting as fast as possible. In addition the varmints had turned our own cannon on us and were using it better than we ever could do. It was said that Bate's division ran first, but I think all ran together. It seemed to me a simultaneous running. We hurried out to the Franklin road and in the gathering gloom and darkness started our retreat from Tennessee.... The Army of Tennessee was completely demoralized and routed. I now felt the Confederacy was indeed gone up, that we were a ruined people.[63]

William Shy stood and fought until a bullet between the eyes ended his life. If he had done nothing else, he had at least christened, with his blood, a hill that would thereafter carry his name.[64]

The ground over which the Confederates traveled was slick and wet causing many to fall, but the sight of the pursuing Yankees urged them to their feet to continue their journey toward safety. Some Rebs, weakened by the lack of food, fell to the ground and were captured before they could regain their feet. Of the withdrawal, Sam Watkins said, "Such a scene I never saw. The army was panic stricken. The woods were full of running soldiers."[65]

But even in the midst of such confusion some Rebs attempted to rally and fight. According to one veteran:

Just as I reached the Franklin Pike some one with a battle flag waved it crying: "Halt and rally round the flag, boys!" Soon there were several hundred of us formed in line across the pike, and we began firing at the bluecoats in the valley below. I don't think there were any officers present. It seemed to be a "private" affair though "free for all." [66]

Such efforts did nothing to stem the advance of the Yankees who seemed intent upon the total destruction of the Confederate Army. "It's no use," yelled a Reb, "let's give it up, or we will be captured," and the entire group fell back in wild confusion.[67]

Farther down the Franklin Pike, a young staff officer who had just arrived at Nashville from a furlough home, yelled at the retreating soldiers to rally and fight. "Halt here, men, halt, form line here," he repeated over and over. According to a witness:

> *An old soldier who had been in the fight all day and was nearly exhausted, with powder all over his face and his garments of rags covered with mud, was trying to keep out of the way of the victorious Yankees. This young officer rode up to him and halting him in the road, said, "Where are you going? Halt and form line here, there is no danger down there." The old soldier said to the staff officer, "You go to hell, I've been there."* [68]

General Thomas Benton Smith, a young Confederate Brigadier General, was surrounded by angry Federal soldiers and forced to surrender. He was immediately struck over the head with a sword whereupon he pled, "I am an unarmed prisoner." His plea had no effect and soon additional strokes landed on his head. As a result of this incident, the young man was forced to spend the remainder of his days in an insane asylum.[69]

The defeat at Nashville completed a tragic circuit for many soldiers in the Army of Tennessee. Three and a half years before, the Tennesseans in this army had marched through the Capitol City with their bright new battle flags waving defiantly. They had marched to camps of instruction amid the city's flag-bedecked buildings from which thousands of enthusiastic voices shouted words of encouragement. They had paused to eat delicately prepared food on the very ground now occupied by Federal munitions of war. They had warmed to the glorious promises of the politicians and the shy smiles of Nashville's most elite young ladies. They had marched out, and in their imaginations would return as the founders of a new nation.

Those who had urged these gawky boys into the terrible maw of war were strangely silent during the Battle of Nashville. There were no mayors with their fiery speeches, no bankers to tell how wealthy the state would be under the new government, and no plantation owners to lavish their attention on the element of the population they had so haughtily ignored before the idea of secession gained prominence. Such men, for the most part, had long since adjusted to Yankee occupation. The fire of Southern Nationalism which had burned so feverishly within their bosoms only three years before, had been extinguished by a counter-flame of economic expediency.

Writing of this period of the war, Thomas Head of the 16th Tennessee said:

> *The destiny of the Confederacy was dark and unpropitious, and its doom was sealed. Its armies, reduced by the casualties of war and by desertions, had dwindled down to a mere handful of worn out veterans, who, though knowing that the cause was lost, and all their brightest anticipations had proved to be mere illusions and permanently put to flight, they felt that they had invested their all in the sequel, and many were ready and willing to follow the fortunes of the sinking Confederacy to the last throes of its expiring agonies, and offer themsleves as a final sacrifice upon its funeral pile. There were others who had long since beheld the hopelessness of further resistance, and had been governed accordingly, especially among the troops from the border States who had families. Many of these men, who had made good soldiers and fought bravely on*

many battlefields, and whose scars told that they had stood where danger was thick and heavy, began to leave the army during the last year and a half of the war. After the Battle of Franklin, many of the Tennessee troops went home and abandoned the service permanently . . . in so doing they did what they believed to be their duty under all the circumstances.[70]

The roads leading from Nashville and Franklin became a final, pathetic, parade-ground for the wounded, ragged, and demoralized men who had fought under the most trying circumstances imaginable. Their blood-soaked bandages and improvised crutches blended well into the backdrop of burned houses, torn-down fences, and ruined farms through which they passed. Horses had scarcely enough strength to pull their suffering cargo along roads whose gullies symbolized that the face of nature itself was not immune to the scars of a ruthless war.

The spirits of these men were severely damaged. Although they had never been specific in their diaries or letters as to what it was they hoped to gain by a Southern victory, they were nevertheless disappointed that they had failed to achieve victory. In any event, the war was over for these men. Whatever had been their secret dreams and expectations under a new government had long since been shattered. Their immediate task was to reach home as quickly as possible. For some, that would not be easy.

Spencer Talley and two of his friends left Franklin for Wilson County. All were severely wounded. Along the way the party was attacked by a gang of outlaws and one of the men was brutally murdered.[71] Spencer made it home safely.

Meanwhile, for the fourth time, the Confederate Army was withdrawing from Tennessee — it would not return.[72]

Chapter XXII

The Immortal Six Hundred

Mrs. Milly Ann Lytle of Rover, Tennessee, in Bedford County, must have felt that she gave more than her share in the effort to establish the Southern Confederacy. In April of 1863, Mrs. Lytle received a letter from a stranger who lived in Farmville, Virginia. The letter said:

In the discharge of my duty as a minister of the gospel, I visited the General Hospital in this town, this morning, and found there William A. Lytle of the third Regiment Tennessee troops, Company F. He says that he is your son — that he has been a prisoner of war at Camp Douglas, Illinois — that he left that place as an exchanged prisoner on 31st March — that he became sick at Petersburg, Virginia, and arrived at this hospital on the eighth day of this month. His disease is Pneumonia, and he is right sick; but he appears to be in no immediate danger of dying. He wished to write these things to you & to say that he would be glad to have a letter from you. He is entirely out of money & wishes you, if you can conveniently, to send him some. He intends to go home to you if it please God to spare his life and enable him to go.

Three days after writing the above letter, its author, the Rev. Micheal Osburne, wrote another. For several paragraphs, the minister reviewed the circumstances under which he had met William and assured the mother that everything possible was done for her son. He then informed her:

I was with him yesterday at noon, & when I took leave of him saw no reason to doubt that he would recover his health after a short time; but my dear madam it grieves me to tell you that I was sadly disappointed. He began to fail immediately after I left him; during the night he continually grew weaker; he was in full possession of his reason, .& said that he suffered no particular pain — and so, a few minutes after midnight he ceased to breathe. I have no power to afford you consolation under so heavy an affliction, but, blessed be God, He is able & willing to comfort you. He is especially the Widow's God, and will hear your prayer. I commend you to the riches of his grace and pray that he may strengthen your heart to bear the present trouble, and may cause all your afflictions to work out for you a far more exceeding and eternal weight of glory.[1]

At the time Mrs. Lytle received the news of William's death, another of her sons, Captain James K. Polk Lytle of the 23rd Tennessee was at Shelbyville, Tennessee, with Bragg's army. Later, James went to Chattanooga and fought the Battle of Chickamauga. Shortly before the Battle of Missionary Ridge, his regiment was ordered to Knoxville to aid General James Longstreet's assault on Fort Sanders, but was held in reserve and did not participate in the actual fighting. On December 1, 1863, the Confederate Army fell back, and in a few days, left the area.

James Lytle was a young man who found humor in the strange incidents that made up his military life. His vivid imagination gave him the ability to superimpose lively interpretations on experiences that to others might well have been commonplace. As his regiment retreated from Knoxville, it was challenged by a sullen bull that refused to surrender the middle of the road. As seen by James the bull

...seemed to have made war against the Rebel column as he stationed himself in the road where there was a mudhole in the center making him a fine position as the Rebels had but one outlet. The mud protecting his flanks, Regiment after Regiment passed without making an attact on the threatening foe, but a soldier marching up as stubborn as himself, and unwilling to walk around the ground, the great warier marched up boldly, but as the advance was made he stood fast in his tracts, took aim and made a desperate lunge at his antaginist. The Rebel coming to a right about, his Knapsack served as a Shield as the horns of the Ox struck the Knapsack instead of the Rebels back, though the Rebel was Lodged in the opposite side of the Mudhole and had nothing to do but continue his march. Though the Battle is not over, for the defendant Sounded the trumpet of war and bid defiance to an invasion of the Sacred Spot while up marched another Rebel closely persued by his Supporters. The advance was thrown against the antagonist, but the reisitance was so sternly made that it terminated in the Rebel being like a pier of winding blades whirled over and over in the air. Fortunate he Struck the earthe on the opposite side of the fence and the Enemy was prevented by the fence from charging again. The Rebel advance rose to his feet in perfect confusion and retreated in disorder. The loss in the Rebel part as well as I remember was Something like one Canteen, one half jacket, one hat, and perhaps the greater portion of the rear of his Pants. By this time the Reserve had taken protection behind the fence with pieces cocked, and were about hurling some minnies through

479

the foe, but when it was taken into consideration the destructiveness the Rebels had exercised on the Beef community, and the Ox was under the impression that our motives were to wod [wad] him in a camp kettle, his life was spared as he was acting on the defencesive, as Rebels simphathized with those who have to Battle in defence of their homes.

Lytle's regiment continued its march away from Knoxville, and on December 10, 1863, camped near Russelville, Tennessee. On the 13th of the month, the young captain visited the home of a prominent secessionist in the area, and after eating a rather elaborate meal, returned to camp. The atmosphere of the home in which he had visited reminded James of his own home in Bedford County, and that night he wrote:

It being Sunday and seeing the comforts and luxuries by which one is surrounded at home caused me [to] look back on the many happy Sabboths I had spent with my generous brothers around my dear mothers hearth Stone. I was mooved to grief when I contemplated the fact that out of 4 brothers, all young men, only 2 Remains. The chairs of the other two are vacant and their songs ceased to echo through the Hall. I now know how to appreciate the worth of my brothers and not until I was deprived of their interest in my well fare . . . Oh, but I could spend my days with them again, I would pride in making myself more useful to them, great is the misfortune that one knows not the worth of a friend until they are deprived of them. Now my advice is to all of you who have parents, Brothers, or Sisters, Oh do not forget their great value and comfort to you. Know it before it is too late for you will see your time will soon pass away and others will fill their place. You may look for others though you will never find them . . .

The visit to the residence which prompted the above observation proved very costly to James Lytle. While he was visiting, his regiment moved to Bean's Station, and there encountered the enemy. By the time James returned to camp, the regiment had gone. In the process of looking for his company, James and a friend were taken prisoner by the 9th Michigan Cavalry. Although their captors were quite considerate of the two captured Rebs, a great despondency overcame the boys as they were hurried toward Knoxville to prison.

Early in January, 1864, James and many other prisoners at Knoxville were transferred to the military prison at Camp Chase, Ohio. Although the trip had its inconveniences, the Yankee guards did all within their power to insure the comfort of their prisoners. The ladies of Louisville brought food to the train, and on at least one occasion the guards impressed beef from farmers along the way and fed it to the prisoners.

On Sunday, January 24, the men arrived at Cincinnati where they were unloaded and marched through the city to another train depot. James wrote in his diary, "I was somewhat surprised at the conduct of the citizens, as I expected to meet with insult and abuse from them, though not a single insult was offered . . ." When the prisoners finally reached Columbus, Ohio, they were unloaded, but before being marched to Camp Chase were allowed to visit a bar in which James "taken a glass of whiskey." It was shortly before sunrise when the prisoners checked into the prison. James remained at Camp Chase for only two weeks and was then transferred to Fort Delaware on the Delaware River. After looking over the surroundings, James wrote, "In a word the fort is a beautiful place." The Confederate captain was impressed with the way the fort was laid out and the way its grounds were kept. If there were any particular hardships associated with his stay at Fort Delaware, James did not record them in his diary. In July he did say that he suffered from the flux, but after a brief stay in the hospital the condition was relieved.

In August, 1864, rumors, called "grape" by the prisoners, spread throughout the camp that an exchange was being arranged for their release. On the 17th of the month, the prisoners were called into formation and the names of some six hundred were read from a prepared list. Ogden Murray, a prisoner from Virginia, told how it felt to stand in line hoping to be among those whose names were called. He said:

> *My agitation and suspense was just as great as that of my comrades, and I did silently, away down in the depths of my heart, beg God for deliverance from Fort Delaware prison. When the M's were called on the roll I could hardly contain myself; when my name was called I could have shouted for joy; and I really felt sorry that all my comrades were not included in the list.*[2]

James Lytle did not record his reaction to the fact that his name was also on the list, but it is safe to assume that his pulse quickened in anticipation of freedom. He was also probably jubilant that the names of J. N. Hastings and W. C. Knox, both Bedford Countians, were also on the list. The fact was that forty-three Tennesseans were on the list.[3] Five hundred and fifty healthy prisoners were mustered in the prison yard, and later, fifty wounded soldiers were brought from the hospital. Of the last fifty, three were Tennesseans.[4] In a lighthearted and joyous state, the men prepared to depart for what they had been led to believe would be their release. James Lytle wrote in his diary that day, "Went on board [the] vessel *Cresent* on Saturday the 20th of August, 1864, 600 officers. Ran out to the mouth of the Bay, there lay until 27/64 on which morning we sailed on the Sea." Although he had no way of knowing it, Captain James Lytle was entering one of the war's most bizarre episodes.

In Confederate history, the six hundred officers who left Fort Delaware on August 20, 1864, would become known as "The Immortal Six Hundred," and their plight would become a rallying point for hate as long as the Civil War generation survived. The chain of events which initiated this event began in June of 1864. On the 16th of that month, Federal authorities were notified that fifty Federal soldiers, five of them generals, were being held prisoners in Charleston, South Carolina. Charleston was at the time under bombardment by Federal artillery stationed on Morris Island off the coast. Federal authorities interpreted the imprisonment of the Union generals as a move designed to halt the bombardment and immediately set about to place five Confederate generals under similar circumstances at Morris Island. On July 1, the five Federal generals at Charleston wrote a letter to their superiors informing them that they were being treated with great consideration and were not unduly exposed to the incoming Federal fire. Because of this message, the five Confederate generals were never placed under fire and in fact they and their comrades were later exchanged.

According to Colonel Abram Fulkerson of the 63rd Tennessee who was among the "Six Hundred,"

> *It was thought after the fortunate termination of this affair that General Gilmore* [Gen. Quincy Adams Gilmore, U.S.A.] *would desist from shelling that part of the city* [Charleston] *occupied by its helpless people, but instead of so doing, shells were thrown into that quarter from day to day. In view of the continued cruel and inhumane conduct of General Gilmore, General Jones* [General Samuel Jones, C.S.A.] *determined again to try the experiment of placing Federal prisoners among the helpless people of the city for their protection, and with this view he made a requisition upon Andersonville prison for 600 Federal officers of all ranks, from colonel down.*[5]

Upon receiving knowledge that the Andersonville prisoners were being used as hostages by the Confederates, Union General Gilmore

...promptly caused requisition to be made upon the prison at Fort Delaware for 600 officers of equal rank of those at Charleston, to be placed on Morris Island, under the fire of the Confederate guns . . .[6]

Because the previous hostage situation had resolved itself so favorably for the soldiers involved, it was assumed the same routine would occur again, but it was not to be. Grant specifically recommended that no further exchanges be made. Thus, instead of being on his way to freedom, James Lytle faced an uncertain and frustrating future.

Unlike most of the diaries of other Confederates in the "Six Hundred," that of James Lytle deals little with the discomforts he experienced. Instead, his mind studies the situations of which he is a part and attempts to bring meaning to his role. James never allowed himself to believe that all choices, and therefore all freedom, were denied him, but instead jealously guarded the freedom of thought which only death could deny him.

The "Six Hundred" arrived at Morris Island on September 7, 1864. Artillery duels began immediately, in spite of the fact that both the Federals and Confederates were firing toward their own men. But artillerists had learned a lot by this stage of the war and each side was expert enough to avoid hitting its own men. It soon became evident that the hostages were ineffective and so on October 27, 1864, the Confederates were transferred to Fort Pulaski, offshore from Savannah, Georgia.

Almost from the beginning of their imprisonment on the offshore islands, the food furnished the "Six Hundred" was unbelievably bad. Colonel Fulkerson explained that, for a while, the food at Fort Pulaski was highly acceptable, but when word reached the fort of how poorly Federal prisoners were faring at Andersonville Prison, matters changed radically.[7]

Captain A.M. Bedford[8] wrote in his diary:

As the Yankees are continually boasting about how well they feed us, I will attempt to give a correct account of each meal. Roll call one and one-half hours by sun for breakfast, three crackers issued, one tablespoon of rice. Twelve o'clock roll call. Rations for dinner, one-half pint bean soup, two crackers wormy and full of bugs. Five o'clock roll call. Rations for supper, two ounces of bacon, two crackers, wormy as usual.[9]

At Fort Pulaski on October 31, James Lytle wrote in his diary:

A portion of [the day] has been spent by me in a game of Chess and the other reading the Book of Job. One might suppose as chess was a game of pleasure and I had engaged in that game, I had realized but little good from the Bible. With all such I must beg to disagree by reminding them that there is a portion of life lotted to man for pleasure.

Where is the evil you claim to find? The game simply consists of maneuvering the pieces on the board in scientific order, thereby giving active exercise to the mind and wearing the monotony of a prison life away or other conchihitions [conscientious?] men are liable to find themselves where a continued uniformity absorbs the whole of one's time. I do not wish to be understood as attempting to convey the idea that it is ones duty to engage in this game, not so, but merely that men may amuse himself in an innocent manner while on the other hand it is undoubtedly ones duty to read the Bible, though by refreshing the mind it is enabled to lay hold of the important subjects that are contained in this great work with more vigor.

The time at Fort Pulaski dragged by slowly for the men. A death among their comrades established the day as a reference point; at least the death shattered the endless monotony that dominated the scene. Even wash days served to establish some purpose in the lives of the prisoners. James wrote:

I have just washed my clothes making today washday. The wash women generally dread this day. I am now prepared to Justify them in so doing since realizing the disagreeable labor that is attached to this day, though my facilities here are quite limited to most of theirs. For instance, I have not had an opportunity of washing my cloths in warm water in near three months and frequently without soap. Generally have soap but no warm water.

James was an astute observer of his fellow prisoners and refused to view their behavior as void of meaning, but the meaning he found was not always flattering. On November 3, 1864, he observed:

Weather warm and cloudy, nothing of importance has transpired to day save a little fight that occurred between two of our officers, however they were soon separated without anyone being hurt. Strange to say, those difficulties are frequently occurring here in prison, men that are selected for intelligence. It only reveals the nature of wicked man when he is taken away from society and his interest does not, in his estimation, directly demand those polished qualities that shields man from his true disposition, therefore the fact is beyond doubt that men generally go, as it were, covered with a veil of beautiful colors [which], when thrown off, leaves the man exposed to all around him in his true state, and the course he follows frequently is a terror to his comrades instead of giving aid and comfort to them which is required of him by a Trust [ing] god whose eye penetrates the veil that obstructs the dull eyes of men in darkness. If that man was what he should be, that he would place the propper value on the sacred law that is handed down to man for his guide, serving for him by day as the cloud that guided the children of Isreal, and at night as a pillow of fire. If he would lean on the arm of this guide, yielding himself subject to its course, he would soon be conveyed through the wilderness and the waters of Jordan would be separated that he might reach the promist land and enjoy the rich treasures laid up there for him by the framer of this law through Eternity for ever and ever without end.

Rumors persisted that the prisoners were to be exchanged, and although the men were aware that rumors seldom materialized, any encouragement was better than none. Each time the men peered from their cells to watch truce boats meet in the river they imagined themselves about to be freed. On November 4th, James wrote:

We live here in hope. What a presious Jewel hope is, without it life would be one continued scene of misery, but it appears to one in solitude or where I am confined within the prison walls, revealing to me happy days and bright prospects. The prisoner in his cold, damp enclosure, shivering with cold and yearning for food in the strong grasp of despair contemplating of near and dear relatives far away who a few years since nourished and cheered him with good food, raiment and lovely smiles. It has been one, two or perhaps three years since he saw them or even heard from them. He comes to the conclusion they live no longer, that they sleep in the cold grave never again to minister to his wants, never again to cast there eyes upon him, over flowing with tears and affection of love, never again to offer a bit of advice worth more than silver or gold. He thinks perhaps he will never see his dear mother again, that she now lives with angels on high, that she will never moisten her pillow again with tears while beseeching god for the pardon of her wicked sons many trans gressions — then kind hope inter poses and hovers around him like the gentle dew at night, relaxing the strong grasp of dispair, then he feels that he will be permitted to return to those dear relatives to comfort and associate with them again, and above all, to comfort that dear old generous mother who would willingly lay down her life for mine, to minister to her wants, to care for and protect her from the troubles of this unfriendly world, and to ask of her pardon for rash words uttered to her through the unthoughtedness of youth, and bestow on her kind words, gently words, smiles that she might be happy in the days of her old age.

Later in the month, James recorded in his diary a summary of his imprisonment at Fort Pulaski. He said:

I will say something of the manner which I have been getting on since I have been at this place.

When we first arrive at this place there was no bunks, consequently we lay on the floor in the casements the first nights though Col Brown[10] soon had good new bunks prepared for us. Our ration consisted of crackers, bacon and soup once a day, about 3 gills. This soup was made of beens and peas at some time and rice at others. We generally grew hungry by the time our Rations came. At this time our rations was sent in to us cooked though we are now doing our own cooking and have been drawing soft bread for sometime, a small loaf to each man. This loaf does not make as much bread as we need, but we are allowed to send out to the Sutler and there we buy Flour at Eleven cts per lb and bake soda bisquites on the stove. We can buy what coffee we want at the Sutler and other articles of food, those that have money. As far myself, I spent the last money I had a few days after my arrival at this place and found myself considerably in need of money, therefore I commenced making gifts for the purpose of making money, and succeeded in making as much as I need to buy every thing I realy need though there are some men here who prefer suffering than to any thing else, it seems from their conduct for they will not Economize and make gifts that they could make. [They] ly up in their bunks and die with scurvey and other loathsome diseases. For a while after my arrival at this place I had not one cent, now I have money sufficient to buy every thing that is really essential to my health except Blankets and they are not kept here to sell to us, though such things as I have to do for money sometimes is rather disagreeable, but much better than to ly up all the time and die from starvation and want of exercise.

Regardless of the circumstances in which he found himself, James always found choices available. On a Saturday in December, he wrote:

As this was Satturday evening we thought we would do as we use to see our people do when we were at home, consequently we bought us a lot of potatoes, sweet milk and cloves. The flour we had on hand as we bought 25 lbs of flour and a lot of molasses a few days since, this being done, we boiled our potatoes, made our doe, mixed our ingredients and soon had three fine larg custards in the stove baking, thus we continued until we had a pile of home made old fashioned custards sufficient to do us some time. I am now as an old miser is by his chest of yellow dolls. I must raise my eyes occassionally and place them in the direction of my safe which is made of an old goods box, and there behold my fine pile of custards and feel independent as an old Apossome with a year old hen in his den.

489

The behavior of his fellow prisoners never ceased to amaze the young Bedford Countian. In describing the scene inside the prison, he observed:

One thing I will say something of so I may know hereafter, also others, how this prison looked. In the first place you might take a promonade up and down our alley and you would see the officers engaged in almost every business and game, perhaps the first object you would see would be a table surrounded with gamesters, their money spread before them, as hard as money is to get here, staked on the chance of the game, and there perhaps you would see a youth participating in the game risking the money his friends had sent him for his comfort and there he would lose every cent he had, then get up and force a dry laugh, rub his fore head, and swear he had lost one, two or perhaps three hundred dollars . . . but had a thousand dollars worth of fun. However, the same person would be groping and mourning for his money for months to come, thus he purchases one days amusement with several days grief, and his ascertain [assertion] is false when he says he has amusement in looseing money. The countenance tells the truth on the heart. Then walk a little further on and you come up with a kind of confection where some one made and sold beer and cakes, pies etc. The confectioneer would also send out to the Post Sutler and buy paper envelopes, a considerable amount of stationary, Candies, vegetables, fruit — dried and green —, molasses and assortment sufficient in quantity and quality to make a considerable little grocery store ... .

Then walk on and you would come to the cooking stove of one of the divisions as we were at this time furnished with one large cooking stove to the division which numbered about one hundred Officers. At this stove you would find three or four to each stove who

490

volunteered their services to do the cooking for their division which was a considerable task, but for the general good of all they taken it on themselves. They would use every exertion and economize to the utmost to prepare our food in a proper manner, and to make it go as far as possible that they might prevent some suffering from hunger as every officer here realized at Morris Island what it was to be hungry.

Walk on and see more despondency than you would have ever imagined that man could be possessed with and live. Here you would see more of this element in one month than you would see elsewhere in perhaps a life time, generally amongst those that could have no communication with friends and destitute of money, consequently they were undergoing all the miseries of a prisoners life. As you would pass on you would see men engaged in about every thing men has a disposition to participate in, and see more pain and suffering than would be pleasant to you.

On Christmas Day 1864, James wrote:

CHRISTMAS — This day is one of gloom to myself. I have been at liberty on former Christmast Most days I have often seen it celebrated. I have often seen on this day the meeting of the youths of my vicinity, with faces bright with smiles as if a trace of sorrow never rolled across their fair countenances. Scarce had they ever seen the frowns of this miserable world. At that time the country was in an elagant condition. It was bountifully supplied with the luxuries of life, therefore one had scarcely been hungry and could not imagine the poor mortals suffering while destitute of the neccessaries of life. While enjoying freedom and the luxuries of a country over flowing as it were with milk and honey, enjoying friendly association and warm receptions by those we loved— at that time I knew the fate of man uncertain. I knew he was a subject of many down falls, that he was subject to disease, the loss of property, friends and &c, but not the first time did I ever think that before I reached the age of 27 years that I would have suffered twelve months the miseries of prison away from my friends and the neccessaries of life, pining away by degrees from the miseries by which I am surrounded, and what my fate may be ere another Christmas may roll by I am just unable to say as I was to tell my present condition this Christmas five years since, however let it be what it may, my motto is contentment under every circumstance let them be as severe as they may, whatsoever is the will of god must be submitted to by man. Though in spite of all the fortitude and resolution one can exercise he will in a life of this kind frequently find himself despondent, however when he takes into consideration that the will of god must be done, and when done, no matter what the suffering of some individuals are, all will terminate for the better. Well at this conclusion one recovers from his despondency and resolves to make the best of his condition and look to the future for better days. Such is the case with me. This Christmas for the present presents nothing pleasant, all is gloom and solemnity mingled with confusion and bustle, thus it passes.

New Year's Day was a time for taking stock for most Confederate soldiers who kept diaries. No matter what the situation was, if they could find the time and writing material, they evaluated their situation. They seemed to believe that the events which made up their lives achieved a unity in terms of the year in which they happened. If the birth of a new year had no other meaning, it at least offered a new twelve-month period of hope. When these twelve months were condensed into one numerical symbol, their longevity seemed shortened. On New Year's Day, 1865, James Lytle wrote in his diary:

The first day of the new year has now made its apperance, the last night of the old year was one of the coldest we have had this winter. It gave birth to the first day of the new year which has now appeared and this day is as cold natured and disagreeable as its parent . . . To day a new year appears. It is not only the beginning of a new year, but to day another change takes place in regard to our treatment, that is the Rations I speak of. The ration commences to day, which consist of about 3 gills of corn meal 2 [pieces] of loaf bread, one ounce of piquals [pickles] a little salt to each man pr day, and nothing else. No meat, no molasses, not anything only corn Bread made of the most inferior quality of meal . . . It seems to me that this fare, no fire of consequences and no blankets scarcely, will carry many to the grave as we are exposed to all the sufferings of hunger, cold, disease and confinement without any means of avoiding any of them, though I find that men can endure more than I would have imagined while I was enjoying the comforts of a peaceful home. If I was going to give you an idea of the condition of a great many in prison, I would simply refer you to an old hog that was scarcely any thing else but skin and bones, at the same time severely diseased with the mange. This, most of persons have seen, therefore I illustrate the sufferings of the sufferer in prison in this manner as the condition of the two are similar.

The lack of meat in their diet drove the Confederate prisoners to desperate measures. On January 8, James wrote:

To day I have witnessed one thing I never expected to see, that is some of the men cooking a cat for their dinner. This they parboiled and baked as they would have a shoat. I saw them eat the whole of it, 4 men eat a large cat.

The next day James recorded:

Cat eating still goes on. There is a number of cats about the Fort and there has several been killed and eat. When a fat cat comes in our quarters she is very apt to be put in the stove and baked for some mans breakfast or dinner. The Yankees are isueing us no meat, no ration except bread and salt, and it seems that the cats has to suffer thereby. It seem to some that this is disgraceful conduct, but we are now only getting bread and water for our ration. The men are ready to sieze on anything that will satisfy hunger, as for myself I have not eat any of the cat meat yet.

The day of deliverance from Fort Pulaski was March 4, 1865. On that day, the men were loaded aboard the steamer, *Illinois*, and returned to Fort Delaware. Colonel Abram Fulkerson wrote, "Our party greatly enjoyed the superior accomodations and privileges of the Deleware prison, and rapidly improved in health."[11] On June 12, 1865, James Lytle was released from prison and returned to his home in Rover, Tennessee.

Captain James K. Polk Lytle

Chapter XXIII

The cards were fairly dealt, but they were mighty badly shuffled

The retreat of the Confederate Army from Nashville ended at Tupelo, Mississippi. The remnants of Hood's army were saved by the well-executed rear-guard action of Stephen D. Lee's infantry and Nathan Beford Forrest's cavalry. Both groups hovered closely to Hood's beaten and demoralized column, protecting it from Yankee cavalry which had, at long last, become a potent military weapon. The retreat was accompanied by intense suffering. The weather was freezing and there was a dramatic scarcity of blankets, coats, and shoes. In addition to these physical discomforts was the realization that the Yankees could never be driven from Tennessee. To infer that the men in the Army of Tennessee were not discouraged would be to insult their intelligence.

One vet remembered:

On our arrival at Franklin my shoes had fallen from my feet, and I was now barefooted in the deep snow, with a hostile army pressing... I did not get a pair of shoes until we reached Tupelo, Miss., a distance of two hundred and fifty miles. I certainly came near to freezing to death.[1]

Many half-frozen soldiers dropped out along the line of march and sought help from farmers who lived close by. Some of these men later rejoined their regiments, but others, seeing the futility of further resistance, wearily made their way toward home. When Resinor Etter reached Franklin, he ate his first meal in several days and stopped to rest before continuing the retreat southward. After resuming the march, he stopped at the home of a Mr. "Willson" where he was invited to sleep on a feathered bed and enjoy comforts he had not known for many trying months. Of the retreat from Nashville, Etter wrote, "It snowed very hard and the ground was hard froze my feet sufferd much as I was barefooted . . . It was so cold I came nigh freezing."[2] It was while at Mr. "Willson's" that Etter decided he had seen enough of war. What was there to look forward to except more marching without shoes, more cold nights without blankets, and more fighting which had no meaning? It was asking too much of men like Resinor Etter, who had given their all in a cause for which hope no longer existed, to continue leaving their families in need, risking death because the South's politicians were too self-centered and blind to see that the war was over.

On the other hand, there were thousands of soldiers determined to follow wherever destiny led. These men doggedly continued the retreat toward Tupelo. Nelse Rainey was one of them. Nelse missed the fighting at Franklin and Nashville, having been allowed to go home under Hood's policy of furloughing men who lived close to the line of march. When the retreating army reached Columbia, he rejoined his regiment. Writing of the retreat south of Columbia, Nelse said:

> *The weather was very cold . . . rain, half sleet, then snow half sleet on the rocky frozen roads. We all suffered. The infantry most of all. Not half of these poor boys had blankets, very few overcoats. More than half without shoes, their feet tied up in gunny sacks or old cloth. We have all read in history that Washington's*

barefoot soldiers left bloody tracks on the ground. I saw such instances, plenty of them, on this retreat. The boys were hungry too, all hungry. At one place, our company commissary officer, Billy Eanes, found a pen of fairly fat hogs. We had a day's ration of pork which we ate <u>raw</u> — everything too wet to make a fire. At a cabin I parched corn in an old shovel. George and I lived on that for two days.[3]

Even during a march as unpleasant as the one from Nashville, Rebel soldiers could be depended upon to extricate themselves from situations which to lesser men would have seemed hopeless. R.J. Cotton's toothache is a case in point. Cotton was on a scouting mission during the Battle of Nashville and it took him several days to evade the Yankees north of the city. While traveling through back country, the young cavalryman developed a severe toothache from which he could find no relief. After consulting with fellow scouts, he decided the tooth must come out, but alas, there was no dentist available. Cotton settled for the only appropriate alternative he could find, a blacksmith.

According to a fellow scout,

The blacksmith had no pullikens... but thought he could get it out. Taking a spike about six inches long, he flattened one end of it carefully and then placed Cotton on a bench, I standing at Cotton's back and holding his head. The blacksmith placed the flattened end of the spike against the tooth near the gum, and with one quick tap of the hammer out flew the tooth. With a few grunts and some expletives Cotton expressed his great relief.[4]

Another pair of indomitable Rebs whose natural bent for tomfoolery remained undampened by the defeat at Nashville were Clabe Perry and J. Walker of the 19th Tennessee. These two half-clad cavaliers strayed from the main column and traveled pretty much to suit themselves. As the two "slightly used" troopers made their way through the countryside, Clabe spied some leaf tobacco hanging by the chimney of a cabin. The pair immediately decided that the tobacco would be their target for the day.

A knock on the cabin door was answered by an elderly lady who explained that she was at home alone while her son was at the mill with a turn of corn. Clabe expressed interest in the tobacco and, after a bit of bargaining, was successful in purchasing a modest portion. Unwilling to stop trading with this conquest, Clabe inquired as to the possibility of purchasing a bit of sorghum. He was informed that there was a small quantity in the smokehouse and sent Walker with the old lady to arrange for the purchase. While they were thusly occupied, he "slipped into the house, and in his prowling, found in the bed a small sack of salt and a pair of yellow jean pants, evidently belonging to the boy . . ." After deftly slipping the sack of salt into his army blanket, Clabe hurried to the smokehouse where the sorghum was being measured. Addressing the old lady, Clabe said, "Madam, we have no money, but will pay you for your sorghum in salt, as we have more than we can carry." To this the woman replied, "La, Me! that is just what I want, I have not had any salt for a month." After paying the lady for the sorghum with her own salt, Clabe and Walker bid her Godspeed and resumed their journey southward! It is probably needless to add that as the two Rebs made their way down the road they traded the unsuspecting son his own yellow jeans for the meal he had just obtained at the mill![5]

C. H. Clark of the 16th Tennessee rejoined the army at Columbia, after having been on the disabled list since the fighting at Atlanta. Of his reunion Clark wrote:

From Corinth I started North "a foot" to find the boys (if any left). I found them and the night we were at Columbia . . . it snowed and the ground froze. I slept

*with Sqr. Jo. Cummings and Ad Fisk, under a little
"dog fly," the size of a table cloth . . . Let me say to you
that those days cannot be forgotten by those who were
there, as long as life and memory last. Empty
haversacks, clothes worn out, our little army, few in
number, discouraged & exhausted. When we got from
under our little dog fly to get ready to flee from the host
in pursuit of us, my hat & shoes were gone, leaving me
barefoot & bare headed, with a little January skift of
snow & the ground frozen. Several of the boys in our
Regiment said "no use going any further," & they
started East. I saw them leave, & never thought hard of
them for leaving . . . I decided to follow on & if alive
would see the end. Before going far my feet got sore &
very cold. My little dog fly was to protect me at night,
but I had to resort to it to save my feet, by tearing off
strips, wrap around my feet & repeat when absolutely
necessary.[6]*

Soon after leaving Columbia, the army reached a chain of
hills north of Pulaski. It had snowed the day before and the
hills were wet and slick. Knowing that the wagons would need
to be pushed by hand over these hills, General Cheatham sought
one hundred men for the job. According to General James D.
Porter, whose job it was to find the hundred men,

*I dismounted and gave my horse to the courier.
The fellows soon found out that I was after men with
shoes on, and they were highly amused. They would
laugh and stick up their feet as I approached. Some
would have a pretty good shoe on one foot and on the
other a piece of rawhide or a part of a shoe made strong
with a string made from a strap of rawhide tied around it,
some of them would have all rawhide, some were
entirely barefooted, and some would have on old shoe
tops with the bottoms of their feet on the ground.[7]*

At one particular stream below Columbia, Generals Forrest and Cheatham almost started a private war as to who would cross first, and the men in both commands made preliminary plans to follow the dispute to its bitter end. Calm eventually prevailed and Cheatham's men crossed first. In view of Forrest's reputation perhaps this incident was symbolic of what had happened to the Confederate Army.[8]

Slowly the main army continued its journey toward Tupelo. Almost daily, Forrest was forced to fight off the Yankees who were determined to strike a death blow to the regiments of Hood's army. At no other time did Forrest render a more valuable service to the Army of Tennessee. Every Federal attack was beaten off until the Confederates were safely across the river at Florence, Alabama. Many times the Rebel rear-guard was forced to remain so long before the enemy that the forward companies were captured, but the desperate action paid off. The army was saved — at least what was left of it.

By Christmas Day 1864, the entire army was across the Tennessee River and on its way to safety. James Cooper wrote:

> *Christmas day dawned bright and beautiful but upon what a scene did that morning's sun rise. A poor half starved, half clad band of ragamuffins fleeing in disgrace from the last chance of freedom and independence.*[9]

By January 10, 1865, Hood and his men were at Tupelo and here, faced with the inevitable truth that his Tennessee campaign had been an utter disaster, the Confederate commander asked for and received a release from command. According to Hood,

> *The President finally complied with my request, and I bid farwell to the Army of Tennessee on the 23d of January, 1865, after having served with it somewhat in excess of eleven months, and having performed my duties to the utmost of my ability.*[10]

Hood took from the war a paralyzed arm and the stump of an amputated leg, but it is almost certain that these infirmities were secondary to his great disappointment.

The men in his army expressed little sorrow at Hood's departure. They were in fact, glad to see him go. Such feelings were not projected from personal dislike; they simply doubted his ability. C. W. Heiskell of the 19th Tennessee said that shortly before Hood left the army he was heard to say, "The cards were fairly dealt at Nashville, boys, but they beat the game." A private soldier replied, "Yes, General, the cards were fairly dealt, but they were mighty badly shuffled."[11] To the men in the Army of Tennessee, Hood's reign as commander was well represented by a rhyme sung during the retreat from Nashville.

You can talk about your desert maids and sing of Rose Lee But the gallant Hood of Texas played hell in Tennessee.

2.

In Richmond, General Robert E. Lee was named the Commanding General of all Confederate forces. Now that it was too late, the politicians were relinquishing the command of the military forces to an authority equipped to deal with it. One of Lee's first official acts was to recall General Joseph E. Johnston from semi-retirement and restore him to a position of command. Johnston was assigned to command troops in North Carolina, and what remained of the Army of Tennessee was ordered to him. Just how many men this involved is impossible to know. Hood would later claim that when he left command there were eighteen thousand men in the Army of Tennessee; Johnston would claim that no more than five thousand ever made it to North Carolina. It really made little difference.

Regardless of the hopelessness of the situation, the men at Tupelo were pleased to be ordered back to Joe Johnston. He was their favorite commander, and anywhere he was, they were willing to be. The trip to North Carolina would not be easy. Railroad tracks were in disrepair, the Yankees were dangerously near the route to be taken, and the roads were so bad that heavy equipment could hardly be moved. The first troops left Tupelo on January 25; most of the others were on their way within the week. The men started on foot, then rode the train, after which they transferred to steamboats, then back to trains, and finally covered the last segment as they had started, on foot.

The train ride was almost as taxing as the walking. One veteran wrote, "The train made only six miles an hour. The boys would climb down off the cars and run out to a house some times a hundred yards away, return, and catch up with the train and climb on again."[12] If such gymnastics were a bit tiring they at least served to keep the boys caught up on their social lives and kept food in their stomachs. The sympathetic smiles of young ladies always had a favorable effect on these soldiers, and as the trip continued, the soldiers regained some of the spirit lost during the Tennessee campaign.

In North Carolina, the men in the Army of Tennessee would renew some old acquaintances. Sherman, his march through Georgia having been deflected by the sea, was on his way north toward Virginia. Schofield was on his way from Nashville. It was the job of Joe Johnston to intercept these two armies and at least keep them at bay — no easy task since Sherman alone outnumbered him over four to one.

It was early March, 1865, when Sherman entered North Carolina. Behind him was a charred trail over which his troops had traveled. To face the victorious Yankees, Johnston had what amounted to a corporal's guard. Although the Army of Tennessee constituted only a part of Johnston's force, it supplied distressing evidence as to the condition of Southern arms. The troops from Tennessee were consolidated into one brigade of four regiments. The 16th Tennessee was only large enough to comprise two under-manned companies. The 19th Tennessee, which at one time numbered 1,297 men, now had 64. The thirty seven Tennessee regiments with Johnston in North Carolina had at one time totaled almost 40,000 men; now they numbered less than 2,000. The troops from other states had dwindled accordingly.

By March 19, Johnston had gathered approximately 15,000 men in North Carolina to strike Sherman's divided army as it moved north toward a juncture with Schofield. At the little town of Bentonville Johnston placed his men directly across the path of Sherman's left column, hoping to defeat it before help could arrive. The fighting which followed resulted in the Confederates holding their ground but it had no real significance. Two days later, Sherman had his entire army in position to attack and Johnston was forced to retreat. By March 23, Sherman had joined forces with Schofield and together their 90,000 men awaited Johnston's 15,000.

On April 4, Bromfield Ridley wrote in his journal:

> *I witnessed to-day the saddest spectacle of my life, the review of the skeleton Army of Tennessee, that but one year ago was replete with men, and now filed by with tattered garments, worn-out shoes, bare-footed and ranks so depleted that each color was supported by only thirty or forty men . . . The march of the remnant was so slow — colors tattered and torn with bullets — that it looked like a funeral procession . . . Oh! it is beginning to look dark in the east, gloomy in the west, and like almost a lost hope when we reflect upon the review today!*[13]

Two days before Ridley made this entry in his journal, Richmond had fallen and while Joseph E. Johnston attempted to concentrate his forces for a last desperate try at containing Sherman, Lee surrendered at Appomattox Court House. In effect, this left Johnston with 15,000 men to fight the entire Federal Army. Reason dictated but one course: surrender.

When Richmond fell, Jefferson Davis started south and by April 12, was at Greensboro, North Carolina. He asked Johnston to meet him there. Assuming the President desired knowledge concerning "the question of continuing or terminating the war," Johnston and General Beauregard went to Davis' quarters prepared to answer questions. "But," wrote Johnston, "the President's object seemed to be to give, not obtain information..." To Johnston's utter astonishment, the President had stopped to give him a pep talk and resented all implications that the Confederacy was through. Davis talked of deserters returning to the army and about those who had previously refused to join rallying around the Rebel flag in a sort of patriotic repentance. Johnston, after conferring with other generals, refused to heed the President's counsel and told him that to continue the war "would be the greatest of human crimes." Johnston explained that the effect of further fighting would be "not to harm the enemy, but to complete the devastation of our country and ruin of its people." With much hesitation, Davis agreed for Johnston to open surrender talks with Sherman.[14]

Joseph E. Johnston and William T. Sherman had never met before April 17, 1865. Although they had served in the "old army" for thirteen years, their paths had never crossed. But they were not exactly strangers. The Georgia campaign had given each man a knowledge and respect for the other, and when they met to discuss the terms of surrender, this respect permeated their deliberations. The meeting was pleasant, marked by every courtesy either side could extend. Staff officers mingled freely in the yard of a log cabin while the generals inside worked on final terms.

As Sherman entered a private room with Johnston he handed the Confederate general a telegram. As Johnston read the telegram, his forehead broke out in perspiration and,

504

according to Sherman, Johnston made no attempt to conceal his distress.

ABRAHAM LINCOLN HAS BEEN ASSASSINATED! Indeed, fate had taken a strange twist. In Washington, Andrew Johnson, the embittered East Tennessean, would become President and accept the surrender of the Army of Tennessee, portions of which had driven him from his home four years before. Nothing could have served more adequately as a final blow to the men from Confederate Tennessee.

Actually, Sherman proved as generous in peace as he had been relentless in war. In fact, he was so generous that the final terms of surrender were delayed two weeks. Grant insisted that Johnston be given no more consideration at Bentonville than Lee had received at Appomattox. On April 26, 1865, the final terms were agreed upon. The Civil War was over — almost.

Handmade Confederate Cavalry Bugle

Chapter XXIV

I could see the fire
in the old boys eyes

The surrender of Johnston's army came as no surprise to the men. There was no hope and they knew it. They had witnessed thousands of their discouraged comrades quitting the army; for months they knew it was only a matter of time.

During the truce arranged for Johnston and Sherman to discuss terms of surrender, Confederate soldiers gathered in small groups in which the usual small talk gave way to the more serious subjects of home and peace. Although Johnston ordered drills and inspections for those who remained in camp, discipline became lax, organization became nonexistent, and morale dipped to a new low. Once, during the truce, rumors spread that the fighting was about to resume and pickets were ordered to the front. George Guild said the men looked like members of a funeral procession as they made their way toward the enemy.[1] Bromfield Ridley believed the rumor "more saddening than the first news of a probable surrender."[2] The men wanted no more fighting. Reason told them that a few more dead Rebels in the piney woods of North Carolina would decide nothing.

When, at last, the news of surrender reached the troops, it was accepted with mixed emotions. G. H. Baskette of the 18th Tennessee said:

It would be imposible fitly to describe the feelings of the officers and men who after so long and heroic a contest were now called upon to lay down their arms. Into the past four years, so fraught with momentous events, were crowded the memories of untold privations and hardships, and of battlefields upon which thousands and thousands of their comrades had offered up their lives in a grand but unavailing obligation of blood.

The paroles were sent to the different regiments signed by the officers, and distributed among the men. The brigade moved slowly and sadly out into an open field where officers sheathed their swords and the men silently stacked their guns. Then the unarmed command moved out of sight.[3]

On the night following the surrender, Bromfield Ridley wrote in his diary:

And now around the campfires to-night we are discussing the surrender. All is confusion and unrest, and the stern realization that we are subdued, and ruined, is upon us. The proud spirited Southern people, all in a state of the veriest, the most sublimated sorrow. Oh! how is it in the Yankee camp to-night? Rejoicing, triumphing and revelling in the idea of glory. Think of it, the big dog has simply got the little dog down.[4]

General Joe Johnston wrote a farewell speech to his men who gathered around to listen to the last official words of their respected commander. As the speech was read, the war weary veterans of Shiloh, Chickamauga, and Franklin stood in silence. The occasional tear which appeared gave notice that somewhere beneath the ugly callouses of war there still remained a sensitivity within these men which had survived four years of useless hell.

Few were sorry that the war was over, but even the happy prospect of returning home could not mask the disappointment of having failed to achieve their objective. Partly because of their love for Joe Johnston, and partly because they had so little else to take home, the men sought copies of their general's speech. Far into the night huge piles of pine brush were burned, and while illiterate soldiers brought wood to feed the flames, their more literate comrades knelt in the unsteady light and made copies of Johnston's speech. Other soldiers got drunk on "red eye" whiskey, and from their overall behavior it could have been assumed that they had won the war. Other soldiers busied themselves taking the names and addresses of those with whom they had fought for so many long and trying months.

Across the South, similar scenes were taking place. In the Trans-Mississippi Department, General E. Kirby-Smith surrendered without incident. At Selma, Alabama, Forrest submitted to the constantly increasing competency of the Federal cavalry. Even before these groups laid down their arms, the men of Robert E. Lee's Army of Northern Virginia were already on their way home.

Nelse Rainey was with Forrest's command when it surrendered. According to him,

> *Four-fifths of the soldiers objected to giving up. I saw many big bearded fellows actually crying with vexation. Many a gun and pistol was smashed against a tree. Many left without paroles . . . We lay in camp without much show of discipline, restless and almost desperate.*[5]

It was May 11, 1865, when Nelse received his parole. It read:

> *Issac N. Rainey, Residence Columbia, Tennessee. Occupation, student. He is permitted to return to his home, with one horse. He is not to be molested by the United States Authorities so long as he does not take up arms against the United States and obeys the laws of the State in which he resides.*[6]

With this document as his guarantee of freedom, Nelse went home.

Perhaps C. H. Clark expressed the sentiments of many Confederates when he said:

> *I was glad & sorry too. Glad the war was over & sorry we had to give it up . . . President Lincoln was assassinated, the news of which brought sorrow and sadness to our little army. We had been slandering and speaking evil of him for four years, but when he was murdered, we would gladly have put flowers on his coffin.*[7]

In North Carolina, each soldier was given $1.15 in silver as final payment for his four years service to the Confederacy. With this and what few personal belongings he had left, the former Rebel soldier started for home. For the most part, the men traveled in small groups. They were allowed to keep enough weapons for protection, or for use in killing game, and those who owned horses were permitted to ride them home. In some instances artillery horses were raffled off to men returning to farms where all the livestock had been appropriated by either army. John B. Blair of the 35th Tennessee observed, "The terms were agreed on and now we drew rations from the Yankees and the boys began to be lively; money in our pockets, bacon and crackers in their haversacks and home in their heads."[8]

Paroled soldiers who traveled through East Tennessee learned quickly that the bitterness generated by four years of war did not end at the surrender table. Many Rebs chose to walk through Georgia rather than face the risks involved in passing through East Tennessee. Ex-Confederate soldiers native to the region would live with the animosity for decades to follow.

One ex-Reb writing of his treatment at the hands of the Unionists said:

> *One of the first indignities was a demand that I remove the brass buttons from my Confederate uniform*

that is if I intended to wear it. It was not a question of choice with me about wearing it; it was all I had, and I hesitated, but they were peremptory. I should remove them that day or they would be cut off.... One indignity followed another in rapid succession until I began to apprehend something serious from men who left our town and who were plundering and picking up everything in the way of guns and horses that they could lay claim to as having been used in Confederate service. Their cruelty and plundering knew no limit.[9]

To prevent their identification as ex-Confederates, men forced to travel through Union territory swapped coats with men along the road. Crude buttons carved from wood replaced those with "C.S.A." on them. Mules branded with a "US" were smeared with mud to prevent their being taken by local residents. Isolated bands of ex-Rebs took no offense at the insults hurled by people who detested them and the cause for which they had fought. They pretended not to hear when townspeople followed along the streets singing "Hang Jeff Davis to a sour apple tree," and they bit their tongues in silence when freed slaves taunted them with "Bottom rail on top now." If the design of such incidents was to goad the returning Rebs into a fight, it was a failure. The homebound men from the Confederate Army had no intention of being held up by the insults of a few stray Yankees.

John B. Blair was appointed captain of the group in which he traveled. Although at one time the rank of captain was something to be proud of, Blair confessed he could salvage little satisfaction from his new appointment. His men were ragged, he had no hat and only a half-way pair of shoes. Some of his men were barefoot and when the small band was assembled, its members looked more like a set of mountain fugitives than soldiers. At Greenville, Tennessee, Blair was ordered to turn over all guns and ammunition. "When I gave orders to stack arms," Blair wrote,

> *...the boys stacked them and I marched them off. One Yankee officer said we looked like mud-daubbers, and another said yes, but mud daubers have stings in their tail, and they laughed heartily over us as we were filthy; we had no clothes to change, and no chance to wash what we had. Some of the Yankees seemed to be sociable, and some of them looked as though they had always lived on sour Kraut.*[10]

The stopover at Greenville had special significance for a soldier from Texas. Samuel T. Foster had experienced about everything the Civil War offered: fierce battles, prison, hunger, scant clothing, and brief moments of jubilation when all went well. But at Greenville, he experienced something entirely new. On May 19, 1865, he wrote in his diary:

> *I saw some negro children going to school this morning, for the first time in my life. In fact I never heard of such a thing before, nor had such a thing ever cross [ed] my mind. — I stopped a little negro girl about 12 years old dressed neat and clean, going to school with her books — I asked her to let me see what she was studying — She pulled out a 4th Reader a Grammar Arithmetic and a Geography — I opened the Grammar about the middle of the book and asked her a few questions — which she answered very readily and correctly. Same with her Geography and Arithmetic. I never was more surprised in my life! The idea was new to me.*
>
> *I asked her who was her teacher. She said "a lady from the North."*

Samuel Foster was not a man who viewed new experiences as ends within themselves. Like Morgan Leatherman, Andrew Jackson Campbell, and James Lytle, such experiences had a symbolic significance and inspired further thought. That night Samuel wrote:

*I returned to camp and think over what I have seen.
I can see that all the negro children will be educated the
same as the white children are. That the present
generation will live and die in ignorance, as they have
done heretofore - I can see that our white children will
have to study hard, and apply themselves closely, else
they will have to ride behind, and let the negro hold the
reins — I can see that the next generation will find
lawyers doctors preachers, school teachers farmers
merchants &c divided some white and some black, and
the smartest man will succeed without regard to color. If
the negro lawyer is more successful than the white one
then the negro will get the practice.*

*The color will not be so much in the future as
knowledge. The smartest man will win — in every
department of life. Our children will have to contend for
the honors in life against the negro in the future — They
will oppose each other as lawyers in the same case.
They will oppose each other as mechanics, carpenters,
house builders, blacksmiths, silver and gold smiths
shoemakers, saddle makers &c.*

*And the man that is the best mechanic   lawyer,
doctor or teacher &c will succeed.*[11]

The vision of at least one man had penetrated the ugly veil
of prejudice which hung so heavily over the South, but the new
reality he foresaw was more than a hundred years away.

For some Confederate veterans the trip home proved a
pleasant experience. The disappearance of military organization
opened the way for the ever-present element of class distinction
to reassert itself. Even as the men in the defeated army made
their way home, it was often easy to distinguish between the
social classes among them. As he walked through Georgia or
East Tennessee, the hill soldier saw once again the shadow of
the social system which had staffed Confederate regiments with
incompetent officers during the first months of the war. The

fact was that, for those who could qualify for special privileges, the trip home was not without its rewards. Sons of prominent politicians sometimes traveled with their private wagons and were attended by private body servants just as they had been throughout the war. When such soldiers traveled in a party of their own kind it was difficult to identify them as members of a recently defeated army.

Bromfield Ridley found the trip home both enlightening and entertaining. Young Ridley enjoyed privileges unknown to most soldiers. His father was one of Tennessee's most prominent citizens and Bromfield himself had been a member of General Alex P. Stewart's staff. The young officer had fortunately been capable of displaying talents equal to every opportunity afforded him. Ridley, in company with General Stewart's son, had been allowed to leave North Carolina ahead of the disbanded army "so we could find forage for man and beast," and a few days later was in Georgia. While there, young Ridley wrote:

> *Fun, now, to drive off the storm-cloud of defeat, is what we are after. These good people, although made poor by raids and robbery, have thrown open their doors and are gorging us with full eating and fine time. Whilst the old gentlemen are pondering over the future and grieving over "what I used to was," we young bloods are delving in boyish hope and dwelling in the bright anticipation of meeting a beautiful blonde or brunette.*[12]

Parties and cock fights were held daily for the entertainment of high-ranking officers and great stores of food were broken out by influential Southern patriots whose pantries had not suffered depletion. Old barrels of whiskey were resurrected from hidden graves, and throughout the night, the fiddle's whine blended with the rhythmic chant of the square dance caller.[13]

While scattered bands of former soldiers made their way home from the battlefield, other soldiers waited for their release from Yankee prisons. Perhaps it was for these men that the surrender held its greatest shock. On the one hand, they welcomed the possibility that the war's end would bring their release from prison, but on the other, the hardships of prison had been endured in the expectation that a Southern victory might be forthcoming. When prisoners learned that their suffering and privations had been in vain, the prospect of freedom was tinged with despair.

Many of the prisoners had been captured when the armies of the Confederacy were still intact and the hopes of victory were yet prominent. They had not witnessed the gradual disintegration of Southern arms, which had been so obvious to the soldiers who remained in the field.

Captain James Lytle was representative of many Confederates who were in prison at the time Johnston surrendered at Bentonville. To Lytle the events leading to the final surrender presented a conflict between what he considered his sworn duty and his intense desire to return home. At Fort Delaware prison on April 10, 1865, Lytle wrote:

> *We have sad news today. It is that genl. R.E. Lee surrendered yesterday with his entire army. At any rate there had been a salute of two hundred guns fired from the fort today and there is firing at some other point in hearing.*

Less than a week later he said:

> *We know not what a day may bring forth Yesterday evening cities, towns, and garrisons were luminated in honor of the hoisting of the Federal Flag over Sumpter: Today they are mourning on account of the death of Abraham Lincoln.*[14]

Following Lee's surrender, the commandant at Fort Delaware was anxious to clear his cells as quickly as possible.

Federal officers utilized every method at their disposal to persuade the prisoners to take the oath of allegiance to the Federal Government, an act required before release was possible. Although many disheartened prisoners did subscribe to the oath, others shunned any pretense of buckling to Yankee pressure. The Rebs had taken an oath to stand by the Confederacy and many considered it treasonous to pledge their support to the very government they had been fighting.

On April 28, James Lytle wrote:

> *They have made a completion of enrolling the names of applicants for the oath today   there has been more than two thirds of the Privates on this island that made application for the oath. There are about two thousand confederate officers confined in the officers barracks with myself and about one half of them made application, the Privates went almost unanimous for it. The cause of this demorrialization among the prisoners at this place was in consequence of General Lee's army being surrendered a few days since and the expectation of General Johnston's surrender in a few days. The Prisoners considering the cause we have so long contending for now being hopeless, and as they were doomed within the prison walls their service could no longer be rendered to the bleeding remains of their country, they resolved at once to return to their homes and leave the horrors of this miserable life . . . The impression is made in my mind that chances for our independence is becoming quite limited. But when I cast a thought toward General Johnston's army yet in the field and relatives, friends, associates, and perhaps, members of my company   (who I promised to act in good faith) still exposed to the dangers and toils of the field I could not think of tareing myself from their cause in this hour of triel, and flying to the victorious colors that is hurling in defiance against my comrades, and*

there hovel down in the climes of safety and ease, while my comrads are undergoing the calamities of defeat and despair, my conscience spoke in thunder tones, Shear their fate, let it be what it may.[15]

Days later, James Lytle heard of Johnston's surrender. After a few hours he wrote:

Today there has been a roll of our names called. That is a roll of those who refused to agree to take the oath during the last three days calling . . . I enrolled my name today to take the oath on some future day . . . If I have erred, it is an error of the head and not of the heart.[16]

On June 12, 1865, Captain Lytle took the oath of allegiance to the United States, and the following day began the long journey to his home in Bedford County.

It had been almost a year since Captain Richard Beard and W.A. Brown were captured following the death of General McPherson at Atlanta. The prospect of freedom overwhelmed such men. Beard wrote:

On the morning of June 1st, 1865, I passed out of the gate of the prison a free man and no one who had not experienced a prison life can realize the sensations that I underwent. The morning was as beautiful as the sun ever rose on. There was not a cloud in the sky; the air was silent as the ocean and the dew sparkled like jewels on the grass. Taking a mint julip with Captain Collings one of the officers of the 128th Ohio, who had been guarding us, we shook hands across the bloody chasm and turned my face toward my home in Tennessee — a home that I had not seen for more than four years.[17]

Far to the south, Tennesseans serving with the Union Army celebrated the end of the war. In Nashville, bands played "Rally Round The Flag," and soldiers marched beneath the victorious Stars and Stripes while politicians hailed the dawning of a new era. The taste of victory was sweet, especially sweet to East Tennesseans who had been forced from their homes early in the war. They lost few opportunities to express their joy even if it meant further humiliation to their former enemies.

For some East Tennesseans, the war harbored a final, tragic chapter. On April 27, 1865, the steamboat *Sultana* plowed its way north through the muddy waters of the Mississippi River. On board was a portion of the 3rd Tennessee Federal Cavalry, captured by Forrest the previous September. Thrilled at their release from prison and the prospect of going home, the men relaxed as the boat churned along its watery course. Sailing under a clear sky and a full head of steam, the *Sultana* suddenly convulsed into an un-natural throb and seconds later exploded into small bits of floating debris. One hundred and seventy-five members of the 3rd Tennessee Regiment U.S.A., died in the explosion.[18]

For the Confederate soldier on his way home there were occasional moments of embarrassment which were only indirectly related to the war. Young Newton Cannon of Forrest's command was on the final leg of his trip home when he stopped at the residence of Ben Harlan in Maury County. After resting a while, Cannon made ready to continue his journey, but his host insisted that he stay for dinner.

According to Cannon:

> *In a very short time, a lot of young ladies began to come in, to whom I was introduced, and who kept me busy answering questions about other boys I knew who were friends of theirs, until Mr. Harlan walked down the hall, with the young ladies seated on each side, and announced that dinner was ready, and when I asked him to let the ladies precede us, said no; that I should have the post of honor, and caught me by the arm and we walked down the hall to the dining room, a very embarrassing thing for me to do, as my little cavalry*

jacket with two bullet holes in it was too short to conceal
the defect in my pants and drawers which had seen too
much service, and were even too defective to hide that
part of my person that had been constantly in the saddle.
So, when we reached the table, some of the girls looked
sad, and some even shed tears.[19]

Amanda McDowell was pleased with the prospect of peace. The White County "school-marm" had lived an almost intolerable existence, having had one brother on each side of the conflict. When the news of Lee's surrender reached her, Amanda wrote:

There is some great news . . . Guess from all
accounts the great Southern Confederacy is about "gone
up for ninety days" as the boys say . . . Some are
already rejoicing over the downfall of their oppressors.
For truly secession has been the greatest tyrant that ever
reigned over this country. For my own part, I try not to
rejoice at any one's downfall, only as far as I think will
be good for their souls. But I do rejoice at the prospect
of peace.[20]

By the middle of May, 1865, the bulk of the Confederate soldiers were arriving at home. It was into a climate of physical destruction, financial ruin, and social confusion that the veterans entered. Nothing they had experienced prepared them for what they found. They had seen the terrible effects left on the countryside by marching and fighting armies, and had watched the desperate look of hopelessness cloud the countenances of Southern sympathizers as they had been driven from their state. Such things were only symptomatic of immediate problems. They failed to reveal the deeper significance of the defeat which was now a reality.

In spite of the chaos and confusion they experienced upon reaching home, there was also relief and happiness. Lieutenant James Cooper perhaps expressed it adequately.

Crowds of men from Lee's and Johnston's armies filled up the village of Eatonton and one would have thought from the mirth and gayety that prevailed that our armies had been successful. The meeting of relatives for the first time in years contributed much to the gayety and all went happy as you please. At our house all felt very blue at the turn our affairs were taking, but with all our sorrow there was a feeling of relief that the war was at last over; that we were at liberty to go home, once more. I was afraid if the truth were known that we were not sorry as we should have been. The feeling of relief was so great that for a time all else was forgotten in the satisfaction that gave. We now began our preparations in earnest for our return home. When the prospect was in view every moment lost, seemed an age.[21]

2.

Upon reaching home the Confederate soldier's first reaction was to the superficial evidence of war which glared at him from every direction. Men who had been unable to maintain contact with relatives were shocked by what they saw. Marcus Toney found

...change written on everything. When I left home, the whole country around Edgefield [a suburb of Nashville] *was a vast forest of large populars, sweet gums, hackberry, hickory, and walnut.... It was all gone, and the stumps dug up. I looked for the old homestead, and there was a piece of house that resembled it; but the weatherboarding had been stripped off for some distance, and not a piece of fence in sight.... I walked near the old house where some mulatto children were playing on the porch. I stopped to look at,*

but could not recognize them. Presently a white woman came to the porch, and I said: "who are you?" She replied: " I'm Jim's wife." I saw at once she was a northern woman, the "Jim" she had reference to was one of my former slaves.[22]

George Guild's regiment arrived home on May 20, 1865. He wrote:

It was a sad homecoming with many of them: to desolated homes, a war-swept country, families suffering for the necessities of life, and, worst of all, with a disreputable militia lording it over a helpless people.[23]

John Blair arrived home to find that "the yankees had come out to my little farm with thirty wagons and had hauled off my rails and burned them, and they or some of the home-made yankees had burned my house, leaving me a naked piece of land."[24]

Following the initial shock of finding their homes and farms either destroyed or run-down, Confederate veterans began to sense a more significant result of the war. Tennessee politicians were initiating their plan of reconstruction. In their plan, the significance of defeat became even more obvious. Former Rebs were forced to surrender their fire-arms, the right to vote was denied them, and at one time, an attempt was made to require an oath of allegiance of every young lady who married a Confederate veteran. The veteran became a target of hate for every candidate who sought public office. Even though the declared war was over, the momentum of hate it had set in motion continued forward in time, entrapping and subjecting its victims to its own unique form of retribution.

Throughout its duration, the war was seen by many as a social and military experiment initiated by the rich and forced on the poor. Andrew Johnson, in his farewell speech before becoming Lincoln's vice president, said:

The folly of destroying their government, and sacrificing their sons to gratify the mad ambitions of political leaders, needs no longer to be told to the laboring masses. The wasted estates — ruined and dilapidated farms—vacant seats around the hearthstones — prostrate business — insecurity of property, and even life itself, everywhere proclaim it in language not to be misunderstood.

But all is not lost. A new era dawns upon the people of Tennessee. They enter upon a career guided by reason, law, order, and reverence. The reign of brute force and personal violence has passed away forever . . . the shackles have been formerly stricken from the limbs of more than 275,000 slaves in the State. The unjust distinctions in society, fostered by an arrogant aristocracy, based upon human bondage, have been overthrown; and our whole social system reconstructed on a basis of honest industry and personal worth. Labor shall now receive its merited reward, and honesty, energy, and enterprise their just appreciation.[25]

Johnson was succeeded as governor by William G. Brownlow, the fiery East Tennessee publisher and preacher. Brownlow's opinions on any subject were never a matter of doubt. In his first speech to the legislature, the new governor said:

Secession is an abomination that I cannot too strongly condemn, and one that you cannot legislate against with too much severity. What has it done for our country in the space of four years? It has plunged our country into civil war, paralyzed our commerce, destroyed our agricultural pursuits, suspended the whole trade and business of our country . . .

What has it done for Tennessee? It has forced odious and unconstitutional leagues, passed military bills, and inaugurated a system of oppressive taxation, without consulting the people . . . It has offered a premium for crime in ordering the discharge of culprits from prison on condition that they would enter the rebel army . . . It has passed laws making it treason to say or do anything in favor of the government of the United States, or against the so-called Confederate States . . . Our people have been arrested and imprisoned; our homes have been rudely entered and shamefully pillaged; our families have been subjected to insults; our women and children have been tied up and scourged, or shot by a ruffian soldiery; our towns have been pillaged; our citizens have been robbed of their horses, mules, grain, and meat, and many of them assassinated and murdered.[26]

Thus spoke the man who possessed the supreme authority in Tennessee at the very time its Confederate soldiers were returning home following their surrender. It was unfortunate for the ex-Confederate soldiers that those against whom the most intemperate actions of their government had been directed, were now in power in Tennessee. From them, little sympathy could be expected.

Finding himself in a situation where the least wrong move could invoke the wrath of a hostile government, the former soldier cautiously bided his time. Torn-up fences, damaged houses, and dilapidated equipment became a natural anesthetic against the sickening pangs of social and political upheaval by which he was surrounded. Time would be his chief ally.

There were many diversions to occupy the mind of the ex-Confederate. He had never been one to let a situation get him down and there was no reason to begin now. As one veteran put it:

There were compensations for even the evils of reconstruction. In those first days after we got home, though defeated, ragged, penniless, and mulattos in complexion, yet we were all heroes in the eyes of our own people. And especially did the girls glorify us, and if one of us had a scar or went on crutches the admiration was so touched with pity that he was a kind of double hero.[27]

At community dances and parties veterans sat surrounded by a bevy of local belles who waited in great anticipation for their every word. With such glamorous attention, it was probably understandable if the defeated warriors sometimes strayed from the less exciting path of truth and entered the world of fantasy. One vet recalled:

It was a tacit understanding that no one of these youthful veterans should discount the story of another, and each would make it as vivid as he pleased without fear of contradiction, and each one of those girls was convinced that if all the soldiers had been as heroic as her own particular hero, then the Yankee army would have been whipped world without end and our independence won.[28]

As the months passed, time accomplished for the Confederate veteran what he had been unable to accomplish for himself. In Nashville, the politicians had their problems. No longer held together by the emotional issues of the war, the solid wall of Unionism began to crack. Old hates and jealousies began to reassert themselves as Union leaders sought favorable positions in the post-war political arena. Political expediency echoed from the throats of some political leaders in the form of tempered reconstruction policies, while from others it echoed in thunderous tones of spiteful retribution. In the compromises that were sure to follow, lay the hope of a defeated army.

Even the men who had fought in the Yankee Army disliked some of the by-products of the victory to which they had contributed. Although the hill and mountain people of Tennessee had, to a large extent, remained loyal to the Union, they never attempted to conceal their contempt for the Negro. East Tennesseans had never liked emancipation as an *objective* of the war; they liked it even less as a *by-product.*

In January of 1866, a Congressional Committee on Reconstruction asked General Clinton B. Fisk, Director of the Freedman's Bureau in Tennessee, if the anti-Negro sentiment was prevalent throughout the state. "It is not," replied Fisk, who explained:

> *It is a melancholy fact that among the bitterest opponents of the negro in Tennessee are the intensely loyalists of the mountain-district — the men who have been in our armies. Take East Tennessee, for instance. The great opposition to the measure in the Tennessee legislature, giving the negro the right to testify and an equality before the law, has come from that section, chiefly. In Middle and West Tennessee the largest and the wealthiest planters of the slaveholding population have more cordially co-operated with me in my duties than the people of East Tennessee.*[29]

When asked the nature of the Negro opposition on the part of East Tennesseans, Fisk said, "In a desire that he should be entirely removed from the State: opposing his education, and right to justice before the law."[30]

While the victors debated policy, the ex-Confederates continued to wait. It was becoming more and more evident that the Unionists, by eliminating Confederate veterans from political activities, had freed themselves to devour each other. To thinking people, it was inevitable that the former soldiers of the South would regain control of the government; the only question was when. Before five years had passed Reconstruction was history in Tennessee; the Rebs were back in control, and from that time forward, their government would be as good as they desired or as poor as they would tolerate.

That the former Confederate soldier and his family suffered during the years immediately following the war cannot be denied, but that this suffering was a direct result of Reconstruction is somewhat doubtful. Most of the hardships experienced were a direct outgrowth of the war and were only indirectly attributable to the policies of post-war politicians. Politicians were affected most by Reconstruction and, unfortunately, recorded the most about it. Many Confederate veterans never knew what a difficult time they had experienced until they read accounts of the period — written by men who had suffered very little.

Tennessee politicians liked to refer to the terror created by Governor Brownlow's militia. But to veterans who had faced George Thomas' men at Chickamauga and Grant's men at Shiloh, Brownlow's homespun militia was far from frightening.

James H. M'Neilly, a former Confederate chaplain, who watched the militia attempt to keep order at an election at Trenton, Tennessee, wrote:

> *These companies were made up largely of boys from East Tennessee, and they seemed to look on their expedition as a kind of jaunt for recreation. They had their camp on a rising ground west of the town. I was then boarding two or three miles in the country, and when I came to town I passed within two hundred yards of their camp, and they were about as harmless looking a crowd as I ever saw. There was nothing warlike in their appearance and if there had been any purpose of resistance to the government, there were enough of us in and around Trenton who had been soldiers to have driven the whole force into the swamps surrounding their quarters. But the Confederates treated them with good-natured contempt.*[31]

Reconstruction was such an anticlimax to four years of war that it passed before many veterans knew it existed. Unlike most other Southern States, Reconstruction in Tennessee was administered by native politicians and although there was unpleasantness, fairness would indicate that Middle and West Tennessee fared much better under East Tennessee Reconstructionists than the eastern portion of the state fared under Confederate occupation during the first two years of the war.

3.

The Civil War and its aftermath had no greater impact on any segment of the population than the widows and orphans left in its wake. The statistics of history include mostly the number of men killed, wounded or missing in battle. Perhaps a more dramatic statistic would be the number of widows and orphans left after such engagements as Shiloh, Chickamauga, and Franklin. While war-time politicians went about the country explaining how right they had been in urging Tennessee's withdrawal from the Union, and post-war politicians sought to exploit their army service into self-serving ends, the war widows and orphans faced an endless struggle for survival. Betty Burford Bobo and her three children were representative of the widows and orphans.

Just how Betty Bobo's husband, a physician, was killed during the war has been lost to history. Family opinion is that he was killed by bushwhackers in the foothills of the Cumberland Mountains. In any event, Betty was left with three small children. Her place of residence was Red Boiling Springs in Macon County.

In the months following the war, Betty set her thoughts toward her situation down in a diary. A portion of that diary has been preserved. Its pages are filled with the anxieties and aggravations of a woman for whom the Civil War will seemingly never end. Long after the politicians had learned to turn the South's defeat into an asset by appealing to the pity of sympathetic citizens, Betty's life was dominated by the loss of her husband. The diary is not exciting, but it reveals the permanent pain which survives the temporary excitement that sometimes causes humans to forget their humaneness. The diary is a recording of the private thoughts of a very intelligent woman who fought her battles without fanfare in the most trying of circumstances.

Being a young, attractive widow, Betty's private life was a source of interest to her friends and neighbors. This fact seemed to seriously annoy her. On the other hand it was probably natural that neighbors would entertain the possibility that a widow with three children might wish to remarry. There was no lack of eligible men since the war had delayed the marriage of soldiers, plus the fact that many women died young in those days, leaving husbands and children to fend for themselves.

In August of 1866, Betty wrote in her diary:

False rumor says Mr. Young [evidently a young man in the community] *and I will marry. Why speak thus? There is no foundation for such a report. He has never manifested to the world any partiality for me. Everyone knows I am not a marrying woman. No sooner than the subject is introduced* [than] *thoughts of my dear Dr. Bobo crowd my mind and in comparing his noble nature and excellent qualities with others I despair of ever being so fortunate as to live with another whose heart would glow with the same warmth of affection, whose only object in life would be to render me and my children comfortable and happy. Without children, I could live happy with any nice warm hearted-high minded man (a second Bobo), but with my children I fear the consequences of a second marriage. Believe me, Little Diary, (for you are my only companion) that my happiest days passed while living with Dr. Bobo and I am contented to remain his widow. My highest ambition is to educate the little Bobo's, both mentally and morally.*

Betty seemed to resent the normality she perceived in the lives of her neighbors. The pain of her own life made her suspicious of pleasure in the lives of others. Writing of a community dance she said:

> *This whole community old and young, rich and poor, widows and widowers are all preparing to start to the picnic (as they term it), To do what? Why to ha! ha! frisk and flirt and dance out several dollars worth of shoes — could not the worth of those shoes and this costly dinner be appropriated to a better purpose? How many are the orphans who would gladly enjoy a piece of bread that will be thrown away and rejoice to have the superfluities of the dinner spent on winter clothing? Have these gay folks forgotten the late war and its consequences and have widows forgotten their husbands who are now in distant graves; doubtless in a better world watching over them and those who are entrusted to their care. Could these seraphas visit our world would they not feel mortified ot see their widows at a Barn Dance?*

During the year following the war, Betty acquired a teaching job in a one-teacher school in Macon County. Much of her time and talents were consumed by its demands. She did manage to visit in the neighborhood and observed that "My Yankee neighbors appeared as glad to see me as the Rebels." The resentment felt by the young teacher was directed more toward the war than toward participants on either side. In September of 1866, she attended church services and noted:

> *In every crowd you can see one or more widow ladies such are the consequences of the late war. How much! I sympathize with this class of unfortunate people. How sad the bereavement! Would that the originators of this war, together with their coadjutators,*

could feel the pang of the heart-felt sorrow that now prevades the bosoms of the widows and orphans, more, may the cries of the distressed banish every thought of subjugation, coercion and everything that tends to excite a warlike spirit and cause our rulers to throw political documents aside and take the Bible as their guide. In all probability, a new order of things would come up; which would redound to the security and happiness of our nation . . .

The following day, Betty Bobo's mood blended with the weather. It was an attitude prominent during the era. People in trouble seemed to find reassurance in the belief that nature reflected their personal situation. Betty wrote on September 10, 1866: "Gloomy day — All nature seems to be weeping — my feeling corresponds with the weather. But I'll wear contentment, smile and conceal my troubles, anxieties and unhappy feelings, bitter tears, etc."

The one thing that diverted Betty's attention from her family was the school in which she taught. She believed herself to be a good teacher, but had doubts about the community's appreciation for her talents. To her diary she wrote, "I defy any one to advance them [scholars] more rapidly than I have and doubt whether half the teachers would have taken the pains and trouble for $20.00 a month. My friends are continually expressing their desires for me to content myself in Macon [County], but unfortunately for them (as well as myself) they are not willing to pay living prices. I can't confine myself in the school room, especially in the Summer Season for $20.00 per month ha ha . . ."

The young widow found herself in conflict with community standards as pertained to her wearing apparel. Tradition demanded that widows wear black as a symbol of their grief for departed husbands. Betty viewed the situation in a different light. On September 17, 1866, she observed:

I went to the store this morning and bought a few things — yes, I purchased a brown calico dress — will I enjoy wearing it? What will the tattler [community gossips] say? I don't care — the world knows I loved Bobo and would prefer him to assist me in raising my Little Brats, but unfortunately for us he can never again be with us on this earth. I'm not going to lay off black, but merely wish my everyday dresses to be serviceable and you know black calico is not as good or durable as other colors — My actions prove whether I'm making any endeavors to captivate any one or not, or even wish to keep company with the gentlemen. I wish their friendship, particularly their assistance in the way of a school etc. but Heaven knows, I'm contented to remain Bobo's widow.

Sunday being a day of leisure prompted reflections on her past, present and future. Inevitably the war occupied a dominant place in her thoughts. Betty had been forced to leave her young son Lacy with her parents in an adjoining county while she met the obligations of a school marm. The situation was much to her dislike. The war may have ended, but its havoc persisted. On this particular Sunday night, she entered in her diary:

Night finds me insconced in my cabin writing in my Diary and reading a good book — titled the Gem. Would that I [could?] see my dear Lacy this moment, but Oh Me! the consequences of the late war. I am now a lone widow in a negro cabin with two children, but separated from my baby — 18 miles from him — and the poor little fellow sick. If Dr. Bobo could have survived the war our condition would be quite different — talk of marrying! How can I ever love another man as I did my dear Doctor. I may someday marry again, but doubt whether I'll ever love and be happy as I was with Dr. Bobo — peace to his tomb.

531

Other Sundays followed and with each came a rehashing of past joys and future hopes. The cloud of war was ever present. On November 4, 1866, Betty reflected:

> *The Sabbath finds me ready to start to Church. How fondly do I hope our meeting proves advantageous to both sinner and christian. Would that I could enjoy such meetings as in days gone by. Whither at home or abroad, in Company or alone, my mind is dwelling on the past lingering and hovering around the image of my dear companion. Though time gradually wears away troubles and produces many a change, yet no change can restore the ravages of the past. Folly may stretch her scepter over the earth, seeming to blight all that is fairest and brightest — Crime may stride haughtily through the world leaving misery and desolation in its path, yet love is still among us in the quiet recesses of life, even exerting its sacred influence; serving as a token and a pledge of a better land where pain and woe will visit never — Friends or companions never will sever but live and love eternally.*

Poverty and loneliness were constant companions to Betty Bobo as she attempted to survive the consequences of civil war. But the negative factors were more than offset by a grim determination that all but insured the survival of her family. In November, she wrote in her diary:

> *Started Dany* [evidently a neighbor or a student] *off with my last cow to sell. Poverty forces me to sell but I hope she will bring a good price and next spring I can buy another . . . In borrowed language there is many a pang to pursue me. They may crush, but they shall not condemn. They may torture, but shall not subdue me. Tis of him I think, not them.*

In spite of her efforts to see hope for a brighter future, the young war widow occasionally stripped from reality its veil of optimism and faced her situation in all its gloomy details. She wrote:

Unfortunate woman! left without stock provisions and only a few dollars to carry me through the winter. I will not take the "Blues" or become a hypochondriac. No! I'll double my energies, use economy and hope for a better day.

A few days later she confided to her diary:

Many things are troubling me this gloomy forenoon and at times I think I'll never be happy again. It may be that I will forget my grief, that time has good in store for me and that my heart will yet find relief from sources unknown. Whatever may be the joys in store, I can never forget the past.

Sometimes memories from the past negated what, otherwise, might have been considered joyous times. On one such occasion, Betty wrote, "Were it not for the memories of 'better days' I might exclaim how happy I am! She then asks, "Tell me what is pleasure?" There is no answer. Sundays continued to be frustrating. On November 23, she wrote:

The Sabbath! were it not for reading and writing I would dread to see the Sabbath. Without employment my mind is ever wandering and particularly dwelling on the past. Time was when I rejoiced at the dawning of the day of rest — for then my dear companion beguiled my weary hours and I was always contented when blessed with society. Oh! that I could once more hear him talk and see him caress his dear little children. His image is ever before me and often for a moment do I forget the torture of my soul when I gazed on his face the last time. Oh! the anguish of that moment. I felt that the

_____ [?] *of the years were blasted and the holiest and purest principles of my nature had been crushed. Oh! the sorrow of widowhood.*

The following day she observed:

The Revolutionary War was a war of principles — but alas! the late war was carried on principally for gain. Our leaders ought to stand by the Washington Platform with absolute disregard of personal consequences. If conciliatory measures are not adopted very soon the most unhappy widows and orphans will not only mourn the loss of the dearest friends but be turned out from their comfortable homes to seek shelter . . . No change however pleasant can restore the ravages of the late War and God grant us a happy reunion — not only of States, but of hearts.

The new year, 1867, came in as unpretentiously as the older had departed. There was no fanfare and no resolutions recorded in Betty's diary, but the drudgery of survival was the topic for January 3rd. The diary reads, "Washing! what a task before me! However, I'll double my energies . . . roll up my sleeves and go to the washtub with a good resolution. Poverty acts as a stimulus with me, but as long as I can shun the washtub, I'll vow someone black or white may have the job." During the same week, she wrote, "My children are pretty smart — interesting Little Brats and hope whispers they will comfort a devoted Mother in old age." About the same time she wrote, "The day has passed when I try to make an impression by fine dressing. If moral worth can not introduce me into society, I'll remain unloved and uncared for."

The final entry in Betty Bobo's diary was made on Feb. 28, 1867. She wrote:

Farewell to February! Wilt thou come again? Yes, but many who welcomed me in 67' will ere 68' be in

their lone grave. Sad thought indeed. Oh God! may I
live with my helpless babies until then and for years to
come — without a father or mother's love how lonely
and desolate they feel — how dark the prospect before
them.

Betty Bobo's prayer was answered. She did live to raise her children and to see them grow up to be well-educated, productive citizens. But the memories of happier days haunted her the remainder of her life. Long after the political issues of Reconstruction had been laid to rest, the emotional issues of her personal loss hovered close to the surface of her consciousness. For Betty, the Civil War never ended.[32]

4.

Following the Civil War, the people of the South assumed a dubious role in American history: they afforded the only opportunity to study Americans who had experienced total military defeat. For at least another century, Southerners would be studied, analyzed, and evaluated. A train ride through the South would make sociologists out of writers who had previously devoted their literary talents to less demanding assignments. Even Northerners who lacked the advantage of the train ride would volunteer suggestions as to how the defeated South could become more worthy of its compulsory membership in the Union.

As a study in defeat, Southerners offer few unique insights. Like most individuals and nations, the Confederate veteran continued to defend his honor long after he ceased defending his home. He had surrendered his arms, not his pride and honor. The former Confederate soldier never quite got around to saying he was wrong in fighting the war, but by implication, he admitted it when he said he was glad the nation survived intact. Former Rebs wrapped their beliefs concerning States' Rights in colorful and elaborate verbalisms, but through the transparency of these verbalisms, the contents of their arguments never seemed worthy of the wrappings. Even while maintaining their satisfaction that the nation had survived intact, they defended their right to fight for its division, an argument that never quite seemed worthy of their mentality. Such an argument reduced them to defending their right to be wrong — an uncomfortable position at best.

They should have argued that what they fought for was ill-advised but fought for valiantly, or better yet, admitted that they fought for personal and sectional pride, but in the process had redefined valor, established new dimensions of sacrifice, and demonstrated that victory is not the only road to honor.

Southerners were emotionally involved in the struggle they had waged for independence and it prevented them from asking questions which might have changed their attitude toward the struggle. In the years following the war, politicians would need only to remind voters that it had been the Yankees who invaded the South, killed Southern men, and ruined Southern property; this alone would hold the voters in line. That the very politician who spoke such words might have helped bring on the war in which these things happened was never mentioned or considered. One of the oddities of the Southern attitude toward defeat was the fact that those who led the South into secession remained heroes amid the ruins they might have avoided through more temperate action.

The Civil War all too often became a reference point in history from which the Confederate veteran and his immediate descendants could never divorce themselves. Somehow, the war had to be defended and the defense dictated attitudes not conducive to progress — social or economical. So much time was spent in honoring the dead that too little time was left to deal

with the problems of the living.   Former Southern soldiers
talked in glowing and emotional terms of the war they had
waged for their state's independence without ever mentioning
that, had they won, it would have meant the continued
enslavement of 275,000 human beings in Tennessee alone; it
seems never to have occurred to them that with the defeat of the
Confederacy, freedom was guaranteed for all.

At least a few soldiers did think upon this matter. Captain
Samuel Foster of Texas recorded in his diary the reaction of his
comrades.

> *It seems curious that mens minds can change so
> sudden, from opinions of life long, to new ones a week
> old.*
>
> *I mean that men who have not only been taught
> from their infancy that the institution of slavery was
> right; but men who actually owned and held slaves up to
> this time, — have now changed in their opinions
> regarding slavery, so as to be able to see the other side of
> the question, — to see that for man to have property in
> man was wrong, and that the   "Declaration of
> Independence meant more than they had ever been able
> to see before. That all men are, and of right ought to be
> free" has a meaning different from the definition they
> had been taught from infancy up....*
>
> *These ideas come not from the Yanks or northern
> people but come from reflection, and reasoning among
> ourselves.*[33]

It would take a century for the war to be accepted as a tragic
tributary of history's mainstream — for Southerners to learn that
answers are not found by fastening the human mind to history
as an object of worship, but rather through studying its
implications for the present and future. Such a view does not
dishonor the past, but rather acknowledges its value as a
reservoir of evidence upon which the present can be better
understood.

If the South presented a worthwhile study of defeat, the North afforded an excellent study of Americans in victory. Northerners somehow gained the impression that their victorious armies reflected on over-all superiority which gave them license, if not the obligation, to criticize, to recommend and expect changes in Southern attitudes and patterns of thought. Naturally enough, the Northerner used himself as a standard of excellence by which he measured the worth of his defeated adversary. To the degree that he did not find himself reflected in the behavior and ideas of the Southerner, he condemned that individual without mercy.

In many ways, the two groups, North and South, reacted similarily to the tragic event which had cut so deeply into their lives. Individuals on both sides divided the events of the war into two categories: the tragic and the commonplace. What was tragic to one, was commonplace to the other — and vice-versa. If it had been a Rebel horse stolen or a Rebel house burned, it was an act of outlawish proportions to the Southerner, but was likely to be much less serious to the Yankee. If a Yankee fell in a grotesque heap before a Rebel's fire, it was evidence of great marksmanship to the Reb, but might very well inspire a patriotic sonnet from the Yank who described it. Roving bands of independent fighters were "fearless patriots" if they were on *our* side, but were common bushwhackers if on *their* side. A thief was a man on *their* side who took things that didn't belong to him; the same man on *our* side was a forager. The "defiant banner" was *their* flag; *ours* was a "glorious emblem." If *our* men retreated before overwhelming numbers it was an indication of patriotic intelligence; if *their* men did the same thing it was an act of downright cowardice. It was military expediency when *our* side burned rail fences; but it was plain banditry when *they* did it. When one of *our* men shot from behind a tree he was a sharpshooter, but when one of *their* men fought from such an advantage he was a cowardly scoundrel. Perhaps such inconsistencies lessened the pain of what war had done to the participants on both sides.

The Civil War would send riplets of discontent through and beyond the century which followed. It would take the Negro another century to gain the rights of citizenship, and even then, it would demand constant vigilence to hold on to the gains made. Nathan Bedford Forrest would emerge from the War as probably its most controversial participant. Rarely would a year pass without his name being prominently displayed as a result of his attack on Fort Pillow. There were matters of less importance that would also make the news. Riverboats were raised from the depths of the Mississippi and Tennessee Rivers. In August of 1975, the body of Confederate General Bushrod Johnson was exhumed from its unmarked grave in Miles Station, Illinois, and moved to Nashville, Tennessee. In 1977, the grave of Colonel William Shy, the hero of the Battle of Nashville, was disturbed by vandals and a subsequent ceremony was held for the reburial. In 1982, during the construction of a new highway through Nashville, a 400-foot section of the Confederate line was uncovered with its wealth of material and information about the battle of which it was a part.

5.

If the Civil War interrupted the lives of those who survived, it by no means threw them permanently off course. Many Confederate soldiers discovered in its outcome their own emancipation from a social system which had relegated them to a secondary role beneath an arrogant aristocracy. Such men thankfully pursued the blessings of peace, while the fallen aristocrats mourned the loss of things the ordinary soldier never believed important in the first place.

For half a century, Confederate veterans of Tennessee would assist in making and administering public policy. While they retained a sentimental allegiance to, and pride in, the fallen Confederacy, many of them prepared to become a valuable part of the future. The angry scars of war disappeared behind the plows of men no longer forced to compete with giant plantations and thousands of slaves; millwheels of the South turned to grind the grain of men no longer ashamed to labor with their hands; and most important of all, the children of the new middle class attended schools to erase the restricting bonds of illiteracy which had so long neutralized their talents. Without apologies for past deeds, the men who made up the Confederate Army from Tennessee prepared to live out their lives along those lines which best fitted the talents, desires, and opportunities of the individual.

For many veterans, there was little time left. Weakened by exposure during long campaigns or the unhealthy conditions of prison, hundreds of former Rébs died in the years immediately following the war. David Phillips returned to his home in Watertown and reopened his school, but the years of hardship had taken their toll and in less than ten years he was dead. Captain James Lytle came home from prison so diseased that he could hardly manage the work on his small farm, and in six years, he too suffered a premature death. Although such men were not listed as casualties of the war, they died of its effects as certainly as did those who fell at Shiloh and Chickamauga.

The wiry constitutions of some Confederates actually seemed to thrive on their hardships. The scar from the wound Resinor Etter received at Perryville never completely healed, but he lived to be ninety-two. He was active until a short time before his death. He became a legend in his community. Returning to the mountain cove which he left in 1861, Etter farmed his land, imported fine cattle, and sat up until all hours of the night reciting his war experiences to any who gathered round his hearth. Members of the community would remember with great admiration how, after he was too feeble to walk, he insisted that his chair be placed in his garden where he would sit and hoe as far as his arms could reach, after which, the procedure was repeated until the garden was cleared of weeds. Fifty years later in the same mountainous cove, the same bloodlines of cattle grazed on the mountain side, and an admiring son continued to relate the stories he heard over and over during the long winter nights of so long ago.

Old John Savage lived until he almost literally withered away. But if the flesh withered, the spirit did not. As long as he lived, Savage referred to Braxton Bragg as a man who wore "the appearance of a broken merchant, or disgraced preacher flying from the wrath of his congregation, accused of immoral conduct," and Jefferson Davis as a "pusillanimous man whose proper place would be an inferior monk in a monastery."[34] Savage would never forgive Southern leaders for what he considered their deplorable blunders in guiding the destiny of the Confederacy. He would never lose the bitterness acquired against his generals at Perryville and Stone's River, but he forever retained pride in his old regiment and its contribution to the Southern cause. He remained ready at the drop of a hat to fight the man who challenged his allegiance to the South.

Jim Womack was not as vocal in his post war ideas as John Savage, nor was he as amply endowed with energy. The ex-captain of the 16th Tennessee Regiment was more content to be a Southern Gentleman of leisure. Like many of his fellow veterans, Captain Jim strolled the streets of his hometown bowing to the respectful greetings received wherever he went and, if prodded a little, would relate for several hours his experiences during the "late, great unpleasantness." Men like Captain Jim lived to become the personification of the "Lost Cause," and were regarded as invaluable symbols of an age which was rapidly disappearing.

C. H. Clark returned to his farm following the war and "began to use the plow, hoe, and ax and decided that farming would suit me better than anything I could do, and thought of leaving the mountains and valleys, the hills and hollows of my

Dedication of the Robert Hatton Monument, Lebanon, Tennessee, 1912.

Confederate and Union veterans at the site of General Joseph McPherson's death during the Battle of Atlanta.

childhood and the rest of the people with whom I had been raised."[35] But the magnetic power of home was too strong and Clark remained close to his roots.

By the dawn of the Twentieth Century, men like Clark, Etter, and Savage were approaching old age. They had become wards of a new generation who respected them for what they had been and were. No group of veterans was ever taken to the heart of a people more than the Confederate veterans. Special medals were designed for them to wear, a modest pension fund was established in their behalf, special homes were maintained for their comfort, and they were given a vehicle through which they could refight the war: the Confederate Veteran's Reunion. Railroad companies ran special trains to convention cities and the old Rebs were welcomed aboard, whether they had the fare or not. Veterans who had never owned a uniform during the war bought a "reunion special" and left for conventions amid attention that would have flattered a real general in 1862.

Although C. H. Clark lived only seventy-five miles from Nashville, it was many years after the war before he revisited the city. The occasion was a Confederate Reunion. According to Clark,

> *When the people began to talk of the Centennial at Nashville, I had no idea of being there, but when it was decided that there would be a reunion of the old confeds, I decided that I would try to go. The thought of meeting the old boys once more had a tendency to spur me up for the occasion. [Clark found] the streets crowded, and it began to look like there was no room for more. The city was beautifully decorated and the citizens with outstretched arms welcomed us. My business was to see the boys, and be seen by them.*
>
> *I saw many wonders in the Centennial, but nothing interested me as much as the old confeds. I intended to be in the parade, but was not well enough to stand the fatigue. I took position on Market Street and saw every*

*one in the parade, and occasionally turned my head to
keep bystanders from seeing the tears roll down my
cheeks. The people along the street had barrels of ice
water, and carried it to the old confeds, who drank
without breaking a step. I could see the fire in the old
boys eyes as they marched to the rolling of the drum. I
am glad I was with the boys, and while writing this, fill
up and have to turn away . . .*

*The young smooth faced boys of 1861 were the old
confeds of 1897 . . . In conclusion let me say that I want
no more of war, but if it must come, let me go with the
old 16th.*[36]

Clark was representative of thousands of veterans who
came home from the war, remained close to the land, and in the
process of providing for their families inevitably grew old. But
with old age came the luxury of having the time to relive the
exciting days of the war. On the porches of country stores and
around the open fires of neighbors' hearthstones, the veterans
told of the Hornet's Nest, the Round Forest, the Dead Angle,
raids with Forrest, and most of all, how their brigade never
withdrew from the line until flanked on both sides by the
enemy.

Old age was a time for remembering. C. W. Heiskell of
the 19th Tennessee wrote:

*Looking backward through the vista of forty years
that elapsed since the Nineteenth shouldered arms, my
soul is stirred with strange and unutterable emotions.*

*I see the company's muster, the regiment organized,
see the daily drill, guard mounting, breakfast, dinner,
and as the westering sun sinks to rest, I see the
companies one by one take their places on dress parade.
What an array! How inspiring the music; how
magnificent that long and symmetrical line, a thousand
men and more; and with what soldierly bearing they*

march and wheel and counter-march. I listen again to the jest and laugh, as we sit and smoke and take our rest, around the camp fire, when the days deeds are done. I hear "taps" sounded, and lights out; and silence reigns; broken save by the tread or challenge of the lone sentinel.[37]

The first quarter of the Twentieth Century was the twilight zone of the Civil War generation, and just as it had emerged unspectacularly from those which preceded it, so did it gradually blend into those which followed. But the deeds of that generation would forever remain distinctive and would prove increasingly more interesting to a maturing nation willing and anxious to study the intemperate actions of its own adolescence.

Confederate Reunion, Lynchburg, Tennessee.

Appendix

General References

1. Nathaniel Cheairs Hughes Jr. "General William J. Hardee, Old Reliable," L.S.U. Press, Baton Rouge, 1965.
2. James Lee McDonough, "Shiloh — in Hell before Night," U.T. Press, Knoxville, 1977.
3. J.P. Young, "The Seventh Tennessee Cavalry," Press of Morningside, Dayton, 1976. (A reprint).
4. J. Harvey Mathes, "General Forrest," D. Appleton and Co., New York, 1902, reprinted by Frank Myers and Gennie Myers, Memphis, and Burke's Book Store, Memphis.
5. T.C. De Leon, "Joseph Wheeler," Byrd Printing Co., Atlanta, 1899, reissued by Continental Book. Co., Kennesaw, 1960.
6. John P. Dyer, "From Shiloh to San Juan," L.S.U. Press, Baton Rouge, 1961.
7. Glenn W. Sunderland, "Lightning at Hoover's Gap," Thomas Yoseloff, New York, 1969.
8. Glenn Tucker, "Chickamauga, Bloody Battle in The West," Press of Morningside, Dayton, 1976.
9. Ed Porter Thompson, "History of The Orphan Brigade 1861-65," Press of Morningside, Dayton, 1973.
10. E.B. Long with Barbara Long, "The Civil War Day by Day," Doubleday & Co. Inc., Garden City, 1971.
11. Joseph H. Parks, "General Leonidas Polk C.S.A.," L.S.U. Press, Baton Rouge, 1962.
12. F. Senour, "Morgan and His Captors," C.F. Vent & Co., Cincinnati, 1865.
13. James Lee McDonough, "Stones River — Bloody Winter in Tennessee," U.T. Press, Knoxville, 1980.
14. Jennie Starks McKee, "Throb Of Drums in Tennessee 1862-1865," Dorrance & Co., Philadelphia, 1973.
15. Stanley Horn, "Tennessee's War 1861-1865," Distributed by Tenn. Historical Society, Nashville, 1965.
16. Larry J. Daniel, "Cannoneers In Gray," Uni. of Alabama Press, University, 1984.
17. T. Harry Williams, "Beauregard, Napoleon in Gray," Collier Books, New York, 1962.
18. Samuel Carter III, "The Siege of Atlanta, 1864," St. Martin's Press, New York, 1973.
19. "The Civil War in Middle Tennessee," Nashville Banner, 1965.
20. Shelbyville Times-Gazette Sesquicentennial, Historical Edition, 1969.

21. Charles M. Cummings, "Yankee Quaker — Confederate General, The Curious Career of Bushrod Rust Johnson," Fairleigh Dickinson, Uni. Press, Associated University Presses, Inc. Cranbury, 1971.
22. Howard Swiggett, "The Rebel Raider," The Garden City Pub. Co., Garden City, 1937.
23. James Lee McDonough, "Chattanooga _ A Death Grip On The Confederacy," U.T. Press, Knoxville, 1984.
24. "Tennessee In The Civil War, Parts I and II," Civil War Centennial Commission of Tennessee, 1964.
25. John Watson Morton, "Forrest's Artillery," Publishing House of the M.E. Church South, Nashville, 1909.
26. Grady McWhiney, "Braxton Bragg and Confederate Defeat," Vol. I, Columbia Uni. Press, New York, 1969.
27. "Through The South With A Union Soldier," Letters of Alburtus A. Dunham and Charles Laforest Dunham, edited by Arthur H. DeRosier Jr., East Tenn. State Uni., Johnson City, 1969.
28. Walter T. Durham, "Rebellion Revisited, A History of Sumner County, Tennessee From 1861 to 1870," Sumner County Historical Society, Gallatin, 1982.
29. Rebel C. Forrester, "Glory and Tears," (A history of Obion County, Tenn.) H.A. Lanzer Co., Union City, 1966.
30. R. W. Banks, "The Battle of Franklin," Morningside Press, Dayton, 1982.
31. Andrew Nelson Lytle, "Bedford Forrest and His Critter Company," G. P. Putnam's Sons, New York, 1931.
32. Robert Self Henry, "First With The Most," The Bobbs-Merill Co., Indianapolis, 1944.
33. Marcus J. Wright, "Tennessee In The War 1861- 1865," Ambrose Lee Publishing Co., New York, 1908.
34. Thomas Lawrence Connelly, "Army Of The Heartland, The Army of Tennessee 1861-1862," L.S.U. Press, 1967.
35. Thomas Lawrence Connelly, "The Autumn of Glory," L.S.U. Press, Baton Rouge, 1971.
36. "Fort Pillow Massacre," Govt. Publishing Office, 38th Congress 1st Session, Report No. 65.
37. Joe Bennett McBrien, "The Tn. Brigade," Hudson Printing & Lithographing Co., Chattanooga, Tn., 1977.
38. Stanley Horn, "Tennessee's War 1861-1865," Tn. Civil War Centennial Commission, Nashville, 1965.
39. Bennett H. Young, "Confederate Wizards of the Saddle," Morningside Press, Dayton, 1979 (Reprint).
40. Walter Durham, "Nashville, The Occupied City," Tn. Historical Soc., Nashville, 1985.

41. Joseph H. Parks, "Gen. Kirby Smith, C.S.A.," L.S.U. Press, Baton Rouge, 1954.
42. James Lee McDonough and Thomas L. Connelly, "Five Tragic Hours — The Battle of Franklin," U.T. Press, Knoxville, Tn., 1983.
43. Robert Penn Warren, "The Legacy of The Civil War," Harvard Uni. Press, Cambridge, 1983.
44. Charles E. Nash, "Bio. Sketches of Gen. Pat Cleburne and Gen. T.C. Hindman," Morningside Press, Dayton, 1977.
45. Kenneth A. Hafendorfer, "Perryville — Battle for Kentucky," McDowell Publishers, Utica, Ky., 1981.
46. Bruce Catton, "The Centennial History of The Civil War," 3 Vols. Doubleday and Co., Garden City, 1963.
47. Stephen Z. Starr, "The Union Cavalry in The Civil War," Vol. III, "The War in The West," L.S.U. Press, Baton Rouge, 1985.
48. James A. Ramage, "Rebel Raider, The Life of General John Hunt Morgan," The University Press of Kentucky, Lexington, 1986.

Chapter Notes

I
There was a call to arms

1. Will T. Hale and Dixon Merritt, "History of Tennessee," Vol. III,The Lewis Publishing Co., New York 1913, p 576. At the time these volumes were written both Hale and Merritt were writers for the Nashville Banner.
2. Samuel W. Scott and Samuel P. Angel, "History of the Thirteenth Regiment, Tennessee Volunteer Cavalry U. S. A.," P. W. Ziegler Co. Philadelphia 1903, p 39. This book was reissued by Toney Marion, Blountville, Tn. in 1973. Scott was Captain of Co. G and Angel was adjutant of the Thirteenth Tennessee Cavalry U.S. A. The unit was made up of men from upper East Tennessee.
3. The Fayetteville Observer, April 25, 1861. The Observer was a dedicated supporter of secession. Its articles and editorials did much to stir the emotions of its readers against the Union.
4. Ibid.
5. Hale and Merritt, Vol. III, p 576.
6. J. G. Carrigan, " The Cheat Mountain Campaign," Albert B. Tavel Co., Nashville 1885, p 16. This book was published anonymously, but its author later became public knowledge.
7. Ibid, p 18.
8. Fayetteville Observer, May 9, 1861.
9. Carrigan, p 17.
10. H. T. Childs, "Turney's 1st Tennessee Regiment C.S.A. " in The Confederate Veteran Magazine, April 1917,p 164. The Confederate Veteran was published in Nashville, Tn. from 1893 until 1934. It was founded by Sumner A. Cunningham, a veteran of the 41st Tennessee Regiment C. S. A. Cunningham was a native of Bedford County in Middle Tennessee and is buried in the Willow Mount Cemetery at Shelbyville. In that cemetery a monument stands commemorating his work with The Confederate Veteran. Local opinion is that the monument is the only one in America dedicated to the memory of a magazine.

11. Jim Womack's Diary, May 16, 1861. Womack was a member of the 16th Tennessee Regiment C. S. A. generally associated with Warren and surrounding counties. The diary was published by Walter Womack, a descendant from McMinnville, Tn. during the

Civil War Centennial. An autobiographical sketch of Womack is found in "The Tennessee Civil War Veterans Questionnaires" Southern Historical Press, Ensley, S.C., Vol . 5, pp 2234-2235.

12. An Address of Miss Sallie Landess to the Norris Creek Guards of Lincoln County. Published in " The Cheat Mountain Campaign," p 19.

13. The Fayetteville Observer , April 25, 1861.

14. J. G. Carrigan, p 18.

15. Memoirs of I. Nelson Rainey (unpublished), copy furnished by Dr. Tom Tracy of Columbia, Tn. Rainey was a member of Gen. William "Red" Jackson's Cavalry which was, generally, attached to the Army of Tennessee. These memoirs were written in 1925, but , according to Rainey "every statement" is true. An autobiographical sketch of Rainey is found in "The Tennessee Civil War Veterans Questionnaires," pp 1787-1788.

16. Memoirs of John Johnston, 20th Tennessee Regiment C. S. A. These memoirs were published in the Tn. Hist. Quarterly in two installments: Dec. 1954, and March 1955, edited by William T. Alderson. The quote referred to in this footnote appeared Dec. 1954, p 75.

17. James Cooper's Diary, Sept. 30, 1861. Cooper was a member of the 20th Tennessee Regiment, C. S. A. The diary was published in the Tn. Hist. Quarterly June, 1956.

18. Marcus Toney, "Privations of a Private," published privately in Nashville, 1905, p 15. Toney enlisted in the Rock City Guards which became a part of Maney's 1st Tennessee Regiment C. S. A.

19. Nelson Rainey's Memoirs.

20. Amanda McDowell's Diary, May 4, 1861. Ms. McDowell was a school-teacher in White County, Tennessee before and during the war. Diary loaned by Mrs. Lela McDowell Blankenship of Morrison, Tn. Much of the material contained in the McDowell Papers which also include letters and essays written by members of the family, were utilized in Mrs. Blankenship's "Fiddles in the Cumberland,"and "When Yesterday was Today."

21. Ibid.

22. Ibid, July 21, 1861.

23. J. G. Carrigan, p 24.

24. Thomas Head, "Campaigns and Battles of the Sixteenth Regiment, Tennessee Volunteers," Cumberland Presbyterian Publishing House, Nashville, 1885, p 197. The book was reissued by Walter Womack of McMinnville in 1961.

25. Robert Gates, 6th Tennessee Regiment C. S. A. in "The Civil War, Tennessee, Roll of Honor," commonly known as *Lindsley's*

Military Annals of Tennessee, J.M. Lindsley & Co., Nashville 1886, p 205. This book represents an attempt on the part of the editor, Dr. J. Berrien Lindsley, to submit "to the public a splendid tribute to the fame and memory of the Confederate soldiery of Tennessee." Lindsley appealed to many veterans for assistance in collecting the material and from many received outstanding cooperation, but from some almost nothing. Therefore, as an overall and consistent history of Tennessee Confederate military units the book is sometimes sketchy. The book was proposed as the first of three to cover the history of Tennessee troops in the Confederate army. A recent duplication of the book has been issued by Charles Elder and Son, Nashville.

26. Memoirs of John Johnson , p 77.
27. Roberts Gates, 6th Tn. Inf. in *Lindsley's Military Annals,* pp 207-8
28. J. R. Thompson's Diary. Entry taken from the original, but its location and the name of its owner have been lost.
29. W. J. McMurray, 10th Tn. Inf. in *Lindsley's Military Annals,* p 386.
30. *Fayetteville Observer,* May 30, 1861.
31. Ibid.
32. Ibid.
33. W.J. McMurray, "The History of the Twentieth Tennessee Volunteer Infantry C. S. A.," the Publishing Committee, Nashville, 1904, pp 116-117. This book has been reissued by Elder Book Shop, Nashville. Following the Civil War McMurray became a prominent physician in Nashville, Tn.
34. H. T. Childs, "Turney's First Tennessee Regiment," article in CVM, April 1917, p 165.
35. Amanda McDowell's Diary, June 9-15, 1861.
36. R. R. Hancock, "Hancock's Diary," or "A History of the Second Tennessee Cavalry, C. S. A.," Brandon Printing Co. Nashville 1887, p 18. Hancock was a sergeant in the 2nd Tennessee Cavalry. The book represents personal reminiscences combined with notes and diaries of regiment members. According to Hugh Walker of the Nashville Tennessean this book is among the "finest" of Middle Tennessee regimental histories.
37. J. G. Carrington, p 30.
38. W. J. McMurray, "Twentieth Tennessee," p 117.
39. J. G. Carrigan, p 24.
40. J. R. Thompson's Diary.
41. This quote is taken from the diary of Sally Ives which is in the State Library in Nashville. It appears, however, that the particular

passage describing the movement of the 1st Tennessee Regiment was written by a young lady identified only as "Mary."

42. Jim Womack's Diary, July 22, 1861.
43. W.J. McMurray, "Twentieth Tennessee," p 189.
44. Marcus Toney, p 16.
45. J. R. Thompson's Diary.
46. J. G. Carrington, p 30.
47. J. R. Thompson's Diary.
48. Jim Womack's Diary, Sept.4, 1861.
49. Thomas Head, p 30; "Lindsley's Military Annals," p 228.
50. J. G. Carrington, p 43.
51. Ibid, p 40.
52. Ibid, pp 81-2.
53. Resinor Etter's Diary, Sept. 29, 1861. Etter was a member of the 16th Tennessee Regiment C. S. A. The original is in the possession of the Stokley Etter family, Viola, Tn.
54. Ibid, Sept. 29 and 30, 1861.
55. David Phillips' Diary, Oct. 26, 1861. The diary is included in the Phillips Family History written by the Hon. Harry Phillips and published by the Lebanon, (Tennessee,) Democrat in 1935. David Phillips was a member of the 7th Tennessee Regiment C. S. A.
56. Oliver P. Temple, "East Tennessee and the Civil War," The Robert Clarke Co., Cincinnati, 1889, p 130. A reprint of the book was issued in 1972 by Burmar Books, Blountville, Tn. Although a slaveholder, when the choice came between the ownership of slaves and the dissolution of the Union, Temple became an ardent Unionist.
57. Scott and Angel, p 56; Thomas B. Alexander, "Political Reconstruction in Tennessee," Vanderbilt Uni. Press, Nashville 1950, Ch. I; W. R. Carter, "History of the First Regiment of Tennessee Volunteer Cavalry [USA]," Gaunt-Ogden Co., Knoxville 1902. This book was later issued by Crowe and Marion of Kingsport and Blountville in 1984.
58. Ibid, p 56.
59. Quoted in Scott and Angel, p 64.
60. Oliver P. Temple, p 385.
61 William Rule, "The Loyalists of Tennessee," H. C. Sherick Co., Cincinnati 1887, p 10. This material appeared originally as a paper read before the Ohio Commandry of the Military Order on April 6, 1887.
62. Governor Isham G. Harris to Jefferson Davis quoted in Temple, p 390
63. Confederate Secretary of War Judah P. Benjamin to Colonel W. B. Wood, Confederate Commander at Knoxville. Quoted in Temple, p 391.

64. Scott and Angel, pp 92-3; Thomas William Humes, "The Loyal Mountaineers," Ogden Brothers & Co. Knoxville 1888, Chapters IX and X; Carter, p 16.

65. Colonel D. Ledbetter C. S. A. to Secretary of War Benjamin on Nov. 30, 1861. Quoted in Temple, p 393.

66. Ibid.

II
It was here we began to understand the seriousness of war

1. Private Burton Warfield to Anna Worley, Jan. 22, 1862, from a camp near Oakland, Kentucky. Private Warfield was later promoted to lieutenant after his regiment was consolidated into the 6th Tennessee Cavalry C. S. A. The Warfield letters contained in this book are taken from transcriptions made by Graham Vick Brown on June 8, 1949. Mr. Brown states, "I saw the original letters at Alma, Arkansas, July 1934." At the time of the Civil War the Warfield family lived at Columbia, Tennessee, where the father of Burton ran the first furniture shop in the town.

2. St. John Liddell, "Liddell's Record," edited by Nathaniel C. Hughes, Morningside Press, Dayton, 1985, p 41. Liddell was a planter from Mississippi and Louisiana who served as a courier for General A.S. Johnston during the early months of the war. He was murdered following the close of the war.

3. Ibid.

4. Raymond E. Myers, "The Zollie Tree," The Filson Club Press, Louisville 1964, pp 24-5. This book depicts a thorough study of Zollicoffer and his family.

5. Ibid p 51.

6. Historians disagree on Zollicoffer's competency as displayed in the Mill Springs campaign. Stanley Horn in "The Army of Tennessee" is highly critical of his movements, while Thomas Lawrence Connelly, author of "The Army of The Heartland," is more sympathetic.

7. W. J. McMurray, "History of the Twentieth Tennessee Regiment Volunteer Infantry [C.S.A.]," The Publishing Committee, Nashville 1904, p 193. The book has been subsequently reissued by Elder Bookshop of Nashville.

8. Memoirs of Spencer Talley, Lt. Co. F, 28th Tennessee Infantry C.S.A. Following the Civil War Talley became a school teacher in Wilson County. Copy of memoirs furnished by Mrs. Sam Bone, Lebanon, Tennessee, grand-daughter of Talley.

554

9. R. R. Hancock, p 126; L. Virginia French's Diary, Jan. 26, 1862.

10. Ibid.

11. Spencer Talley's Memoirs.

12. A. S. Marks, Capt of Co. E, 17th Tennessee Regiment C.S.A. in "Lindsley's Military Annals," p 350.

13. W. J. Worsham, "The Old Nineteenth Tennessee C.S.A.," Press of Paragon Printing Co., Knoxville 1902. The book has been reissued by Tony Marion of Blountville (1973). Worsham was chief musician of his regiment.

14. R. M. Kelly, Colonel U.S. Volunteers, in "Battles and Leaders of the Civil War," Vol. 1, p 390, The Century Co., New York 1884.

15. W. J. Worsham, p 27.

16. Bromfield Ridley, "Battles and Sketches of the Army of Tennessee," Missouri Printing & Publishing Co., Mexico, Missouri, 1906, p 41. This book was reissued by Morningside Press, Dayton, Ohio, in 1978. Ridley was a native of Rutherford County who was too young to join the army at the war's opening. He later volunteered and young Ridley's father was one of Tennessee's most prominent politicians.

17. W. J. McMurray, p 202; Worsham pp 29-30.

18. A. S. Marks, 17th Tennessee Infantry, in "Lindsley's Military Annals," p 350.

19. Edward A. Pollard, "The Lost Cause," E.B. Treat & Co., New York 1866, p 201.

20. Burton Warfield to "Anna," Jan. 22, 1862, from Oakland, Ky.

21. Gen. Lew Wallace "Battles and Leaders," Vol. I, p 399.

22. Capt. Jesse Taylor, Weller's Light Artillery, in "Battles and Leaders," Vol. 1, p 369. Captain Taylor was a native of Lexington, Tennessee. His father had been with Andrew Jackson at New Orleans and he himself had graduated from the Naval Academy at Annapolis with honors. It was reported that Admiral Farragut thought so much of the young officer that he offered him duty outside American waters so that he might escape the necessity of fighting against his own people. Taylor refused and with his two brothers joined the Confederate Army. He died during his 71st year near Nashville in 1903.

23. Ibid.

24. Ibid, p 363.

25. Official Records of the War of the Rebellion, Series I, Vol. VII, pp 140-1, Hereinafter referred to as OR.

26. Jesse Taylor, "Battles and Leaders," Vol. I, p 371.

27. Ibid, p 372.

28. Ulysses S. Grant in OR, Series I, Vol. VII, p 125
29. Gen. Lew Wallace in "Battles and Leaders," Vol. I, p 398.
30. Ibid, p 401.
31. The Journal of Reuben Ross, published in CVM Nov. 1896, pp 393-7, entries not dated. Captain Ross was the son of James Ross who later wrote a book detailing the life and times of his own father, also named Reuben. The family played a prominent role in the religious life of the area around Clarksville, Tennessee. James Ross' book was entitled "Elder Reuben Ross," and in it, on page 265, the younger Ross is mentioned in regard to his appointment to West Point. In The Confederate Veteran Magazine article it is stated that the Civil War soldier was promoted to brigadier general. Captain Ross had a brother who was also a captain in the Confederate Army and is the subject of an article in Vol. 20 (1912), p 176 of The Confederate Veteran Magazine. In the book "Courageous Caroline" by Josephine M. Turner of Louisville, Ky. it is stated on page 59, that Captain Ross is buried in the Meriville Cemetery in south central Kentucky.
32. Ibid.
33. James D. Porter, "Confederate Military History," Vol.III (Tennessee) p 21. The series of books were edited by General Clement A. Evans who was, at the time, a member of the Methodist Episcopal Ministry.
34. J. P. McGuire, 32nd Tennessee Regiment C.S.A., in "Lindsley's Military Annals," p 471.
35. Thomas A. Turner, 42nd, Tennessee Regiment C.S.A. in "Lindsley's Military Annals," p 516.
36. Journal of Reuben Ross.
37. Ibid.
38. Ibid.
39. Ibid.
40. Adm. Henry Walke, U.S. Navy, quoted in CVM, Nov. 1896, p 398.
41. Journal of Reuben Ross.
42. M. L. Vesey in CVM, Oct. 1929, p 370.
43. Major William Brown, 20th Mississippi Infantry C.S.A. in OR, Series I, Vol. VII, pp 381-2.
44. J. J. Montgomery in CVM, Jan. 1899, p 11.
45. Lt. Col. D. C. Kelly, quoted in a footnote in the "Life of Nathan Bedford Forrest," by John Allan Wyeth, p 50. This book was reissued in 1975, by Morningside Press of Dayton, Ohio.
46. U. S. Grant, "Personal Memoirs," Vol. I, Charles L. Webster & Co., New York 1885, p 311.

47. Gen. Lew Wallace in "Battles and Leaders," Vol. I, p 428. For further reading on Buckner see Albert Feldman, "The Strange Case of Simon Bolivar Buckner," Civil War History, Uni. of Iowa, June 1959, pp 199-204.
48. Simon Bolivar Buckner in CVM, July 1913, p 357; W.E. Woodward, "Meet General Grant," Horace Liveright Inc., U.S., 1928, p 121.
49. CVM, Nov. 1896, p 398.
50. Ibid.

III
The situation did look gloomy

1. William G. Stevenson, "Thirteen Months in the Rebel Army," Sampson, Low, Son & Co., London 1862, p 86. Stevenson was a native of New York who, at the outbreak of the war, was in business in Arkansas. Finding himself faced with possible imprisonment if he did not join the Confederate Army, he reluctantly enlisted in the 2nd Tennessee volunteer Infantry. Following the Battle of Shiloh he left the Confederate Army and made his way north. According to his publishers Stevenson's motive in writing "Thirteen Months in the Rebel Army" was to alert Northerners as to the total dedication of Southerners toward the war.
2. John Miller McKee, "The Great Panic," Elder-Sherbourne, Nashville, 1977, p 8. This book was originally published as a pamphlet in 1862, and was described as depicting "Incidents Connected With Two Weeks Of The War In Tennessee."
3. Ibid, p 9.
4. John M. Taylor, 27th Tennessee Infantry C.S.A. in "Lindsley's Military Annals," p 417.
5. McKee, p 14.
6. John Allan Wyeth, "Forrest," p 73.
7. Gen. John Floyd in OR Series I, Vol. VII, p 428.
8. Wyeth, "Forrest," p 73.
9. Stanley F. Horn, "The Army of Tennessee," Uni. of Oklahoma Press, Norman, 1941, p 99. Horn was for many years the Dean of Tennessee Civil War Historians. His "Army of Tennessee" is considered a classic in the field.
10. Major Charles W. Anderson in The Confederate Veteran Magazine, Sept. 1896, p 289. Major Anderson was a native of Rutherford County who served on the staff of Nathan Bedford Forrest.

According to his private papers Anderson wrote most of Forrest's official communications including his farewell address to the soldiers at Selma, Alabama.

11. Telegram to Quarter-Master Charles Anderson from Gen. Albert Sidney Johnston quoted in CVM Sept., 1896, p 289.

12. Major Charles Anderson, CVM Sept., 1896, p 289.

13. Ibid.

14. Mrs. Ben Hardin Helm in CVM, Sept., 1896, p 290. Mrs Helm was a half-sister to Mrs. Abraham Lincoln. Mrs. Helm's husband, a colonel in the famous Kentucky "Orphan Brigade," was killed at the Battle of Chickamauga whereupon she went to Washington and resided with the Lincolns for several weeks.

15. Maj. Charles Anderson, CVM, Sept. 1896, p 289.

16. Capt. Napoleon Monroe Bearden, 8th Tennessee Regiment C.S.A. to his parents in Lincoln County, Tennessee, March, 1862. The original is in the possession of Mrs. Margaret Sullivan, Fayetteville, Tennessee. The letter was written in South Carolina as the 8th was making its way toward Corinth, Mississippi.

17. Colonel Robert Hatton, 7th Tennessee Regiment C.S.A. to his wife from Winchester, Virginia, Feb. 21, 1862. This letter along with others quoted in this book are found in "The Life of Robert Hatton," by J. V. Drake, published by the author in Lebanon, Tennessee in 1867, p 409.

18. Robert Hatton to his wife, Feb. 21, 1862, Drake, p 409.

19. Robert Hatton to his wife, Feb. 21, 1862, Drake, p 408.

20. Robert Hatton to his wife, Feb. 12, 1862, Drake, p 407.

21. Capt. D.C. Spurlock 16th Tennessee Regiment C.S.A. to his sister Florence , Feb. 25th, 1862. Original in possession of Mrs. Chatham Ross, McMinnville, Tn. The letter was written from Pocataligo, South Carolina.

22. McMurray, pp 124-5.

23. Worsham, p 32.

24. Stevenson, p 88.

25. John Taylor, 27th Tennessee Regiment C.S.A. in "Lindsley's Military Annals," p 418.

26. Private John Gumm, 23rd Tennessee Regiment C.S.A. to his wife March 15th, 1862, from Huntsville, Alabama. The original in possession of Ms. Maggie Lowe, Kittrell, Tn.

27. Stevenson, p 89.

28. Ibid.

29. Diary of Thomas Fuller, regiment unknown. Typewritten copy in possession of author.

30. Ibid.

31. Memoirs of I. Nelson Rainey.

32. Ibid.

33. Francis Shoup in CVM, May 1894, p 137. General Shoup was a native of Indiana, but was in Florida at the outbreak of the war. He had graduated from West Point in 1855. Following the war Shoup taught mathmatics at the University of Mississippi and at the University of the South at Sewanee, Tn. He later accepted the directorship of the Columbia, Tennessee Institute for Young Ladies. (Ezra J. Warner, "Generals in Gray," L.S.U. Press, Baton Rouge, 1959).

34. William Preston Johnston in The Century Magazine, Feb., 1885, p 620. William Preston was the son of General Albert Sidney Johnston.

IV
They call it Shiloah

1. Sam Watkins, "Company Aytch," McCowat-Mercer Press, Jackson 1952, p 63. "Company Aytch" must be considered a Civil War classic. Its contents originally appeared as a series of newspaper articles in The Columbia Herald some twenty years following the war. Watkins was a member of the Maury Grays, Maney's 1st Tennessee Regiment. He died at the age of 62 and is buried at the Old Zion Church near Columbia, Tn.

2. Basil W. Duke, "A History of Morgan's Cavalry," Miami Printing and Publishing Co. Cincinnati, 1867, p 138. Duke was a brother-in-law to Morgan and rode in his command through much of the war. The book was reissued by Indiana University Press in 1960.

3. Diary of W. W. Wilson, April 3, 1862. Owner of the original unknown, typewritten copy in possession of author. There are two "W.W. Wilsons" listed in "Tennesseans in The Civil War," Part 2, and since only one of these was an infantryman it is assumed the diary belonged to him. If so he was a member of the 40th Tennessee Infantry C.S.A.

4. Diary of John Gumm, 23rd Tennessee Regiment C.S.A. April 3, 1862. Original in possession of Ms. Mary Hall, Murfreesboro, Tn.

5. Ibid, April 4, 1862.

6. Diary of W. W. Wilson, April 4, 1862.

7. Stevenson, p 104.

8. Ibid.

9. Ibid, p 105.
10. "Battles and Leaders," Vol. I, p 558.
11. Diary of W.W. Wilson, April 5, 1862.
12. John M. Taylor in "Lindsley's Military Annals," p 419.
13. Mrs. W. H. Cherry in CVM, Jan., 1893, p 44. The Cherry residence
    on the east bank of the Tennessee River at Savannah, Tn., played a
    prominent role in the events that transpired during the Civil War.
    The house was built in 1830, by slave labor and was presented by
    James Robinson to his daughter as a wedding present. In addition
    to serving as Grant's headquarters, two Federal generals, C.F. Smith
    and W.H. L. Wallace, died there after receiving wounds at Shiloh.
    The residence is at present (1985) owned by Mr. and Mrs. Robert B.
    Guinn, Jr.
14. Capt. W. S. Hillyer in a letter to his wife dated April 11, 1862.
    Published in CVM, Oct. 1893, p 298.
15. Robert Gates in "Lindsley's Military Annals," pp 210-11.
16. William Preston Johnston in The Century Magazine, Vol. 29, p 626.
17. Ibid.
18. J. A. Cochran, Culleoka, Tn., Lt. Co. "F" 6th Cav. C.S.A. in CVM
    Feb., 1898, p 66.
19. Official Report of Col. B.J. Hill, 5th Tennessee Regiment C.S.A. in
    OR, Series I, Vol. X, p 589.
20. Sam Watkins, p 64.
21. OR, Series I, Vol. X, Part I, p 469.
22. John M. Taylor in "Lindsley's Military Annals," p 420.
23. Ibid, p 418.
24. W. J. McMurray, p 209.
25. R. R. Hancock, p 195.
26. Diary of W. W. Wilson, April 7, 1862.
27. Ibid.
28. John Gumm's Diary, April 6, 1862.
29. W. S. Hillyer, CVM, Oct. 1893, p 299.
30. Ibid.
31. Ulysses S. Grant, "Memoirs," Vol. I, p 349; The Century
    Magazine, Vol. 29, p 603.
32. Wyeth, "Forrest," p 79.
33. Ibid.
34. Worsham, p 43.
35. Maj. John R. Chamberlain, 81st Ohio Regiment, in CVM, June
    1905, p 254. The article is entitled "The Burial of Joel Allen Battle
    of Tennessee." The featured article, of which Chamberlain's
    contribution is a part, was written by Gen. G.P. Thruston, U.S.A.

Following the Civil War Thruston married a Nashville girl and made the city his home. According to the "Veteran", the former Federal general became a defender of the rights of former Confederate soldiers "during the troubles and disorders of the reconstruction . . .

Thruston was also a classmate of Allen Battle at Miami University. He wrote, "I remember him as if he were before me now — a handsome young southern student, refined, with intellectual face, graceful and cordial in manner...

"In March, 1862, my regiment, the 1st Ohio Infantry, was encamped south of Nashville, and I had charge of the picket line on the Franklin Pike near the Overton residence. One day a physician of the neighborhood came to the picket post on the pike seeking to pass the lines. He proved to be Dr. W.C. Blackman . . . I at once asked him if he knew Joel Allen Battle. "Know him?" he replied; "he is my kinsman." Dr. Blackman insisted later that I go to his house and meet and dine with Allen's wife and sisters. His invitation was so hearty that I consented . . . There I met Allen's family and friends. Far apart as we were in other ways, we all loved Allen, and I was received by them with kind, cordial consideration...

As I rose to leave the party, I remarked to the young ladies, that when we got down there [Shiloh] and captured Col. Battle and Allen, I would see that they received the kindest treatment. "I assure you sir," said one of the sisters with a smile, "that they will have no occasion to accept your kindness. It will be more than you can do to take care of your own scalp," and thus we parted.

36. Ibid.
37. John Gumm's Diary at Corinth, Mississippi, April 8, 1862.
38. Ibid.
39. Ibid.
40. W. W.Wilson's Diary, April 9 and April 14, 1862.
41. Ibid.
42. Captain Monroe Bearden to his parents, March, 1862.
43. Resinor Etter's Diary, Dec. 22, 1861.
44. Ibid, Mar. 12, 1862.
45. Jim Womack's Diary, Mar.9, 1862.
46. Ibid.
47. Resinor Etter's Diary, April 15, 1862.
48. Ibid, April 5, 1862.
49. Ibid, April 16, 1862.
50. Burton Warfield to Anna Worley, Feb. 2, 1862, from Kentucky.
51. Monroe Bearden to his parents, March, 1862.
52. Sam Watkins, p 69.

53. Thomas Head, p 196.
54. Ibid.
55. Resinor Etter's Diary, May 8, 1862.
56. W. J. McMurray, pp 214-15.
57. W. W. Wilson's Diary, May 12, 1862.
58. Edwin H. Reynolds, "A History of the Henry County Commands," originally published by Sun Publishing Co., Jacksonville, Florida, 1904. Reissued by Centennial Book Co., Kennesaw, Georgia, 1961, pp 39-40.
59. Ibid, p 43.
60. Stevenson, p 128.
61. Jim Womack's Diary, May 14, 1862.
62. John Gumm's Diary, May, 1862.
63. Ibid, May 30, 1862.
64. Resinor Etter's Diary, June 16, 1862.
65. Ibid, June 4, 1862.

V

Virginia Interlude
We go to attack the enemy

1. David Phillips' Diary, Nov. 16, 1861. According to Harry Phillips, "David returned to Wilson County broken in body. The long marches, the brutal exposure, the slow starvation, particularly during his imprisonment at Fort Deleware, had wrecked the physique once strong and stalwart.
   ... Probably his poor health was responsible for his never marrying. After the war he went back to his old profession of school teaching. He sought vainly to regain his lost health, but the ravages of war were too great. The white plague took root in the body that had marched courageously under the Stars and Bars, and on May 18, 1869, the loyal brave heart was stilled. David is buried in the Phillips Cemetery near Watertown."
2. Ibid, Nov. 20, 1861.
3. Ibid, Dec. 25, 1861.
4. Ibid, Dec. 31, 1861.
5. John Williams' Diary, 7th Tennessee Regiment C.S.A. Original in possession of Mrs. Dorothy White, Murfreesboro, Tn. Loaned to the author by Mrs. Gutha Williams of Murfreesboro. According to family legend John Williams found the diary he kept on the body of a dead federal soldier. When Williams decided to continue the diary

as his own he paid little or no attention to the dates printed on its pages, therefore it is impossible to identify the exact dates of his entries.

6. Ibid.
7. David Phillips' Diary, Feb. 26, 1862.
8. Ibid, March 2, 1862.
9. Ibid.
10. Letters of General Robert Hatton to his wife and parents published in Drake's "The Life of General Robert Hatton," p 363. This particular letter was written July 9, 1861.
11. Ibid, p 413, letter written Mar. 18, 1862.
12. Ibid, p 418, letter written May 28, 1862.
13. Ibid.
14. John Williams' Diary.
15. David Phillips' Diary, May 31, 1862.
16. John Williams' Diary.
17. Ibid — A statue of Robert Hatton stands on the public square in Lebanon, Tennessee.

VI
I must demand an unconditional surrender

1. Grant, "Personal Memoirs," Vol. I, p 368.
2. Charles Anderson Papers, a collection of letters and reminiscences of Anderson who was on the staff of Gen. Nathan Bedford Forrest. His home was in Rutherford County, Tn. The original papers are in the possession of the Ewing family of Murfreesboro, Tn.
3. L. Virginia French's Diary, June 15, 1862, original in TSL, Nashville. For further reading on Mrs. French see Virginia Lewis Peck, "Life and works of L. Virginia French," Ph.D. Dissertation, Vanderbilt University, 1939; Herschel Gower, "Beersheba Springs and L. Virginia French: The Novelist as Historian," Tn. Hist. Quarterly, Summer 1983, pp 115-137.
4. Sterling Spurlock Brown, "The History of Cannon County, Tennessee," Doak Printing Co., Manchester, Tn. 1936, p 120.
5. Thomas Jordan and J.P. Pryor, "The Campaigns of Lieut. Gen. Forrest," Blelock & Co., New York, 1868, p 163. This book was reissued by Morningside Press, Dayton, Ohio, in 1973.
6. John Allan Wyeth, "Forrest," p 51.
7. Bromfield Ridley, p 107.
8. Carlton C. Sims, "History of Rutherford County," published by author, 1947, p 93.

9. Ibid.
10. Jordan and Pryor, p 166.
11. Statement of William Richardson in Wyeth (Forrest) pp 91-2.
12. Diary of Salley Ives, Tennessee State Library, Nashville.
13. L. Virginia French gives a vivid picture of the captured Federal troops as they entered McMinnville on July 14th. French Diary July 14th, 1862.

VII
When they fout, I fit

1. Sam Watkins, p 70.
2. "B" Reaves to Anna Worley June 18, 1862, from Charlotte, Tn. Letter a part of the Burton Warfield Papers.
3. Diary of John Gumm, June, 1862.
4. Diary of Wiley Noblett, April 7, 1862. Noblett was a member of the 44th Tennessee Regiment C.S.A. His home was in Lincoln County, Tennessee. The diary covers a period of time from March 20th, 1862, until November 11, the same year. A typewritten copy was furnished by Mr. J. D. Walters of Antioch, Tn.
5. Ibid, May 18, 1862.
6. Ibid, June 2, 1862, at Baldwin, Mississippi.
7. Sam Watkins, pp 70-1.
8. Wiley Noblett's Diary, June 11, 1862.
9. Resinor Etter's Diary, July 22, 1862.
10. Ibid, July 24, 1862.
11. Memoirs of Spencer Talley.
12. Wiley Noblett's Diary, July 29, 1862, at Montgomery, Ala.
13. John Gumm's Diary.
14. Ibid.
15. W. W. Wilson's Diary.
16. Wiley Noblett's Diary, Aug. 21, 1862.
17. Ibid.
18. Because of her prominence in the literary field Mrs. French became acquainted with several Confederate leaders. Among them, besides Morgan, were General Nathan Bedford Forrest and General Joseph Wheeler.
19. L. Virginia French's Diary, Mar. 22, 1863; Walter Durham, "Rebellion Revisited," Sumner County Historical Society, 1982, pp 80-92; Dee Alexander Brown, "The Bold Cavaliers," J.P. Lippincott Co., New York, 1959, pp 104-108.

20. Resinor Etter's diary. Aug. 22, 1862.
21. Ibid, Aug. 27, 1862.
22. Thomas Head, pp 198-9.
23. Resinor Etter's diary, Sept. 4, 1862.
24. Ibid.
25. Marcus Toney, p 40.
26. Ibid.
27. Jim Womack's Diary, Sept. 20, 1862.
28. Sam Watkins, p 80.
29. Quoted in SHSP, Vol. 7, p 172.
30. Wiley Noblett's Diary, Sept. 16, 1862.
31. Simon Bolivar Buckner in CVM, Feb., 1909, p 85; B.A. Botkin, "A
    Civil War Treasury of Tales, Legends and Folklore," Promontory
    Press, New York, 1960, pp 85-6.
32. Ibid.
33. Wiley Noblett's Diary, Sept.17, 1862.
34. Ibid, Oct. 7, 1862.
35. Ibid, Oct. 8, 1862.
36. Interview with Stokley Etter, son of Resinor Etter in about 1960.
37. Jim Womack's Diary, Oct. 8, 1862.
38. Ibid.
39. C. W. Frazer, 5th Confederate Regiment, in "Lindsley's Military
    Annals," p 148.
40. Ibid.
41. Ibid.
42. Ibid.
43. Memoirs of Thomas H. Malone, Baird-Ward Publishing Co.,
    Nashville, 1928, p 133. Following the Civil War Malone became
    a very prominent member of the Bar in Nashville serving at one
    time as the Dean of the Vanderbilt University Law School. He died
    at the age of 73, on Sept. 15, 1906.
44. Ibid.
45. Ibid, p 135; CVM, Dec., 1922, p 468.
46. Marcus Toney, pp 46-7; CVM, Aug., 1926, p 290.
47. Ibid, pp 44-5.
48. Thomas Malone, pp 138-40.
49. A. J. Vaughn, "Personal Record of the Thirteenth Regiment,
    Tennessee Infantry, C.S.A." S.C. Toof & Co., Memphis, 1897, p
    23. This book has been reissued by the Mayers' and Burke Book
    Store, Memphis.
50. Sam Watkins, p 87.
51. Robert Gates in "Lindsley's Military Annals," p 214.

52. Ibid.
53. Marcus Wright's Diary, Tennessee State Library, Nashville, Tn.
54. Diary of Wiley Noblett, Oct. 9 to Oct. 28, 1862.
55. Memoirs of Carroll Clark, 16th Tennessee Regiment. Original in possession of the Charles M. Clark family, McMinnville, Tn.
56. Ibid.
57. Col. David Urquhart, C.S.A. in "Battles and Leaders," Vol. III, p 603. Urquhart was a member of Bragg's Staff; for further reading see Grady McWhiney, "Controversy in Ky: Braxton Bragg's Campaign of 1862, Civil War History, Uni. of Iowa.

VIII
What a scene of confusion, of bloodshed, of war

1. Memoirs of Spencer Talley.
2. Basil Duke, p 320.
3. Ibid, p 309.
4. Henry L. Stone, 9th Kentucky Cavalry C.S.A., in The Confederate Veteran, April, 1906, p 188. Stone, at the time the article was written was General Counsel of the Louisville and Nashville Railroad.
5. Jim Womack's Diary, Dec. 13, 1862.
6. Ibid.
7. Spencer Talley's Memoirs.
8. Government literature on the Battle of Stone's River omits the apostrophe in the word "Stone's." It can be assumed that some copy clerk long ago made a mistake in transcribing documents and that the government believed it better to perpetuate a mistake than to correct it.
9. W. D. Pickett, Assistant Inspector General to Gen. William J. Hardee C.S.A., in The Confederate Veteran, Sept., 1908, p 450.
10. Ibid.
11. W. J. McMurray, p 226.
12. Monroe Bearden to his parents, Mar., 1862, from South Carolina.
13. Jim Womack's Diary, Dec. 28, 1862.
14. W. J. Worsham, p 69.
15. John G. Parkhurst, "Recollections of Stone's River" War Paper No. 15, Michigan Commandry, Winn & Hammond, Printers and Binders, Detroit, 1890, p 6-7.
16. Ibid.
17. J. T. Tunnell, 1st Lieut. Co. "B" 14th Texas C.S.A., in The Confederate Veteran, Nov., 1908, p 574.

18. Memoirs of Thomas Malone, p 149.
19. Ibid.
20. A. J. Vaughn, "Thirteenth Regiment Tenn. Infantry," C.S.A., privately published, 1897, pp 24-5. Vaughn was the Colonel of the 13th.
21. A. F. Stevenson, "The Battle of Stone's River," James R. Osgood & Co., Boston, 1884, p 65. This book was reissued in 1974 by the Civil War Times Illustrated, Gettysburg; for further information on the Battle of Stone's River see Stanley Horn, "The Army of Tennessee," Ch. XI and James Lee McDonough, "Stones River," Uni. of Tenn. Press, Knoxville, 1980.
22. Memoirs of Thomas Malone, p 149.
23. Jim Womack's diary, Dec. 31, 1862.
24. Stanley Horn, "Army of Tennessee," p 203; Head, p 107; Confederate Military History, Vol. VIII, p 68. There are slight differences recorded in these separate accounts.
25. W. J. McMurray, p 234.
26. Memoirs of Spencer Talley.
27. Sam Watkins, p 93.
28. W. J. McMurray, p 236.
29. Memoirs of Spencer Talley.
30. Letter written by the mother of Bromfield Ridley quoted in The Confederate Veteran, Feb., 1903, p 67.
31. Gervis Grainger, "Four Years With The Boys in Gray," printed at the Favorite Office, Franklin, Ky., 1902, pp 13-4. Reissued by Morningside Press, Dayton, Ohio 1972.
32. A. F. Stevenson, p 132.
33. W. J. McMurray, p 239.
34. Ibid.
35. A. F. Stevenson, p 138.
36. Memoirs of Spencer Talley.
37. W. J, McMurray, p 238.
38. L. D. Young, Lt. in Kentucky [Orphan] Brigade C.S.A., "Reminiscences of a Soldier of the Orphan Brigade," published privately, Paris, Ky., (no date), pp 49-50; For an account played by the Orphan Brigade in this action see Ed Porter Thompson, "History of The Orphan Brigade," Morningside Press, reissued in 1973, Dayton, Ohio, pp 177-203.
39. Memoirs of Spencer Talley.
40. Mrs. L. D. Whitson, "Gilbert St. Maurice," Tavel, Eastmen and Howell, Nashville, 1874, pp 115-17.

41. Bearden Papers, a collection of letters along with a journal or diary kept by Monroe Bearden's father. The little black book had formerly served as a farm record book, but upon the father hearing of his son's being wounded at Stone's River it became a day by day record of the subsequent events which transpired. This particular entry was made within a few days of the battle. Originals in possession of Mrs. Margaret Sullivan, Fayetteville, Tn.
42. Ibid, Jan. 20, 1863.
43. Ibid, Jan.21, 1863.
44. Ibid, Jan. 22, 1863.
45. Monroe Bearden to parents Mar., 1862, from South Carolina.
46. Bearden Papers, father's diary, Mar. 12, 1863.

IX
The women sit in the hall and chew tobacco

1. Frank Moore, "The Civil War in Song and Story," P.F. Collier, New York, 1882, p 220.
2. Ibid.
3. Joseph G. Vale, "Minty and the Cavalry," E. K. Meyers Printers, Harrisburg, 1886, p 17.
4. W. D. Bickham, "Rosecrans Campaigns," Keys and Co. Cincinnati, 1863, p 50.
5. Ibid, p 114.
6. Ibid.
7. An Officer, "Annals of the Army of the Cumberland," J. P. Lippincott & Co., Philadelphia, 1863, p 606.
8. Ibid.
9. Ibid, pp 607-8.
10. Ibid, p 606. When Andrew Johnson became Military Governor of Tennessee he had Mayor Cheatham and the entire City Council of Nashville ousted for being unwilling to take the Oath of Allegiance to the Federal Government. Cheatham and other public officials who refused to take the oath were subsequently arrested and imprisoned. But, according to Thomas B. Alexander in "Political Reconstruction in Tennessee," in those parts of "Tennessee controlled by the Confederate Government, prominent Unionists were receiving similar treatment."
11. Ibid, p 603-4. In 1868, Harding's daughter, Selene, married former Confederate General William Hicks "Red" Jackson, a noted cavalryman during the war.

12. <u>Report on the Conduct of the War</u>, Government Printing Office, Vol. III, p 348.
13. Ibid.
14. James A. Connolly, "Three Years in the Army of the Cumberland," Indiana Uni. Press, Bloomington, 1959, edited by Paul M. Angle, p 57. Connolly was a member of the 123rd Illinois Infantry U.S.A. Before the war he was a lawyer in Charleston, Ill. His birthplace was Newark, New Jersey. He was 21 years old when the war began.
15. Hans Christian Heg, "The Civil War Letters of Hans Christian Heg," Norwegian-American Historical Assn., Northfield, Minn. 1936, edited by Theodore C. Blegen, p 95. Hans Heg came to America when he was 11 years old. His family settled in what is now Wind Lake, Wisconsin. In 1861 he recruited a Scandinavian regiment, the 15th WisconsinVolunteer Infantry. He was killed at the Battle of Chickamauga on September 19, 1863. A handsome monument marks the place where Heg was killed. His home in Wisconsin has become a historical landmark. (The Milwaukee Journal, June 18, 1980.)
16. John Beatty, "Memoirs of a Volunteer," W.W. Norton & Co., New York, 1946, edited by Harvey S. Ford, p 96. Beatty was a member of the 3rd Ohio Volunteer Infantry. From the business of banking he entered the service as a private, but eventually rose to the rank of brigadier general. He was recognized for outstanding gallantry at Perryville, Ky. and Murfreesboro, Tn.
17. Ibid, p 9.
18. Hans Heg, p 182.
19. Scott and Angel, p 140.
20. Ibid, p 141.
21. Ibid.
22. Ibid, p 149.
23. Ibid.
24. Beatty, p 159.

X
The uncertain future opens out to us

1. This chapter is based primarily on the diary of Major Andrew Jackson Campbell of the 48th Tennessee Regiment C.S.A. A typewritten copy of this diary, edited by Ms. Gill Garrett of Columbia, Tenn., is in the Tennessee Room of the Middle Tennessee State University library. Major Campbell is buried in the Shaves Cemetery near Culleoka, Tennessee.

XI
God help us in our need

1. Fayette McDowell to Amanda McDowell, Jan. 9, 1863, from Tullahoma, Tenn.
2. Pvt. Lewis Peach's Diary, 8th Tenn. Regiment, C.S.A. published in CVM, Nov., 1915, p 520.
3. W. J. McMurray, pp 95,96.
4. A. A. Abernathy, 18th Tennessee Regiment C.S.A. to his grandmother, Oct. 16, 1861. Original in possession of Ms. Polly Dinges, Murfreesboro, Tn.
5. L. Virginia French Diary, Dec. 31, 1862.
6. Ibid.
7. Ibid, Jan. 4, 1863.
8. Ibid.
9. Memoirs of Spencer Talley.
10. Col. John Savage, "Life of John H. Savage," published by author, 1903, p 147. Savage was the colonel of the 16th Tennessee. He was known as "The Old Man of the Mountains" by the people of his area. Savage expressed contempt for Jefferson Davis, Braxton Bragg and many other Confederate leaders. He died on April 6, 1904, in his 89th year.
11. Marcus Toney, p 56.
12. "Three Deserters Shot at Shelbyville," author unknown, CVM, Mar., 1908, p 128.
13. Wyeth, "Forrest," p 151.
14. William Pittenger, "Capturing A Locomotive," The National Tribune, Washington, 1897. The book records the planning and execution of the Federal attempt to disrupt the railroad between Chattanooga and Atlanta during the summer of 1862.
15. Wyeth, "Forrest," p 218; CVM, "The Pursuit and Capture of Colonel Streight," by Capt. James Dinkins, Jan., 1928, pp 15-18.

    It was during the Streight surrender that one of the classic tales concerning Forrest's cunning came into being. Capt. Dinkins wrote in The Confederate Veteran:

    Meeting the flag [flag of truce] Colonel Streight asked to communicate with General Forrest, and they met in a woods, where a parley ensued. Streight, however, declined to capitulate unless it could be shown to his satisfaction that he was doing so to a force at least equal in number to his own . . . At this moment the section of Confederate artillery came in sight at a full gallop, remarking which, Colonel Streight urged that no more troops should be brought up nearer than three hundred yards. Forrest assented to the request, at the same time secretly instructed an aide-de-camp to keep the two pieces of artillery moving in a circle, so as to appear like several batteries coming up.

That was done so adroitly by Captain Ferrell that Colonel Streight inquired of Forrest how much artillery he had. "Enough," was the prompt answer, "to destroy your command in thirty minutes."

... It was still thought to be necessary to keep the enemy deceived in regard to the actual force that had captured them, and Captain Pointer asked Forrest what disposition should be made of some three or four imaginary bodies of troops. At the same time, General Forrest explained to his prisoners that as forage was very scarce at Rome, [Georgia], he would send only his Escort and one regiment to accompany them there . . . one thousand seven hundred and forty officers and men and a rifle gun battery stacked their arms... The Confederates in line at the surrender numbered less than five hundred officers and men.

16. J. T. Garretson letter to his family, original in possession of Ms. Annie Macon estate, Woodbury, Tn.

17. Henry Martyn Cist, "The Army of the Cumberland," C. Schribners' Sons, New York, 1882, p 586; Statement of Rush O'Dill, Spring Hill, Tn., 1947, copy in possession of author. An excellent biography of Van Dorn was written by Robert G. Hartje, Vanderbilt University Press, 1967. An account of the General's death is found on pp 317-27.

18. Ibid.

19. Memoirs of Nelson Rainey.

20. General Jackson was a native of Paris, Tn. He graduated from West Point in 1856. In later life he became the manager of Belle Meade Plantation at Nashville, Tn.

21. James Parrott, 28th Tennessee Regiment C.S.A. to his wife, June 15th, 1863, from Shelbyville, Tn. Original in possession of Ms. Alberta Buntley, Fayetteville, Tn.

22. Lee Edwards, 45th Tennessee Regiment C.S.A. to his sister Feb. 11th, 1863, from Tullahoma, Tn. Original in possession of the Christine Vaughn estate in Manchester, Tn.

23. Corporal William Tripp, Co. B, 44th Tennessee Regiment C.S.A. to his wife Martha on March 29th, 1863. The Tripp letters are in the possession of William C. Fanning, Lynchburg, Tn.

24. Ibid.

25. James Parrott to his wife, no date, from Shelbyville, Tn.

26. Ibid.

27. Lee Edwards to his mother Feb. 15, 1863, from Tullahoma.
28. Lee Edwards to his sister, Mar. 16, 1863, from Tullahoma.
29. T. M. Webb, 24th Infantry Battalion, C.S.A., to his family.
    Published in the Park City News, Sunday, Nov. 24, 1957.
30. Margaret Leech and Harry J. Brown, "The Garfield Orbit," Harper and
    Row, New York, 1978, pp 135-37.
31. William Tripp to Martha, April 30, 1863.
32. Ibid, May 20, 1863.
33. Ibid, May 30, 1863, from Fairfield, Tn.
34. Ibid, June 22, 1863.
35. J. B. Clark, Supt. of Hospital, location unknown, to Martha Tripp,
    June 24, 1865.

XII
The Confederate soldier was growing weary

1. Thomas Head, p 114.
2. John Allan Wyeth, "With Sabre & Scapel," Harper and Brothers, New
   York, 1914, p 218.
3. W. W. Heartsill, "Fourteen Hundred and 91 Days in the Confederate
   Army," McCowat-Mercer Press, Jackson, 1954, p 134. Heartsill
   was born in Louisville, Tennessee, near Knoxville. He later moved
   to Nashville and still later to Texas. He died at Waco, Texas on
   July 28, 1916.
4. Sam Watkins, p 105.
5. Ibid, p 108.
6. Resinor Etter's Diary, July 10, 1863.
7. Ibid, July 11, 1863.
8. George Guild, "The Fourth Tennessee Cavalry Regiment [C.S.A.],"
   published privately, 1913, pp 20-1.
9. W. R. Dyer's Diary, July 13, 1863. Dyer was a member of Forrest's
   Escort. The original diary is in the possession of Mrs. John Dyer,
   Eagleville, Tn.
10. William Rule, "The Loyalists of Tennessee," H.C. Sherick & Co.,
    Cincinnati, 1899, p 472.
11. Oliver P. Temple, p 472.
12. Ibid, p 476.
13. J. J. Blair's Diary, Aug. 27, 1863. Blair was a member of the 4th
    Tennessee Regiment C.S.A. He was a native of Louden, Tn. He
    died at the age of 29 from complications of a disease contracted at
    Vicksburg, Miss. The original diary is in the possession of Mrs.
    Cynthia Cummings. McMinnville, Tn.

14. Ibid, Aug. 31, 1863.
15. W. W. Heartsill, p 145.

XIII
Soldiers... You must seek the contest

1. Bromfield Ridley, pp 208-9.
2. Braxton Bragg's General Order, LaFayette, Ga. Sept. 16, 1863.
   Quoted in Ridley's Journal, pp 206-7.
3. Sam Watkins, p 114.
4. Marcus Toney, p 60.
5. Sam Watkins, pp 114-116.
6. A. J. Vaughn, p 30.
7. W. J. Worsham, pp 88-9.
8. Bromfield Ridley, p 221.
9. W. C. Brown, 93rd Regiment of Ohio Volunteer Infantry, in The
   Confederate Veteran, May, 1905, p 228.
10. Ibid.
11. J. P. McGuire, 32nd Tennessee Infantry C.S.A., in "Lindsley's
    Military Annals," p 475.
12. George Guild, p 26.
13. Bronfield Ridley, p 223.
14. OR, Series I, Vol. XXX, Part II, p 457.
15. W. J. McMurray, p 276.
16. Marcus Toney, p 61.
17. Diary of Captain James K. Polk Lytle, 23rd Tennessee Infantry
    C.S.A., Sept. 20, 1863. Lytle was a native of Rover, Tennessee,
    in Bedford County. Original in possession of Ms. Wanda Elmore
    and Ms. Ethel Elmore of Eagleville, Tennessee.
18. W. R. Carter, "History of the First Regiment of Tennessee Volunteer
    Cavalry [USA]," Gaut-Ogden Co., Knoxville, 1902, pp 96-7. This
    book was reissued by Dan Crowe and Tony Marion of Kingsport
    and Blountville, Tn., 1984.
19. Ibid, p 97.
20. Memoirs of Spencer Talley.
21. Diary of Captain James K. Polk Lytle, Sept. 20, 1863.
22. George Guild, p 31.
23. Sam Watkins, p 120.
24. Diary of Resinor Etter, Sept. 20, 1863.
25. H. H. Dillard, 16th Tennessee Regiment C.S.A., "Lindsley's Military
    Annals," p 343.

XIV
The very air smelt of battle

1. H. H. Dillard, 'Lindsley's Military Annals," p 342.
2. John Allan Wyeth, "Forrest," p 265.
3. Diary of W. R. Dyer, Oct. 13, 1863.
4. John Allan Wyeth, "With Sabre and Scapel," pp 265-66.
5. George Guild, p 37.
6. Ibid, p 39; John Allan Wyeth, "With Sabre and Scapel," pp 271-73; Calvin L. Collier, "The War Child's Children," published privately. 1965, pp 71-72.
7. Ibid, p 42.
8. Ibid.
9. J. L. Hudson, "Old Times in Bedford County," pamphlet published by Lions Club of Shelbyville, Tn., no date, p14.
10. Ibid.
11. George Guild, p 43.
12. OR, Series I, Vol. XXX, Part II, p 666.
13. Liddell, pp 133-34.
14. Most historians have assumed that the lack of charges against Forrest for his confrontation with Bragg indicated a recognition of talent on the part of the Confederate High Command. There can be little doubt that such an assumption is justified. But the recently published memoirs of St. John Liddell introduces another element into the situation. According to Liddell Bragg did not hold either Forrest or Wheeler in high regard as concerned their military leadership. Bragg is quoted as saying:
    I have not a single general officer of cavalry fit for command. Look at Forrest! I sent him with express orders to cross the Tennessee above and get around in the rear of the enemy to destroy his provision trains coming to Chattanooga through Sequatchie Valley, and the man instead of attending to this has allowed himself to be drawn off toward Knoxville on a general rampage, capturing villages and towns that are of no use whatever to me in the result . . . The man is ignorant and does not know anything about cooperation. He is nothing more than a good raider. I have sent General Wheeler to relieve him. Chattanooga is short of supplies, and if Forrest had executed my orders, the place would have by this time surrendered. (Liddell, p 150)
15. Sam Watkins, p 123.
16. Ibid, p 122.
17. OR, Series I, Vol. XXX, Part I, p 215.

18. Ulysses S. Grant,"Memoirs," Vol. II, pp 26-7.
19. Horace Porter, "Campaigning With Grant," Bonanza Books, New York, 1961, p11.
20. Diary of Resinor Etter, Oct. 4, 1863.
21. Marcus Toney, p 62.
22. W. J. Worsham, p 96.
23. Joseph Fullerton, Brevet Brig.—Gen. USV, in "Battles and Leaders," Vol. III, p 719.
24. William T. Sherman, "Personal Memoirs of Gen'l W.T. Sherman," Charles L. Webster & Co., New York, 1891, Vol. I, p 376.
25. Pvt. H. M. Woodson, Co. "E" 34th Mississippi Regiment C.S.A., in The Confederate Veteran, Jan. 1898, p 34.
26. J. J. Turner, 30th Tennessee Regiment, C.S.A. in "Lindsley's Military Annals," p 452.
27. W. J. McMurray, p 135.
28. Ibid, p 136.
29. Ulysses S. Grant, "Personal Memoirs," Vol. II, pp 39-40.
30. W. J. Worsham, p 100.
31. Ibid.
32. W. J. McMurray, p 136.
33. Joseph S. Fullerton, "Battles and Leaders," Vol. III, p 725.
34. Pvt. William K. Poston in The Confederate Veteran, Sept., 1901, p 389.
35. W. J. Worsham, p 100.
36. " Private Goodloe," quoted by Luke Finlay in "Lindsley's Military Annals," p 189.
37. W. J. McMurray, p 137.
38. The Confederate Veteran, June, 1909, p 276; B.A. Botkin, "A Civil War Treasury of Tales, Legends and Folklore," Promontory Press, New York, 1960, pp 339-342; John Bakeless, "Spies of the Confederacy," J.P. Lippincott Co., Philadelphia, 1970, pp 216-245.
39. Ibid, Oct., 1908, p 522.
40. Ibid.
41. Ibid, p 523. The source here quoted is one Josha Brown, a member of the Coleman Scouts, reported as resulting from a conversation between himself and General Grenville Dodge. Brown died in 1924. When in 1902, money was being collected for the Sam Davis Monument on the capitol grounds in Nashville, General Dodge is listed as contributing $10.00. (CVM, June, 1902, p 245, p 243.)
42. Report of the Court Martial Commission, as reported in The Confederate Veteran, Oct., 1908, p 523.

43. Joshua Brown in <u>The Confederate Veteran</u>, Oct., 1908, p 523.
44. Original in possession of Tennessee State Museum, Nashville, Tenn.
45. Joshua Brown, <u>The Confederate Veteran</u>, Oct., 1908, pp 523-4.
46. L. W. Forgaves in <u>The Confederate Veteran</u>, Aug., 1909, p 375.
47. Sumner A. Cunningham, <u>The Confederate Veteran</u>, 1908, p 524. The statement is credited to a "Captain Armstrong," the official executioner.
48. L. W. Forgaves, <u>The Confederate Veteran</u>, Aug., 1909, p 375; Edythe Johns Whitely, "Sam Davis, Hero of Confederacy," Nashville, 1971. For another perspective see Stanley P. Hirshon, "Granville M. Dodge," Indiana University Press, Bloomington, 1967, pp 81-84.

Letters from eyewitnesses:

Pulaski, Tennessee

Nov. 30th 1863

Addressed to "Dear Friends at Home."

... I witnessed the hanging of a spy the other day   he was caught inside our lines with papers in his pockets stateing how many men we have here   the number of the regt   the name and number of our Batterys and a plot of the Country ad Railroad   they tryed him by court marshall and sentenced him to be hung. I was close by when he was hung   it was a sad sight to see a man in the prime of life and in the enjoyment of health to see him hung till he is dead
  I tell you tis a sad Sight   his was a very slender man perhaps 25 years old   he was a Brave man and if ever a man Died game he did for he talked and laughed with his executioners till the very last he walked upon the scaffold without any aid and stood there while the rope was put around his neck and I dont think he trembled in a single muscle. tis a pitty such men should be hung But he was a spy and an enemy to his Country and according to the laws of our country he should be hung, and tis necessary to execute such men as a warning to others.

Amos Spencer

Dec. 11/63

Miss Emma Guthrie
Baldwinville, Edgar Co. Ill.

Dear Emma,

... The honest just & true we should ever love and try to emulate their example. To those who are led astray in an unjust cause & are yet honest true & faithful to the cause & their friends I have respect for them. A young rebel spy of this description was executed 27th last month in this town. Some soldier or citizen had given him information as to our strength & position & he was brought back tried & found guilty. When informed of his fate he did not seem to care much. The Genl offered to pardon him if he would tell who gave him the information but this he refused to do. Just before going onto the scaffold the chaplain asked him if he had not better tell. This seemed to insult him said he   do you think I would betray a friend. No I would die a thousand deaths first. I stood near by him as I could get for the guard. He died like a soldier a brave boy he was — though a spy. I almost hated to see him die. I guess he was 21 years of age, hair, eyes & complexion dark, five ft 8 inches high & weighed about 150 lbs. Samuel Davis was his name . . .

Yours truly,

John Doak

49. For a very readable account of the Fort Sanders fight see Digby Gordon Seymour, "Divided Loyalties," U.T. Press, Knoxville, 1963.
50. Linda Millgate, "The Almanac of Dates," Harcourt Brace Co., New York, 1977 ; Stanford M. Mirkin, "What happened When," Ives Washburn, Inc., New York, 1966, p 380.

XV
No armistice on sea or land

1. Bearden Papers.
2. Thomas William Humes, "The Loyal Mountaineers," Ogden Brothers & Co., Knoxville, 1888, p 392. The quote is from Appendix: Note X, "Martyrdom of Union People," by N.G. Taylor.
3. Ibid — The quote is from C.W. Hall, "Threescore Years and Ten, "by a lawyer," Cincinnati, 1884.

4. The book referred to is "Adventures of Dan Ellis The Union Guide." Ellis leveled severe accusations at many East Tennesseans, then alive, involving their roles in the war. He did not hesitate to call names and relate specific incidents. His book was published in 1867, by Harper & Brothers in New York. It has recently been reissued by Dan Crowe and Tony Marion of Kingsport and Blountville, Tn. The new edition has come under some criticism from people who charge that the events related are overdrawn. Put into the context of what other writers of the time have said of affairs in East Tennessee and the southwestern part of Virginia during the war Ellis' book seem perfectly plausible. The fact that wealthy Confederate sympathizers bought up and burned as many of the books as they could may imply credibility.

5. Ellis Merton Coulter, "Parson Brownlow," University of North Carolina Press, 1937, p 251.

6. The diary of L. Virginia French, Dec. 7, 1862.

7. Emma Inman Williams, "Historic Madison," Madison County Historical Society, Jackson, 1946, pp 178-9.

8. Diary of Amanda McDowell, July 27, 1863.

9. Merritt and Hale, Vol. III, p 646.

10. Paul Turner Papers, Tullahoma, Tn. Turner was for many years the principal of the Cannon County High School at Woodbury. As a class project he directed his students in collecting material pertaining to the Civil War. Included in the material are former interviews with participants in the war as well as other interviews with older people in the community.

11. Rutherford County Courier, Aug. 4, 1950.

12. Rufus Dennis, part of the Paul Turner Papers.

13. Basil Duke, p 182.

14. Thurman Sensing, "Champ Ferguson," Vanderbilt University Press, Nashville, Tenn., 1942, p. 98.

15. "Report of The Adjutant General of The State of Tennessee From 1861 to 1866," S. C. Mercer, Nashville, 1866, p 442.

16. Basil Duke as quoted in Merritt and Hale, Vol. III, p 650.

17. Albert R. Hogue, "Mark Twain's Obedstown and Knobs of Tennessee," Cumberland Printing Co., Jamestown, 1950, p 47.

18. Ibid, pp 48-9.

19. The Nashville Dispatch, Oct. 21, 1865.

20. Captain Wirtz was executed in Washington, D. C. for his alleged role in the many deaths that occurred at Andersonville Prison.

21. "Goodspeed's History of Tennessee," The Goodspeed Publishing Co., Nashville, 1886, (Stewart County) p 913.

22. Ibid.
23. Livernia Webb in "Ridley's Journal," p 551.
24. Ibid, p 552.
25. Amanda McDowell's Diary. At the time Amanda kept her diary she was very much in love with a young man named Larkin Craig. For some reason their romance did not work out. Following the war, she married Hazel Burns.
26. Leland Jordan, "Triune in the Civil War." So far as is known this manuscript has never been published. Jordan was a retired army officer when the material was written after World War II; copy in possession of author; John W. Headly, "Confederate Operations in Canada and New York," Neale Publishing Co., New York, 1906, p 444. The book has recently (1984) been reissued by Time-Life Books Inc., New York; Rutherford Co. Hist. Soc., Publication No. 25, Sumner 1985 , Murfreesboro, Tn., pp 38-53.
27. Thomas Frank Gailor, "Some Memories," Southern Publishers Inc., Kingsport, Tn., 1937, pp 6-7.
28. Ibid.
29. Rebel C. Forrester, "Glory and Tears, Obion County, Tennessee 1860-1870," Lanzer Co., Union City, 1966, p 67.
30. Charles L. Lufkin, "Not Heard From Since April 12, 1864," an article scheduled to be published in the Tennessee Historical Quarterly, 1986.
31. Rebel C. Forrester, pp 67-74.
32. Ibid.
33. Ibid.
34. Emma Inman Williams, p 178.
35. John Allan Wyeth, "Forrest," p 369.
36. Ibid, pp 369-70.
37. Diary of William Dyer.
38. Jordan and Pryor, p 423.
39. John Allan Wyeth, "Forrest," p 354.
40. OR, Series I, Vol. XXXII, Part I, p 520.
41. R. R. Hancock, P 367.
42. "Fort Pillow Revisited: New Evidence About An Old Controversy," edited by John Cimprich and Robert C. Mainfort, Jr. in the Civil War History, Kent State Uni., Dec., 1982, pp 293-306; Albert Castel. "The Fort Pillow Massacre: A Fresh Examination of Evidence," Civil War History, March, 1958, pp 37-50.
43. Ibid.
44. Ibid.
45. "Report of the Adjutant General of the State of Tennessee From 1861 to 1866," p 646.

46. John Allan Wyeth, "Forrest," p 368.
47. Diary of William Dyer, April 12, 1864.
48. A wealth of material has been written on the Battle of Fort Pillow. One interesting and informative source is Dr. Charles Fitch who wrote General James R. Chalmers in 1879, concerning an accusation that Chalmers, a Confederate officer, had murdered a baby during the fight. Fitch, a Union physician from Iowa, defended Chalmers. Fitch's letter to Chalmers was published in the Southern Historical Society Papers, Vol. 7, pp 440-1. More recently a report that Fitch wrote on the affair has been discovered by John Cimprich and John Mainfort Jr. This report in its entirety was published in the Tennessee Historical Quarterly in the spring issue of 1985. In his official report Fitch gives dramatic testimony not only to the fact that a massacre occurred, but eyewitness accounts of specific incidents involved.

The article cited by Charles Lufkin is designed to offset the traditional attitude of Southern writers toward Major Bradford's Battalion. Most Southern writers have been very unkind to the men who composed this battalion, but Lufkin pleads that they were just as upstanding in their personal lives as their counterparts in the Confederate Army.

XVI
Everything here is at present quite dull

1. Resinor Etter's Diary, Dec. 11, 1863.
2. W. J. Worsham, p 104.
3. Diary of an unknown soldier of the 49th Tennessee Regiment C.S.A. from Robertson County, Tn. Typewritten copy in possession of author. Owner of original not known.
4. George Guild, p 57.
5. Resinor Etter's Diary, Dec. 25, 1863.
6. John Farris' Diary, Dec. 26, 1864. Farris was a physician in the 41st Tennessee Regiment C.S.A. The original diary is in Emory University, Atlanta, Ga. A photostatic copy was furnished by Ms. Shirley Farris Jones of Murfreesboro, Tn.
7. Sam Watkins, p 131.
8. Ibid.
9. W. J. Worsham, p 105.
10. Sam Watkins, pp 131-2.
11. Joseph E. Johnston, "Johnston's Narrative," D. Appleton and Co., New York, 1874, p 279.

12. Thomas H. Davenport's Diary, May 4, 1864. Davenport was a chaplain in the 3rd Tennessee Regiment C.S.A. Original in Tennessee State Library, Nashville; John Berrien Lindsley, p 487; CVM, Mar., 1903, p 113.
13. Bromfield Ridley, p 282.
14. Ibid, p 283.
15. Ibid.
16. Memoirs of Carroll H. Clark, 16th Tennessee Regiment C.S.A. Original in possession of the Charles M. Clark estate, McMinnville, Tennessee.
17. Bromfield Ridley, p 283.
18. Stanley Horn, "Army of Tennessee," p 313; OR, Vol. 52, Part 2, p 586; SHSP Vol. 31, pp 215-228.
19. Ulysses S. Grant, Vol. I, p 376.
20. Morgan Leatherman to "Dear Uncle," April, 1864, from Dalton, Ga. Leatherman was from Rutherford County. Original in possession of author.
21. Ibid.
22. Resinor Etter's Diary, April 8, 1864.
23. Ibid, April 24-28, 1864.
24. Morgan Leatherman to "Dear Uncle," April, 1864, from Dalton, Ga.
25. Edward A. Pollard, "The Lost Cause," E.B. Treat & Co., New York, 1866, p 541.

XVII
Be aisey: Old Joe will get them yet

1. G. W. Waggoner, 20th Tennessee Infantry, to Lt. J. H. Hastings, 17th Tennessee Infantry, Mar. 8, 1864, from Tilton, Ga. Original in possession of Mrs. Nancy Hastings Stowers, Shelbyville, Tn.
2. William T. Sherman, "Sherman's Memoirs," Vol. II, p 34.
3. Thomas Head, p 126.
4. Morgan Leatherman to parents, April 3, 1864, from Dalton, Ga.
5. Memoirs of Spencer Talley.
6. W. C. Dodson of A. P. Stewart's Division in CVM, Feb., 1911, p 71.
7. Resinor Etter's Diary, May 16, 1864.
8. George Guild, p 62.
9. Col. J. N. Wyatt to J. B. Cunningham, Aug. 10, 1864, in CVM, Oct., 1897, p 519.
10. Ibid.

11. Bromfield Ridley, p 303.
12. Ibid, p 305.
13. Gen. Oliver O. Howard, U.S.A., "Battles and Leaders," Vol. IV, pp 306-7.
14. Memoirs of Nelson Rainey.
15. Memoirs of C. H. Clark.
16. Samuel Robinson, "Maney's 1st Tennessee Regiment C.S.A.," in "Lindsley's Military Annals," p 164.
17. Ibid.
18. George Guild, p 63.
19. W. J. Worsham, p 118.
20. Resinor Etter's diary. June 12 and 13, 1864.
21. Ibid, June 14, 1864.
22. Morgan Leatherman to "Dear Uncle," June 15th, 1864, from Marietta, Ga.
23. Thomas Head, p 134.
24. Ibid.
25. Col. J. N. Wyatt to J. B. Cunningham, Aug. 10, 1864, in CVM, Oct., 1897, p 520.
26. Bob Whitaker to his sister, July 16, 1864, in CVM, July, 1908, p 332. Whitaker was from Union City, Tn.
27. Robert Gates in "Lindsley's Military Annals," p 219.
28. Bromfield Ridley, p 319.
29. Ibid.
30. Col. A. J. Vaughn, "History of Thirteenth Regiment C.S.A." p 33.
31. Sam Watkins, p 157.
32. Ibid, p 158.
33. Bob Whitaker in CVM, July, 1908, p 332.
34. W. J. Worsham. p 123.

XVIII
Well Johnny, how many of you are left?

1. Gen. Francis A. Shoup in CVM, Sept., 1895, pp 262-65. Shoup was a native of Indiana. He graduated from West Point in 1855. Following the Civil War he became a Professor of Mathematics at the Uni. of Mississippi and later became a priest in the Episcopal Church. In 1869, he accepted the position of chaplain at the University of the South at Sewanee, Tn. and still later ended his career at a girl's preparatory school in Columbia, Tn.
2. Nelson Rainey's Memoirs.

582

3. A. J. Vaughn, pp 86-7.
4. Nelson Rainey's Memoirs.
5. Sherman, Vol. II, p 66.
6. OR, Series I, Vol. 38, Part 5, p 876.
7. Ibid, p 962.
8. Nelson Rainey's Memoirs.
9. Ibid.
10. Bob Whitaker to his sister July 16, 1864, from Atlanta, in CVM, July, 1908, p 332.
11. Col. J. N. Wyatt to J B. Cunningham Aug. 10, 1864, in CVM, Oct., 1897, p 521.
12. W. J. Worsham, p 127.
13. Morgan Leatherman to parents July, 1864, from "Dixie."
14. Ibid.
15. Resinor Etter's Diary, July 20, 1864.
16. Memoirs of Spencer Talley.
17. John Bell Hood, "Advance and Retreat," Indiana Uni. Press, Bloomington, 1959, p 177.
18. Hood later expressed frustration with his subordinate generals, especially Hardee. A defense of Hardee was published in the SHSP, Vol. 8, pp 337-87, by Colonel T.B. Roy. Also see "William J. Hardee, Old Reliable," by Nat Hughes, Chapter XIII.
19. Sam Watkins, pp 176-77.
20. Gervis Grainger, p 19.
21. Spencer Talley's Memoirs.
22. Captain Richard Beard was the grandfather of Mrs. Douglas MacArthur.
23. Captain Richard Beard, 18th Tennessee Regiment C.S.A. in "Ridley's Journal," p 325; CVM, Mar., 1903, p 118; The Atlanta Hist. Journal, Vol. XXVIII, No. 3, Fall 1984, pp 55-6; James P. Jones, "The Battle of Atlanta and McPherson's Successor," Civil War History Uni. of Iowa, Dec., 1961, p 395.
24. Ibid.
25. Sherman, Vol. II, p 80.
26. John Bell Hood, p 162.
27. Memoirs of Spencer Talley.
28. Ibid.
29. Resinor Etter's Diary, July 22, 1864.
30. Thomas Head, p 140.
31. Sam Watkins, p 179.
32. Ibid.
33. J. W. Jackson to his mother July 12, 1864. Original in possession of Mrs. James Latimer, Old Hickory, Tn.

34. Willie Jackson to the parents of J. W. Jackson, July 29, 1864.
    Original in possession of Mrs. James Latimer, Old Hickory, Tn.
35. Robert Gates, 6th Tennessee Regiment C.S.A. in "Lindsley's
    Military Annals," p 220.
36. Quoted in Horn's, "Army of Tennessee," p 362.
37. Walter R. Houghton, "The Biography of Gen. John A. Logan," N.G.
    Hamilton Co., Cleveland, 1884, p 286.
38. W. J. Worsham, p 132.
39. C. W. Heiskell, 19th Tennessee Regiment C.S.A. in "Lindsley's
    Military Annals," p 377; Worsham, p 132.
40. Spencer Talley's Memoirs.
41. Ibid.
42. Resinor Etter's Diary, Aug. 14, 1864.
43. Jim Parrott to his wife in Lincoln County from Atlanta, Aug. 18,
    1864.
44. Resinor Etter's Diary, Aug. 19, 1864.
45. Nelson Rainey's Memoirs.
46. Ibid.
47. Joseph Love, 48th Tennessee Regiment C.S.A. in "Lindsley's
    Military Annals," p 548.
48. Nelson Rainey's Memoirs.
49. Joseph Love, "Lindsley's Military Annals," p 548.
50. Nelson Rainey's Memoirs.
51. Ibid.
52. Ibid.
53. Ibid.
54. Gervis Grainger, p 20.
55. Ibid.
56. Ibid.
57. Nelson Rainey's Memoirs.
58. James Parrott to his wife, Sept. 10, 1864.
59. Resinor Etter's Diary, Sept. 12, 1864.
60. Thomas Head, p 144.
61. John Bell Hood, p 206.
62. W. J. Worsham, p 134.
63. Resinor Etter's Diary, Sept. 25, 1864.

XIX
Bring Morgan out dead or alive

1. This account of John Hunt Morgan's death is based on material found
    in Basil Duke, "A History of Morgan's Cavalry," op cit;

Bromfield Ridley, "Ridley's Journal," op cit; Dee Alexander Brown, "The Bold Cavaliers," J. P. Lippincott Co., Philadelphia, 1959; F. Senour, "Morgan and his Captors," C.F. Vent & Co., Chicago, 1865; The Report of the Adjutant General, State of Tennessee, 1861-1866, op cit; Howard Swiggett, "The Rebel Raiders," The Garden City Publishing Co., Garden City, 1934.

2. Scott and Angel, p 184.
3. Ibid, p 152.
4. Ibid.
5. Basil Duke, p 532.
6. Scott and Angel, p 166.
7. Ibid, p 169.
8. Ibid, p 176.
9. Many sensational stories emerged as to the circumstances surrounding John Hunt Morgan's death and the treatment of his body afterwards. Scott, Angel, and Duke were in the vicinity when the event occurred and each is considered a reliable source. Major Charles A. Withers, an assistant adjutant general of Morgan's command signed an affidavit in 1920, as to the circumstances of the general's death. A copy may be found in The Confederate Veteran, Aug., 1920, p 300. Another version may be found in The Filson Club History Quarterly, "The Death of John Hunt Morgan," by Harry Harris, pp 46-51, Jan., 1965 (Louisville, Ky.)

An excellent book, "Rebel Raider," has recently been published on the life of John Hunt Morgan. Authored by James A. Ramage, it is published by the University Press of Kentucky, Lexington, 1986.

XX
I begin now to look forward to the worst

1. Diary of L. Virginia French, Sept. 25, 1864.
2. Thomas Head, p 145.
3. Ibid.
4. Since the war's end a controversy has developed as to whether Federal troops were actually approaching. The subject is discussed in the Southern Historical Society Papers, Vol. 10, pp 402-06.
5. Memoirs of Spencer Talley.
6. Ibid.
7. Diary of Resinor Etter, Oct. 5, 1864.
8. G. W. Gordon, 11th Tennessee Regiment C. S. A. in "Lindsley's Military Annals," p 300.

9. Ibid.
10. George Dallas Mosgrove, "Kentucky Cavaliers in Dixie," Courier-Journal Press, Louisville, 1895, p 206.
11. George Guild, p 100.
12. Memoirs of Benjamin Rogers, Co. "B," Starnes 4th Tennessee Cavalry, C.S.A. Typewritten copy in possession of author.
13. Ibid.
14. George Mosgrave, p 207.
15. Benjamin Rogers' Memoirs.
16. Dr. L. B. Murfree in "Ridley's Journal," pp 528-9.
17. George Guild, p 99.
18. Diary of Brevet Major George Ward Nichols, Aid-de-camp to Sherman, Harper's Monthly Magazine, Vol. XXXI, pp 574-5.
19. George Guild, pp 107-8.

XXI

The desperate venture of a desperate man

1. Diary of Thomas H. Davenport, original in TSL, Nashville. Chaplain 3rd, Tenn. Reg., C.S.A., Sept. 23, 1864.
2. Ibid, November 8, 1864.
3. Thomas Head, p 147.
4. Diary of Resinor Etter, Nov. 3, 1864.
5. Memoirs of Spencer Talley.
6. Jordan and Pryor, p 609.
7. Ibid, p 609.
8. Diary of Resinor Etter, Nov. 16, 1864.
9. Memoirs of Spencer Talley.
10. Diary of Resinor Etter, Nov. 22, 1864.
11. Memoirs of Nelson Rainey.
12. Thomas Robson Hay, "Hood's Tennessee Campaign," Walter Neale Co., New York, 1929, pp 77-8. This book was subsequently reissued by Morningside Press, Dayton, 1976.
13. Diary of Resinor Etter, Nov. 27, 1864.
14. Memoirs of Spencer Talley.
15. Levi T. Schofield, "Retreat From Pulaski to Nashville," H. C. Sherick Co., Cincinnati, 1886, p 8.
16. E. Shepard, sergeant in the consolidated regiment composed of remnants of the 19th, 24th, and 41st Tennessee Regiments C.S.A., in The Confederate Veteran, Mar., 1916, p 138.
17. Diary of Resinor Etter, Nov. 29, 1864.

18. John Bell Hood, p 290.
19. Ibid, p 291.
20. Memoirs of Spencer Talley.
21. Diary of Resinor Etter, Nov. 30, 1864.
22. Sumner A. Cunningham in The Confederate Veteran, April, 1893, p 101.
23. Letter of Gen. John M. Schofield to Sumner A. Cunningham published in The Confederate Veteran, Sept., 1895, p 274.
24. H. P. Figuers in The Confederate Veteran, Jan., 1915, p 5.
25. Jacob Cox, "The Battle of Franklin," Charles Scribner's Sons, New York, 1897, p 62.
26. Sumner A. Cunningham in The Confederate Veteran, Jan., 1910, p 18. Cunningham says, "It is perhaps given to me . . . to know . . . certain extraordinary facts of this battle [Franklin] . . . I happened to be . . . where General Hood . . . rode over a crest and down to a linden tree . . . and with glasses examined the area of Franklin . . . I watched him closely, while there, meditating upon his responsibility."
27. Ibid, p 19.
28. Irving A. Buck, "Cleburne and His Command," McCowat-Mercer Press Inc., Jackson, 1959, p 281.
29. Tillman H. Stevens, a Union veteran, in The Confederate Veteran, April, 1903, p 166.
30. Schofield, p 12.
31. Tillman H. Stevens, The Confederate Veteran, April, 1903, p 166.
32. G. W. Gordon, "Lindsley's Military Annals," p 301.
33. Capt. Edwins Parsons, Wisconsin Adjutant, quoted in Douglas MacArthur's "Reminiscences," McGraw-Hill Co., New York, 1964, p 10.
34. Ibid.
35. C. W. Heiskell in "Lindsley's Military Annals," p 378.
36. Memoirs of Spencer Talley.
37. Irving A. Buck, pp 290-1.
38. Sumner A. Cunningham in The Confederate Veteran, Jan., 1910, p 19.
39. Ibid, p 20.
40. Tillman H. Stevens in The Confederate Veteran, April, 1903, p 167.
41. Lt. Col. Edward Adams Baker, 61st Ind. Infantry U.S.A., in Confederate Military History, Vol. VIII, p 2861, p 160; CVM, 1903, p 166.
42. Mrs. John C. Gaut in The Confederate Veteran, Sept., 1904, p 422.
43. H. P Figuers in The Confederate Veteran, Jan., 1915, p 6.

44. Memoirs of Spencer Talley.
45. Ibid.
46. Sam Watkins, p 219.
47. W. J. Worsham, p 146.
48. Park Marshall, "A Life of William B. Bate," Cumberland Press, Nashville, 1908, p 148. Bate became the governor of Tennessee in 1882.
49. Letter of Col. W. D. Gale to his wife dated Jan. 14, 1865. Published in "Ridley's Journal," pp 409-12. Mrs. Gale was the daughter of General and Mrs. Leonidas Polk.
50. H. P. Figuers in The Confederate Veteran, Jan., 1915, p 7.
51. Diary of Resinor Etter, Dec. 1, 1864.
52. Stanley Horn, "The Army of Tennessee," p 403.
53. H. P. Figuers in The Confederate Veteran, Jan., 1915, p 7.
54. Diary of James L. Cooper, 20th Tennessee Infantry C.S.A., Nov., 1864. Original in Tennessee State Library, Nashville. Published in the Tennessee Historical Quarterly, Vol. 15, June, 1956, pp 141-173.
55. Diary of Resinor Etter, Dec. 7, 1864.
56. W. J. Worsham, pp 151-2.
57. Journal of Dr. John Berrien Lindsley in Lindsley Family Papers, Tennessee State Library, Nashville.
58. Col. Henry Stone, Brevet Col. U.S.V., member of Gen. George H. Thomas' staff in "Battles and Leaders," Vol. IV, p 454.
59. Ibid, p 455.
60. Sam Watkins, p 222.
61. Diary of James L. Cooper, Dec., 1864.
62. The Confederate Veteran, author not listed, April, 1899, p 154.
63. Diary of James L. Cooper, Dec., 1864.
64. An account of Shy's death can be found in W.J. McMurray's "History of The Twentieth Tennessee Regiment," p 348; The Tennessean Sunday Magazine, Dec. 15, 1974.
65. Sam Watkins, p 224.
66. The Confederate Veteran, author not listed, April, 1899, p 154.
67. Ibid.
68. W. J. McMurray, p 349-50.
69. Ibid, p 348.
70. Thomas Head, pp 154-5.
71. Memoirs of Spencer Talley.
72. For a detailed account of the Battle of Nashville see; Stanley Horn, "The Decisive Battle of Nashville," Uni. of Tenn. Press, Knoxville, 1968.

XXII
The Immortal Six Hundred

1. Letter from Michael Osbourne, Farmville, Va., April 17, 1863, to Mrs. Millie Ann Lytle, Rover, Tenn. Original in possession of Ms. Wanda Elmore and Ms. Ethel Elmore, Eagleville, Tennessee. Since this chapter is based primarily on the diary of Capt. James K. Polk Lytle, 23rd Tennessee Regiment, C.S.A., and each quotation from it is identified in the text, only those references from other sources are footnoted.
2. Ogden Murray, "The Immortal Six Hundred," Stone Printing & Manufacturing Co., Roanoke, 1911, p 67.
3. Southern Historical Society Papers, Vol. 17, pp 44-5.
4. Ibid.
5. Col. Abram Fulkerson, 63rd Tennessee Regiment C.S.A., "The Prison Experiences Of A Confederate Soldier," Southern Historical Society Papers, Vol. 22, p 132.
6. Ibid.
7. Ibid, p 140.
8. The name of A. M. Bedford does not appear in the list of the "Six Hundred" published by the SHSP in Vol. 17. However the name does appear in Murray's list as published in 1905.
9. A. M. Bedford in "The Immortal Six Hundred," p 256.
10. Col. Abram Fulkerson says of Brown, "Colonel Brown was not only an accomplished and humane officer, but was a kind and courteous gentleman." SHSP, Vol. 22, p 140.
11. SHSP, Vol. 22, p 144.

For further reading on the "Six Hundred" see:
The Confederate Veteran Magazine
1893, p 49
1897, pp 116 and 219
1898, p 118
1899, pp 149, 313, 364, 415, 255
1900, p 116
1915, p 485

SHSP, Vol. 29, p 229
Civil War History Ill., Feb., 1981, p 20
"Six Hundred," by Fritz Fuzzlebug, Joseph Funk's Sons Printers, Singer's Glen, Va., 1869. T.H. Pearce, "The Immortal Six Hundred," The CVM, Vol. 34, No. 1, p 7. This Vol. represents the re-establishment of the Confederate Veteran Magazine by the Sons of Confederate Veterans, 1985, Ronald T. Clemmons, Editor, Murfreesboro, Tn.

XXIII
The cards were fairly dealt, but they were mightly badly shuffled

1. Capt. R. N. Rea, 13th Miss. Regulars C.S.A., in CVM, Aug., 1922, p 288.
2. Resinor Etter's diary, Dec. 22, 1864.
3. Memoirs of Nelson Rainey.
4. John Smith, 7th Tennessee Cavalry C.S.A., in CVM, Jan., 1922, p 14.
5. W. J. Worsham, p 163.
6. Memoirs of C. H. Clark.
7. Gen. James D. Porter, quoted in "The Battle of Nashville," by M. B. Morton in CVM, Jan., 1909, p 20.
8. W. J. Worsham, pp 156-7; Cooper's Diary, Tn. Hist. Quarterly, June, 1956, p 170.
9. James Cooper's diary, Dec., 1864, published in Tn. Hist. Quarterly, June, 1956.
10. Hood, p 311.
11. C. W. Heiskell in "Lindsley's Military Annals," p 378.
12. W. J. Worsham, p 167.
13. Bromfield Ridley, p 456.
14. Joseph E. Johnston, pp 396-7.

XXIV
I could see the fire in the old boys eyes

1. George Guild, p 148.
2. Bromfield Ridley, p 464.
3. G. H. Baskette in "Lindsley's Military Annals," p 368.
4. Bromfield Ridley, pp 465-6.
5. Memoirs of Nelson Rainey.
6. Ibid.
7. Memoirs of C. H. Clark.
8. Diary of John B. Blair, 35th Tennessee Regiment , C.S.A. Typewritten copy in possession of author. Owner of original unknown.
9. The Confederate Veteran, March, 1914, p 122. (Author not listed.)
10. John B. Blair's Diary.
11. Samuel T. Foster, "One of Cleburne's Command," The Civil War Reminiscences and Diary of Capt. Samuel T. Foster, Granbury's Texas Brigade, CSA, edited by Norman D. Brown, Uni. of Texas, Austin, 1980, pp 178-9.

12. Bromfield Ridley, p 479.
13. Ibid.
14. Diary of James K. Polk Lytle, Ft. Delaware Prison, April 10 & 15, 1865.
15. Ibid, April 28, 1865.
16. Ibid, May 2, 1865.
17. Captain Richard Beard in "Ridley's Journal," p 327.
18. Report of the Adjutant General, State of Tennessee, 1861-1866, p 387; James W. Elliott, "Transport To Disaster," Holt, Rinehart and Winston, New York, 1962; Merritt and Hale, Vol. III, p 602.
19. Reminiscences of Newton Cannon, edited by Campbell Brown, The Carter House, Franklin, Tn. , 1963, p 67.
20. Diary of Amanda McDowell, April 17, 1865.
21. Diary of James Cooper, April, 1865.
22. Marcus Toney, p 122.
23. George Guild, p 152.
24. Diary of John B. Blair.
25. Philip M. Hamer, "Tennessee, A History," The American Historical Society, New York, 1933, Vol, II, p 597.
26. The Report of the Joint Committee on Reconstruction, Government Printing Office, Washington, 1866, p 13.
27. The Rev. James H. M'Neilly in The Confederate Veteran, Aug., 1920, p 298.
28. Ibid.
29. The Report of the Joint Committee on Reconstruction, p 112.
30. Ibid.
31. M'Neilly, The Confederate Veteran, Sept., 1920, p 342.
32. Based on diary of Betty Burford Bobo. Typewritten copy provided by Anna Burford, original in possession of C. C. Jones, Glasco, Ky.
33. Samuel Foster, pp 178-9.
34. John Savage, "Life of John Savage," printed privately, 1903, pp 144 and 114.
35. Memoirs of C. H. Clark.
36. Ibid.
37. C. W. Heiskell in "The Old Nineteenth Tennessee C.S.A.," Press of Paragon Printing Co., Knoxville, p 180.

Index

Burns, Hazel 337.

Burnside, Ambrose 296, 304, 307, 322, 325, 275-76.

Cairo, Illinois 241.

Caldwell, Samuel H. 347.

Calfkiller Creek, Tn. 333.

Camp Beech Grove, Ky. 53-60.

Camp Chase, Il. 238, 481.

Camp Dick Robinson, Ky. 332.

Camp Douglas, Illinois 477.

Campbell, Andrew 198-99, 386, 420, 425, 428, 430.

Campbell, Andrew Jackson 235-46.

Campbell, Joe 284.

Campbell, John 235.

Campbell, Sarah 235.

Cannon County, Tn. 150, 328.

Cannon, Newton 518.

Capt. Holman 146.

Carrigan, J. G. 17, 36.

Carroll, William 55.

Carter, William B. 42.

Carter, Theo 466.

Carter, W. R. 291.

Carter, William B. 41.

Case, Almon 342-43.

Cassville, Ga. 372-73.

Castilian Springs, Tn. 196.

Cate, A. M. 43.

Cave City, Ky. 175.

Central Academy 229.

Chalmers, James R. 175, 186.

Chamberlain, John R. 125.

Champion's Hill, Ms. 86.

Charleston, South Carolina 483.

Chattahoochee River 389, 398, 417-19, 431, 388, 391, 393.

Chattanooga, Tn. 91-94, 162-71, 246, 251, 256-59, 268-78, 285, 292-323, 351, 362, 367, 418, 433.

Cheat Mountain, Va. 34-36, 49, 140.

Cheatham County, Tn. 337.

Cheatham's Division 178, 316, 284.

Cheatham, Ben 177, 184, 186, 205, 283-84, 361, 389, 419, 451, 453, 465, 499-500.

Cheatham, Richard 225.

Cherry Creek, Tn. 337.

Cherry Mansion 115.

Cherry, Mrs. W.H. 339, 115.

Chickahominy River 141, 144.

Chickamauga 38, 229, 278-82, 287, 291, 303-4, 312, 316-17, 355, 395, 416.

Chickasaw 319-20.

Clark, Achilles V. 347.

Clark, C. H. 377, 498, 510, 541, 543, 544.

Clark, Carroll 190, 362.

Clark, J. B. 268.

Clarksville, Tn. 138, 222.

Cleburne, Pat. 180, 198, 266, 308-11, 316, 362-63, 377, 383, 390, 400, 425, 444, 457, 461, 465.

Clemenson, Charlie 59.

Clinch River 188.

Cobb, Emma 23.

Coleman's Scouts 317-18, 339.

Coleman, Bob 400-01.

Coleman, Capt. 320.

Collins, G. O. 44.

Columbia, Tn. 103-04, 258, 261.

Columbus, Mississippi 132.

Commings, Denny 190.

Congressional Committee on Reconstruction 525.

Connelly, James A. 227.

Conscription Act 130-33, 159.

Cooper, James L. 19, 467, 471-72, 500, ,519.

Corinth, Mississippi 98, 101-19, 123-37, 159-63, 193, 260, 318.

Cotton, R. J. 497.

Cowan, J. B. 297.

Cox, Jacob 455.

Crisp, Garrett 336.

Crittenden, George 54-63.

Fort Monroe 141, 340.
Fort Pillow 344-49, 435.
Fort Pulaski 484-494.
Fort Sanders 322.
Fort Sumter 51.
Fort Henry 68.
Foster, Samuel T. 512, 537.
Fosterville, Tn. 217.
Franklin Pike 473-74.
Franklin, Tn. 457.
Fraser, C. W. 180.
Freedman's Bureau 525.
French, John Hopkins 148.
French, L. Virginia 148-49, 158, 169, 249-51, 325, 431, 433.
Frogg, William 332.
Fry, Henry 46.
Fulkerson, Abram 483, 494.
Fulkerson, Arthur 460.
Fuller, Thomas 102.
Fullerton, Joseph 306.
Fulton, John S. 267.
Gailor, Thomas 341.
Galbreath, James 399.
Gale, W. D. 466.
Gallatin, Tn. 169, 177, 230, 425.
Gander pulling 361.
Garfield, James A. 257, 267.
Garretson, J. T 259.
Gates, Robert 22-23, 47, 116, 185, 383.
Gaut, Mrs. John C. 463.
Gettysburg 269, 395.
Gillem, A. C. 425-27, 429-30.
Gilmer, Jeremy 65-66.
Gist, States Rights 444, 462.
Gordon, G. W. 436-37, 458.
Grainger, Gervis 212, 399, 413-15.
Granbury, Hiram 444, 462.
Grant, Ulysses S. 52, 64-71, 82-85, 105, 112-22, 147-48, 162, 222, 255, 260, 269, 304-12, 340, 363, 367, 434, 484, 505.
Gray, James 336.

Greely, Horace 267.
Greenville, Tn. 198, 427.
Griffin, Micajah 119.
Guild, George 273, 280, 288, 292, 298-301, 355, 378, 438-39, 441-42, 506-507, 521.
Gumm, John 101, 109, 120, 126-27, 135, 159-60, 166
Gunboat Carondelet 66.
Gunship Essex 67.
Guntersville, Alabama 435-36.
Hackett, Wright 208, 403.
Half Acre 330.
Hamilton, Mrs. R. 184.
Hamilton, Robert 183-84.
Hardee, William J. 51, 104, 110, 200, 302, 355, 368, 372, 389, 390, 395, 398, 413, 415, 419.
Harding, William G. 225.
Harlan, Ben 518.
Harmon, Jacob 46.
Harmon, Thomas 46.
Harpeth River 453-54.
Harris, H. W. 343.
Harris, Isham G. 12, 25, 28, 40, 45, 63, 98, 117, 122, 142, 418.
Harrison, Tom 200.
Hartsville, Tn. 169, 195-96.
Hastings, J. N. 482.
Hatton, Robert 95-97, 137, 138, 140, 142-46, 542.
Hatton, Sophie 142-44.
Hawkinsville, Ga. 409, 417.
Head, Thomas 18, 21, 35, 172, 370, 446, 475.
Hearn, Isham 119.
Heartsill, W. W. 270, 278.
Heg, Hans Christian 228-29.
Heiskell, C. W. 408, 503, 544.
Helm, Mrs. Ben Hardin 92-94.
Henderson County, Tn. 405.
Henderson, Pink 59.
Henry County, Tn. 347.

Lytle, Mrs. Milly Ann 477-78.
Lytle, William A. 477.
Macon, Georgia 403, 408-09.
Magoffin, Beriah 53.
Malone, Thomas 181, 204, 206.
Manassas (see Bull Run) 110.
Maney Mansion 156.
Maney's 1st Tn. Reg. 30, 34, 49, 108.
Maney's Grove, Tn. 157.
Maney, George 49, 179, 182, 184, 205, 282, 362.
Marietta, Georgia 378, 381, 388, 390, 441.
Market Street, Chattanooga 294.
Marks, A. S. 58.
Martin, Demon 118.
Martin, W. H. 384.
Mason and Dixon Line 14.
Masonic College 72.
Maury County Artillery 72.
Maury Grays 283.
McArthur, Arthur 459.
McClellan, George 141.
McCook's Cavalry 148.
McDonald, John 23.
McDowell, Amanda 20, 27-28, 37, 326, 337, 519.
McDowell, Fayette 21, 247.
McGavock, John 466.
McGavock, Mrs. John 466.
McGuire, J. P. 75.
McKee, John Miller 89.
McLaws, Lafayette 286.
McMinnville, Tn. 97, 134, 148-49, 168-69, 249, 255, 272, 300, 431.
McMullen, J. P. 371.
McMurray, William J. 48, 61, 214, 290, 313, 473.
McNairy County, Tn. 343.
McPherson, James 368-69, 386, 398-401, 406.
Meadow Bridge 144.
Memphis and Charleston Railroad 102.

Memphis, Tn. 241, 340, 408.
Methodist Printing Co. 183.
Mexican War 52.
Miles Station, Illinois 539.
Mill Springs, Kentucky 52-53, 61, 63, 65, 69.
Miller, Rueben 43.
Missionary Ridge 293, 303, 308-15, 321, 351-52, 355, 358, 367-68.
Mobile, Alabama 164-65.
Mobile and Ohio Railroad 102.
Mobile Bay 167.
Montgomery, Alabama 404.
Montgomery, J. J. 81
Moore, William 207.
Morgan , John Hunt 109, 168-69, 194-99, 266, 269, 282, 331, 386, 420-29, 441.
Morris Island 483-494.
Morrow, W.R. 118.
Mosgrove, George 438-39.
Moss, William 339.
Mount Pleasant, Tn. 284.
Munfordville, Ky. 175, 180.
Murfree, L. B. 440.
Murfreesboro, Tn. 63, 89, 92, 97-101, 150-52, 157, 177, 189, 193-200, 209, 211, 215-16, 229, 231, 247-48, 253, 261, 266, 268, 300, 323, 338, 363, 371, 395, 416.
Murray, Ogden 482.
Nashville, Tn. 87, 89, 90-93, 142, 169, 194, 198-200, 223-26, 257, 266, 296, 317-18, 323, 333, 335, 339, 425, 436, 448, 465, 467, 470.
Nashville Banner 25.
Nashville Pike 204.
Nashville Republican Banner 52.
Neely, Jack 329.
New Hope Church 374-78.
New Orleans, La. 425.
Nichol, Dr. William 184.
Noble Ellis 60-61.

Military Units